STUDY GUIDE

for

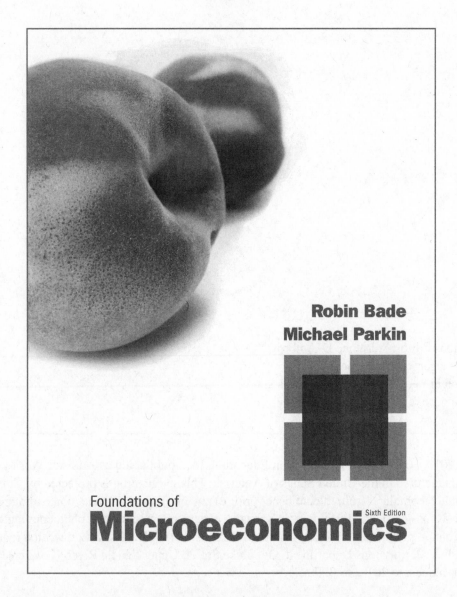

Robin Bade
Michael Parkin

Foundations of
Microeconomics
Sixth Edition

Mark Rush
University of Florida

PEARSON

Boston Columbus Indianapolis New York San Francisco Upper Saddle River
Amsterdam Cape Town Dubai London Madrid Milan Munich Paris Montreal Toronto
Delhi Mexico City Sao Paulo Sydney Hong Kong Seoul Singapore Taipei Tokyo

Executive Acquisitions Editor: Adrienne D'Ambrosio
Editorial Project Manager: Sarah Dumouchelle
Associate Production Project Manager: Alison Eusden
Senior Manufacturing Buyer: Carol Melville

10 9 8 7 6 5 4 3 2 1

www.pearsonhighered.com

PEARSON

ISBN-10:   0-13-283095-7
ISBN-13: 978-0-13-283095-9

Table of Contents

■ **Part 7 Incomes and Inequality**

Your Complete Learning Package

■ The Complete Package

Your *Foundations of Microeconomics* package consists of:

- Textbook
- Study Guide
- MyEconLab Access Kit

MyEconLab is a powerful and tightly integrated homework and tutorial system that puts you in control of your own learning. MyEconLab includes

- Practice Tests that let you test your understanding and identify where you need to concentrate your studying
- A personalized Study Plan that evaluates your test results and provides further practice
- Tutorial instruction that will guide you through the areas you have difficulty with
- eText—the entire textbook online with animated figures accompanied by audio explanations prepared by us and with hyperlinks to all the other components of the Web site.
- Economics in the News updated daily during the school year
- Online "Office Hours"—ask a question via e-mail, and one of us will respond within 24 hours!
- Economic links—links to sites that keep you up to date with what's going on in the economy and that enable you to work end-of-chapter Web Exercises

Each new textbook arrives with a MyEconLab Student Access Card that unlocks protected areas of the Web site.

■ Checklist and Checkpoints: The Glue That Holds Your Tools Together

Each chapter of your textbook opens with a Chapter Checklist that tells you what you'll be able to do when you've completed the chapter. The number of tasks varies from two to five and most often is three or four. Begin by reviewing this list thoughtfully and get a good sense of what you are about to learn.

Each part of a chapter in the textbook, Study Guide, and MyEconLab Web site is linked directly to a Checklist item to enable you to know exactly what you're studying and how it will enable you to accomplish your learning objective.

Each part of a chapter in the textbook ends with a Checkpoint—a page that offers you Practice Problems to test your understanding of the key ideas of the part. For each Practice Problem there is a worked and illustrated solution. The Checkpoints enable you to review material when it's fresh in your mind—the most effective and productive time to do so. The Checkpoints guide you through the material in a step-by-step approach that takes the guesswork out of learning. The Study Guide reinforces each Checkpoint by providing Additional Practice Problems. Use these if you're still not sure you understand the material or if you want to review before an exam.

The self-test questions in the Study Guide, the Study Plan Exercises on the MyEconLab Web site, and the chapter resources on the MyEconLab Web site are organized by Checkpoint so that you can maintain your focus as you work through the material.

■ Practice Makes Perfect

As you study, distinguish between *practice* and *self-test*. Practice is part of the learning process, learning by doing. Self-test is a check. It shows you where you need to go back and reinforce your understanding, and it helps you build confidence in your knowledge of the material.

The Checkpoint Practice Problems and Exercises, the end-of-chapter Exercises, and the Checkpoint Exercises in MyEconLab are designed for practice. The self-test questions in the Study Guide, the pre- and post-tests, and Study Plan Exercises in MyEconLab are designed to reveal your gaps in understanding and to target your final examination of the material.

■ Learn Your Learning Style

It is unlikely that you'll need to use all the tools that we've created all of the time. Try to discover how you learn best. Then exploit what you discover.

If you learn best by reading with a marker or pencil in your hand, you'll use the textbook and Study Guide more often than the other items. If you learn best by seeing the action, you'll often use the eText and MyEconLab tutorials. If you learn best by hearing, you'll use the eText audio explanations of the action in key figures. If you learn best by participating and acting, you'll often use the Study Plan Exercises.

■ Tell Us What Works for *You*

Please tell us the tools that you find most helpful. And tell us what you think we can improve. You can email us at robin@econ100.com or michael.parkin@uwo.ca, or use the Office Hours in your MyEconLab Web site.

Robin Bade
Michael Parkin
Ontario, Canada
January, 2012

Your Course and Your Study Guide

SUGGESTIONS FOR CLASS

■ Introduction

My experience has taught me that what students want most from a study guide is help in mastering course material in order to do well on examinations. This Study Guide has been created to respond specifically to that demand. Using this Study Guide alone, however, is not enough to guarantee that you will earn an A or do well in your course. In order to help you overcome the problems and difficulties that most students encounter, I have some general advice on how to study, as well as some specific advice on how best to use this Study Guide.

Economics requires a different style of thinking than what you may encounter in other courses. Economists make extensive use of assumptions to break down complex problems into simple, analytically manageable parts. This analytical style, while ultimately not more demanding than the styles of thinking in other disciplines, feels unfamiliar to most students and requires practice. As a result, it is not as easy to do well in economics on the basis of your raw intelligence and high school knowledge as it is in many other courses. Many students who come to my office are frustrated and puzzled by the fact that they are getting A's and B's in their other courses but only a C or worse in economics. They have not recognized that economics is different and requires practice. In order to avoid a frustrating visit to your instructor after your first test, I suggest you do the following.

■ Don't rely solely on your high school economics.

If you took high school economics, you have seen the material on supply and demand which your instructor will lecture on in the first few weeks. Don't be lulled into feeling that the course will be easy. Your high school knowledge of economic concepts will be very useful, but it will not be enough to guarantee high scores on exams. Your college or university instructors will demand much more detailed knowledge of concepts and ask you to apply them in new circumstances.

■ Keep up with the course material on a weekly basis.

Skim or read the appropriate chapter in the textbook before your instructor lectures on it. In this initial reading, don't worry about details or arguments you can't quite follow — try to get a general understanding of the basic concepts and issues. You may be amazed at how your instructor's ability to teach improves when you come to class prepared. After the lecture, return to the book and read the material more thoroughly and completely. As soon as your instructor has finished covering a chapter, complete the corresponding Study Guide chapter. Avoid cramming the day before or even just the week before an exam. Because economics requires practice, cramming is an almost certain recipe for failure.

■ Keep a good set of lecture notes.

Good lecture notes are vital for focusing your studying. Your instructor will only lecture on a subset of topics from the textbook. The topics your instructor covers in a lecture should usually be given priority when studying. Also give priority to studying the figures and graphs covered in the lecture.

Instructors differ in their emphasis on lecture notes and the textbook, so ask early on in the course which is more important in reviewing for exams — lecture notes or the textbook. If your instructor answers that both are important, then ask the following, typical economic question: which will be more beneficial — spending an extra hour re-reading your lecture notes or an extra hour re-reading the textbook? This question assumes that you have read each textbook chapter twice (once before lecture for a general understanding, and then later for a thorough understanding); that you have prepared a good set of lecture notes; and that you have worked through all of the problems in the appropriate Study Guide chapters. By applying this style of analysis to the problem of efficiently allocating your study time, you are already beginning to think like an economist!

■ Use your instructor and/or teaching assistants for help.

When you have questions or problems with course material, come to the office to ask questions. Remember, you are paying for your education and instructors are there to help you learn. Don't be shy. The personal contact that comes from one-on-one tutoring is professionally gratifying for instructors as well as (hopefully) beneficial for you.

■ Form a study group.

A very useful way to motivate your studying and to learn economics is to discuss the course material and problems with other students. Explaining the answer to a question out loud is a very effective way of discovering how well you understand the question. When you answer a question only in your head, you often skip steps in the chain of reasoning without realizing it. When you are forced to explain your reasoning aloud, gaps and mistakes quickly appear, and you (with your fellow group members) can quickly correct your reasoning. The Exercises at the end of each textbook chapter are extremely good study group material. You might also get together after having worked the Study Guide problems, but before looking at the answers, and help each other solve unsolved problems.

■ Work old exams.

One of the most effective ways of studying is to work through exams your instructor has given in previous years. Old exams give you a feel for the style of question your instructor might ask, and give you the opportunity to get used to time pressure if you force yourself to do the exam in the allotted time. Studying from old exams is not cheating, as long as you have obtained a copy of the exam legally. Some institutions keep old exams in the library, others in the department. If there is a class web page, check there—many instructors now post old exams on their class web pages. Students who have previously taken the course are usually a good source as well. Remember, though, that old exams are a useful study aid only if you use them to understand the reasoning behind each question. If you simply memorize answers in the hopes that your instructor will repeat the identical question, you are likely to fail. From year to year, instructors routinely change the questions or change the numerical values for similar questions.

■ Use All Your Tools

The authors of your book, Robin Bade and Michael Parkin, have created a rich array of learning tools that they describe in the preceding section, "Your Complete Learning Package." Make sure that you read this section because it makes sense to use *all* your tools!

USING THE STUDY GUIDE

You should only attempt to complete a chapter in the Study Guide after you have read the corresponding textbook chapter and listened to your instructor lecture on the material. Each Study Guide chapter contains the following sections.

Chapter Checklist

This first section is a short summary of the key material. It is designed to focus you quickly and precisely on the core material that you must master. It is an excellent study aid for the night before an exam. Think of it as crib notes that will serve as a final check of the key concepts you have studied.

Additional Practice Problems

In each checkpoint in the textbook there are practice problems. These problems are extremely valuable because they help you grasp what you have just studied. In the Study Guide are additional Practice Problems. These Practice Problems are either similar to the one in your textbook, extend the Practice Problem in your textbook, or cover another important topic from the Checkpoint. Although the answer is given to the additional Practice Problem, try to solve it on your own before reading the answer.

Following the additional Practice Problem is the Self Test section of the Study Guide. This section has fill in the blank, true or false, multiple choice, complete the graph, short answer and numeric questions, and additional exercises. The questions are designed to give you practice and to test skills and techniques you must master to do well on exams. Before I describe the parts of the Self Test section, here are some general tips that apply to all parts.

First, use a pencil to write your answers in the Study Guide so you have neat, complete pages from which to study and recall how you answered a question when the test approaches. Draw graphs wherever they are applicable. Some questions will ask explicitly for graphs; many others will not but will require a chain of reasoning that involves shifts of curves on a graph. Always draw the graph. Don't try to work through the reasoning in your head — you are much more likely to make mistakes that way. Whenever you draw a graph, even in the margins of the Study Guide, label the axes. You might think that you can keep the labels in your head, but you will be confronting many different graphs with many different variables on the axes. Also, be sure to understand what the axes are measuring. After finishing Chapter 4, some students think that the vertical axis always shows the price. That belief is simply not so. Hence you must be careful with the axes. In other words, avoid confusion and label. As an added incentive, remember that on exams where graphs are required, instructors often will deduct points for unlabelled axes.

Do the Self Test questions as if they were real exam questions, which means do them without looking at the answers. This is the single most important tip I can give you about effectively using the Study Guide to improve your exam performance. Struggling for the answers to questions that you find difficult is one of the most effective ways to learn. The adage — no pain, no gain — applies well to studying. You will learn the most from right answers you had to struggle for and from your wrong answers and mistakes. Only after you have attempted all the questions should you look at the answers. When you finally do check the answers, be sure to understand where you went wrong and why the right answer is correct.

Fill in the Blanks

This section covers the material in the checkpoint and has blanks for you to complete. Often suggested phrases are given but sometimes there are no hints—in that case you are on your own! Well, not really, because the answers are given at the end of each Study Guide chapter. This section also can help you review for a test because, once completed, they serve as a *very* brief statement of the important points within the important points within the checkpoint.

True or False

Next are true or false questions. Some instructors use true or false questions on exams or quizzes, so these questions might prove very valuable. The answers to the questions are given at the end of the chapter. The answer also has a page reference to the textbook. If you missed the question or did not completely understand the answer, definitely turn to the textbook and study the topic so that you will not miss similar questions on your exams.

Multiple Choice

Many instructors use multiple choice questions on exams, so pay particular attention to these questions. Similar to the true or false questions, the answers are given at the end of the Study Guide chapter and each answer references the relevant page in the text. If you had any difficulty with a question, use this page reference to look up the topic and then study it to remove this potential weakness.

Complete the Graph

The complete the graph questions allow you to practice using one of economists' major tools, graphs. If you will have essay questions on your exams, it is an extremely safe bet that you will be expected to use graphs on at least some of the questions. This section is designed to ensure that you are well prepared to handle these questions. Use the graph in the Study Guide to answer the questions. Although the answer is given at the end of the Study Guide chapter, do *not* look at the answer before you attempt to solve the problem. It is much too easy to deceive yourself into thinking you understand the answer when you simply look at the question and then read the answer. Involve yourself in the material by answering the question and then looking at the answer. If you cannot answer the question or if you got the answer wrong, the Study Guide again has a reference to the relevant page number in the text. Use the text and study the material!

Short Answer and Numeric Questions

The next set of questions are short answer and numeric questions. Short answer and numeric questions are classic exam questions, so pay attention to these questions. Approach them similarly to how you approach all the other questions: Answer them before you look at the answers in the back of the Study Guide. These questions are also excellent for use in a study group. If you and several friends are studying for an exam, you can use these questions to quiz your understanding. If you have disagreements about the correct answers, once again there are page references to the text so that you can settle these disagreements and be sure that everyone has a solid grasp of the point!

Additional Exercises

The final set of questions are exercises that link very closely to the Checkpoint material. These questions (and answers) are also available in your MyEconLab Test A, so you can practice with these questions using either your Study Guide or your computer! Regardless of how you tackle them, as always answer them before you look at the answers. These questions are similar to the short answer and numeric questions because they work very well in a study group.

FINAL COMMENTS

This Study Guide combines the efforts of many talented individuals. Save for Chapter 12, the author of the Chapter Checklists and many of the additional Practice Problems and answers is Tom Meyer, from Rochester Community and Technical College. It was a pleasure to work with Tom; I always looked forward to his emails and the resulting conversations.

For the multiple choice questions, we assembled a team of truly outstanding teachers:

- Ali Ataiifar, Delaware County Community College
- Diego Mendez-Carbajo, Illinois Wesleyan University

- William Mosher, Assumption College
- Cynthia Tori, Valdosta State University
- Nora Underwood, University of California, Davis
- Seemi Ahmad, Dutchess Community College
- Susan Bartlett, University of South Florida
- Jack Chambless, Valencia Community College
- Paul Harris, Camden County Community College
- William Mosher, Assumption College
- Terry Sutton, Southeast Missouri State University

I added a few multiple choice questions and wrote the fill in the blank, true or false, complete the graph, and short answer and numeric questions. I also served as an editor to assemble the material into the book before you.

The Study Guide and other supplements were checked for accuracy by a team of instructors. For previous editions, the team included:

- David Bivin, Indiana University-Purdue University
- Geoffrey Black, Boise State University
- Jeffrey Davis, ITT Technical Institute
- Ken Long, New River Community College
- Barbara Wiens-Tuers, Penn State University, Altoona
- Joachim Zietz, Middle Tennessee State University
- Armand Zottola, Central CT State University
- Carol Conrad, Cerro Coso Community College
- Marie Duggan, Keene State University
- Steven Hickerson, Mankato State University
- Douglas Kinnear, Colorado State University
- Tony Lima, California State University, at Eastbay (Tony, I believe you were one of my instructors when I was an under-graduate—thanks for helping excite me about economics!)
- Michael Milligan, Front Range Community College
- Barbara Ross-Pfeiffer, Kapiolani Community College
- John Daly and his class at St. Andrews

Jeannie Shearer-Gillmore, University of Western Ontario, checked every word, every sentence, every paragraph, and every page of the first edition of this book and many of the words, sentences, paragraphs, and pages of the third edition. She made a huge number of corrections and comments. The easiest way to distinguish her work and mine is to determine if there is an error in a passage. If there is, it's my work; if there is not, it's her work.

Looking over this edition of the book have been Alison Eusden and Sarah Dumouchelle, both with Pearson Publishers. Both played a key role in finding blunders, errors, and typos and for that I am eternally grateful. However, beyond that, both also were remarkable in how they remained so chipper and cheerful even in face of what I had presumed were insurmountable obstacles.

Students and professors who have used this book in earlier editions also have found errors that I did not catch. I think we owe them a special thanks for their conscientious work and generous initiative to report the errors:

- Lisa Salazar-Rich, at Cal Poly Pomona
- Professor Tom McCaleb's class at Florida State University and Professor McCaleb himself.
- Professor Lisa Gladstone, at St. Louis University

Robin Bade and Michael Parkin, the authors of your book, also need thanks. Not only have they written such a superior book that it was easy to be enthusiastic about writing the Study Guide to accompany it, both Robin and Michael played a very hands-on role in creating this Study Guide. They corrected errors and made suggestions that vastly improved the Study Guide.

I want to thank my family: Susan, Tommy, Bobby, and Katie, who, respectively: allowed me to work all hours on this book; helped me master the intricacies of FTPing computer files; let me postpone working on our trains with him until after the book was concluded; and would run into my typing room to share her new discoveries. Thanks a lot!

Finally, I want to thank Pearl, Lucky Tu, and Sphynx (and the late, beloved Butterscotch, Snowball, Mik, and Lucky Bunny) who, while I typed, sometimes sat on my lap and sometimes sat next to the computer in a box peering out the window (and occasionally meowed).

We (well, all of us except the cats) have tried to make the Study Guide as helpful and useful as possible. Undoubtedly I have made some mistakes; mistakes that you may see. If you find any, I, and following generations of students, would be grateful if you could point them out to me. At the end of my class at the University of Florida, when I ask my students for their advice, I point out to them that this advice won't help them at all because they have just completed the class. But comments they make will influence how future students are taught. Thus just as they owe a debt of gratitude for the comments and suggestions that I received from students before them, so too will students after them owe them an (unpaid and unpayable) debt. You are in the same situation. If you have questions, suggestions, or simply comments, let me know. My address follows, or you can reach me via e-mail at MARK.RUSH@CBA.UFL.EDU. Your input probably won't benefit you directly, but it will benefit following generations. And if you give me permission, I will note your name and school in following editions so that any younger siblings (or, years down the road, maybe even your children!) will see your name and offer up thanks.

Mark Rush
Economics Department
University of Florida
Gainesville, Florida 32611
January, 2012.

Chapter 1

Getting Started

Chapter 1 defines economics, microeconomics and macroeconomics; discusses the three major questions of *what, how,* and *for whom*; covers the six core economic ideas that shape how economists think about issues; and, examines methods used by economists.

1 Define economics and explain the kinds of questions that economists try to answer.

Economic questions exist because of scarcity, the point that wants exceed the ability of resources to satisfy them. Economics is the social science that studies the choices that individuals, businesses, government, and entire societies make as they cope with scarcity, the incentives that influence those choices, and the arrangements that coordinate them. The field of economics is divided into microeconomics, the study of the choices that individuals and businesses make and the way these choices interact and are influenced by governments, and macroeconomics, the study of the aggregate effects on the national economy and the global economy of the choices that individuals, businesses, and governments make. Economics studies how choices wind up determining: *what* goods and services get produced?; *how* goods and services are produced?; and *for whom* goods and services are produced? Economics also studies when choices made in a person's self-interest also serve the social interest. For instance, do the self-interested choices made about globalization, the information age, climate change and social security also promote the social interest?

2 Explain the ideas that define the economic way of thinking.

The six ideas that are the core of the economic approach: a choice is a tradeoff; people make rational choices by comparing benefits and costs; benefit is what you gain from something; cost is what you must give up to get something; most choices are "how much" choices made at the margin; and choices respond to incentives. Choices are tradeoffs—giving up one thing to get another. A rational choice uses the available resources to most effectively meet the objective of the person making the choice. The benefit from something is the gain or pleasure it brings. Benefit is measured by what someone is willing to give up to get something. The opportunity cost of something is the best thing that must be given up. Making choices on the margin means comparing all the relevant alternatives systematically and incrementally to determine the best choice. The marginal cost is the opportunity cost of a one-unit increase in an activity; the marginal benefit is the gain from a one-unit increase in an activity. Rational choices compare the marginal benefit of an activity to its marginal cost and undertake it if the marginal benefit exceeds or equals the marginal cost. Statements about "what is" are positive statements; statements about "what ought to be" are normative statements. Economists are interested in positive statements about cause and effect so they develop economic models. Economists use natural experiments, statistical investigations, and economic experiments to test if their models are making correct predictions.

CHECKPOINT 1.1

■ **Define economics and explain the kinds of questions that economist try to answer.**

Quick Review

- *Self-interest* The choices that people make that they think are the best for them.
- *Social interest* The choices that are best for society as a whole.

Additional Practice Problems 1.1

1. Which of the following headlines deals with *what, how,* and *for whom* questions?:
   a. A new government program is designed to provide high-quality school lunches for children from poorer families.
   b. Intel researchers discover a new chip-making technology.
   c. Regis Hairstyling sets a record for hairstylings in month of July

2. Which of the following headlines concern social interest and self interest?
   a. A new government program is designed to provide high-quality school lunches for children from poorer families.
   b. Intel researchers discover a new chip-making technology.
   c. Regis Hairstyling sets a record for hairstylings in month of July.

Solutions to Additional Practice Problems 1.1

1a. "More lunches" is a *what* question and "for children from poorer families" is a *for whom* question.

1b. "New chip-making technology" is a *how* question because it deals with how computer chips will be manufactured.

1c. "Record for hairstylings" is a *what* question because it notes that a record number of hairstylings have taken place in July.

2a. The decision to implement a new government program is a decision that is most likely made in the social interest. The self-interest of the government bureaucrat who made the decision might also be involved, particularly if the bureaucrat also will help manage the program.

2b. Intel's decision to research new chip-making technology is made in Intel's self-interest.

2c. Regis's decision to offer hairstylings is made in its self-interest as are the decisions of the people who had their hair styled by Regis.

■ **Self Test 1.1**

Fill in the blanks

Economic questions arise because ____ (human wants; resources) exceed the ____ (human wants; resources) available to satisfy them. Faced with ____, people must make choices. (Macroeconomics; Microeconomics) ____ is the study of the choices the individuals and businesses make and the way these choices interact and are influenced by governments. Choices that are the best for the person who makes them are made in ____ (self-interest; social interest).

True or false

1. Faced with scarcity, we must make choices.
2. The question of *what* refers to what production method should a firm use?
3. The answers to the *what, how* and *for whom* questions depend on the interactions of the choices people, businesses, and governments make.
4. If Sam buys a pizza because she is hungry, her choice is made in the social interest.
5. Because everyone is a member of society, all choices made in self-interest are also in the social interest.

Multiple choice

1. The characteristic from which all economic problems arise is
   a. political decisions.
   b. providing a minimal standard of living for every person.
   c. how to make a profit.
   d. hunger.
   e. scarcity.

2. Scarcity results from the fact that
   a. people's wants exceed the resources available to satisfy them.
   b. not all goals are desirable.
   c. we cannot answer the major economic questions.
   d. choices made in self-interest are not always in the social interest.
   e. the population keeps growing.

3. To economists, scarcity means that
   a. limited wants cannot be satisfied by the unlimited resources.
   b. a person looking for work is not able to find work.
   c. the number of people without jobs rises when economic times are bad.
   d. there can never be answers to the *what, how* or *for whom* questions.
   e. unlimited wants cannot be satisfied by the limited resources.

4. Which of the following is a microeconomic issue?
   a. Why has unemployment risen nationwide?
   b. Why has economic growth been rapid in China?
   c. What is the impact on the quantity of Pepsi purchased if consumers' tastes change in favor of non-carbonated drinks?
   d. Why is the average income lower in Africa than in Latin America?
   e. Why did overall production increase within the United States last year?

5. The question "Should we produce LCD televisions or computer monitors?" is an example of a ____ question.
   a. what
   b. how
   c. for whom
   d. where
   e. why

6. The question "Should we produce houses using bricks or wood?" is an example of a ____ question.
   a. what
   b. how
   c. for whom
   d. where
   e. why

7. The question "Should economics majors or sociology majors earn more after they graduate?" is an example of a ____ question.
   a. what
   b. how
   c. for whom
   d. where
   e. why

8. If a decision is made and it is the best choice for society, the decision is said to be
   a. a valid economic choice.
   b. made in self-interest.
   c. made in social interest.
   d. consistent with scarcity.
   e. a want-maximizing choice.

Short answer and numeric questions

1. Will there ever come a time without scarcity?

2. If there was no scarcity, would there be a need for economics?

3. Explain the difference between microeconomics and macroeconomics.

4. What are the three major questions answered by people's economic choices?

5. Why is the distinction between choices made in self-interest and choices made in social interest important?

Additional Exercises (also in MyEconLab Test A)

1. Every day, we make many choices. Why can't we avoid having to make choices?

2. Which of the following headlines deals with *what, how,* and *for whom* questions?
   a. "Major league baseball's turf keepers earn about $85,000, umpires earn about $350,000, and players make millions a year"

b. "Many full-service gas stations are switching to self-serve"

c. "Retail trends analysts make as much as $300,000 a year, while retail salespeople make less than $10 an hour"

3. Explain how the following headlines concern self-interest and social interest:

a. "Former-president George W. Bush powers his Texas ranch with solar electricity"

b. "Today's upper-class traveler goes on safari in southern Africa or stays at eco-resorts that cost $1,000 a night but do not have electricity"

CHECKPOINT 1.2

■ **Explain the ideas that define the economic way of thinking.**

Quick Review

- *Opportunity cost* The opportunity cost of something is the best thing you must give up to get it.
- *Marginal cost* The opportunity cost from a one-unit increase in an activity.
- *Marginal benefit* The benefit that arises from a one-unit increase in an activity.
- *Rational choice* A choice that compares the marginal benefit and marginal cost of the activity and takes the action if the marginal benefit exceeds or equals the marginal cost.
- *Positive statement* A statement that tells what is currently believed about the way the world operates. Positive statements can be tested.
- *Normative statement* A statement that tells what ought to be. It depends on values and cannot be tested.

Additional Practice Problems 1.2

1. What are the opportunity costs of *using* this *Study Guide*?

2. Kate usually plays tennis for two hours a week and her grade on each math test is usually 70 percent. Last week, after playing two hours of tennis, Kate thought long and hard about playing for another hour. She decided to play another hour of tennis and cut her study time by one additional hour. But the grade on last week's math test was 60 percent.

a. What was Kate's opportunity cost of the third hour of tennis?

b. Given that Kate made the decision to play the third hour of tennis, what can you conclude about the comparison of her marginal benefit and marginal cost of the second hour of tennis?

c. Was Kate's decision to play the third hour of tennis rational?

3. Classify each of the following statements as positive or normative:

a. There is too much poverty in the United States.

b. An increase in the gas tax will cut pollution.

c. Cuts to social security in the United States have been too deep.

Solutions to Additional Practice Problems 1.2

1. The opportunity cost is mainly the time spent using the *Study Guide* because that time could be devoted to other activities. The best activity given up, be it studying for another class, or sleeping, or some other activity, which is lost because of the time spent using the *Study Guide* is the opportunity cost. Once you have purchased this *Study Guide*, its price is not an opportunity cost of *using* the *Study Guide* because you have already paid the price.

2a. The opportunity cost of the third hour of tennis was the 10 percentage point drop on her math test grade because she cut her studying time by one hour to play an additional hour of tennis. If Kate had not played tennis for the third hour, she would have studied and her grade would not have dropped.

2b. Kate chose to play the third hour of tennis, so the marginal benefit of the third hour of tennis was greater than the marginal cost of the third hour. If the marginal benefit of the third hour of tennis was less than the marginal cost of the third hour, Kate would have chosen to study rather than play tennis.

2c. Even though her grade fell, Kate's choice used the available time to most effectively satisfy her wants because the marginal benefit of the third hour of playing tennis exceeded the marginal cost of the third hour. This was a choice made in her self-interest.

3a. A normative statement because it depends on the speaker's values and cannot be tested.

3b. A positive statement because it can be tested by increasing the gas tax and then measuring the change in pollution.

3c. A normative statement because it depends on the speaker's values (someone else might propose still deeper cuts) and cannot be tested.

■ Self Test I.2

Fill in the blanks

A ____ choice uses the available resources to most effectively satisfy the wants of the person making the choice. The opportunity cost of an activity is ____ (all of the activities given up; the best alternative given up). The benefit of an activity is measured by what you ____ (are willing to; must) give up. We make a rational choice to do an activity if the marginal benefit of the activity ____ the marginal cost. A statement that tells "what is" is a ____ (positive; normative) statement. A statement that tells "what ought to be" is a ____ (positive; normative) statement.

True or false

1. Instead of attending his microeconomics class for two hours, Jim can play a game of tennis or watch a movie. For Jim the opportunity cost of attending class is forgoing the game of tennis *and* watching the movie.

2. Marginal cost is what you gain when you get one more unit of something.

3. A rational choice involves comparing the marginal benefit of an action to its marginal cost.

4. A change in marginal benefit or a change in marginal cost brings a change in the incentives that we face and leads us to change our actions.

5. The statement, "When more people volunteer in their communities, crime rates decrease" is a positive statement.

Multiple choice

1. Jamie has enough money to buy either a Mountain Dew, or a Pepsi, or a bag of chips. He chooses to buy the Mountain Dew. The opportunity cost of the Mountain Dew is
   a. the Pepsi and the bag of chips.
   b. the Pepsi or the bag of chips, whichever the best alternative given up.
   c. the Mountain Dew.
   d. the Pepsi because it is a drink, as is the Mountain Dew.
   e. zero because he enjoys the Mountain Dew.

2. The benefit of an activity is
   a. purely objective and measured in dollars.
   b. the gain or pleasure that it brings.
   c. the value of its opportunity cost.
   d. measured by what must be given up to get one more unit of the activity.
   e. not measurable on the margin.

3. The marginal benefit of an activity is
   i. the benefit from a one-unit increase in the activity.
   ii. the benefit of a small, unimportant activity.
   iii. measured by what the person is willing to give up to get one additional unit of the activity.
   a. i only.
   b. ii only.
   c. iii only.
   d. i and iii.
   e. ii and iii.

4. The cost of a one-unit increase in an activity
   a. is called the total one-unit cost.
   b. is called the marginal cost.
   c. decreases as more of the activity is done.
   d. is called the marginal benefit/cost.
   e. is called the unit cost.

5. If the marginal benefit of the next slice of pizza exceeds the marginal cost, you will
   a. eat the slice of pizza.
   b. not eat the slice of pizza.
   c. be unable to choose between eating or not eating.
   d. eat half the slice.
   e. More information is needed about how much the marginal benefit exceeds the marginal cost to determine if you will or will not eat the slice.

6. When people make rational choices, they
   a. behave selfishly.
   b. do not consider their emotions.
   c. weigh the costs and benefits of their options and act to satisfy their wants.
   d. necessarily make a decision in the social interest.
   e. are necessarily making the best decision.

7. A positive statement
   a. must always be right.
   b. cannot be tested.
   c. can be tested against the facts.
   d. depends on someone's value judgment.
   e. cannot be negative.

Short answer and numeric questions

1. What is an opportunity cost?

2. You have $12 and can buy a pizza, a movie on a DVD, or a sketch pad for drawing. You decide to buy the pizza and think that if you hadn't been so hungry, you would have purchased the DVD. What is the opportunity cost of your pizza?

3. What is benefit and how is it measured?

4. What is a marginal cost? A marginal benefit? How do they relate to rational choice?

5. Becky is writing an essay about the law that requires all passengers in a car to use a seat belt and its effectiveness. What might be a positive statement and a normative statement that she will include in her essay?

Additional Exercises (also in MyEconLab Test A)

1. Bill Gates has donated billions of dollars through the Bill and Melinda Gates Foundation to support universities, cancer research, a children's hospital, the Seattle Symphony, etc. Are his donations rational? In making these donations, might Bill Gates have responded to any incentive? Does he make his decision about his donations on the margin?

2. Tony is an engineering student, who is considering taking an extra course in history. What things might be part of his costs and benefits of the history course? Think of an incentive that might encourage him to take the course.

SELF TEST ANSWERS

■ CHECKPOINT 1.1

Fill in the blanks

Economic questions arise because <u>human wants</u> exceed the <u>resources</u> available to satisfy them. Faced with <u>scarcity</u>, people must make choices. <u>Microeconomics</u> is the study of the choices the individuals and businesses make and the way these choices interact and are influenced by governments. Choices that are the best for the person who makes them are made in <u>self-interest</u>.

True or false

1. True; page 2
2. False; page 3
3. True; page 4
4. False; page 4
5. False; page 5

Multiple choice

1. e; page 2
2. a; page 2
3. e; page 2
4. c; page 2
5. a; page 3
6. b; page 3
7. c; page 4
8. c; page 4

Short answer and numeric questions

1. There will never be a time without scarcity because human wants are unlimited; page 2.

2. If there was no scarcity, then there likely would be no need for economics. Economics studies the choices that people make to cope with scarcity, so if there was no scarcity, then people's choices would not be limited by scarcity; page 2.

3. Microeconomics studies individual units within the economy, such as a consumer, a firm, a market, and so forth. Macroeconomics studies the overall, or aggregate, economy, such as the overall unemployment rate, or overall economic growth rate; pages 2-3.

4. The questions are *"What* goods and services get produced and in what quantities?", *"How* are goods and services produced?", and *"For whom* are the goods and services produced?" pages 3-4.

5. In general economists believe that people make choices according to their self-interest. These choices might or might not be in the social interest. Part of what economists study is when choices made in people's self-interest also further the social interest; page 5.

Additional Exercises (also in MyEconLab Test A)

1. The only way to avoid making choices is to either limit our wants or conjure up unlimited resources. Because neither is possible, we will always face choices; page 2.

2. a. The differences in incomes between turf keepers, umpires, and players is directly a *for whom* question. In addition, because it's likely that the consumption choices of the turf keepers, umpires, and players are different, there is also a *what* question involved; pages 3-4.

   b. The switch to self serve directly reflects a *how* question, that is, how will gasoline be delivered. In addition, because the switch means people previously employed at gas stations will be fired, there is a *for whom* question also involved; pages 3-4.

   c. The differences in incomes between retail trend analysts and retail salespeople is directly a *for whom* question. Because it's likely that the consumption choices of the analysts and salespeople are different, there is also a *what* question involved; pages 3-4.

3. a. Former-president Bush's decision to power his ranch with solar power is in his self interest because it affects what he pays for power; pages 4-5.

   b. The travelers' decisions are in their self interest. And, if they are also best for society, then they are in the social interest; pages 4-5.

■ CHECKPOINT 1.2

Fill in the blanks

A <u>rational</u> choice uses the available resources to most effectively satisfy the wants of the person making the choice. The opportunity cost of an activity is <u>the best alternative given up</u>. The benefit of an activity is measured by what you <u>are willing to</u> give up. We make a rational choice to do an activity if the marginal benefit of the activity <u>exceeds</u> the marginal cost. A statement that tells "what is" is a <u>positive</u> statement. A statement that tells "what ought to be" is a <u>normative</u> statement.

True or false

1. False; page 9
2. False; page 10
3. True; page 11
4. True; page 11
5. True; page 13

Multiple choice

1. b; page 9
2. b; page 9
3. d; page 10
4. b; page 10
5. a; page 11
6. c; page 11
7. c; page 13

Short answer and numeric questions

1. The opportunity cost of something is the best thing that must be given up. The opportunity cost is only the *single* best thing, not *all* the other things given up; page 9.
2. The opportunity cost of the pizza is the best thing given, which in this case is the DVD. The opportunity cost is *not* the DVD and the sketch pad because you would not have been able to purchase both of them with your $12; page 9.

3. The benefit of something is the gain or pleasure that it brings. Economists measure the benefit of something by what a person is willing to give up to get it; pages 9-10.
4. Marginal cost is the cost of a one-unit increase in an activity. Marginal benefit is the benefit of a one-unit increase in an activity. A rational choice is made by comparing the marginal cost and marginal benefit, so that if the marginal benefit of an activity exceeds or equals the marginal cost, the activity is undertaken; pages 10-11.
5. A positive statement is "People who wear seat belts are involved in fewer road deaths." This statement can be tested. A normative statement is "People should be free to choose whether to wear a seat belt or not." This statement cannot be tested; page 13.

Additional Exercises (also in MyEconLab Test A)

1. As long as Mr. Gates compares the marginal benefits and marginal costs of his donations and made the best decision he could, his donations are the result of rational decisions. Mr. Gates perhaps responded to incentives when making these donations. For example, by making these donations, he reduced his taxable income. Mr. Gates made his decisions on the marginal as long as he compared all the alternatives available to him. For instance, he could consider giving more or less money to AIDs initiatives or more or less money to cancer research.
2. The costs of any extra course include the extra tuition as well as less time available for studying for other courses, for work, or for leisure. The benefits include increased knowledge of history. An incentive to taking the course might be the promise of a better job or perhaps the fact that he is required to take a history class as a general education requirement in order to graduate.

Appendix: Making and Using Graphs

Chapter 1

APPENDIX CHECKLIST

After you have completed the appendix, you will have thoroughly reviewed the graphs used in your economics course.

▌ Making and using graphs.

Graphs represent quantities as distances. The vertical axis is the y-axis and the horizontal axis is the x-axis. A scatter diagram plots a graph of one variable against the value of another variable. A time-series graph measures time along the x-axis and the variable (or variables) of interest along the y-axis. A cross-section graph shows the values of an economic variable for different groups in the population at a point in time. Graphs can show the relationship between two variables in an economic model. Variables that move in the same direction have a positive, or direct, relationship. Variables that move in the opposite direction have a negative, or inverse, relationship. Some relationships have minimum or maximum points. The slope of a relationship is the change in the value of the variable measured on the y-axis divided by the change in the value of the variable measured on the x-axis. Using the symbol "Δ" to mean "change in", the slope of a relationship equals $\Delta y \div \Delta x$. To graph a relationship among more than two variables, we use the *ceteris paribus* assumption and graph the relationship between two of the variables, holding the other variables constant.

CHECKPOINT 1

■ Making and using graphs.

Additional Practice Problems

1. You have data on the average monthly rainfall and the monthly expenditure on umbrellas in Seattle, Washington. What sort of graph would be the best to reveal if any relationship exists between these variables?

2. In Figure A1.1, draw a straight line showing a positive relationship and another straight line showing a negative relationship.

■ FIGURE A1.1

Year	Price (dollars per gallon)
1998	1.12
1999	1.22
2000	1.56
2001	1.53
2002	1.44
2003	1.64
2004	1.92
2005	2.34
2006	2.64
2007	2.85
2008	3.32

3. The table has the average price of a gallon of gasoline, including taxes, for eleven years. In Figure A1.2, measuring years along the horizontal axis, label the axes and then plot these data. What type of graph are you creating? What is the general trend of gas prices during this decade?

■ **FIGURE A1.2**

4. Figure A1.3 shows the relationship between the price of a paperback book and the quantity of paperback books a publisher is willing to sell. What is the slope of the line in Figure A1.3?

■ **FIGURE A1.3**

Price (dollars per paperback book)

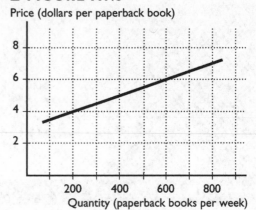

Quantity (paperback books per week)

Solutions to Additional Practice Problems 1

1. A scatter diagram would be the best graph to use. A scatter diagram would plot the monthly value of, say, rainfall along the vertical axis (the y-axis) and the monthly value of umbrella expenditure along the horizontal axis (the x-axis).

■ **FIGURE A1.4**

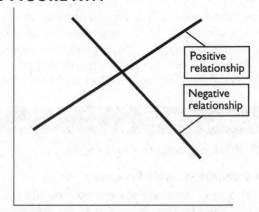

Positive relationship

Negative relationship

2. Figure A1.4 has two lines, one showing a positive relationship and the other showing a negative relationship. Your figure does not need to have identical lines. The key point your figure needs is that the line for the positive relationship slopes up as you move rightward along it and the line for the negative relationship slopes down as you move rightward along it.

■ FIGURE A1.5

Price (dollars per gallon)

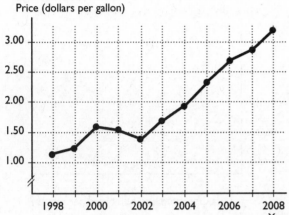

3. Figure A1.5 labels the axes and plots the data in the table. The graph is a time-series graph. The trend is positive because gas prices generally increased during these years.

■ FIGURE A1.6

Price (dollars per paperback book)

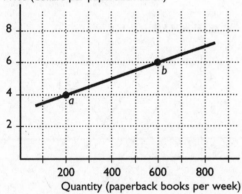

Quantity (paperback books per week)

4. The slope of a line is the change the variable measured on the y-axis divided by the change in the variable measured on the x-axis. To calculate the slope of the line in the figure, use points a and b in Figure A1.6. Between a and b, y rises by 2, from 4 to 6. And x increases by 400, from 200 to 600. The slope equals $2/400 = 0.005$.

■ Self Test 1

Fill in the blanks

In a graph, the vertical line is called the ____ (x-axis; y-axis) and the horizontal line is called the ____ (x-axis; y-axis). A ____ (scatter diagram; time-series graph; cross-section graph) is a graph of the value of one variable against the value of another variable. A ____ (scatter diagram; time-series graph; cross-section graph) measures time along the x-axis and the variable along the y-axis. A ____ (scatter diagram; time-series graph; cross-section graph) shows the values of an economic variable for different groups in the population at a point in time. If the graph of a relationship between two variables slopes up to the right, the two variables have a ____ (positive; negative) relationship. If the graph between two variables is a vertical line, the two variables ____ (are; are not) related. The slope of a relationship is the change in the value of the variable measured along the ____ (x-axis; y-axis) divided by the change in the value of the variable measured along the ____ (x-axis; y-axis). By using the *ceteris paribus* assumption, it ____ (is; is not) possible to graph a relationship that involves more than two variables.

True or false

1. A point that is above and to the right of another point will have a larger value of the x-axis variable and a larger value of the y-axis variable.

2. A scatter diagram shows the values of an economic variable for different groups in a population at a point in time.

3. A time-series graph compares values of a variable for different groups at a single point in time.

4. A trend is a measure of the closeness of the points on a graph.

5. A positive relationship is always a linear relationship.

6. A relationship that starts out sloping upward and then slopes downward has a maximum.

7. A graph that shows a horizontal line indicates variables that are unrelated.

8. The slope at a point on a curve can be found by calculating the slope of the line that touches the point and no other point on the curve.

Multiple choice

1. Demonstrating how an economic variable changes from one year to the next is best illustrated by a
   a. scatter diagram.
   b. time-series graph.
   c. linear graph.
   d. cross-section graph.
   e. trend-line.

2. To show the values of an economic variable for different groups in a population at a point in time, it is best to use a
   a. scatter diagram.
   b. time-series graph.
   c. linear graph.
   d. cross-section graph.
   e. trend diagram.

3. If whenever one variable increases, another variable also increases, then these two variables are ____ related.
   a. positively
   b. negatively
   c. inversely
   d. cross-sectionally
   e. not

4. A graph of the relationship between two variables is a line that slopes down to the right. These two variables are ____ related.
   a. positively
   b. directly
   c. negatively
   d. not
   e. trend-line

5. Two variables are unrelated if their graph is
   i.   a vertical line.
   ii. a 45 degree line.
   iii. a horizontal line.
   a. i only.
   b. ii only
   c. iii only
   d. i and iii.
   e. i, ii, and iii.

■ FIGURE A1.7

Price (dollars per pound of rutabagas)

Quantity (rutabagas purchased per month)

6. In figure A1.7, between points *A* and *B*, what is the slope of the line?
   a. 12
   b. 3
   c. 9
   d. –9
   e. 0

■ FIGURE A1.8

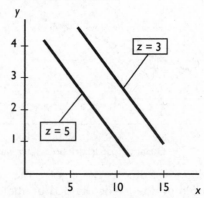

7. In Figure A1.8, an increase in z leads to a
   a. movement up along one of the lines showing the relationship between x and y.
   b. movement down along one of the lines showing the relationship between x and y.
   c. rightward shift of the line showing the relationship between x and y.
   d. leftward shift of the line showing the relationship between x and y.
   e. trend change in both x and y.

8. In Figure A1.8, *ceteris paribus*, an increase in x is associated with
   a. an increase in y.
   b. a decrease in y.
   c. an increase in z.
   d. a random change in z.
   e. no change in either y or z.

Complete the graph

Year	Workers (millions)
1999	7.9
2000	8.1
2001	8.3
2002	8.4
2003	8.5
2004	8.7
2005	9.0
2006	9.2
2007	9.5
2008	9.7

1. The table above gives the number of people working in restaurants and bars in the United States during 10 previous years.

■ **FIGURE A1.9**

In Figure A1.9, measure time on the horizontal axis and the number of workers on the vertical axis, and then plot these data.
a. What type of graph are you creating?

b. Using your figure, what was the trend in the number of people working in restaurants and bars during these years?

Year	Revenue (billions of dollars)	Workers (millions)
1999	285	7.9
2000	306	8.1
2001	318	8.3
2002	332	8.4
2003	350	8.5
2004	372	8.7
2005	393	9.0
2006	418	9.2
2007	438	9.5
2008	453	9.7

2. The table above gives the annual revenue for restaurants and bars and the number of people employed in restaurants and bars in the United States during 10 previous years. In Figure A1.10, measure the revenue along the horizontal axis and the number of workers along the vertical axis and plot the data.

a. What type of graph are you creating?
b. What relationship do you see in your figure between the revenue and the number of workers?

■ **FIGURE A1.10**

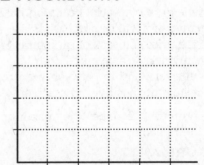

Price (dollars per sack of cat food)	Quantity (sacks of cat food per month)
1	10,000
2	8,000
3	7,000
4	4,000

3. The number of sacks of premium cat food that cat lovers will buy depends on the price of a sack of cat food. The relationship is given in the table above. In Figure A1.11, plot this relationship, putting the price on the vertical axis and the quantity on the horizontal axis.

■ **FIGURE A1.11**

a. If the price of a sack of cat food is $2, how many sacks will be purchased?
b. If the price of a sack of cat food is $3, how many sacks will be purchased?
c. Is the relationship between the price and the quantity positive or negative?

4. In Figure A1.12, label the maximum and minimum points.

■ **FIGURE A1.12**

5. In Figure A1.13, draw a line through point A with a slope of 2. Label the line "1." Draw another line through point A with a slope of –2. Label this line "2."

■ **FIGURE A1.13**

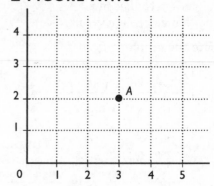

x	y	z
1	4	0
2	3	2
3	1	6
4	0	8

■ **FIGURE A1.14**

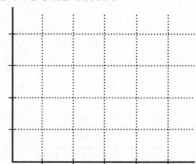

6. The table above contains data for three variables.

a. In Figure A1.14, put y on the vertical axis and x on the horizontal axis. Show the relationship between x and y. Is this relationship positive or negative?
b. What is the slope between $x = 2$ and $x = 3$?
c. In Figure A1.15 (on the next page), put z on the vertical axis and x on the horizontal axis. Show the relationship between x and z. Is this relationship positive or negative?

■ **FIGURE A1.15**

Price (dollars per DVD)	Quantity of DVDs purchased, low income	Quantity of DVDs purchased, high income
11	4	5
12	3	4
13	1	3
14	0	2

7. Bobby says that he buys fewer DVDs when the price of a DVD is higher. Bobby also says that he will buy more DVDs after he graduates and his income is higher. The table above shows the number of DVDs Bobby buys in a month at different prices when his income is low and when his income is high.

■ **FIGURE A1.16**

a. In Figure A1.16, put the price on the vertical axis and the quantity purchased on the horizontal axis. Show the relationship be-tween the number of DVDs purchased and the price when Bobby's income is low.

b. On the same figure, draw the relationship between the number of DVDs purchased and the price when his income is high.

c. Does an increase in Bobby's income shift the relationship between the price of a DVD and the number of DVDs purchased rightward or leftward?

Short answer and numeric questions

1. What are the three types of graphs?

2. If two variables are positively related, will the slope of a graph of the two variables be positive or negative? If two variables are negatively related, will the slope of a graph of the two variables be positive or negative?

3. If a line slopes upward to the right, is its slope positive or negative? If a line slopes downward to the right, is its slope positive or negative?

4. In Figure A1.17, what is the slope of the curved line at point *A*? At point *B*?

■ **FIGURE A1.17**

SELF TEST ANSWERS

■ CHECKPOINT I

Fill in the blanks

In a graph, the vertical line is called the _y-axis_ and the horizontal line is called the _x-axis_. A _scatter diagram_ is a graph of the value of one variable against the value of another variable. A _time-series graph_ measures time along the _x_-axis and the variable along the _y_-axis. A cross-section graph shows the values of an economic variable for different groups in the population at a point in time. If the graph of a relationship between two variables slopes up to the right, the two variables have a _positive_ relationship. If the graph between two variables is a vertical line, the two variables _are not_ related. The slope of a relationship is the change in the value of the variable measured along the _y-axis_ divided by the change in the value of the variable measured along the _x-axis_. By using the _ceteris paribus_ assumption, it _is_ possible to graph a relationship that involves more than two variables.

True or false

1. True; page 21
2. False; page 22
3. False; page 22
4. False; page 22
5. False; page 24
6. True; page 26
7. True; page 26
8. True; page 27

Multiple choice

1. b; page 22
2. d; page 22
3. a; page 24
4. c; page 25
5. d; page 26
6. d; page 27
7. d; page 28
8. b; page 28

Complete the graph

■ **FIGURE A1.18**

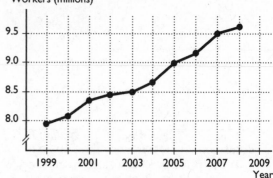

Workers (millions)

1. Figure A1.18 plots the data.
   a. This is a time-series graph; page 22.
   b. The trend is positive. During these 10 years there is an increase in the number of people working in restaurants and bars; page 22.

■ **FIGURE A1.19**

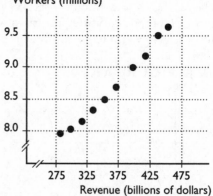

Workers (millions)

2. Figure A1.19 plots the data.
   a. The figure is a scatter diagram; page 22.
   b. The relationship between the revenue and the number of workers is positive; page 24.

■ **FIGURE A1.20**

3. Figure A1.20 plots the relationship.
   a. If the price is $2 per sack, 8,000 sacks are purchased; page 21.
   b. If the price is $3 per sack, 7,000 sacks are purchased; page 21.
   c. The relationship between the price and quantity of sacks is negative; page 25.

■ **FIGURE A1.21**

4. Figure A1.21 labels the two maximum points and one minimum point; page 26.

■ **FIGURE A1.22**

5. Figure A1.22 shows the two lines; page 27.

■ **FIGURE A1.23**

6. a. Figure A1.23 plots the relationship. The relationship is negative; page 25.
   b. The slope equals $(3 - 1) \div (2 - 3)$, which is -2; page 27.

■ **FIGURE A1.24**

   c. Figure A1.24 plots the relationship. The relationship is positive; page 24.

■ **FIGURE A1.25**

Price (dollars per DVD)

7. a. Figure A1.25 plots the relationship; page 28.

b. Figure A1.25 plots the relationship; page 28.

c. An increase in Bobby's income shifts the relationship rightward; page 28.

Short answer and numeric questions

1. The three types of graphs are scatter diagram, time-series graph, and cross-section graph; page 22.

2. If two variables are positively related, a graph of the relationship will have a positive slope. If two variables are negatively related, a graph of the relationship will have a negative slope; pages 24, 25, 27.

3. If a line slopes upward to the right, its slope is positive. If a line slopes downward to the right, its slope is negative; page 27.

4. The slope of a curved line at a point equals the slope of a straight line that touches that point and no other point on the curve. The slope of the curved line at point A is –20 and the slope of the curved line at point B is 10; page 27.

Chapter 2

The U.S. and Global Economies

CHAPTER CHECKLIST

Chapter 2 introduces the circular flow model which shows how goods and services and expenditures flow from and to households, firms, the government, and the rest of the world.

1 Describe what, how, and for whom goods and services are produced in the United States.

The production of goods and services, the "what" question, is divided into four broad categories defined in terms of the ultimate buyer: individuals (consumption goods and services), businesses (capital goods), governments (government goods and services), and other countries (export goods and services). The "how" of production involves the factors of production: land, labor, capital, and entrepreneurship. Goods and services are sold to those who have income, so the personal distribution of income is one way of showing who ends up with our national output. The functional distribution of income shows how much is paid to the owners of each type of productive resource. The largest share of national income is wages, so workers get the largest share of our nation's goods and services.

2 Describe what, how, and for whom goods and services are produced in the global economy.

Countries are divided into advanced economies, the richest 29 countries, and emerging market and developing economies. The advanced economies produce 53 percent of the world's total output, with 20 percent produced in the United States. The advanced economies have more human capital and physical capital than the developing countries. In the world, the lowest-paid 20 percent of the population receives 2 percent of world income and the highest-paid 20 percent receives 70 percent of world income. Inequality of incomes across the entire world has decreased during the past twenty years, primarily because incomes in China have grown rapidly

3 Use the circular flow model to provide a picture of how households, firms, and governments interact in the U.S. economy and how the U.S. and other economies interact in the global economy.

The circular flow model shows that households provide the services from the factors of production, and firms hire these services in factor markets. The circular flow also shows that households purchase goods and services and firms sell goods and services in goods markets. In the circular flow, the government purchases goods and services in goods markets. It makes transfers to firms and households and also taxes them. The decisions made by households and firms in these markets determine the answers to the "what," "how," and "for whom" questions. Households and firms in the United States buy goods and services from firms in other countries (U.S. imports) and U.S. firms sell goods and services to households and firms in other countries (U.S. exports). Using financial inflows, we borrow from other countries (when the value of imports exceeds that of exports) and using financial outflows, we lend to other countries (when the value of exports exceeds that of imports).

CHECKPOINT 2.1

■ **Describe what, how, and for whom goods and services are produced in the United States.**

Quick Review

- *Consumption goods and services* Goods and services that are bought by individuals and used to provide personal enjoyment and contribute to a person's standard of living.
- *Capital goods* Goods that are bought by businesses to increase their productive resources.
- *Government goods and services* Goods and services that are bought by governments.
- *Exports* Goods and services produced in the United States and sold in other countries.

Additional Practice Problems 2.1

1. Tell whether the following goods and services are consumption goods and services, capital goods, government goods and services, or exports.
   a. A taco at Taco Bell purchased for lunch by Shaniq.
   b. An HP printer manufactured in Idaho purchased by Maria in Peru.
   c. A new grill purchased by Taco Bell.
   d. A tour down the Colorado river from Rimrock Adventures purchased by the Miller family.
   e. CamelBak drinking packs purchased by the U.S. Marine Corp.
   f. CamelBak drinking packs purchased by Rimrock Adventures for use by their customers during tours.
   g. A CamelBak drinking pack purchased by Anne for use while mountain biking.
   h. A CamelBak drinking pack purchased by Sebastian, a German racing in the Tour de France.

2. How much labor is there in the United States? What determines the quantity of labor?

Solutions to Additional Practice Problems 2.1

1a. Shaniq's taco is a consumption good.
1b. Maria's printer is an export good.
1c. The new grill is a capital good.
1d. The tour is a consumption service.
1e. The drinking pack purchased by the Marines is a government good because it is purchased by the government.
1f. The drinking pack purchased by Rimrock Adventures is a capital good because it is purchased by a business.
1g. The drinking pack purchased by Anne is a consumption good.
1h. The drinking pack purchased by Sebastian is an export good.

2. In the United States, in 2011 about 153 million people had jobs or were available for work and they provided about 250 billion hours of labor a year. The quantity of labor depends on the size of the population, the percentage of the population that takes jobs, and on social relationships that influence things such as how many women take paid work. An increase in the proportion of women who have taken paid work has increased the quantity of labor in the United States over the past 50 years.

■ **Self Test 2.1**

Fill in the blanks

Goods and services that are bought by individuals and used to provide personal enjoyment and to contribute to a person's standard of living are ____ (consumption; capital; export) goods. Goods that are bought by businesses to increase their productive resources are ____ (consumption; capital; export) goods. Goods that are produced in the United States and sold in other countries are ____ (consumption; capital; export) goods. Of the four large groups of goods and services in the United States, ____ (consumption goods and services; capital goods; government goods and services; export goods and services) have the largest share of total production. Productive resources are called ____ and are grouped into four categories: ____,

____, ____, and ____. In 2010, ____ (labor; capital) received 69 percent of total income. The distribution of income among households is called the ____ (functional; personal) distribution of income.

True or false

1. Consumption goods and services include a slice of pizza purchased to eat at home.

2. A gold mine is included in the "land" category of productive resources.

3. Michael Dell, the person who founded and manages Dell computers, is an example of an entrepreneur.

4. In the United States, the factor of production that earns the most income is labor.

5. In the United States, the richest 20 percent of individuals earn approximately 30 percent of total income.

Multiple choice

1. When the total U.S. production of goods and services is divided into consumption goods and services, capital goods, government goods and services, and export goods and services, the largest component is
   a. consumption goods and services.
   b. capital goods.
   c. government goods and services.
   d. export goods and services.
   e. capital goods and government goods and services tie for the largest component.

2. An example of a capital good is
   a. a fiber optic cable TV system.
   b. an insurance policy.
   c. a hair cut.
   d. an iPod.
   e. a slice of pizza.

3. Goods and services produced in the United States and sold in other countries are called
   a. consumption goods and services.
   b. capital goods.
   c. government goods and services.
   d. export goods and services.
   e. import goods and services.

4. Which of the following correctly lists the factors of production?
   a. machines, buildings, land, and money
   b. hardware, software, land, and money
   c. capital, money, and labor
   d. owners, workers, and consumers.
   e. land, labor, capital, and entrepreneurship

5. Human capital is
   a. solely the innate ability we are born with.
   b. the money humans have saved.
   c. the knowledge humans accumulate through education and experience.
   d. machinery that needs human supervision.
   e. any type of machinery.

6. Wages are paid to ____ and interest is paid to ____.
   a. entrepreneurs; capital
   b. labor; capital
   c. labor; land
   d. entrepreneurs; land
   e. labor; entrepreneurs

7. Dividing the nation's income among the factors of production, the largest percentage is paid to
   a. labor.
   b. land.
   c. capital.
   d. entrepreneurship.
   e. labor and capital, with each receiving about 41 percent of the total income.

8. The personal distribution of income shows
   a. that labor earn the largest percentage of total income.
   b. how profit accounts for the largest fraction of total income.
   c. that the richest 20 percent of households earn 23 percent of total income.
   d. that interest accounts for most of the income of the richest 20 percent of households.
   e. that the poorest 20 percent of households earn 3 percent of total income.

Short answer and numeric questions

1. Is an automobile a consumption good or a capital good?

2. Compare the incomes received by the poorest and richest 20 percent of individuals.

Additional Exercises (also in MyEconLab Test A)

1. What is the distinction between consumption goods and services and capital goods? Which one of them brings an increase in productive resources?

2. If everyone in the United States were to consume an equal quantity of goods and services, what percentage of total income would the poorest 20 percent of households have to receive from higher-income groups?

3. Compare the percentage of total U.S. income that labor earns with the percentage earned by all the other factors of production combined.

CHECKPOINT 2.2

■ **Describe what, how, and for whom goods and services are produced in the global economy.**

Quick Review

- *Advanced economies* The 29 countries (or areas) that have the highest living standards.

- *Emerging markets and Developing economies* Emerging markets are the 28 countries in Europe and Asia that were until the early 1990s part of the Soviet Union or its satellites and are changing the way they organize their economies. Developing economies are the 119 countries in Africa, the Middle East, Europe, and Central and South America that have not yet achieved a high standard of living for their people.

Additional Practice Problems 2.2

1. What percentage of the world's population live in developing economies? In places such as China, India, and Africa, what was the average income per day?

2. What percentage of the world's population live in advanced economies? In countries such as the United States, Canada, and Japan, what was the average income per day?

3. How does the total production within the advanced economies, the emerging market economies, and the developing economies compare?

4. How is it possible that income inequality within most countries has increased in recent years yet income inequality across the whole world has decreased in recent years?

Solutions to Additional Practice Problems 2.2

1. The world's population is about 7 billion. More than 5 billion of the people live in developing economies. So, approximately 80 percent of the world's population lives in developing economies. Average daily income in China is $16, in India is $8, and in Africa is $7. Because these are the average, many people live on less than these amounts.

2. About 1 billion people, or 15 percent of the world's population live in the 28 advanced economies. The average income per day in the United States was $129, in Canada was $126, and in Japan was $116.

3. Of the world's total production, the advanced economies produce 53 percent (20 percent is produced in the United States). The emerging market economies produce 8 percent of the world's production and the developing economies produce the remainder, 39 percent.

4. While income inequality within nations has been increasing, the difference in incomes among different nations has been decreasing. In particular, China has seen extremely rapid growth in income. The growth in income for this poor but populous nation has decreased income inequality in the world as a whole.

■ **Self Test 2.2**

Fill in the blanks

Most of the world's population lives in the ____ (advanced economies; emerging market economies; developing economies). The lowest average income is in the ____ (advanced economies; emerging market economies; developing economies). Advanced economies produce about ____ (24; 53; 72) percent of the world's total production and the United States, alone, produces about ____ (6; 20; 33) percent of the world's total production. As a fraction of total output, agricultural is a ____ (larger; smaller) part of the economy in developing economies than in advanced economies. Factories in advanced economies generally are much ____ (less; more) capital intensive than in developing economies. During the past 20 years, the distribution of income in the world economy has become ____ (more; less) equal.

True or false

1. About 50 percent of the world's population lives in the advanced economies.

2. Mexico is classified as an emerging market economy.

3. Taken as a group, the 119 developing economy nations produce a larger percentage of total world production than do the 29 advanced economy nations.

4. Most of the world's electricity is generated by coal.

5. Workers in the advanced economies have much more human capital than workers in the developing economies.

6. Income inequality within most nations has increased over the past years.

Multiple choice

1. The world population is approximately ____ people.
   a. 7 million
   b. 2 trillion
   c. 7 billion
   d. 1.4 trillion
   e. 70 million

2. The percentage of the world's population that lives in the advanced economies is
   a. more than 71 percent.
   b. between 51 percent and 70 percent.
   c. between 31 percent and 50 percent.
   d. between 20 percent and 30 percent.
   e. less than 20 percent.

3. Which of following groups of countries are *all* advanced economies?
   a. Australia, Brazil, and the United States
   b. Hong Kong, Japan, France, and the United Kingdom
   c. Italy, the United States, China, and Russia
   d. Singapore, Russia, France, and Chad
   e. Mexico, Canada, Germany, and Egypt

4. The emerging market economies are
   a. the largest grouping including the nations of China and India.
   b. in transition from state-owned production to free markets.
   c. most of the nations of Western Europe.
   d. the nations that are currently agricultural in nature.
   e. the nations with the highest standards of living.

5. As a percentage of total world production, production in the 29 advanced economies is about ____ percent of total world production and in the 119 developing economies is about ____ percent of total world production.
   a. 53; 39
   b. 23; 62
   c. 53; 12
   d. 30; 46
   e. 19; 73

6. Compared to the developing economies, the advanced economies have ____ human capital and ____ physical capital.
   a. more; more
   b. more; less
   c. the same; the same
   d. less; more
   e. less; less

7. In the advanced economies, ____ of the factories use advanced capital equipment and in the developing economies ____ of the factories use advanced capital equipment.
   a. virtually all; virtually all
   b. some; some
   c. virtually all; none
   d. some; none of
   e. virtually all; some

8. Among the United States, Canada, Russia, India, and the United Kingdom, the country with the highest average income per person is
   a. the United States.
   b. Russia.
   c. India.
   d. Canada.
   e. the United Kingdom.

Short answer and numeric questions

1. What are the groups the International Monetary Fund uses to classify countries? Describe each group. Which group has the largest number of countries? The largest number of people?

2. As a fraction of total world production, how does production within the advanced economies compare to production within the developing economies? As a fraction of total population, how does the population within the advanced economies compare to the population within the developing economies?

3. How does the amount of human capital in the advanced economies compare to that in the developing economies?

4. How does the distribution of income within the United States compare to the distribution of income in the world economy?

Additional Exercises (also in MyEconLab Test A)

1. Describe how inequality around the world has changed over the past few decades.

CHECKPOINT 2.3

■ **Use the circular flow model to provide a picture of how households, firms, and governments interact in the U.S. economy and how the U.S. and other economies interact in the global economy.**

Quick Review

- *Circular flow model* A model of the econ-

omy, illustrated in Figure 2.1, that shows the circular flow of expenditures and incomes that result from firms', households', and governments' choices.

■ FIGURE 2.1

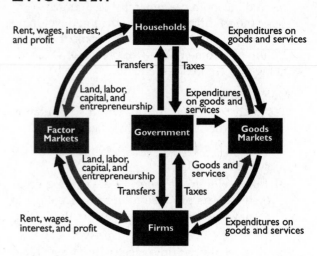

Additional Practice Problems 2.3

1. Describe where the following money flows fit in the circular flow.
   a. Shaniq pays for a taco at Taco Bell.
   b. Sam receives his monthly Social Security payment.
   c. Jennifer gets a $10,000 end of the year bonus from Bank of America, where she works.
   d. Exxon pays landowners in Texas $20,000 for the oil under their land.
   e. Bill pays property tax of $6,000.

2. In the circular flow, what is the relationship between the flow of expenditures into the goods markets (from households and the government) and the flow of revenues out of the goods markets to firms?

Solutions to Additional Practice Problems 2.3

1a. Shaniq's payment is an expenditure on a good that flows from households through the goods market to Taco Bell, a firm.

1b. Sam's check is a transfer payment from the government to households.

1c. Jennifer's payment is wages flowing from a firm, Bank of America, through the factor market to households.

1d. Exxon's payment is rent flowing from a firm, Exxon, through the factor market to households.

1e. Bill's payment is a tax flowing from households to government.

2. The flow of expenditures into the goods markets–the funds that households and the government spend on the goods and services they purchase–equals the flow of revenue out of the goods markets.

■ Self Test 2.3

Fill in the blanks

The ____ model shows the flows of expenditure and incomes. An arrangement that brings buyers and sellers together is a ____ (firm; household; market). A market in which goods and services are bought and sold is a ____ (goods; factor) market and a market in which the services of the factors of production are bought and sold is a ____ (goods; factor) market. In 2010, the federal government spent about ____ (24; 13) percent of the total value of the goods and services produced in the United States. A large part of what the federal government spends is ____ (social security benefits; personal income taxes). The two components that account for most of the federal government's tax revenue are ____. The largest part of the expenditures of state and local governments is spending on ____ (education; highways). When the value of U.S. imports exceeds the value of U.S. exports, U.S. residents ____ (borrow from; lend to) the rest of the world.

True or false

1. Firms own the factors of production.

2. A market is any arrangement where buyers and sellers meet face-to-face.

3. Factors of production flow from households to firms through goods markets.

4. Rent, wages, interest, and profit are the payments made by firms to households through factor markets.

5. Social security payments are made by state and local governments.

6. The largest part of the expenditures of state and local government is on education.

Multiple choice

1. Within the circular flow model, economists define households as
   a. families with at least 2 children.
   b. families living in their own houses.
   c. individuals or groups living together.
   d. married or engaged couples.
   e. individuals or groups within the same legally defined family.

2. A market is defined as
   a. the physical place where goods (but not services) are sold.
   b. the physical place where goods *and* services are sold.
   c. any arrangement that brings buyers and sellers together.
   d. a place where money is exchanged for goods.
   e. another name for a store.

3. In the circular flow model,
   a. only firms sell in markets.
   b. only households buy from markets.
   c. some firms only sell and some firms only buy.
   d. the money used to buy goods and the goods themselves travel in the same direction.
   e. both firms and households buy or sell in different markets.

4. ____ choose the quantities of goods and services to produce, while ____ choose the quantities of goods and services to buy.
   a. Households; firms
   b. Firms; households and the government
   c. The government; firms
   d. Firms; only households
   e. Households; the government

5. A circular flow model shows the interrelationship between the ____ market and the ____ markets.
   a. household; goods
   b. household; factor
   c. business; household
   d. expenditure; income
   e. goods; factor

6. In the circular flow model, the expenditures on goods and services flow in the
   a. same direction as goods and services in all cases.
   b. same direction as goods and services *only if* they both flow through the goods market.
   c. same direction as goods and services *only if* they both flow through the factor market.
   d. opposite direction as goods and services.
   e. same direction as factor markets.

7. Of the following, the largest source of revenue for the federal government is
   a. personal income taxes.
   b. sales taxes.
   c. corporate income taxes.
   d. property taxes.
   e. lottery revenue.

8. U.S. exports of goods and services flow to households and firms in ____ and U.S. financial inflows of capital flow to households and firms in ____.
   a. the United States; the United States
   b. the United States; the rest of the world
   c. the rest of the world; the United States
   d. the rest of the world; the rest of the world
   e. the United States; the rest of the world and the United States

Complete the graph

■ **FIGURE 2.2**

1. Figure 2.2 ignores the government and shows the flows into and out of households. Label the flows and identify who they come from and who they go to.

■ **FIGURE 2.3**

2. Figure 2.3 ignores the government and shows the flows into and out of firms. Label the flows and identify who they come from and who they go to.

■ **FIGURE 2.4**

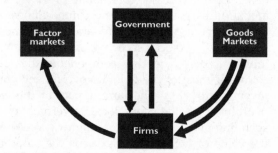

3. Figure 2.4 now includes the government and shows the money flows into and out of firms. Label the money flows.

Short answer and numeric questions

1. Ignoring taxes and transfer payments, what funds flow into firms and what funds flow out of them?

2. Is it possible for something to affect households and not firms? To affect firms and not households? Explain your answers.

3. The circular flow reveals that which two groups interact to determine what will be the payments to the factors of production?

4. In the circular flow model, what are the sources of expenditures on goods and services?

5. In recent years, which spent more, the federal government or state and local governments?

Additional Exercises (also in MyEconLab Test A)

1. What are the choices made by households and firms that determine what, how, and for whom goods and services are produced? Where, in the circular flow model, do those choices appear?

2. How do the actions of governments modify what, how, and for whom goods and services are produced? Where, in the circular flow model, do those choices appear?

SELF TEST ANSWERS

■ CHECKPOINT 2.1

Fill in the blanks

Goods and services that are bought by individuals and used to provide personal enjoyment and to contribute to a person's standard of living are <u>consumption</u> goods. Goods that are bought by businesses to increase their productive resources are <u>capital</u> goods. Goods that are produced in the United States and sold in other countries are <u>export</u> goods. Of the four large groups of goods and services in the United States, <u>consumption goods and services</u> have the largest share of total production. Productive resources are called <u>factors of production</u> and are grouped into four categories: <u>labor</u>, <u>land</u>, <u>capital</u>, and <u>entrepreneurship</u>. In 2010, <u>labor</u> received 69 percent of total income. The distribution of income among households is called the <u>personal</u> distribution of income.

True or false

1. True; page 32
2. True; page 34
3. True; page 36
4. True; page 37
5. False; page 37

Multiple choice

1. a; page 32
2. a; page 32
3. d; page 32
4. e; page 34
5. c; page 35
6. b; page 37
7. a; page 37
8. e; page 37

Short answer and numeric questions

1. An automobile might be either a consumption or a capital good. It is a consumption good if it is purchased by a household. It is a capital good if it is purchased by a business for use within the business; page 32.
2. The richest 20 percent of households receive 51 percent of the total U.S. income. The poorest 20 percent of households receive 3 percent of the total U.S. income; page 37.

Additional Exercises (also in MyEconLab Test A)

1. Consumption goods and services are items that are bought by individuals and used to provide personal enjoyment. They contribute to a person's standard of living. Capital goods are goods that are bought by businesses to increase their productive resources and thereby help produce additional goods and services. Capital goods increase the nation's capital, which is a productive resource; page 32.
2. If everyone were to consume an equal quantity of goods and services, the poorest 20 percent of individuals would need to receive about 17 percent of total income from the higher-income groups; page 37.
3. Labor earns by far the largest share of the nation's total income, about 69 percent. The other factors of production earn only 31 percent of the nation's total income; page 37.

■ CHECKPOINT 2.2

Fill in the blanks

Most of the world's population lives in the <u>developing economies</u>. The lowest average income is in the <u>developing economies</u>. Advanced economies produce about <u>53</u> percent of the world's total production and the United States, alone, produces about <u>20</u> percent of the world's total production. As a fraction of total output, agricultural is a <u>larger</u> part of the economy in developing economies than in advanced economies. Factories in advanced economies generally are much <u>more</u> capital intensive than in developing economies. During the past 20 years, the distribution of income in the world economy has become <u>more</u> equal.

True or false

1. False; page 39
2. False; page 39

3. False; page 40
4. True; page 42
5. True; page 42
6. True; page 44

Multiple choice
1. c; page 39
2. e; page 39
3. b; page 39
4. b; page 39
5. a; page 40
6. a; pages 42-43
7. e; page 43
8. a; pages 43-44

Short answer and numeric questions
1. The groups are the advanced economies and the emerging market and developing economies. Advanced economies have the highest standard of living. Emerging market and developing economies have yet to achieve a high standard of living. The emerging market economies are changing their economies from government management and state-ownership of capital to market-based economies similar to that in the United States. There are more nations, 119, and more people, almost 5 billion, in developing economies; page 39.
2. Production in the advanced and emerging economies accounts for 61 percent of world production and production in the developing economies accounts for 39 percent. The population within the advanced and emerging economies accounts for 22 percent of the world's population and the developing economies account for 78 percent of the world's population; page 40.
3. The human capital possessed by workers in the advanced economies is *much* larger than that in the developing economies. People in the advanced economies have vastly more education, more on-the-job training and, in general, better health than in the developing economies; page 42.
4. The distribution of income within the United States is more equal than the distribution of income in the world economy. In the United States, the poorest 20 percent of households receive about 3 percent of the total income and the richest 20 percent of households receive about 50 percent of total income. In the world economy, the poorest 20 percent of households receive about 2 percent of total income and the richest 20 percent receive about 70 percent of total income; page 43.

Additional Exercises (also in MyEconLab Test A)
1. Inequality around the world has decreased over the past few decades. Extreme poverty has fallen, largely because of income growth in China, the largest nation in the world and a nation that was the source of much of the extreme poverty of a few decades ago; page 44.

■ CHECKPOINT 2.3

Fill in the blanks
The circular flow model shows the flows of expenditures and incomes. An arrangement that brings buyers and sellers together is a market. A market in which goods and services are bought and sold is a goods market and a market in which the services of the factors of production are bought and sold is a factor market. In 2010, the federal government spent about 24 percent of the total value of the goods and services produced in the United States. A large part of what the federal government spends is social security benefits. The two components that account for most of the federal government's tax revenue are personal income tax and social security tax. The largest part of the expenditures of state and local governments is spending on education. When the value of U.S. imports exceeds the value of U.S. exports, U.S. residents borrow from the rest of the world.

True or false
1. False; page 46
2. False; page 46
3. False; pages 46-47

4. True; pages 46-47

5. False; page 48

6. True; page 51

Multiple choice

1. c; page 46

2. c; page 46

3. e; pages 46-47

4. b; pages 47, 49

5. e; pages 46-47

6. d; page 47

7. a; page 50

8. c; page 53

Complete the graph

■ FIGURE 2.5

1. Figure 2.5 labels the flows. Rent, wages, interest, and profits (or losses) flow from the factor markets while the services from land, labor, capital, and entrepreneurship flow to the factor markets. In addition, expenditures on goods and services flow to the goods market, and goods and services flow from the goods market; page 47.

■ FIGURE 2.6

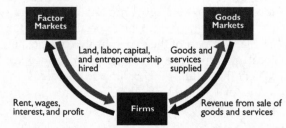

2. Figure 2.6 labels the flows. Revenue from the sale of goods and services, which are the expenditures on goods and services, flow to firms from the goods market and payments

of rent, wages, interest, and profit (or loss) flow from firms into the factor market. The services from land, labor, capital, and entrepreneurship flow to firms from the factor markets, and goods and services flow from firms into the goods markets; page 47.

■ FIGURE 2.7

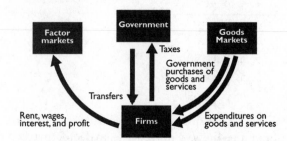

3. Figure 2.7 labels the money flows into and out of firms. The difference between this figure and Figure 2.6 is the addition of transfers and taxes; page 49.

Short answer and numeric questions

1. Funds that flow into firms are households' expenditures and government purchases of goods and services. Funds that flow out of firms are payments for rent, wages, interest, and profit (or loss) to households in exchange for the factors of production; pages 47, 49.

2. The circular flow shows that at the macroeconomic level it is impossible for something to influence only firms or only households. An influence that changes households' buying behavior in goods markets affects firms because they sell to households in goods markets; page 47.

3. Payments to the factors of production are determined by the interaction of households, who own and provide the services from the factors of production, and firms, who employ the services from these factors; page 47.

4. The circular flow identifies two sources of expenditures on goods and services, expenditures by households and expenditures by the government; page 49.

5. In 2010, the federal government spent $3.5 trillion and in 2008 state and local governments spent $2.1 trillion. The federal government spends significantly more than state and local governments; page 48.

Additional Exercises (also in MyEconLab Test A)

1. Households choose the quantities of land, labor, capital, and entrepreneurship services to provide to firms. Households decide what goods and services they will buy. Firms choose the quantities of services of the factors of production to hire and the quantities of goods and services to produce. Households decide what to buy in goods markets and what quantities of the services of factors of production to provide in factor markets. Firms decide the quantities of services of factors of production to hire in factor markets and the quantity of goods and services to produce in goods markets; pages 46-47.

2. Governments modify the answers to the "what," "how," and "for whom" questions by their interactions with firms and households. In the goods market, governments decide what goods to buy, thereby affecting the "what" question. Governments also tax firms and households and give firms and households transfer payments. These directly effect the "for whom" question because taxes decrease the payer's ability to buy goods and services while transfers enhance the recipient's buying power. The taxes and transfer payments also affect households' and firms' decisions about what services of the factors of production to provide and what services to buy, so these taxes and transfer payments also affect the "how" question; page 49.

The Economic Problem

Chapter 3

Chapter 3 develops an economic model, the production possibilities frontier, or *PPF*, model. The *PPF* shows how the opportunity cost of a good or service increases as more of the good or service is produced. It can be used to illustrate economic growth and to demonstrate societies and individuals gain by specializing according to comparative advantage.

1 Explain and illustrate the concepts of scarcity, production efficiency, and tradeoff using the production possibilities frontier.

The production possibilities frontier, *PPF*, is the boundary between the combinations of goods and services that can be produced and those that cannot be produced, given the available factors of production and technology. Production points outside the *PPF* are unattainable. Points on and inside the *PPF* are attainable. Production points on the *PPF* are production efficient while production points within the *PPF* are inefficient. Moving along the *PPF* producing more of one good, less of another good is produced—a tradeoff. Moving from inside the *PPF* to a point on the *PPF*, more of some goods and services can be produced without producing less of others—a free lunch.

2 Calculate opportunity cost.

Along the *PPF* all choices involve a tradeoff. Along the *PPF*, the opportunity cost of the good on the *x*-axis is the loss of the good measured along the *y*-axis and is equal to the decrease in the good on the *y*-axis divided by the increase in the good on the *x*-axis. As more of a good is produced, its opportunity cost increases, so the *PPF* is bowed outward. The opportunity cost increases because resources are not equally productive in all activities. In the real world, most activities have increasing opportunity cost.

3 Explain what makes production possibilities expand.

Economic growth is the sustained expansion of production possibilities. If more capital is accumulated production possibilities increase and the *PPF* shifts outward. The (opportunity) cost of economic growth is that resources used to increase capital cannot be used to produce current consumption goods and services.

4 Explain how people gain from specialization and trade.

A person (or nation) has an absolute advantage when the person (or nation) is more productive than another—needs fewer inputs or less time to produce the good. A person (or nation) has a comparative advantage in an activity or producing a good if the person (or nation) can perform the activity or produce the good at lower opportunity cost than another. A person (or nation) can have an absolute advantage in all activities but cannot have a comparative advantage in all activities. People can gain from specializing in production according to comparative advantage and then trading with others. In this situation people (and nations) can consume combinations of goods and services that lie beyond their production possibilities frontiers.

CHECKPOINT 3.1

■ **Explain and illustrate the concepts of scarcity, production efficiency, and tradeoff using the production possibilities frontier.**

Quick Review

- *Production possibilities frontier* The boundary between combinations of goods and services that can be produced and combinations that cannot be produced, given the available factors of production and the state of technology.
- *Unattainable points* Production points outside the *PPF* are unattainable.
- *Tradeoff* A constraint or limit to what is possible that forces an exchange or a substitution of one thing for something else.

Additional Practice Problem 3.1

Possibility	Fish (pounds)		Fruit (pounds)
A	0.0	and	36.0
B	4.0	and	35.0
C	7.5	and	33.0
D	10.5	and	30.0
E	13.0	and	26.0
F	15.0	and	21.0
G	16.5	and	15.0
H	17.5	and	8.0
I	18.0	and	0.0

1. The table above shows Crusoe's *PPF*. Can Crusoe gather 21 pounds of fruit and catch 30 pounds of fish? Explain your answer. Suppose that Crusoe discovers another fishing pond with more fish, so that he can catch twice as many fish as before. Now can Crusoe gather 21 pounds of fruit and catch 30 pounds of fish? Explain your answer.

Solution to Additional Practice Problem 3.1

1. Initially, Crusoe cannot gather 21 pounds of fruit and catch 30 pounds of fish. This production point lies outside his *PPF* and so is unattainable. Once Crusoe discovers the new pond, however, he can gather 21 pounds of fruit and catch 30 pounds of fish. (In Row *F*, double the amount of Crusoe's fish.) The *PPF* depends on the available factors of production and when the factors of production increase, Crusoe's production possibilities change.

■ Self Test 3.1

Fill in the blanks

The ____ is the boundary between the combinations of goods and services that can and that cannot be produced given the available ____ (goods; factors of production) and ____ (number of services; state of technology). Production points outside the *PPF* ____ (are unattainable; are attainable; represent a free lunch). Production points ____ (on; beyond; within) the *PPF* are production efficient. Society has the possibility of a free lunch if production occurs ____ (inside; on; outside) the *PPF*. When resources are fully employed we face a ____ (free lunch; tradeoff).

True or false

1. A point outside the production possibilities frontier is unattainable.

2. If all the factors of production are fully employed, the economy will produce at a point on the production possibilities frontier.

3. Moving from one point on the *PPF* to another point on the *PPF* illustrates a free lunch.

4. All production points on the *PPF* are production efficient.

Multiple choice

1. The production possibilities frontier is a graph showing the
   a. exact point of greatest efficiency for producing goods and services.
   b. tradeoff between free lunches.
   c. maximum combinations of goods and services that can be produced.
   d. minimum combinations of goods and services that can be produced.
   e. resources available for the economy's production uses.

2. The production possibilities frontier is a boundary that separates
   a. the combinations of goods that can be produced from the combinations of services.
   b. attainable combinations of goods and services that can be produced from unattainable combinations.
   c. equitable combinations of goods and services that can be produced from inequitable combinations.
   d. fair combinations of goods and services that can be consumed from unfair combinations.
   e. affordable production points from unaffordable points.

3. Points inside the *PPF* are all
   a. unattainable and have fully employed resources.
   b. attainable and have fully employed resources.
   c. unattainable and have some unemployed resources.
   d. attainable and have some unemployed resources.
   e. unaffordable.

4. Points on the *PPF* are all
   a. unattainable and have fully employed resources.
   b. free lunches.
   c. inefficient.
   d. attainable and have some unemployed resources.
   e. production efficient.

5. During a time with high unemployment, a country can increase the production of one good or service
   a. without decreasing the production of something else.
   b. but must decrease the production of something else.
   c. and must increase the production of something else.
   d. by using resources in the production process twice.
   e. but the opportunity cost is infinite.

6. Moving along the production possibilities frontier itself illustrates
   a. the existence of tradeoffs.
   b. the existence of unemployment of some factors of production.
   c. the benefits of free lunches.
   d. how free lunches can be exploited through trade.
   e. how tradeoffs need not occur if the economy is efficient.

Complete the graph

■ **FIGURE 3.1**

Computers (millions per year)

1. In Figure 3.1, draw a production possibilities frontier showing combinations of computers and food. Label the points that are attainable and unattainable. Label the points that have full employment and the points that have unemployment.

Short answer and numeric questions

1. What factors limit the amount of production in the United States?
2. What points are production efficient? Moving between these points, is there a tradeoff or a free lunch?
3. What is the relationship between unemployment of a resource and a free lunch? Between full employment of all factors of production and a tradeoff?

Additional Exercises (also in MyEconLab Test A)

The table shows the production possibilities frontier of a small Pacific island economy.

Possibility	Fish (pounds)		Berries (pounds)
A	0	and	20
B	1	and	18
C	2	and	15
D	3	and	11
E	4	and	6
F	5	and	0

Use this table to work these exercises.

1. Explain why this economy cannot produce 2 pounds of fish and 18 pounds of berries.

2. Explain why 3 pounds of fish and 11 pounds of berries achieves production efficiency.

3. Explain why it would be inefficient to produce 4 pounds of fish and 5 pounds of berries.

4. Explain why moving from row A to row B of the table involves a tradeoff.

5. Explain why the citizens of this economy could enjoy a free lunch if they were producing 4 pounds of fish and 5 pounds of berries.

CHECKPOINT 3.2

■ Calculate opportunity cost.

Quick Review

- *Opportunity cost is a ratio* Along a *PPF*, the opportunity cost of one good equals the quantity of the other good forgone divided by the increase in the first good.

Additional Practice Problem 3.2

Possibility	Fish (pounds)		Fruit (pounds)
A	0.0	and	36.0
B	4.0	and	35.0
C	7.5	and	33.0
D	10.5	and	30.0
E	13.0	and	26.0
F	15.0	and	21.0
G	16.5	and	15.0
H	17.5	and	8.0
I	18.0	and	0.0

1. The table above shows Robinson Crusoe's production possibilities. How does Crusoe's op-portunity cost of a pound of fish change as he catches more fish?

Solution to Additional Practice Problem 3.2

Move from	Increase in fish (pounds)	Decrease in fruit (pounds)	Opportunity cost of fish (pounds of fruit)
A to B	4.0	1.0	0.25
B to C	3.5	2.0	0.57
C to D	3.0	3.0	1.00
D to E	2.5	4.0	1.60
E to F	2.0	5.0	2.50
F to G	1.5	6.0	4.00
G to H	1.0	7.0	7.00
H to I	0.5	8.0	16.00

1. The table above shows Crusoe's opportunity cost of a pound of fish. His opportunity cost of a pound of fish increases as he catches more fish. As he moves from point A to point B and catches his first fish, the opportunity cost is only 0.25 pounds of fruit per pound of fish. But as he moves from point H to point I and catches only fish, the opportunity cost has increased to 16.0 pounds of fruit per pound of fish.

■ Self Test 3.2

Fill in the blanks

Along a production possibilities frontier, the opportunity cost of obtaining one more unit of a good is the amount of another good that is ____ (gained; forgone). The opportunity cost is equal to the quantity of the good forgone ____ (plus; divided by) the increase in the quantity of the other good. As more of a good is produced, its opportunity cost ____.

True or false

1. Moving from one point on the *PPF* to another point on the *PPF* has no opportunity cost.

2. When moving along the *PPF*, the quantity of CDs increases by 2 and the quantity of DVDs decreases by 1, so the opportunity cost is 2 CDs minus 1 DVD.

3. Increasing opportunity costs are common.

Multiple choice

1. The opportunity cost of one more slice of pizza in terms of sodas is the
   a. number of pizza slices we have to give up to get one extra soda.
   b. number of sodas we have to give up to get one extra slice of pizza.
   c. total number of sodas that we have divided by the total number of pizza slices that we have.
   d. total number of pizza slices that we have divided by the total number of sodas that we have.
   e. price of a pizza slice minus the price of a soda.

2. Moving between two points on a *PPF*, a country gains 6 automobiles and forgoes 3 trucks. The opportunity cost of 1 automobile is
   a. 3 trucks.
   b. 6 automobiles – 3 trucks.
   c. 2 trucks.
   d. 1/2 of a truck.
   e. 1 automobile.

3. Moving between two points on a *PPF*, a country gains 8 desktop computers and forgoes 4 laptop computers. The opportunity cost of 1 desktop computer is
   a. 4 laptops.
   b. 8 desktops.
   c. 1 desktop.
   d. 2 laptops.
   e. 1/2 of a laptop.

4. A country produces only cans of soup and ink pens. If the country produces on its bowed outward *PPF* and increases the production of cans of soup, the opportunity cost of additional
   a. cans of soup is increasing.
   b. cans of soup is decreasing.
   c. cans of soup remain unchanged.
   d. ink pens is increasing.
   e. More information is needed to determine what happens to the opportunity cost.

5. Moving along a country's *PPF*, a reason opportunity costs increase is that
   a. unemployment decreases as a country produces more and more of one good.
   b. unemployment increases as a country produces more and more of one good.
   c. technology declines as a country produces more and more of one good.
   d. some resources are better suited for producing one good rather than the other.
   e. technology must advance in order to produce more and more of one good.

6. Increasing opportunity costs exist
   a. in the real world.
   b. as long as there is high unemployment.
   c. only in theory but not in real life.
   d. for a country but not for an individual.
   e. inside the *PPF* but not on the *PPF*.

Complete the graph

Production point	MP3 players (millions per year)		DVD players (millions per year)
A	4.0	and	0.0
B	3.0	and	3.0
C	2.0	and	4.0
D	1.0	and	4.7
E	0.0	and	5.0

1. The table shows the production possibilities for a nation.
   a. Placing MP3 players on the vertical axis, label the axes in Figure 3.2 and graph the production possibilities frontier.

■ **FIGURE 3.2**

b. What is the opportunity cost per DVD player of moving from point *A* to point *B*? *B* to *C*? *C* to *D*? *D* to *E*? How does the opportunity cost change as more DVD players are produced?

Short answer and numeric questions

Production point	Cans of soda (millions per year)		Candy bars (millions per year)
A	8.0	and	0.0
B	6.0	and	4.0
C	4.0	and	6.0
D	2.0	and	7.0
E	0.0	and	7.5

1. The table above shows the production possibilities for Sweetland.
   a. What is the opportunity cost per candy bar player of moving from point *A* to point *B*? *B* to *C*? *C* to *D*? *D* to *E*?
   b. What is the opportunity cost per can of soda of moving from point *E* to point *D*? *D* to *C*? *C* to *B*? *B* to *A*?
   c. How does the opportunity cost of a candy bar change as more candy bars are produced? How does the opportunity cost of a soda change as more sodas are produced?

2. What is the opportunity cost of increasing the production of a good while moving along a *PPF*? Why does this opportunity cost increase?

3. What does it mean for the opportunity cost to be a ratio?

Additional Exercises (also in MyEconLab Test A)

Possibility	Fish (pounds)		Berries (pounds)
A	0	and	20
B	3.0	and	18
C	5.5	and	15
D	7.5	and	11
E	9.0	and	6
F	10.0	and	0

The table shows Robinson Crusoe's production possibilities in winter. Use the information in this table to work the exercises.
1. If Crusoe currently catches 5.5 pounds of fish and picks 11 pounds of berries a day, what is his opportunity cost of an extra pound of berries? And what is his opportunity cost of an extra pound of fish? Explain your answers.

2. If Crusoe produces efficiently, does his opportunity cost of a pound of berries increase as he spends more time picking berries? Explain.

CHECKPOINT 3.3

■ **Explain what makes production possibilities expand.**

Quick Review
- *Opportunity cost of growth* The opportunity cost of economic growth is the current consumption goods and services forgone.

Additional Practice Problem 3.3
1. Does economic growth eliminate scarcity?

Solution to Additional Practice Problem 3.3
1. Economic growth does not eliminate scarcity. Scarcity exists as long as people's wants exceed what can be produced. Economic growth increases the goods and services that can be produced but people's wants will continue to outstrip the ability to produce. While economic growth means that additional wants can be satisfied, people's wants are infinite and so scarcity will continue to be present even with economic growth.

■ **Self Test 3.3**

Fill in the blanks
A sustained expansion of production possibilities is called ____. Economic growth shifts the *PPF* ____ (inward; outward). The *PPF* shows that economic growth requires ____ (a decrease; an increase) in the current production of consumption goods. The opportunity cost of increasing economic growth is the loss of the ____ (current; future) goods that can be consumed.

True or false
1. Economic growth abolishes scarcity.

2. The opportunity cost of economic growth is less consumption goods in the future.

3. Production possibilities per person in the United States have remained constant during the last 30 years.

Multiple choice

1. To increase its economic growth, a nation should
   a. limit the number of people in college because they produce nothing.
   b. encourage spending on goods and services.
   c. encourage education because that increases the quality of labor.
   d. increase current consumption.
   e. eliminate expenditure on capital goods.

2. Other things equal, if Mexico devotes more resources to train its population than Spain,
   a. Mexico will be able to eliminate opportunity cost faster than Spain.
   b. Mexico will be able to eliminate scarcity faster than Spain.
   c. Spain will grow faster than Mexico.
   d. Mexico will grow faster than Spain.
   e. Mexico will have more current consumption than Spain.

3. If a nation devotes a larger share of its current production to consumption goods, then
   a. its economic growth will slow down.
   b. its *PPF* will shift outward.
   c. its *PPF* will shift inward.
   d. some productive factors will become unemployed.
   e. it must produce at a point within its *PPF*.

4. Which of the following is correct?
   i. As an economy grows, the opportunity costs of economic growth decrease.
   ii. Economic growth has no opportunity cost.
   iii. The opportunity cost of economic growth is current consumption forgone.
   a. i only.
   b. ii only.
   c. iii only.
   d. i and iii.
   e. i and ii.

5. When a country's production possibilities frontier shifts outward over time, the country is experiencing
   a. no opportunity cost.
   b. economic growth.
   c. higher unemployment of resources.
   d. a decrease in unemployment of resources.
   e. an end to opportunity cost.

6. The opportunity cost of economic growth is ____ and the benefit of economic growth is ____.
   a. increased current consumption; increased future consumption
   b. increased current consumption; decreased future consumption
   c. decreased current consumption; increased future consumption
   d. decreased current consumption; decreased future consumption.
   e. nothing; increased future consumption.

Complete the graph

■ **FIGURE 3.3**

Automobiles (millions per year)

Computers (millions per year)

1. In the above figure, illustrate what happens if there is a technological breakthrough in the production of computers but not in the production of automobiles.
   a. Suppose the economy was initially producing at point *A*. After the breakthrough, is it possible for the economy to produce more computers *and* more automobiles?

Short answer and numeric questions

1. What is the opportunity cost of economic growth?

2. What is the benefit of economic growth?

Additional Exercises (also in MyEconLab Test A)

Possibility	Education services (graduates)		Consumption goods (units)
A	1,000	and	0
B	750	and	1,000
C	500	and	2,000
D	0	and	3,000

1. If the nation shown in the table above uses all its resources to produce consumption goods, at what rate will the nation grow? If the nation increases the number of graduates from 0 to 750, will the nation experience economic growth? Explain your answer.

CHECKPOINT 3.4

■ **Explain how people gain from specialization and trade.**

Quick Review

- *Comparative advantage* The ability of a person to perform an activity or produce a good or service at a lower opportunity cost than someone else.

Additional Practice Problem 3.4

1. Tony and Patty produce scooters and snowboards. The figure shows their production possibilities per day. With these production possibilities, the opportunity cost of a snowboard for Patty is 1/2 a scooter and for Tony is 2 scooters. Patty has a lower opportunity cost and therefore she has the comparative advantage in snowboards. The opportunity cost of a scooter for Patty is 2

snowboards and for Tony is 1/2 of a snowboard. Tony has a lower opportunity cost and so he has the comparative advantage in scooters.

Suppose Patty acquires new equipment for scooter production that lets her produce a maximum of 60 rather than 10 scooters a day, should Patty and Tony specialize and trade?

Solution to Additional Practice Problem 3.4

1. Once Patty can produce 60 scooters a day, her opportunity costs change. Her opportunity cost of a scooter falls to 1/3 of a snowboard per scooter and her opportunity cost of a snowboard rises to 3 scooters per snowboard. With these opportunity costs, the comparative advantages have switched: Patty now has a comparative advantage in scooters and Tony in snowboards. Patty and Tony should still specialize and trade, only now Patty will specialize in scooters and Tony will specialize in snowboards. Comparative advantage can switch as the production possibilities frontier shifts outward.

■ **Self Test 3.4**

Fill in the blanks

A person (or nation) has ____ (a comparative; an absolute) advantage if they are more productive than another in producing a good. A person has ____ (a comparative; an absolute) advantage in an activity if that person can perform the activity at a lower opportunity cost than someone else. It ____ (is; is not) possible for someone to have a comparative advantage in all activities. It ____ (is; is not) possible for someone to have an absolute advantage in all activities. If people specialize according to ____ (comparative; absolute) advantage and then trade, they can get to a consumption ____ (outside; inside) their production possibilities frontiers.

True or false

1. A person has an absolute advantage in an activity if the person can perform the activity at lower opportunity cost than someone else.

2. To achieve the gains from trade, a producer specializes in the product in which he or she has a comparative advantage and then trades with others.

3. Specialization and trade can make both producers better off even if one of them has an absolute advantage in producing all goods.

Multiple choice

1. "Comparative advantage" is defined as a situation in which one person can produce
   a. more of all goods than another person.
   b. more of a good than another person.
   c. a good for a lower dollar cost than another person.
   d. a good for a lower opportunity cost than another person.
   e. all goods for lower opportunity costs than another person.

For the next three questions, use the following information: Scott and Cindy both produce only pizza and tacos. In one hour, Scott can produce 20 pizzas or 40 tacos. In one hour, Cindy can produce 30 pizzas or 40 tacos.

2. Scott's opportunity cost of producing 1 taco is
   a. 1/2 of a pizza.
   b. 1 pizza.
   c. 2 pizzas.
   d. 20 pizzas.
   e. 2 tacos.

3. Cindy's opportunity cost of producing 1 taco is
   a. 3/4 of a pizza.
   b. 1 pizza.
   c. 30 pizzas.
   d. 40 pizzas.
   e. 1 taco.

4. Based on the data given,
   a. Cindy has a comparative advantage in producing tacos.
   b. Scott has a comparative advantage in producing tacos.
   c. Cindy and Scott have the same comparative advantage in producing tacos.
   d. neither Cindy nor Scott has a comparative advantage in producing tacos.
   e. Cindy and Scott have the same comparative advantage in producing pizzas.

5. In one hour John can produce 20 loaves of bread or 8 cakes. In one hour Phyllis can produce 30 loaves of bread or 15 cakes. Which of the following statements is true?
   a. Phyllis has a comparative advantage in producing bread.
   b. John has a comparative advantage in producing cakes.
   c. Phyllis has an absolute advantage in both goods.
   d. John has an absolute advantage in both goods.
   e. Phyllis has a comparative advantage in producing both cakes and bread.

6. In one hour John can produce 20 loaves of bread or 16 cakes. In one hour Phyllis can produce 30 loaves of bread or 15 cakes. Which of the following statements is true?
   a. Phyllis has a comparative advantage in producing cakes.
   b. John has a comparative advantage in producing cakes.
   c. Phyllis has an absolute advantage in both goods.
   d. John has an absolute advantage in both goods.
   e. Phyllis has a comparative advantage in producing both cakes and bread.

7. In one hour John can produce 20 loaves of bread or 16 cakes. In one hour Phyllis can produce 30 loaves of bread or 15 cakes. John and Phyllis will reap the largest gains from specialization and trade if John produces ____ and Phyllis produces ____.
   a. only bread; only cakes
   b. only cakes; only bread
   c. both bread and cakes; only loaves
   d. only cakes; both bread and cakes
   e. both bread and cake; both bread and cake

Complete the graph

■ **FIGURE 3.4**

Shirts (per day)

1. Figure 3.4 shows Mark and Sue's *PPFs*.
   a. What is Sue's opportunity cost of producing a shirt? What is Mark's opportunity cost of producing a shirt?
   b. Who has the comparative advantage in producing shirts?
   c. What is Sue's opportunity cost of producing a blouse? What is Mark's opportunity cost of producing a blouse?
   d. Who has the comparative advantage in producing blouses?
   e. Who should specialize in producing blouses and who should specialize in producing shirts?
   f. If Mark and Sue specialize according to their comparative advantage, indicate the total production of shirts and blouses by putting a point in Figure 3.4 showing the total production. Label the point *A*.
   g. How does point *A* show the gains from trade?

Short answer and numeric questions

1. Why should people specialize according to their comparative advantage?
2. When it comes to trading one good for another, why is comparative advantage crucial and absolute advantage unimportant?

Additional Exercises (also in MyEconLab Test A)

Sara and Fran produce boards and sails for windsurfing. The tables show their production possibilities. Each week Sara produces 6 boards and 6 sails, and Fran produces 24 boards and 24 sails.

Sara's Production Possibilities		
Boards (per week)		**Sails (per week)**
15	and	0
12	and	2
9	and	4
6	and	6
3	and	8
0	and	10

Fran's Production Possibilities		
Boards (per week)		**Sails (per week)**
40	and	0
32	and	12
24	and	24
16	and	36
8	and	48
0	and	60

1. Who has a comparative advantage in producing boards? And who has a comparative advantage in producing sails?
2. Can Sara and Fran gain by changing their production and trading 1 board for 1 sail? Explain why or why not.

SELF TEST ANSWERS

■ CHECKPOINT 3.1

Fill in the blanks

The production possibilities frontier or *PPF* is the boundary between the combinations of goods and services that can and that cannot be produced given the available factors of production and state of technology. Production points outside the *PPF* are unattainable. Production points on the *PPF* are production efficient. Society has the possibility of a free lunch if production occurs inside the *PPF*. When resources are fully employed we face a tradeoff.

True or false
1. True; page 62
2. True; page 62
3. False; page 63
4. True; pages 62-63

Multiple choice
1. c; page 60
2. b; pages 61-62
3. d; page 62
4. e; pages 62-63
5. a; page 64
6. a; pages 63-64

Complete the graph

■ FIGURE 3.5

Computers (millions per year)

Points outside the *PPF* are unattainable

Points on the *PPF* are attainable and have full employment

Points inside the *PPF* are attainable and have unemployed resources

1. Figure 3.5 shows a *PPF* between computers and food; pages 61-62.

Short answer and numeric questions
1. The factors that limit the amount of production in *any* economy are the available resources and the state of technology; page 60.
2. All points *on* the production possibilities frontier are production efficient. Moving from one point to another incurs an opportunity cost so there is tradeoff; pages 62-64.
3. When the nation is producing at a point with unemployment of a resource, there are free lunches available because the production of some goods and services can be increased without decreasing the production of anything else. When the nation is producing at full employment of all factors of production, the production point is on the *PPF* and so only tradeoffs are available: If the production of one good or service is increased, the production of something else must be decreased; pages 63-64.

Additional Exercises (also in MyEconLab Test A)
1. The combination of 2 pounds of fish and 18 pounds of berries is not attainable. After the economy produces 2 pounds of fish, the maximum amount of berries it can produce is 15 pounds, not 18 pounds; page 62.
2. The combination of 3 pounds of fish and 11 pounds of berries is production efficient because it lies on the nation's production possibilities frontier. After producing 3 pounds of fish, the production possibilities frontier indicates that the maximum amount of berries that can be produced is 11 pounds, which is the amount produced in the question; pages 62-63.
3. It is inefficient to produce 4 pounds of fish and 5 pounds of berries because it is possible to more berries (or more fish). In particular, after producing 4 pounds of fish the production possibilities frontier indicates that it is possible to produce 6 pounds of berries, 1 pound *more* than the (inefficient) amount in the question, 5 pounds of berries; page 63.

4. Moving from row *A* to row *B* involves a tradeoff because the production of more fish is traded off against the production of fewer berries; pages 63-64.

5. The citizens could enjoy a free lunch if they were producing 4 pounds of fish and 5 pounds of berries because this production combination is inefficient. According to the production possibilities frontier, after producing 4 pounds of fish if resource use is rearranged so that it efficient, the nation could produce 6 pounds of berries, 1 pound *more* than the (inefficient) amount in the question, 5 pounds of berries. Hence by using resources more efficiently, the citizens could have more berries and not lose any fish, a free lunch; pages 63-64.

■ CHECKPOINT 3.2

Fill in the blanks

Along a production possibilities frontier, the opportunity cost of obtaining one more unit of a good is the amount of another good that is forgone. The opportunity cost is equal to the quantity of the good forgone divided by the increase in the quantity of the other good. As more of a good is produced, its opportunity cost increases.

True or false

1. False; page 66
2. False; page 67
3. True; page 68

Multiple choice

1. b; page 66
2. d; page 66
3. e; page 66
4. a; page 67
5. d; page 68
6. a; page 68

Complete the graph

1. a. Figure 3.6 illustrates the production possibilities frontier; page 66.
   b. The opportunity cost of moving from point

■ FIGURE 3.6

MP3 players (millions per year)

DVD players (millions per year)

A to point *B* to is 0.33 MP3 players per DVD player; from *B* to *C* is 1.00 MP3 player per DVD player; from *C* to *D* is 1.43 MP3 players per DVD player; and, from *D* to *E* is 3.33 MP3 players per DVD player. The opportunity cost increases; page 66.

Short answer and numeric questions

1. a. The opportunity cost of moving from point *A* to point *B* to is 0.5 cans of soda per candy bar; from *B* to *C* is 1.0 can of soda per candy bar; from *C* to *D* is 2.0 cans of soda per candy bar; and, from *D* to *E* is 4.0 cans of soda per candy bar; page 66.
   b. The opportunity cost of moving from point *E* to point *D* to is 0.25 candy bars per can of soda; from *D* to *C* is 0.50 candy bars per can of soda; from *C* to *B* is 1.00 candy bar per can of soda; and, from *B* to *A* is 2.00 candy bars per can of soda; page 66.
   c. As more candy bars are produced, the opportunity cost increases. As more cans of soda are produced, the opportunity cost increases; page 67.

2. The opportunity cost of increasing production of one good is the production of some other good forgone. The opportunity cost increases, so that increasingly large amounts of the other good are forgone, because resources are not equally productive in all activities. When initially increasing the production of one good, resources that are well suit-

ed for its production are used. When still more of the good is produced, resources that are less well suited must be used. Because the resources are ill suited, more are necessary to increase the production of the first good, and the forgone amount of the other good increases; page 68.

3. The opportunity cost is the amount of a good forgone to gain an additional unit another good. We divide the quantity of the good forgone by the increase in the other good. So opportunity cost is a ratio—the change in the quantity of one good divided by the change in the quantity of another good; page 68.

Additional Exercises (also in MyEconLab Test A)

1. His opportunity cost of a pound of berries and a pound of fish are both zero. The opportunity cost is zero because he is operating inside his production possibilities frontier. He could pick 4 more pounds of berries without giving up any fish or catch 2 more fish without giving up any berries; page 64.

Move from	Increase in berries picked (pounds)	Decrease in fish caught (pounds)	Opportunity cost of berries (pounds of fish)
F to E	6.0	1.0	0.17
E to D	5.0	1.5	0.30
D to C	4.0	2.0	0.50
C to B	3.0	2.5	0.83
B to A	2.0	3.0	1.50

2. Crusoe's opportunity cost of a pound of berries is the fish he forgoes. To calculate the opportunity cost, compute the increase in fruit and the decrease in fish as he increases the time he spends picking berries and decreases the time he spends catching fish. Then, divide the decrease in fish by the increase in berries to get the opportunity cost of a pound of berries. The table above shows the opportunity cost of a pound of berries moving along the *PPF*. As Crusoe moves from point *F* to point *E* and then to point *D* and so forth, his opportunity cost of a pound of berries increases. His opportunity cost increases as he picks more berries because initially he picks from the most productive bushes and so must spend a short period of

time picking berries, that is, a short period of time away from fishing. But as he picks more berries, he must pick from less productive bushes and so spends increasing more time away from fishing; pages 66 and 68.

■ CHECKPOINT 3.3

Fill in the blanks

A sustained expansion of production possibilities is called <u>economic growth</u>. Economic growth shifts the *PPF* <u>outward</u>. The *PPF* shows that economic growth requires <u>a decrease</u> in the current production of consumption goods. The opportunity cost of increasing economic growth is the loss of the <u>current</u> goods that can be consumed.

True or false

1. False; page 71
2. False; pages 71-72
3. False; page 72

Multiple choice

1. c; page 71
2. d; pages 71-72
3. a; page 71
4. d; page 71
5. b; page 71
6. c; page 71

Complete the graph

■ FIGURE 3.7

Automobiles (millions per year)

Computers (millions per year)

1. Figure 3.7 illustrates the new production

possibilities frontier. Because the technological breakthrough did not affect automobile production, the maximum amount of automobiles that can be produced on the vertical axis does not change; pages 71-72.

1. a. Figure 3.7 shows that it is possible for the production of *both* automobiles and computers to increase, as a movement from the initial point *A* to a possible new point *B* illustrates; page 71.

Short answer and numeric questions

1. Economic growth requires either developing new technologies, accumulating more human capital, or accumulating more capital. All of these avenues require resources, so the opportunity cost of economic growth is the decrease in the current production of goods and services; page 71.

2. The benefit from economic growth is increased consumption per person in the future after the production possibilities frontier has expanded; page 71.

Additional Exercises (also in MyEconLab Test A)

1. If the nation uses all of its resources to produce consumption goods, it will not grow because it does not increase its human capital, which is its only source of economic growth. If the nation increases its graduates from 0 to 750, the nation will experience economic growth because its human capital increases; page 71.

■ CHECKPOINT 3.4

Fill in the blanks

A person (or nation) has <u>an absolute</u> advantage if they are more productive than another in producing a good. A person has <u>a comparative</u> advantage in an activity if that person can perform the activity at a lower opportunity cost than someone else. It <u>is not</u> possible for someone to have a comparative advantage in all activities. It <u>is</u> possible for someone to have an absolute advantage in all activities. If people specialize according to <u>comparative</u> advantage and then trade, they can get to a consumption point <u>outside</u> their production possibilities frontiers.

True or false

1. False; pages 73-74
2. True; page 76
3. True; pages 76-77

Multiple choice

1. d; page 74
2. a; page 74
3. a; page 74
4. b; pages 75-76
5. c; pages 75-76
6. b; pages 75-76
7. a; pages 75-76

Complete the graph

1. a. Sue's opportunity cost of a shirt is 1/2 of a blouse because, when moving along her *PPF* to produce 1 more shirt she gives up 1/2 of a blouse. Mark's opportunity cost of a shirt is 2 blouses; page 75

   b. Sue has the comparative advantage in producing shirts because her opportunity cost is lower; pages 75-76.

   c. Sue's opportunity cost of a blouse is 2 shirts because, when moving along her *PPF*, to produce 1 more blouse she gives up 2 shirts. Mark's opportunity cost of a blouse is 1/2 of a shirt; page 75.

   d. Mark has the comparative advantage in producing blouses because his opportunity cost is lower; pages 75-76.

   e. Mark should specialize in producing blouses and Sue should specialize in producing shirts; page 76.

   f. Mark produces 4 blouses and Sue produces 4 shirts, so a total of 4 shirts and 4 blouses are produced. Figure 3.8 (on the next page) shows this production as point *A*; pages 76-77.

   g. If Mark and Sue agree that the total production at point *A* should be divided evenly, then both Mark and Sue will receive 2 shirts and 2 blouses. When both were producing only for themselves, neither could produce 2 shirts and 2 blouses because this point is beyond both their *PPFs*. By specializing and trading, *both*

Mark and Sue can consume at a point outside of their *PPFs*; page 77.

■ **FIGURE 3.8**

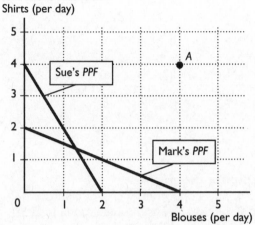

Short answer and numeric questions

1. A person's comparative advantage is the good that the person can produce at a lower opportunity cost than can other people. When this person specializes in the production of the good, it is produced at the lowest cost; page 75.

2. People are willing to trade if they can obtain a good at lower opportunity cost than what it costs them to produce the good. Comparative advantage tells which person has a lower opportunity cost. Even if a person has an absolute advantage in all goods, he or she does not have a comparative advantage in all goods. So comparative advantage determines who produces a product and who does not; page 75.

Additional Exercises (also in MyEconLab Test A)

1. For each board Sara makes, she forgoes 2/3 of a sail, so for her the opportunity cost of 1 board is 2/3 of a sail. For each board Fran makes, she forgoes 1½ sails, so for her the opportunity cost of 1 board is 1½ sails. The opportunity cost of producing a board is lower for Sara, so she has the comparative advantage in producing boards.

   For each sail Sara makes, she forgoes 1½ boards, so for her the opportunity cost of 1 sail is 1½ boards. For each sail Fran makes, she forgoes 2/3 of a board, so for her the opportunity cost of 1 sail is 2/3 of a board. The opportunity cost of producing a sail is lower for Fran, so she has the comparative advantage in producing sails; pages 75-76.

2. Yes, Sara and Fran can gain by changing their production and then trading 1 board for 1 sail. Sara will trade boards with Fran in exchange for sails. With trade, each sail has the opportunity cost for Sara of 1 board, less than her opportunity cost of 1½ boards if she does not trade. Fran will trade sails with Sara in exchange for boards. With trade, each board has the opportunity cost for Fran of 1 sail, less than her opportunity cost of 1½ sails if she does not trade. Sara and Fran can both have more boards and more sails if they specialize and trade; pages 76-77.

Chapter 4

Demand and Supply

Demand and supply determine the quantities and prices of goods and services.

1 Distinguish between quantity demanded and demand, and explain what determines demand.

The quantity demanded is the amount of any good, service, or resource that people are willing and able to buy during a specified period at a specified price. Demand is the relationship between the quantity demanded and the price of a good when all other influences on buying plans remain the same. The law of demand states: Other things remaining the same, if the price of a good rises, the quantity demanded of that good decreases; and if the price of a good falls, the quantity demanded of that good increases. A demand curve is a graph of the relationship between the quantity demanded of a good and its price when all other influences on buying plans remain the same. The market demand is the sum of the demands of all the buyers in a market. A change in price leads to a *change in the quantity demanded* and a movement along the demand curve. Factors that *change demand* and shift the demand curve are: prices of related goods; expected future prices; income; expected future income and credit; number of buyers; and preferences. If demand increases, the demand curve shifts rightward.

2 Distinguish between quantity supplied and supply, and explain what determines supply.

The quantity supplied is the amount of any good, service, or resource that people are willing and able to sell during a specified period at a specified price. Supply is the relationship between the quantity supplied and the price of a good when all other influences on selling plans remain the same. The law of supply states that other things remaining the same, if the price of a good rises, the quantity supplied of that good increases; and if the price of a good falls, the quantity supplied of that good decreases. A supply curve is a graph of the relationship between the quantity supplied of a good and its price when all other influences on selling plans remain the same. A change in price leads to a *change in the quantity supplied* and a movement along the supply curve. Factors that *change supply* and shift the supply curve are: prices of related goods; prices of resources and other inputs; expected future prices; number of sellers; and productivity. If supply increases, the supply curve shifts rightward.

3 Explain how demand and supply determine price and quantity in a market, and explain the effects of changes in demand and supply.

The equilibrium price and equilibrium quantity occur when the quantity demanded equals the quantity supplied. An increase in demand raises the price and increases the quantity. An increase in supply lowers the price and increases the quantity. An increase in both demand and supply increases the quantity but the price might rise, fall, or not change. An increase in demand and a decrease in supply raises the price but the quantity might increase, decrease, or not change. Changes in demand and supply in the opposite direction to those given above lead to opposite changes in price and quantity.

CHECKPOINT 4.1

■ **Distinguish between quantity demanded and demand, and explain what determines demand.**

Quick Review

- *Change in the quantity demanded* A change in the quantity of a good that people plan to buy that results from a change in the price of the good.
- *Law of demand* If the price of a good rises, the quantity demanded of that good decreases, and if the price of a good falls, the quantity demanded of that good decreases.
- *Change in demand* A change in the quantity that people plan to buy when any influence on buying plans, other than the price of the good, changes. These other influences include: prices of related goods, expected future prices; income, expected future income and credit, number of buyers, and preferences.

Additional Practice Problems 4.1

1. In the market for motor scooters, several events occur, one at a time. Explain the influence of each event on the quantity demanded of scooters and on the demand for scooters. Illustrate the effects of each event either by a movement along the demand curve or a shift in the demand curve for scooters and say which event (or events) illustrates the law of demand in action. These events are:
   a. The price of a scooter falls.
   b. The price of a car falls.
   c. Citing rising injury rates, cities and towns ban scooters from busy streets.
   d. Scooters are a normal good and income increases.
   e. Scooters become unfashionable and the number of buyers decreases.

2. Suppose that each year Anna, Ben, Carol, and Dana are willing and able to buy scooters as shown in the table.

Price (dollars per scooter)	Quantity demanded			
	Anna	Ben	Carol	Dana
100	0	0	0	0
75	1	0	0	0
50	2	1	1	0
25	2	1	2	1

■ **FIGURE 4.1**

Using the information in the table:
   a. Label the axes in Figure 4.1 above.
   b. Graph the market demand curve.

Solutions to Additional Practice Problems 4.1

1a. This problem emphasizes the distinction between a change in the quantity demanded and a change in demand. A fall in the price of a scooter brings an increase in the quantity

demanded of scooters, which is illustrated by a movement down along the demand curve for scooters as shown in the figure. This event illustrates the law of demand in action.

1b. A car is a substitute for a scooter. With the lower price of a car, some people who previously would have bought a scooter will now buy a car instead. So a fall in the price of cars decreases the demand for scooters. The demand curve for scooters shifts leftward, as shown in the figure below.

1c. Rising injury rates and banning scooters from streets changes preferences and makes scooters less desirable. The demand for scooters decreases and the demand curve

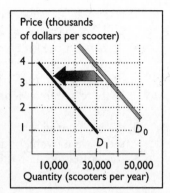

for the scooters shifts leftward as shown in the figure leftward as shown in the figure by the shift from demand curve D_0 to demand curve D_1.

1d. A scooter is a normal good, so people will buy more scooters when their income increases. The demand for scooters increases and the demand curve shifts right-

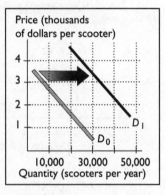

ward as illustrated in the figure.

1e. A decrease in the number of buyers decreases the demand for scooters. The demand curve shifts leftward.

■ **FIGURE 4.2**

Price (dollars per scooter)

Quantity (scooters per year)

2a. Figure 4.2 labels the axes.

2b. The market demand curve is derived by adding the quantities demanded by Anna, Ben, Carol, and Dana at each price. The market demand curve is illustrated in Figure 4.2.

■ **Self Test 4.1**

Fill in the blanks

The ____ (demand schedule; law of demand) states that other things remaining the same, if the price of a good rises, the ____ (quantity demanded of; demand for) that good decreases. A ____ is a graph of the relationship between the quantity demanded of a good and its price. Demand curves are ____ (downward; upward) sloping. An increase in demand shifts the demand curve ____. Factors that change demand lead to a ____ (shift of; movement along) the demand curve. Factors that change demand are ____, ____, ____, ____, ____, and ____.

True or false

1. The law of demand states that other things remaining the same, if the price of a good rises, the quantity demanded of that good increases.

2. If the quantity of ice cream demanded at each price increases, there is a movement along the demand curve for ice cream.

3. When Sue's income increases, her demand for movies increases. For Sue, movies are a normal good.

4. A rise in the price of a computer increases the demand for computers because a computer is a normal good.

5. If people's incomes fall and all other influences on buying plans remain the same, the demand for computers will decrease and there will be a movement along the demand curve.

Multiple choice

1. The "law of demand" indicates that if the University of Maine increases the tuition, all other things remaining the same,
   a. the demand for classes will decrease at the University of Maine.
   b. the demand for classes will increase at the University of Maine.
   c. the quantity of classes demanded will increase at the University of Maine.
   d. the quantity of classes demanded will decrease at the University of Maine.
   e. both the demand for and the quantity of classes demanded will decrease at the University of Maine.

2. Other things remaining the same, the quantity of a good or service demanded will increase if the price of the good or service
   a. rises.
   b. falls.
   c. does not change.
   d. rises or does not change.
   e. rises or falls.

3. Teenagers demand more soda than other age groups. If the number of teenagers increases, everything else remaining the same,
   a. market demand for soda increases.
   b. market demand for soda decreases.
   c. market demand for soda does not change.
   d. there is a movement along the market demand curve for soda.
   e. None of the above answers is correct because the effect on the demand depends whether the supply curve shifts.

4. One reason the demand for laptop computers might increase is a
   a. fall in the price of a laptop computers.
   b. fall in the price of a desktop computer.
   c. a change in preferences as laptops have become more portable, with faster processors and larger hard drives.
   d. poor quality performance record for laptop computers.
   e. a decrease in income if laptops are a normal good.

5. The number of buyers of sport utility vehicles, SUVs, decreases sharply. So the
   a. demand curve for SUVs shifts leftward.
   b. demand curve for SUVs shifts rightward.
   c. demand curve for SUVs does not shift nor is there a movement along the demand curve.
   d. demand curve for SUVs does not shift but there is a movement downward along it.
   e. the supply curve for SUVs shifts rightward.

■ **FIGURE 4.3**

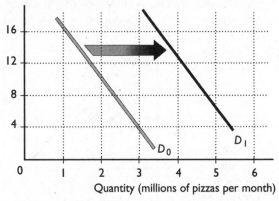

6. The shift of the demand curve for pizza illustrated in Figure 4.3 could be the result of
   a. a rise in income if pizza is a normal good.
   b. a fall in the price of fried chicken, a substitute for pizza.
   c. consumers coming to believe that pizza is unhealthy.
   d. the belief that pizza will fall in price next month.
   e. a fall in the price of a pizza.

7. The shift of the demand curve for pizza illustrated in Figure 4.3 could be the result of
   a. a rise in income if pizza is an inferior good.
   b. a fall in the price of soda, a complement for pizza.
   c. a decrease in the number of college students if college students eat more pizza than other age groups.
   d. a rise in the price of a pizza.
   e. a fall in the price of a pizza.

8. When moving along a demand curve, which of the following changes?
   a. the consumers' incomes
   b. the prices of other goods
   c. the number of buyers
   d. the price of the good
   e. the consumers' preferences

9. If the price of a DVD falls,
   i. the demand curve for DVDs shifts rightward.
   ii. the demand curve for DVDs will not shift.
   iii. there is a movement along the demand curve for DVDs.
   a. i only.
   b. ii only.
   c. iii only.
   d. ii and iii.
   e. i and iii.

10. Pizza and tacos are substitutes and the price of a pizza increases. Which of the following correctly indicates what happens?
    a. The demand for pizzas decreases and the demand for tacos increases.
    b. The demand for both goods decreases.
    c. The quantity of tacos demanded increases and the quantity of pizza demanded decreases.
    d. The quantity of pizza demanded decreases and the demand for tacos increases.
    e. The demand for each decreases because both are normal goods.

Complete the graph

Price (dollars per bundle of cotton candy)	Quantity (bundles of cotton candy per month)
1	10,000
2	8,000
3	7,000
4	4,000

1. The demand schedule for cotton candy is given in the following table. In Figure 4.4, draw the demand curve. Label the axes.
   a. If the price of cotton candy is $2 a bundle, what is the quantity demanded?

■ FIGURE 4.4

   b. If the price of cotton candy is $3 a bundle, what is the quantity demanded?
   c. Does the demand curve you drew slope upward or downward?

■ FIGURE 4.5

Price (dollars per pound of butter)

Quantity (tons of butter per month)

2. Butter is a normal good and margarine is substitute for butter. Figure 4.5 shows the demand curve for butter.
   a. In Figure 4.5, show how the demand curve shifts if incomes rise. Label this demand curve D_1.
   b. In Figure 4.5, show how the demand curve shifts if margarine falls in price. Label this demand curve D_2.
   c. If the price of butter falls from $4 a pound to $3 a pound, does the demand curve shift toward demand curve D_1, D_2, or neither? Explain your answer.

Short answer and numeric questions

Price (dollars per gallon)	Quantity demanded (gallons per week)
3.20	316
3.30	310

1. The table above gives the demand schedule for gasoline for a group of students. If the price of gasoline falls from $3.30 to $3.20 per gallon, how much gas will the students buy?

2. Explain the difference between a change in quantity demanded and a change in demand.

3. What is the difference between a movement along a demand curve and a shift in a demand curve?

Additional Exercises (also in MyEconLab Test A)

The following events occur one at a time in the market for Caribbean cruises.

   a. Caribbean cruises become more popular.

   b. The price of a Caribbean cruise rises.

   c. The price of a cruise to Asia falls.

   d. Celebrity Cruises launches its new "students only" Caribbean cruises.

   e. People expect the price of a Caribbean cruise to fall next season.

   f. Cruise companies increase the number of leading rock artists booked for their onboard entertainment.

1. Explain the effect of each event on the demand for Caribbean cruises.

2. Use a graph to illustrate the effect of each event.

3. Does any event (or events) illustrate the law of demand?

CHECKPOINT 4.2

■ **Distinguish between quantity supplied and supply, and explain what determines supply.**

Quick Review

   • *Change in quantity supplied* A change in the quantity of a good that suppliers plan to sell that results from a change in the price of the good.

   • *Change in supply* A change in the quantity that suppliers plan to sell when any influence on selling plans other than the price of the good changes.

Additional Practice Problems 4.2

1. In the market for motor scooters, several events occur, one at a time. Explain the effect of each on the quantity supplied of scooters and on the supply of scooters. Illustrate the effects of each either by a movement along the supply curve or a shift in the supply curve and say which illustrate the law of supply. These events are:

   a. The price of a scooter rises.

   b. The price of the steel used to make scooters rises.

   c. The number of firms making scooters decreases.

   d. Technological change increases the productivity of the factories making scooters.

Price (dollars per ton of plywood)	Quantity supplied (tons of plywood per month)			
	Eddy	Franco	George	Helen
100	2	2	1	1
75	2	1	1	1
50	1	1	1	0
25	0	0	1	0

■ **FIGURE 4.6**

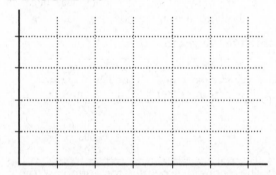

2. Each month Eddy, Franco, George, and Helen are willing and able to sell plywood as shown in the table above.

   a. Label the axes in Figure 4.6.

   b. Graph the market supply curve.

Solutions to Additional Practice Problems 4.2

1a. This problem emphasizes the distinction between a change in the quantity supplied and a change in supply. A rise in the price of a scooter increases the quantity of scooters sup-

plied, which is illustrated by a movement up along the supply curve as shown in the figure. There is no change in the supply and the supply curve does not shift. This event illustrates the law of supply in action.

1b. When the price of the steel used to make scooters rises, the cost to produce scooters increases, which decreases the supply of scooters. The supply curve shifts leftward as shown.

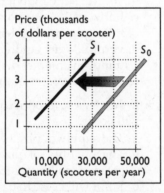

1c. A decrease in the number of firms producing scooters decreases the supply of scooters. The supply curve shifts leftward, as illustrated in the figure above.

1d. An increase in the productivity of the factories making scooters lowers the costs of producing scooters. The supply of scooters increases and the supply curve shifts rightward, as illustrated in the figure.

■ FIGURE 4.7

Price (dollars per ton of plywood)

Price (dollars per ton of plywood)	Quantity supplied (tons per month)
100	6
75	5
50	3
25	1

2a. The axes are labeled in Figure 4.7.

2b. The market supply curve is derived by adding the quantities supplied by Eddy, Franco, George, and Helen at each price. The table above gives the resulting sum and the market supply curve is illustrated in Figure 4.7.

■ Self Test 4.2

Fill in the blanks

The ____ (quantity supplied; supply) of a good is the amount people are willing and able to sell during a specified period at a specified price. The law of supply states that other things remaining the same, if the price of a good rises, the quantity supplied ____. A supply curve is ____ (upward; downward) sloping. A change in the price of a good changes ____ (supply; the quantity supplied) and is illustrated by a ____ the supply curve. Factors that change supply are ____, ____, ____, ____, and ____.

True or false

1. The law of supply states that other things remaining the same, if the price of a good rises, the supply of the good increases.

2. When new technology for producing computers is used by manufacturers, the supply of computers increases.

3. If the wage rate paid to chefs rises and all other influences on selling plans remain the same, the supply of restaurant meals will increase.

4. If the price of coffee is expected to rise next month, the supply of coffee this month will decrease.

5. The supply of a good will increase and there will be a movement up along the supply curve of the good if the price of one of its substitutes in production falls.

Multiple choice

1. The quantity supplied of a good, service, or resource is ____ during a specified period and at a specified price.
   a. the amount that people are able to sell
   b. the amount that people are willing to sell
   c. the amount that people are able and willing to sell
   d. the amount that people are willing and able to buy
   e. the amount sold

2. One reason supply curves have an upward slope is because
   a. increased supply will require increased technology.
   b. people will pay a higher price when less is supplied.
   c. a higher price brings a greater profit, so firms want to sell more of that good.
   d. to have more of the good supplied requires more firms to open.
   e. None of the above answers is correct because supply curves have a downward slope.

3. Which of the following indicates that the law of supply applies to makers of soda?
   a. An increase in the price of a soda leads to an increase in the demand for soda.
   b. An increase in the price of a soda leads to an increase in the supply of soda.
   c. An increase in the price of a soda leads to an increase in the quantity of soda supplied.
   d. A decrease in the price of a soda leads to an increase in the quantity of soda demanded.
   e. A decrease in the price of a soda leads to an increase in the supply of soda.

4. The market supply curve is the ____ of the ____.
   a. horizontal sum; individual supply curves
   b. vertical sum; individual supply curves
   c. horizontal sum; individual supply curves minus the market demand
   d. vertical sum; individual supply curves minus the market demand
   e. vertical average; individual supply curves

5. If the costs to produce pizza increase, which will occur?
   a. The supply of pizza will decrease.
   b. The quantity of pizzas supplied will increase as sellers try to cover their costs.
   c. Pizza will cease to be produced and sold.
   d. The demand curve for pizza will shift leftward when the price of a pizza increases.
   e. The demand curve for pizza will shift rightward when the price of a pizza increases.

6. A rise in the price of a substitute in production for a good leads to
   a. an increase in the supply of that good.
   b. a decrease in the supply of that good.
   c. no change in the supply of that good.
   d. a decrease in the quantity of that good supplied.
   e. no change in either the supply or the quantity supplied of the good.

7. An increase in the productivity of producing jeans results in
   a. the quantity of jeans supplied increasing.
   b. the supply of jeans increasing.
   c. buyers demanding more jeans because they are now more efficiently produced.
   d. buyers demanding fewer jeans because their price will fall, which signals lower quality.
   e. some change but the impact on the supply of jeans is impossible to predict.

■ **FIGURE 4.8**
Price (dollars per pizza)

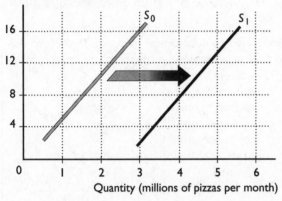

8. The shift of the supply curve of pizza illustrated in Figure 4.8 could be the result of
   a. a rise in the price of cheese used to produce pizza.
   b. a decrease in the number of firms producing pizza.
   c. an increase in the productivity of the firms producing pizza.
   d. a rise in the price of a substitute in production.
   e. a rise in the price of a pizza.

9. The shift of the supply curve of pizza illustrated in Figure 4.8 could be the result of
   a. a rise in income if pizza is a normal good.
   b. a fall in the price of soda, a consumer complement for pizza.
   c. an increase in the number of firms producing pizza.
   d. a rise in the price of a pizza.
   e. a rise in the wage paid the workers who make pizza.

10. The price of leather used to produce shoes rises, so the supply of shoes ____ and the supply curve of shoes ____.
    a. increases; shifts rightward
    b. increases; shifts leftward
    c. decreases; shifts rightward
    d. decreases; shifts leftward
    e. does not change; does not shift

Complete the graph

Price (dollars per bundle of cotton candy)	Quantity (bundles of cotton candy per month)
1	4,000
2	8,000
3	10,000
4	12,000

1. The supply schedule for cotton candy is given in the table above. In Figure 4.4, you previously drew a demand curve for cotton candy. Now use the supply schedule to draw the supply curve in Figure 4.4.
   a. If the price of cotton candy is $2 a bundle, what is the quantity supplied?
   b. If the price of cotton candy is $3 a bundle, what is the quantity supplied?
   c. Does the supply curve you drew slope upward or downward?

■ **FIGURE 4.9**
Price (dollars per ton of rubber bands)

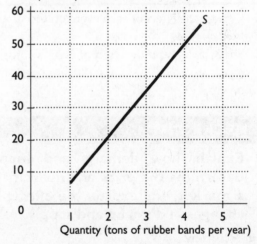

2. Figure 4.9 shows a supply curve for rubber bands. Suppose the productivity of produc-

ing rubber bands increases. In Figure 4.9, illustrate the effect of this event.

Short answer and numeric questions

1. What is the law of supply?
2. What influence(s) lead to a change in the quantity supplied? A change in supply?

Price (dollars per pizza)	Quantity supplied (pizza per day)			
	Tom	Bob	Kate	Market supply
14	20	12	15	____
12	16	10	10	____
10	12	8	5	____
8	8	6	0	____

3. The table gives the supply schedules for the three pizza producers in a small town. Calculate the market supply schedule.

Additional Exercises (also in MyEconLab Test A)

Factories can use their resources to produce either DVDs or CDs. In the market for DVDs, the following events occur one at a time:

    a. The price of a CD falls.

    b. A new robot technology lowers the cost of producing DVDs.

    c. The price of a DVD falls.

    d. The price of a DVD is expected to rise next year.

    e. The wage rate paid to DVD factory workers increases.

1. Explain the effect of each event on the supply of DVDs.
2. Show on a graph the effect of each event.
3. Does any event (or events) illustrate the law of supply?

CHECKPOINT 4.3

■ **Explain how demand and supply determine the price and quantity in a market, and explain the effects of changes in demand and supply.**

Quick Review

- *Market equilibrium* When the quantity demanded equals the quantity supplied.

Additional Practice Problems 4.3

1. Hot dogs are an inferior good and people's incomes rise. What happens to the equilibrium price and quantity of hot dogs?

2. Hot dog producers develop new technology that increases their productivity. What happens to the price and quantity of hot dogs?

3. The price of a hot dog bun falls and, simultaneously, the number of hot dog producers increases. The effect of the fall in the price of a hot dog bun is less than the effect of the increase in the number of producers. What happens to the equilibrium price and quantity of hot dogs?

Solutions to Additional Practice Problems 4.3

1. When income increases, the demand for an inferior good decreases and the demand curve shifts leftward. The supply does not change and the sup- ply curve does not shift. The equilibrium price of a hot dog falls and the equilibrium quantity decreases, as illustrated in the figure.

2. When the productivity of producing a good increases, the supply of the good increases and the supply curve shifts rightward. So the supply curve of hot dogs shifts rightward. The demand does not change and so the demand curve does not shift. As illustrated, the price of a hot dog falls and the quantity increases.

3. The fall in the price of a complement, hot dog buns, increases the demand for hot dogs and the demand curve for hot dogs shifts rightward. The increase in the number of producers increases the supply of hot dogs and the supply curve shifts rightward. Because the increase in supply exceeds the increase in demand, the price of a hot dog falls and the quantity increases, as shown in the figure.

Price (dollars per hot dog)

Quantity (hot dogs per month)

■ Self Test 4.3

Fill in the blanks

The price at which the quantity demanded equals the quantity supplied is the ____. In a diagram, the ____ is determined where the supply and demand curves intersect. If the price exceeds the equilibrium price, the price ____ (rises; falls). An increase in demand ____ (raises; lowers) the equilibrium price and ____ (increases; decreases) the equilibrium quantity. An increase in supply ____ (raises; lowers) the equilibrium price and ____ (increases; decreases) the equilibrium quantity. If both the demand and supply increase, definitely the equilibrium ____ increases but the effect on the equilibrium ____ is ambiguous.

True or false

1. If the price of asparagus is below the equilibrium price, there is a shortage of asparagus and the price of asparagus will rise until the shortage disappears.

2. When the demand for skateboards decreases and the supply of skateboards remains unchanged, the quantity supplied of skateboards decreases as the price rises.

3. Gasoline refiners expect the price of oil will fall next month. If the supply of oil does not change, the equilibrium price of oil today falls and the equilibrium quantity today decreases.

4. As summer comes to an end and winter sets in, the demand for and supply of hamburger buns decrease. The price of a hamburger bun definitely remains the same.

5. The number of buyers of grapefruit juice increases and at the same time severe frost decreases the supply of grapefruit juice. The price of grapefruit juice will rise.

Multiple choice

1. The equilibrium price of a good occurs if the
   a. quantity of the good demanded equals the quantity of the good supplied.
   b. quantity of the good demanded is greater than the quantity of the good supplied.
   c. quantity of the good demanded is less than the quantity of the good supplied.
   d. demand for the good is equal to the supply of the good.
   e. price of the good seems reasonable to most buyers.

2. Which of the following is correct?
   i. A surplus puts downward pressure on the price of a good.
   ii. A shortage puts upward pressure on the price of a good
   iii. There is no surplus or shortage at equilibrium.
   a. i and ii..
   b. i and iii.
   c. ii and iii.
   d. i, ii, and iii.
   e. only iii.

3. The number of people looking to buy ceiling fans increases, so there is an increase in the
   a. quantity of ceiling fans demanded and a surplus of ceiling fans.
   b. demand for ceiling fans and a rise in the price of a ceiling fan.
   c. demand for ceiling fans and a surplus of ceiling fans.
   d. supply of ceiling fans and no change in the price of a ceiling fan.
   e. demand for ceiling fans and in the supply of ceiling fans.

4. Which of the following is the best explanation for why the price of gasoline increases during the summer months?
   a. Oil producers have higher costs of production in the summer.
   b. Sellers have to earn profits during the summer to cover losses in the winter.
   c. There is increased driving by families going on vacation.
   d. There is less competition among oil refineries in the summer.
   e. The number of gas stations open 24 hours a day rises in the summer months and so the price must rise to cover the higher costs.

5. Suppose that the price of lettuce used to produce tacos increases. This change means that the equilibrium price of a taco ____ and the equilibrium quantity ____.
   a. rises; increases
   b. rises; decreases
   c. falls; increases
   d. falls; decreases
   e. does not change; decreases

6. The technology associated with manufacturing computers has advanced enormously. This change has led to the price of a computer ____ and the quantity ____.
   a. rising; increasing
   b. rising; decreasing
   c. falling; increasing
   d. falling; decreasing
   e. falling; not changing

7. Candy makers accurately anticipate the increase in demand for candy for Halloween so that the supply of candy and the demand for candy increase the same amount. As a result, the price of candy ____ and the quantity of candy ____.
   a. rises; does not change
   b. falls; increases
   c. does not change; increases
   d. does not change; does not change
   e. rises; rises

8. During 2010 the supply of gasoline decreased while at the same time the demand for gasoline increased. If the magnitude of the increase in demand was greater than the magnitude of the decrease in supply, then the equilibrium price of gasoline ____ and the equilibrium quantity ____.
   a. increased; increased
   b. increased; decreased
   c. increased; did not change
   d. decreased; did not change
   e. did not change; increased

Complete the graph

1. In Checkpoint 4.1 you drew a demand curve in Figure 4.4; in Checkpoint 4.2, you drew a supply curve in that figure. Return to Figure 4.4 and answer the following questions.
   a. If the price of cotton candy is $1, what is the situation in the market?
   b. If the price of cotton candy is $3, what is the situation in the market?
   c. What is the equilibrium price and equilibrium quantity of cotton candy?

Price (dollars per sweatshirt)	Quantity demanded (sweatshirts per season) Hockey team	Soccer team	Quantity supplied (sweatshirts per season)
35	5	8	32
30	6	9	25
25	8	11	19
20	12	15	12
15	17	20	8

2. The table gives the demand and supply schedules for sweatshirts. What is the market demand schedule? At what price will the quantity demanded be equal to the quantity supplied? What is the equilibrium quantity?

■ FIGURE 4.10
Price (dollars per piece of gold jewelry)

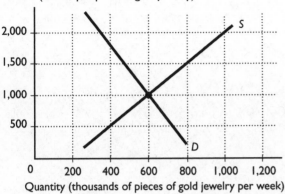

3. Figure 4.10 shows the supply and demand for gold jewelry. In the figure, show what happens to the price and quantity if gold jewelry is a normal good and people's incomes rise.

■ FIGURE 4.11
Price (dollars per piece of gold jewelry)

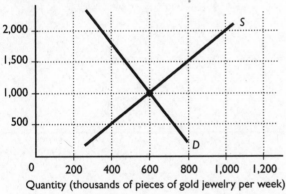

4. Figure 4.11 shows the supply and demand for gold jewelry. Suppose that consumers think that silver jewelry is a substitute for gold jewelry. In Figure 4.12, show what happens to the price and quantity if the price of silver jewelry falls.

■ FIGURE 4.12
Price (dollars per piece of gold jewelry)

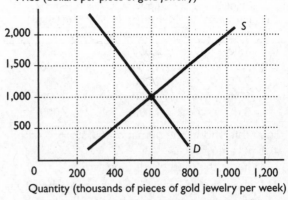

5. Figure 4.12 shows the supply and demand for gold jewelry. Suppose the price of the gold that is used to produce gold jewelry rises. In the figure, show what happens to the price and quantity of gold jewelry.

Short answer and numeric questions

1. How is a shortage different from a surplus?

2. People read that drinking orange juice helps prevent heart disease. What is the effect on the equilibrium price and quantity of orange juice?

3. The cost of memory chips used in computers falls. What is the effect on the equilibrium price and quantity of computers?

4. New cars are a normal good and people's incomes increase. Simultaneously, auto manufacturers must pay more for their workers' health insurance. What is the effect on the price and quantity of new cars?

5. The Eye on Your Life on page 103 points out that supply and demand will be a big part of your life. How can you use the model to make day-to-day decisions, such as when to buy gasoline?

Additional Exercises (also in MyEconLab Test A)

Price (dollars per bar)	Quantity demanded	Quantity supplied
	(bars per week)	
1.00	3,000	1,000
1.50	2,500	1,500
2.00	2,000	2,000
2.50	1,500	2,500
3.00	1,000	3,000

The table shows the demand and supply schedules for energy bars.

1. What is the market equilibrium?

2. If the price of bar is $1.50, describe the situation in the energy bar market. Explain how market equilibrium is restored.

3. A rise in income increases the quantity demanded by 1,000 bars a week at each price. Explain how the market adjusts to its new equilibrium.

4. A fire knocks out a large energy-bar factory and a fitness craze sends more people to the gym. How do these events influence demand and supply? Describe how the equilibrium price and equilibrium quantity change.

SELF TEST ANSWERS

■ CHECKPOINT 4.1

Fill in the blanks

The <u>law of demand</u> states that other things remaining the same, if the price of a good rises, the <u>quantity demanded of</u> that good decreases. A <u>demand curve</u> is a graph of the relationship between the quantity demanded of a good and its price. Demand curves are <u>downward</u> sloping. An increase in demand shifts the demand curve <u>rightward</u>. Factors that change demand lead to a <u>shift of</u> the demand curve. Factors that change demand are <u>prices of related goods</u>, <u>expected future prices</u>, <u>income</u>, <u>expected future income and credit</u>, <u>number of buyers</u>, and <u>preferences</u>.

True or false

1. False; page 85
2. False; page 84
3. True; page 89
4. False; page 89
5. False; page 90

Multiple choice

1. d; page 85
2. b; page 85
3. a; page 89
4. c; page 89
5. a; page 89
6. a; page 89
7. b; page 89
8. d; page 90
9. d; page 90
10. d; pages 89-90

Complete the graph

1. Figure 4.13 illustrates the demand curve, labeled *D* in the diagram. (The supply curve is from the first "Complete the Graph" question in Checkpoint 4.2.)
   a. 8,000 bundles per month
   b. 7,000 bundles per month
   c. The demand curve slopes downward; page 90.

■ FIGURE 4.13

Price (dollars per bundle of cotton candy)

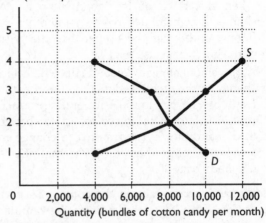

■ FIGURE 4.14

Price (dollars per pound of butter)

2. a. The demand increases and the demand curve shifts rightward, as shown in Figure 4.14 by the shift to *D₁*; page 90
   b. The demand decreases and the demand curve shifts leftward, as shown in Figure 4.14 by the shift to *D₂*; page 90
   c. The demand curve does not shift. The fall in the price of butter leads to an increase in the quantity demanded and a movement along the demand curve, not a shift of the demand curve; page 90.

Short answer and numeric questions

1. When the price falls from $3.30 a gallon to $3.20 a gallon, the quantity of gasoline de-

manded increases from 310 gallons to 316 gallons; page 86.

2. A change in the quantity demanded occurs when the price of the good changes. A change in demand occurs when any other influence on buying plans other than the price of the good changes; page 88.

3. A movement along a demand curve reflects a change in the quantity demanded and is the result of a change in the price of the product. A shift in a demand curve reflects a change in demand and is the result of a change in any factor, other than the price, that affects demand; page 90.

Additional Exercises (also in MyEconLab Test A)

1. a. Caribbean cruises becoming more popular reflects a change in preferences. The demand increases; page 89.

   b. The price of a cruise rising decreases the quantity of cruises demanded; page 90.

   c. Cruises to Asia are substitutes for cruises in the Caribbean. The fall in the price of a cruise to Asia decreases the demand for Caribbean cruises; page 88.

   d. Launching a new "students only" Caribbean cruise makes cruises more attractive to students and so increases the number of demanders. The demand increases; page 89.

   e. People expecting the price of a Caribbean to fall next season decreases the number of people who want to take a cruise this season. The fall in the expected future price decreases the demand today; page 89.

   f. Increasing the number of leading rock artists performing on cruses increases people's preferences to take a cruise. The demand increases; page 89.

2. a. Caribbean cruises becoming more popular increases demand and the demand curve shifts rightward. Figure 4.15 illustrates this change with the rightward shift of the demand curve from D_0 to D_1; page 90.

   b. The price of a cruise rising decreases the quantity of cruises demanded. There is a movement up along the demand curve as

■ **FIGURE 4.15**

Price (thousands of dollars per cruise)

Quantity (millions of cruises per year)

■ **FIGURE 4.16**

Price (thousands of dollars per cruise)

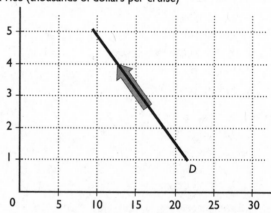

Quantity (millions of cruises per year)

illustrated in Figure 4.16 by the gray arrow. This change reflects the law of demand; page 90.

c. The fall in the price of a cruise to Asia decreases the demand for Caribbean cruises and the demand curve shifts leftward. Figure 4.15 illustrates this change with the leftward shift of the demand curve from D_0 to D_2; page 89.

d. Launching a new "students only" Caribbean cruise makes cruises more attractive to students so demand increases and the demand curve shifts rightward. Figure 4.15 illustrates this change with the rightward shift of the demand curve from D_0 to D_1; page 90.

e. People expecting the price of a Caribbean to fall next season decreases demand today so the demand curve shifts leftward, from D_0 to D_2 in Figure 4.15; page 90.

f. Increasing the number of leading rock artists performing on cruses increases demand so the demand curve shifts rightward, as illustrated in Figure 4.15 by the shift from D_0 to D_1; page 90.

3. Only the second event, the rise in the price of a Caribbean cruise, reflects the law of demand. All the other events reflect a change in demand; page 90.

■ CHECKPOINT 4.2

Fill in the blanks

The quantity supplied of a good is the amount people are willing and able to sell during a specified period at a specified price. The law of supply states that other things remaining the same, if the price of a good rises, the quantity supplied increases. A supply curve is upward sloping. A change in the price of a good changes the quantity supplied and is illustrated by a movement along the supply curve. Factors that change supply are prices of related goods, prices of resources and other inputs, expected future prices, number of sellers, and productivity.

True or false

1. False; page 92
2. True; page 96
3. False; page 96
4. True; page 96
5. False; page 96

Multiple choice

1. c; page 92
2. c; page 92
3. c; page 92
4. a; page 94
5. a; page 96
6. b; page 96
7. b; page 96
8. c; page 96
9. c; page 96
10. d; page 97

Complete the graph

1. The supply curve is illustrated in Figure 4.13, labeled S in the diagram.
   a. 8,000 bundles per month.
   b. 10,000 bundles per month.
   c. The supply curve slopes upward; page 93.

■ FIGURE 4.17

Price (dollars per box of rubber bands)

Quantity (boxes of rubber bands per year)

2. Figure 4.17 illustrates the shift; pages 96-97.

Short answer and numeric questions

1. If other things remain the same, when the price of a good falls (rises), sellers decrease (increase) the quantity supplied; page 92.

2. A change in the price of the product leads to a change in the quantity supplied. Changes in: prices of related goods; prices of resources and other inputs; expectations; number of sellers; and productivity lead to changes in supply; page 97.

Price (dollars per pizza)	Market supply (pizzas per day)
14	47
12	36
10	25
8	14

3. The market supply schedule is in the table above; page 94.

Additional Exercises (also in MyEconLab Test A)

1. a. CDs and DVDs are substitutes in production. When the price of a CD falls, the supply of DVDs increases; page 95.

   b. The new robot technology lowers the cost of producing DVDs and increases the supply of DVDs; page 96.

   c. When the price of a DVD falls, the quantity of DVDs supplied decreases and there is a movement down along the supply curve of DVDs; page 97.

   d. If the price of a DVD is expected to rise next year, supply decreases now; page 96.

   e. If the wage rate paid to DVD factory workers increases, the supply of DVDs decreases because the price of a resource used to produce DVDs has risen; page 96.

2. a. When the price of a CD falls, the supply of DVDs increases and the supply curve of DVDs shifts rightward. In Figure 4.18 the supply curve shifts from S_0 to S_1; page 97.

   b. The new robot technology lowers the cost of producing DVDs and shifts the supply curve of DVDs rightward. In Figure 4.18 this shift is illustrated by the shift from S_0 to S_1; page 97.

   c. When the price of a DVD falls, the quantity of DVDs supplied decreases and there is a movement down along the supply curve of DVDs. In Figure 4.19 as the price falls from $20 per DVD to $10 per DVD the arrow shows that quantity supplied decreases from 200 million to 100 million; page 97.

   d. If the price of a DVD is expected to rise next year, the supply curve shifts leftward, as illustrated in Figure 4.18 by the shift from S_0 to S_2; page 97.

   e. If the wage rate paid to DVD factory workers increases, the supply curve shifts leftward, as illustrated in Figure 4.18 by the shift from S_0 to S_2; page 97.

3. Only the third event, the fall in the price of a DVD, reflects the law of supply. All the other events reflect a change in supply; page 97.

■ **FIGURE 4.18**

Price (dollars per DVD)

Quantity (millions of DVDs per year)

■ **FIGURE 4.19**

Price (dollars per DVD)

Quantity (millions of DVDs per year)

■ **CHECKPOINT 4.3**

Fill in the blanks

The price at which the quantity demanded equals the quantity supplied is the equilibrium price. In a diagram, the equilibrium price is determined where the supply and demand curves intersect. If the price exceeds the equilibrium price, the price falls. An increase in demand raises the equilibrium price and increases the equilibrium quantity. An increase in supply lowers the equilibrium price and increases the equilibrium quantity. If both the demand and supply increase, definitely the equilibrium quantity increases but the effect on the equilibrium price is ambiguous.

True or false

1. True; page 99
2. False; page 101
3. True; page 102
4. False; page 104
5. True; page 104

Multiple choice

1. a; page 99
2. d; page 100
3. b; page 101
4. c; page 101
5. b; page 102
6. c; page 102
7. c; page 104
8. a; page 104

Complete the graph

1. a. A shortage of 6,000 bundles a month; page 100.
   b. A surplus of 3,000 bundles a month; page 100.
   c. The equilibrium price is $2 a bundle of cotton candy and the equilibrium quantity is 8,000 bundles a month; page 100.

Price (dollars per sweatshirt)	Quantity demanded (sweatshirts per season)
35	13
30	15
25	19
20	27
15	37

2. In the table, the market demand schedule is obtained by summing the Hockey team's demand and the Soccer team's demand. The equilibrium price is $25 and the equilibrium quantity is 19 sweatshirts; page 100.

3. Figure 4.20 shows the effect of the increase in income. The increase in income increases the demand for normal goods, such as gold jewelry. The demand curve shifts rightward and the supply curve does not shift. The price of gold jewelry rises, to $1,500 in the figure, and the quantity increases, to 800,000 pieces per week in the figure; page 101.

■ **FIGURE 4.20**
Price (dollars per piece of gold jewelry)

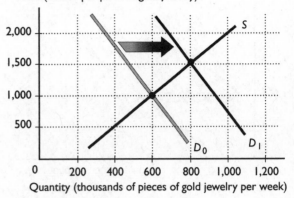

■ **FIGURE 4.21**
Price (dollars per piece of gold jewelry)

4. Figure 4.21 shows the effect of the fall in price of silver jewelry. A fall in the price of a substitute decreases the demand gold jewelry. The demand curve shifts leftward and the supply curve does not shift. The price of gold jewelry falls, to $500 in the figure, and the quantity decreases, to 400,000 pieces per week in the figure; page 101.

5. Figure 4.22 (on the next page) shows the effect of the fall in the price of gold. The price of gold is a cost to the producers of gold jewelry. A rise in the cost decreases the supply of the good. The supply curve shifts leftward and the demand curve does not shift. The price of gold jewelry rises, to $1,750 in the figure, and the quantity decreases, to 400,000 pieces per week in the figure; page 102.

■ **FIGURE 4.22**

Price (dollars per piece of gold jewelry)

Quantity (thousands of pieces of gold jewelry per week)

Short answer and numeric questions

1. When a shortage exists, the price of the good is below the equilibrium price. The quantity demanded is greater than the quantity supplied. When a surplus exists, the price of the good is above the equilibrium price. The quantity demanded is less than the quantity supplied; page 100.

2. The increase in preferences increases the demand for orange juice and the demand curve shifts rightward. The price of orange juice rises and the quantity increases; page 101.

3. The fall in cost increases the supply of computers. The supply curve of computers shifts rightward. The price falls and the quantity increases; page 102.

4. The increase in income increases the demand for normal goods and shifts the demand curve for new cars rightward. The increase in health insurance premiums decreases the supply of new cars and shifts the supply curve of new cars leftward. The price of a new car definitely rises. The effect on the quantity is ambiguous: it rises if the demand effect is larger, falls if the supply effect is larger, and does not change if the two effects are the same size; page 104.

5. You can use supply and demand to determine if you want to buy gasoline immediately or perhaps hold off for a few days. For in-

stance, if you read that a hurricane threatens oil derricks in the Gulf of Mexico, you can reason that if the hurricane actually strikes, the supply of oil will decrease and price of oil will soar. In this case, you ought to fill up your car today to avoid the possibility of paying a higher price next week.

Additional Exercises (also in MyEconLab Test A)

1. The market equilibrium is a price of $2.00 a bar and a quantity of 2,000 bars a week; page 99.

2. If the price of an energy bar is $1.50, the quantity demanded, 2,500 bars, is greater than the quantity supplied, 1,500 bars, so there is a shortage of 1,000 bars a week and the price rises. As the price rises, the quantity demanded decreases, the quantity supplied increases, and the shortage decreases. The price rises until it reaches $2.00, when the shortage disappears; page 99.

3. If the demand for energy bars increases by 1,000 bars at each price, the new equilibrium price is $2.50 a roll of film and the new equilibrium quantity is 2,500 bars a week. There is a shortage of energy bars at the original equilibrium price of $2.00 a bar, after the increase in demand. The shortage leads to the price rising. As the price rises, the quantity demanded decreases, the quantity supplied increases, and the shortage decreases. The price rises until the shortage disappears at a price of $2.50 a bar; page 101.

4. The fire decreases the supply and shifts the supply curve leftward. The fitness craze increases demand and shifts the demand curve rightward. At the initial equilibrium price, there is a shortage of energy bars and the price rises. If the magnitude of the decrease in supply is greater than the magnitude of the increase in demand, the equilibrium quantity decreases. If the magnitude of the decrease in supply is less than the magnitude of the increase in demand, the equilibrium quantity increases. In both cases the price rises; page 102.

Elasticities of Demand and Supply

Chapter 5

In Chapter 5 we study the price elasticity of demand, the price elasticity of supply, the cross elasticity of demand, and the income elasticity of demand.

1 Define the price elasticity of demand, and explain the factors that influence it and how to calculate it.

The price elasticity of demand is a measure of the responsiveness of the quantity demanded of a good to a change in its price when all other influences on buyers' plans remain the same. The price elasticity of demand equals the percentage change in the quantity demanded divided by the percentage change in price, with the negative sign ignored. When the percentage change in the quantity demanded exceeds the percentage change in price, demand is elastic and the elasticity of demand is greater than 1. When the percentage change in the quantity demanded equals the percentage change in price, demand is unit elastic and the elasticity of demand is equal to 1. When the percentage change in the quantity demanded is less than the percentage change in price, demand is inelastic and the elasticity of demand is less than 1. The more substitutes available for the good and the larger the proportion of income spent on the good, the larger the elasticity of demand. The total revenue from the sale of a good equals the price of the good multiplied by the quantity sold. If price and total revenue change in the opposite direction, demand is elastic. If a price change does not change total revenue, demand is unit elastic. If price and total revenue change in the same direction, demand is inelastic.

2 Define the price elasticity of supply, and explain the factors that influence it and how to calculate it.

The price elasticity of supply is a measure of the responsiveness of the quantity supplied of a good to a change in its price when all other influences on sellers' plans remain the same. The two main influences on the price elasticity of supply are production possibilities and storage possibilities. If the good can be stored, supply is more elastic. The price elasticity of supply equals the percentage change in the quantity supplied divided by the percentage change in the price. If the price elasticity of supply is greater than 1, supply is elastic. If the price elasticity of supply equals 1, supply is unit elastic. If the price elasticity of supply is less than 1, supply is inelastic.

3 Define the cross elasticity of demand and the income elasticity of demand, and explain the factors that influence them.

The cross elasticity of demand is a measure of the responsiveness of the demand for a good to a change in the price of a substitute or complement when other things remain the same. The cross elasticity of demand is positive for substitutes and negative for complements. The income elasticity of demand is a measure of the responsiveness of the demand to a change in income when other things remaining the same. The income elasticity of demand equals the percentage change in the quantity demanded divided by the percentage change in income. It is positive for a normal good and negative for an inferior good.

CHECKPOINT 5.1

■ **Define the price elasticity of demand, and explain the factors that influence it and how to calculate it.**

Quick Review

- *Price elasticity of demand* The price elasticity of demand equals the magnitude of the percentage change in the quantity demanded divided by the percentage change in the price.
- *Elastic demand* When the percentage change in the quantity demanded exceeds the percentage change in price. The elasticity of demand is greater than 1 in value.
- *Inelastic demand* When the percentage change in the quantity demanded is less than the percentage change in price. The elasticity of demand is less than 1 in value.
- *Factors affecting elasticity* The demand for a good is more elastic if a large proportion of income is spent on it and if substitutes for it are easy to find. The factors that influence the ability to find substitutes for a good are whether the good is a luxury or a necessity, how narrowly it is defined, and the amount of time available to find substitutes for it.

Additional Practice Problems 5.1

1. For each of the following price changes, calculate the price elasticity of demand. Is the demand elastic, unit elastic, or inelastic?
   a. A 10 percent increase in price results in a 5 percent decrease in the quantity demanded.
   b. A 6 percent increase in price results in a 12 percent decrease in the quantity demanded.
   c. A 4 percent increase in price results in a 4 percent decrease in the quantity demanded.

Price (dollars per bag of cat food)	Quantity (bags of cat food per year)	Total revenue (dollars)
5	4	____
4	8	____
3	12	____
2	16	____
1	20	____

2. The table above gives the demand schedule for bags of cat food. A graph of this demand schedule gives a linear demand curve.
   a. Finish the table by calculating the total revenue for each row.
   b. When is the demand elastic? inelastic? unit elastic?
   c. Explain your answers to part (b).

Solutions to Additional Practice Problems 5.1

1a. The price elasticity of demand equals the magnitude of the percentage change in the quantity demanded divided by the percentage change in the price. So the elasticity of demand equals (5 percent) ÷ (10 percent) = 0.5. Because the elasticity of demand is less than 1, demand is inelastic.

1b. The price elasticity of demand equals (12 percent) ÷ (6 percent) =2.0. Because the elasticity of demand is greater than 1, demand is elastic.

1c. The price elasticity of demand equals (4 percent) ÷ (4 percent) = 1.0. Because the elasticity of demand equals 1, demand is unit elastic.

Price (dollars per bag of cat food)	Quantity (bags of cat food per year)	Total revenue (dollars)
5	4	20
4	8	32
3	12	36
2	16	32
1	20	20

2a. The completed table is above. Total revenue equals the price times the quantity sold.

2b. The demand is elastic at prices greater than $3 a bag. The demand is inelastic at prices less than $3 a bag. The demand is unit elastic at a price of $3 a bag.

2c. Demand is unit elastic at the midpoint of the demand curve. When demand is unit elastic, a price change leaves total revenue unchanged. The midpoint of the curve occurs when the price is $3 a bag, so demand is unit elastic at a price of $3 a bag.

Demand is elastic at all points above the midpoint of the demand curve. So when the price is greater than $3 a bag, demand is elastic. When demand is elastic, price and total revenue change in opposite directions. For example, when the price *rises* from $4 to $5, total revenue *decreases* from $32 to $20.

Demand is inelastic at all points below the midpoint of the demand curve. So when the price is less than $3 a bag, demand is inelastic. When demand is inelastic, price and total revenue change in the same direction. For example, when the price *rises* from $1 to $2, total revenue *increases* from $20 to $32.

■ Self Test 5.1

Fill in the blanks

To calculate the percentage change in price, the midpoint formula divides the change in price by the ____ (initial price; new price; average of the initial and the new price) and then multiplies by 100. If the percentage change in the quantity demanded exceeds the percentage change in the price, demand is ____ (elastic; inelastic). The demand for a product is more elastic if there are ____ (more; fewer) substitutes for it. The demand for a necessity is generally ____ (elastic; inelastic). The price elasticity of demand equals the percentage change in the ____ (price; quantity demanded) divided by the percentage change in the ____ (price; quantity demanded). Moving along a straight-line demand curve, the slope ____ (is constant; varies) and the elasticity ____ (is constant; varies). If demand is elastic, an increase in price ____ (increases; decreases) total revenue.

True or false

1. The price elasticity of demand equals the magnitude of the slope of the demand curve.

2. If the price increases by 10 percent and the quantity demanded decreases by 8 percent, the price elasticity of demand equals 1.25.

3. As the price of a good increases, if the quantity demanded of it remains the same, then demand for the good is perfectly inelastic.

4. Above the midpoint of a straight-line demand curve, demand is elastic.

5. When the price of a service increases by 5 percent and the quantity demanded decreases by 5 percent, total revenue remains unchanged.

6. If the price of tuna increases by 5 percent and the total revenue of tuna producers increases, then the demand for tuna is inelastic.

Multiple choice

1. The price elasticity of demand is a measure of the extent to which the quantity demanded of a good changes when ____ changes and all other influences on buyers' plans remain the same.
   a. income
   b. the price of a related good
   c. the price of the good
   d. the demand alone
   e. both the demand and supply simultaneously

2. Suppose the price of a movie falls from $9 to $7. Using the midpoint method, what is the percentage change in price?
   a. 33 percent
   b. −33 percent
   c. 25 percent
   d. −25 percent
   e. −97 percent

3. Suppose the price of a tie rises from $45 to $55. Using the midpoint method, what is the percentage change in price?
   a. 10 percent
   b. −10 percent
   c. 20 percent
   d. −20 percent
   e. 100 percent

4. Demand is elastic if
   a. consumers respond strongly to changes in the product's price.
   b. a large percentage change in price brings about a small percentage change in quantity demanded.
   c. a small percentage change in price brings about a small percentage change in quantity demanded.
   d. the quantity demanded is not responsive to price changes.
   e. the demand curve is vertical.

5. During the winter of 2011–2012, the price of fuel oil increased enormously but the quantity demanded decreased only a little. This response indicates that the demand for fuel oil was
   a. inelastic.
   b. elastic.
   c. unit elastic.
   d. perfectly elastic.
   e. perfectly inelastic.

6. If substitutes for a good are readily available, the demand for that good
   a. does not change substantially if the price rises.
   b. does not change substantially if the price falls.
   c. is inelastic.
   d. is elastic.
   e. Both answers (a) and(b) are correct.

7. If the price of a product increases by 5 percent and the quantity demanded decreases by 5 percent, then the elasticity of demand is
   a. 0.
   b. 1.
   c. indeterminate.
   d. 5.
   e. 25.

8. The price of a bag of pretzels rises from $2 to $3 and the quantity demanded decreases from 100 to 60. What is the price elasticity of demand?
   a. 1.0
   b. 1.25
   c. 40.0
   d. 20.0
   e. 0.80

9. When a firm raises the price of its product, what happens to total revenue?
   a. If demand is elastic, total revenue decreases.
   b. If demand is unit elastic, total revenue increases.
   c. If demand is inelastic, total revenue decreases.
   d. If demand is elastic, total revenue increases.
   e. If demand is unit elastic, total revenue decreases.

Complete the graph

■ **FIGURE 5.1**

1. In Figure 5.1, label the axes and then draw a demand curve for a good that has a perfectly elastic demand.

■ **FIGURE 5.2**

2. In Figure 5.2, label the axes and then draw a demand curve for a good that has a perfectly inelastic demand.

■ **FIGURE 5.3**

Price (dollars per unit)

Quantity (units per month)

3. In Figure 5.3, darken the part of the demand curve along which demand is elastic. Label the point on the demand curve at which demand is unit elastic.

Short answer and numeric questions

	Percentage change in price	Percentage change in quantity demanded	Price elasticity of demand
A	5	10	____
B	8	4	____
C	3	0	____
D	6	6	____
E	1	8	____

1. Complete the table above by calculating the price elasticity of demand.
   a. Which row has the most elastic demand?
   b. Which row has the least elastic demand?

2. Suppose the price elasticity of demand for oil is 0.3. If the quantity of oil decreases by 6 percent, what is the effect on the price of oil?

3. What does it mean when the demand for a good is inelastic?

4. What is the relationship between how narrowly a good is defined and the number of substitutes it has?

5. The Eye on Your Life explains how you can use elasticity in your personal life. You can also use it in your business life. Suppose you are a brand manager for Crest toothpaste and you are thinking about raising its price. How will this price hike affect the total revenue from sales of Crest?

Additional Exercises (also in MyEconLab Test A)

When the price of Internet service rises from $24 to $26 a month, the quantity demanded decreases from 204 million to 196 million subscribers.

1. Calculate the percentage change in the price of Internet service, the percentage change in the quantity demanded of Internet service, and the price elasticity of demand for Internet service.

2. Is the demand for Internet services elastic or inelastic? Would the demand for AOL service be more elastic or less elastic than the demand for Internet service? Why?

3. What is the change in the total revenue of Internet service providers? Why is the concept of price elasticity of demand useful to Internet service providers? If the demand curve for Internet service is a straight line, is the price at which the demand for Internet service is unit elastic above or below $25 a month? Why?

CHECKPOINT 5.2

■ **Define the price elasticity of supply, and explain the factors that influence it and how to calculate it.**

Quick Review
• *Price elasticity of supply* A measure of the

extent to which the quantity supplied of a good changes when the price of the good changes and all other influences on sellers' plans remain the same.

Additional Practice Problems 5.2

1. For each of the following price changes, calculate the price elasticity of supply.
   a. A 10 percent increase in price results in a 15 percent increase in the quantity supplied.
   b. A 6 percent increase in price results in a 3 percent increase in the quantity supplied.
   c. A 7 percent increase in price results in a 7 percent increase in the quantity supplied.

2. Over one month the elasticity of supply of avocados is 0.1 and over 5 years the elasticity of supply of avocados is 2.0. If the price of avocados rises 10 percent, what is the increase in the quantity supplied in one month and in 5 years? Why is there a difference in the quantities?

Solutions to Additional Practice Problems 5.2

1a. The elasticity of supply equals the percentage change in the quantity supplied divided by the percentage change in price, which is (15 percent) ÷ (10 percent) = 1.5.

1b. The elasticity of supply equals (3 percent) ÷ (6 percent) = 0.5.

1c. The elasticity of supply equals (7 percent) ÷ (7 percent) = 1.0.

2. The increase in the quantity supplied equals the percentage change in the price times the elasticity of supply. In one month the quantity supplied increases by (10 percent) × (0.1), which is 1 percent. In 5 years the quantity supplied increases by (10 percent) × (2.0), which is 20 percent. The increase in the quantity supplied is much greater after 5 years because more changes can be made as more time passes. Existing avocado trees can be more carefully cultivated and additional fertilizer used. Eventually additional avocado trees can be planted, mature, and then be harvested. The supply of avocados increases as time passes, making the supply more elastic.

■ Self Test 5.2

Fill in the blanks

When supply has a vertical supply curve, then the supply of the good is perfectly ____ (elastic; inelastic). Goods that can be produced at an almost constant opportunity cost have an ____ (elastic; inelastic) supply. As time passes, the elasticity of supply ____ (increases; decreases). The price elasticity of supply equals the percentage change in the ____ (price; quantity supplied) divided by the percentage change in the ____ (price; quantity supplied). If the elasticity of supply is greater than 1, supply is ____ (elastic; inelastic).

True or false

1. If the percentage change in the quantity supplied is zero when the price changes, supply is perfectly elastic.

2. Goods that can be produced at a constant (or very gently rising) opportunity cost have an elastic supply.

3. The supply of apples is perfectly elastic on the day of a price change.

4. The supply of a storable good is perfectly inelastic.

5. When the price of a pizza is $20, 10 pizzas are supplied and when the price rises to $30 a pizza, 14 pizzas are supplied. The price elasticity of supply of pizzas is 0.83.

6. If a 5 percent increase in price increases the quantity supplied by 10 percent, the elasticity of supply equals 2.0.

Multiple choice

1. The price elasticity of supply is a measure of the extent to which the quantity supplied of a good changes when only the
   a. cost of producing the product increases.
   b. quantity of the good demanded increases.
   c. supply increases.
   d. price of the good changes.
   e. number of firms changes.

2. When the percentage change in the quantity supplied exceeds the percentage change in price, then supply is
   a. elastic.
   b. inelastic.
   c. unit elastic.
   d. perfectly inelastic.
   e. perfectly elastic.

3. The supply of beachfront property on St. Simon's Island is
   a. elastic.
   b. unit elastic.
   c. negative.
   d. inelastic.
   e. perfectly elastic.

4. For a product with a rapidly increasing opportunity cost of producing additional units,
   a. demand is price elastic.
   b. supply is price elastic.
   c. demand is price inelastic.
   d. supply is price inelastic.
   e. the demand curve is vertical.

5. The greater the amount of time that passes after a price change, the
   a. less elastic supply becomes.
   b. more elastic supply becomes.
   c. more negative supply becomes.
   d. steeper the supply curve becomes.
   e. more vertical the supply curve becomes.

6. The price elasticity of supply equals the percentage change in the
   a. quantity demanded divided by the percentage change in the price of a substitute or complement.
   b. quantity supplied divided by the percentage change in price.
   c. quantity demanded divided by the percentage change in price.
   d. supply divided by the percentage change in the demand.
   e. quantity supplied divided by the percentage change in income.

7. If a firm supplies 200 units at a price of $50 and 100 units at a price of $40, using the midpoint formula what is the price elasticity of supply?
   a. 0.33
   b. 1.00
   c. 3.00
   d. 5.00
   e. 8.50

8. If the quantity supplied increases by 8 percent when the price rises by 2 percent, the price elasticity of supply is ____ percent.
   a. 10.0
   b. 6.0
   c. 0.25
   d. 16.0
   e. 4.0

9 If the price of a good increases by 10 percent and the quantity supplied increases by 5 percent, then the elasticity of supply is
   a. greater than one and supply is elastic.
   b. negative and supply is inelastic.
   c. less than one and supply is elastic.
   d. less than one and supply is inelastic.
   e. greater than one and supply is inelastic.

Complete the graph

■ FIGURE 5.4

1. In Figure 5.4, label the axes and then draw a supply curve for a good that has a perfectly inelastic supply.

Short answer and numeric questions

1. The elasticity of supply of wheat is 0.3 and the elasticity of supply of magazines is 1.3. If the prices of wheat and magazines both rise 10 percent, what is the increase in the quantity of wheat supplied and the increase in the quantity of magazines supplied?

	Price (dollars)	Quantity supplied (units per week)
A	5	10
B	15	30
C	25	50
D	35	90

2. The table above gives a supply schedule. Calculate the price elasticity of supply between points A and B; between points B and C; and between points C and D.

	Percentage change in price	Percentage change in quantity supplied	Price elasticity of supply
A	6	8	___
B	8	4	___
C	4	8	___

3. Complete the table above by calculating the price elasticity of supply.

4. Describe the elasticity of supply of a good that can be stored.

5. Why does the elasticity of supply increase as time passes after a price change?

Additional Exercises (also in MyEconLab Test A)

In 2002, the price of asparagus crashed from $45 a crate to $15 a crate. A typical Californian asparagus farmer would have supplied 2,000 crates a day at $45 a crate but at $15 a crate would plow the crop into the ground and supply nothing.

1. Is the Californian supply of asparagus elastic, unit elastic, or inelastic? How do you think production possibilities and storage possibilities influence the price elasticity of supply of asparagus?

2. Calculate the price elasticity of supply of Californian asparagus. If the price of asparagus remains at $15 a crate, do you think the elasticity of supply will change over the coming years? Explain your answer.

■ Define the cross elasticity of demand and the income elasticity of demand, and explain the factors that influence them.

Quick Review

- *Cross elasticity of demand* A measure of the extent to which the demand for a good changes when the price of a substitute or complement changes, other things remaining the same.
- *Income elasticity of demand* A measure of the extent to which the demand for a good changes when income changes, other things remaining the same.

Additional Practice Problems 5.3

1. For each of the following, calculate the cross elasticity of demand. Are the goods substitutes or complements?
    a. A 10 percent increase in the price of lettuce results in a 15 percent increase in the quantity of spinach demanded.
    b. A 5 percent increase in the price of beef results in a 10 percent increase in the quantity of pork demanded.
    c. A 4 percent increase in the price of a golf club results in a 2 percent decrease in the quantity of golf balls demanded.

2. For each of the following, calculate the income elasticity of demand. Are the goods normal or inferior goods?
    a. A 3 percent increase in income results in a 1 percent increase in the quantity demanded.
    b. A 6 percent increase in income results in a 3 percent decrease in the quantity demanded.
    c. A 2 percent increase in income results in a 4 percent increase in the quantity demanded.

3. Pepsi and Coke are substitutes. Pepsi and Tropicana orange juice also are substitutes. But

quite likely the two cross elasticities of demand differ in size. Which cross elasticity do you think is larger and why?

Solutions to Additional Practice Problems 5.3

1a. The cross elasticity of demand equals the percentage change in the quantity demanded of one good divided by the percentage change in the price of the other good, which is (15 percent) ÷ (10 percent) = 1.5. The cross elasticity of supply is positive for substitute and negative for complements, so lettuce and spinach are substitutes.

1b. The cross elasticity of demand equals (10 percent) ÷ (5 percent) = 2.0. Beef and pork are substitutes.

1c. The cross elasticity of demand equals (−2 percent) ÷ (4 percent) = −0.5. Golf clubs and golf balls are complements.

2a. The income elasticity of demand equals the percentage change in the quantity demanded divided by the percentage change in income, which is (1 percent) ÷ (3 percent) = 0.33. The income elasticity is positive for a normal good and negative for an inferior good, so this good is a normal good.

2b. The income elasticity of demand equals (−3 percent) ÷ (6 percent) = −0.5. The good is an inferior good.

2c. The income elasticity of demand equals (4 percent) ÷ (2 percent) = 2.0. The good is a normal good.

3. The cross elasticity between Pepsi and Coke is likely much larger than the cross elasticity between Pepsi and Tropicana orange juice. For many people, Pepsi and Coke are close to indistinguishable. Even a slight rise in the price of a Coke will increase the quantity of Pepsi demanded significantly, so their cross elasticity is large. Pepsi and Tropicana orange juice are less close substitutes. So, although an increase in the price of Tropicana orange juice will increase the demand for Pepsi, the increase will be relatively slight and the cross elasticity will be small.

■ Self Test 5.3

Fill in the blanks

The ____ (price; cross; income) elasticity of demand is a measure of the extent to which the demand for a good changes when the price of a substitute or complement changes, other things remaining the same. The cross elasticity of demand is ____ (positive; negative) for a substitute and ____ (positive; negative) for a complement. The income elasticity of demand equals the percentage change in ____ (the quantity demanded; income) divided by the percentage change in ____ (quantity demanded; income). The income elasticity of demand is ____ (positive; negative) for a normal good and ____ (positive; negative) for an inferior good.

True or false

1. If the cross elasticity of demand is negative, the two goods are substitutes.

2. If the cross elasticity between hamburgers and hot dogs is positive, then hamburgers and hot dogs are substitutes.

3. An inferior good has a negative income elasticity of demand.

4. When the income elasticity of demand is positive, the good is a normal good.

5. A normal good is a good that has a positive cross elasticity of demand.

Multiple choice

1. The measure used to determine whether two goods are complements or substitutes is called the
   a. price elasticity of supply.
   b. cross elasticity of demand.
   c. price elasticity of demand.
   d. income elasticity.
   e. substitute elasticity of demand.

2. If beef and pork are substitutes, the cross elasticity of demand between the two goods is
   a. negative.
   b. positive.
   c. indeterminate.
   d. elastic.
   e. greater than one.

3. When the price of a pizza is $10, the quantity of soda demanded is 300 drinks. When the price of pizza is $15, the quantity of soda demanded is 100 drinks. The cross elasticity of demand equals
   a. –0.25.
   b. –0.40.
   c. –2.50.
   d. –25.00.
   e. 4.0.

4. When the price of going to a movie rises 5 percent, the quantity of DVDs demanded increases 10 percent. The cross elasticity of demand equals
   a. 10.0.
   b. 0.50.
   c. –0.50.
   d. –2.0.
   e. 2.0.

5. If two goods have a cross elasticity of demand of –2, then when the price of the one increases, the demand curve of the other good
   a. shifts rightward.
   b. shifts leftward.
   c. remains unchanged.
   d. may shift rightward, leftward, or remain unchanged.
   e. remains unchanged but the supply curve shifts leftward.

6. The income elasticity of demand is the percentage change in the ____ divided by the percentage change in ____.
   a. quantity demanded; the price of a substitute or complement
   b. quantity supplied; price
   c. quantity demanded; price
   d. quantity demanded; income
   e. quantity demanded; the quantity supplied

7. When income increases from $20,000 to $30,000 the number of home-delivered pizzas per year increases from 22 to 40. The income elasticity of demand for home-delivered pizza equals
   a. 1.45.
   b 0.69.
   c. 0.58.
   d. 0.40.
   e. 2.86.

8. When income increases by 6 percent, the demand for potatoes decreases by 2 percent. The income elasticity of demand for potatoes equals
   a. –2.00.
   b. 3.00.
   c. –3.00.
   d. 0.33.
   e. –0.33.

9. If a product is a normal good, then its income elasticity of demand is
   a. zero.
   b. positive.
   c. negative.
   d. indeterminate.
   e. greater than one.

10. The income elasticity of demand for used cars is less than zero. So, used cars are
    a. an inferior good.
    b. a normal good.
    c. an inelastic good.
    d. a perfectly inelastic good.
    e. substitute goods.

Complete the graph
■ FIGURE 5.5

Price (dollars per large screen television)

Quantity (millions of large screen televisions per year)

1. The income elasticity of demand for large screen televisions is positive. In Figure 5.5, show the change when income increases.

Short answer and numeric questions

1. Do you think the cross elasticity of demand between Pepsi and Coke is positive or negative, large or small? Why?

	Percentage change in price of good A	Percentage change in quantity demanded of good B	Cross elasticity of demand
A	3	6	____
B	5	−10	____
C	−4	−8	____
D	8	4	____

2. Complete the table above. Which row has substitutes and which row has complements?

3. The income elasticity of demand for inter-city bus trips is negative. What does this fact tell you about inter-city bus trips?

	Percentage change in income	Percentage change in quantity demanded	Income elasticity of demand
A	5	10	____
B	5	−10	____
C	5	2	____
D	6	6	____

4. Complete the table above. Which row indicates an inferior good and which row indicates a good that is income elastic?

Additional Exercises (also in MyEconLab Test A)

When the price of a pizza falls from $9 to $7 and other things remain the same, the quantity demanded of pizza increases from 100 to 200 an hour, the quantity demanded of burgers decreases from 200 to 100 an hour, and the quantity demanded of cola increases from 150 to 250 cans an hour. Use this information to answer Exercises 1, 2, and 3.

1. Calculate the cross elasticity of demand for cola with respect to pizza.

2. Calculate the cross elasticity of demand for burgers with respect to pizza.

3. Of what use are these two cross elasticities of demand to the owner of a business that sells burgers and cola?

When incomes in Miami rise by 10 percent and other things remain the same, the quantity demanded of frozen fish cakes decreases by 5 percent and the quantity demanded of fresh fish increases by 15 percent. Use this information to answer Exercises 4, 5, and 6.

4. Calculate the income elasticity of demand for frozen fish cakes.

5. Calculate the income elasticity of demand for fresh fish.

6. How could a fish shop owner in Miami use these two income elasticities?

SELF TEST ANSWERS

■ CHECKPOINT 5.1

Fill in the blanks

To calculate the percentage change in price, the midpoint formula divides the change in price by the <u>average of the initial and the new price</u> and then multiplies by 100. If the percentage change in the quantity demanded exceeds the percentage change in the price, demand is <u>elastic</u>. The demand for a product is more elastic if there are <u>more</u> substitutes for it. The demand for a necessity is generally <u>inelastic</u>. The price elasticity of demand equals the percentage change in the <u>quantity demanded</u> divided by the percentage change in the <u>price</u>. Moving along a straight-line demand curve, the slope <u>is constant</u> and the elasticity <u>varies</u>. If demand is elastic, an increase in price <u>decreases</u> total revenue.

True or false

1. False; page 116
2. False; page 116
3. True; page 114
4. True; page 118
5. True; page 120
6. True; page 120

Multiple choice

1. c; page 112
2. d; page 112
3. c; page 113
4. a; page 114
5. a; page 114
6. d; page 114
7. b; page 116
8. b; page 116
9. a; page 120

Complete the graph

1. Figure 5.6 labels the axes and illustrates a demand curve for a good with a perfectly elastic demand; page 115.
2. Figure 5.7 labels the axes and illustrates a demand curve for a good with a perfectly inelastic demand; page 115.

■ **FIGURE 5.6**

■ **FIGURE 5.7**

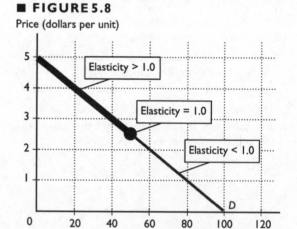

■ **FIGURE 5.8**

Price (dollars per unit)

3. In Figure 5.8, demand is elastic along the dark portion of the demand curve. Demand

is unit elastic at the midpoint of curve. Demand is inelastic along the demand curve below the midpoint; page 118.

Short answer and numeric questions

	Percentage change in price	Percentage change in quantity demanded	Price elasticity of demand
A	5	10	2.0
B	8	4	0.5
C	3	0	0.0
D	6	6	1.0
E	1	8	8.0

1. The complete table is above; page 116.
   a. The most elastic demand is in row E; page 116.
   b. The least elastic demand is in row C (the demand is perfectly inelastic); page 116.
2. The price rises by 20 percent; page 116.
3. Demand is inelastic if the percentage change in the quantity demanded is less than the percentage change in the price; page 114.
4. The more narrow the definition of the good, the more substitutes exist. For example, there are more substitutes for a slice of Pizza Hut pizza than for pizza in general; page 116.
5. When the price of a good rises, total revenue increases if demand is inelastic, does not change if demand is unit elastic, and decreases if demand is elastic. As brand manager, you can use this relationship to predict whether the total revenue from Crest will rise, fall, or stay the same if you boost its price; page 120.

Additional Exercises (also in MyEconLab Test A)

1. The percentage change in price is 8 percent. The midpoint formula shows the percentage change is:

$$\left(\frac{\$26 - \$24}{(\$24 + \$26) \div 2}\right) \times 100.$$

The percentage change in the quantity demanded is 4 percent. The percentage is:

$$\left(\frac{196 \text{ million} - 204 \text{ million}}{(204 \text{ million} + 196 \text{ million}) \div 2}\right) \times 100.$$

The price elasticity of demand equals (4 percent)÷(8 percent), which is 0.50; page 113.

2. The demand for Internet services is inelastic because the percentage change in quantity demanded is less than the percentage change in price. More specifically, the price elasticity of demand for Internet services is 0.50, which indicates that it is inelastic. The demand for AOL service is more elastic than the demand for Internet service because more substitutes exist for AOL service in particular than for Internet service in general. AOL service is a more narrowly defined service; pages 114, 116.

3. The initial total revenue is $24 a month × 204 million subscribers, which is $4,896 million a month. The new total revenue is $26 a month × 196 million subscribers, which is $5,096 million a month. So total revenue increases by $5,096 million a month – $4,896 million a month, which is $200 million a month.

The price elasticity of demand is useful because it allows us to make precise predictions about how much demanders change the quantity they demand when the price changes. For instance, if the price elasticity of demand for AOL is 0.5, then AOL can determine that a 10 percent increase in the price of their service will decrease the quantity that people demand by 5 percent; page 122.

The demand for Internet service is unit elastic at a price higher than $25 a month. At $25 a month, the elasticity equals 0.5. As we move up along a linear demand curve, the price elasticity of demand increases. So the demand for Internet service is unit elastic at the midpoint of the demand curve, which is at a price greater than $25 a month; page 118.

■ CHECKPOINT 5.2

Fill in the blanks

When supply has a vertical supply curve, then the supply of the good is perfectly <u>inelastic</u>. Goods that can be produced at an almost constant opportunity cost have an <u>elastic</u> supply. As time passes, the elasticity of supply increases. The price elasticity of supply equals the percentage change in the <u>quantity supplied</u> divided by the percentage change in the <u>price</u>. If the elasticity of supply is greater than 1, supply is <u>elastic</u>.

True or false
1. False; page 124
2. True; page 124
3. False; page 126
4. False; page 126
5. True; page 126
6. True; page 126

Multiple choice
1. d; page 126
2. a; page 126
3. d; page 126
4. d; page 126
5. b; page 126
6. b; page 126
7. c; page 126
8. e; page 126
9. d; page 126

Complete the graph

■ FIGURE 5.9
Price (dollars)

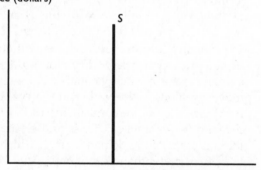

Quantity (units per year)

1. Figure 5.9 labels the axes and illustrates a supply curve for a good with a perfectly inelastic supply; page 125.

Short answer and numeric questions
1. If the price of wheat rises 10 percent, the increase in the quantity supplied is (10 percent) × (0.3), which is 3 percent. If the price of a magazine rises 10 percent, the increase in the quantity supplied is (10 percent) × (1.3), which is 13 percent; pages 124 and 126.

2. The price elasticity of supply between points A and B is 1.00; between points B and C is 1.00; and between points C and D is 1.71; page 126.

	Percentage change in price	Percentage change in quantity supplied	Price elasticity of supply
A	6	8	<u>1.33</u>
B	8	4	<u>0.50</u>
C	4	8	<u>2.00</u>

3. The completed table is above; page 126.

4. The elasticity of supply of a good that can be stored depends on the decision to keep the good in storage or offer it for sale. A small price change can make a big difference to this decision, so the supply of a storable good is highly elastic; page 126.

5. As time passes after a price change, it becomes easier to change production plans and supply becomes more elastic. For example, many manufactured goods have an inelastic supply if production plans have had only a short period in which to change. But after all the technologically possible ways of adjusting production have been exploited, supply is extremely elastic for most manufactured items; page 126.

Additional Exercises (also in MyEconLab Test A)
1. The supply of asparagus is elastic. The percentage change in the quantity supplied is greater than the percentage change in the price. The supply of asparagus over this large price range is elastic because there is the possibility of plowing the crop under and producing nothing. Once harvested, asparagus is not very storable, which makes supply more inelastic; pages 124-125.

2. The percentage change in the quantity supplied of asparagus is:

$$\left(\frac{2,000 - 0}{(2,000 + 0) \div 2}\right) \times 100,$$

which is 200 percent. The percentage change in the price of asparagus is

$$\left(\frac{\$45 \text{ a crate } - \$15 \text{ a crate}}{(\$45 \text{ a crate } + \$15 \text{ a crate}) \div 2}\right) \times 100,$$

which is 100 percent. So the price elasticity of supply = (200 percent) ÷ (100 percent) = 2.0.

As time passes, the elasticity of supply increases. After all the technologically possible ways of adjusting production have been exploited, the supply of asparagus becomes extremely elastic; pages 126-127.

■ CHECKPOINT 5.3

Fill in the blanks

The <u>cross</u> elasticity of demand is a measure of the extent to which the demand for a good changes when the price of a substitute or complement changes, other things remaining the same. The cross elasticity of demand is <u>positive</u> for a substitute and <u>negative</u> for a complement. The income elasticity of demand equals the percentage change in <u>quantity demanded</u> divided by the percentage change in <u>income</u>. The income elasticity of demand is <u>positive</u> for a normal good and <u>negative</u> for an inferior good.

True or false

1. False; page 129
2. True; page 129
3. True; page 130
4. True; page 130
5. False; page 130

Multiple choice

1. b; page 129
2. b; page 129
3. c; page 129
4. e; page 129
5. b; page 130
6. d; page 130
7. a; page 130
8. e; page 130
9. b; page 130
10. a; page 130

Complete the graph

■ FIGURE 5.10

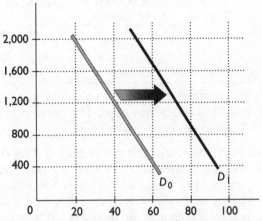

Price (dollars per large screen television)

Quantity (millions of large screen televisions per year)

1. Because the income elasticity of demand is positive, we know that large screen televisions are a normal good. In Figure 5.10 an increase in income shifts the demand curve rightward from D_0 to D_1; page 130.

Short answer and numeric questions

1. The cross elasticity of demand between Pepsi and Coke is most likely positive and large. Pepsi and Coke are substitutes for most people, so their cross elasticity of demand is positive. They are close substitutes for many people, so their cross elasticity of demand is large; page 129.

	Percentage change in price of good A	Percentage change in quantity demanded of good B	Cross elasticity of demand
A	3	6	<u>2.0</u>
B	5	−10	<u>−2.0</u>
C	−4	−8	<u>2.0</u>
D	8	4	<u>0.5</u>

2. The completed table is above. The goods in row B are complements; the goods in rows A, C, and D are substitutes; page 129.

3. The fact that the income elasticity of demand for inter-city bus trips is negative indicates that an inter-city bus trip is an inferior good. When people's incomes increase, they take

fewer inter-city bus trips and instead fly, drive, or take the train; page 130.

	Percentage change in income	Percentage change in quantity demanded	Income elasticity of demand
A	5	10	2.0
B	5	−10	−2.0
C	5	2	0.4
D	6	6	1.0

4. The completed table is above. The good in Row B is an inferior good. The good in row A is income elastic; page 130.

Additional Exercises (also in MyEconLab Test A)

1. The cross elasticity of demand for cola with respect to pizza equals the percentage change in the quantity of cola divided by the percentage change in the price of a pizza. The percentage change in the quantity of cola equals

$$\left(\frac{250 \text{ an hour} - 150 \text{ an hour}}{(150 \text{ an hour} + 250 \text{ an hour}) \div 2}\right) \times 100,$$

which is 50 percent. The percentage change in the price of a pizza is

$$\left(\frac{\$7 \text{ a pizza} - \$9 \text{ a pizza}}{(\$9 \text{ a pizza} + \$7 \text{ a pizza}) \div 2}\right) \times 100,$$

which is −25 percent. So the cross elasticity of demand for cola with respect to pizza is (50 percent) ÷(−25 percent), which is −2.00. Because the cross elasticity of demand for the two is negative the two are complements; page 129.

2. The cross elasticity of demand for burgers with respect to pizza equals the percentage change in the quantity of burgers divided by the percentage change in the price of a pizza. Part (a) shows that the percentage change in the price of pizza is −25 percent. The percentage change in the quantity of burgers is

$$\left(\frac{100 \text{ an hour} - 200 \text{ an hour}}{(200 \text{ an hour} + 100 \text{ an hour}) \div 2}\right) \times 100,$$

or −66.67 percent. The cross elasticity of demand for burgers with respect to pizza is equal to (−66.67 percent) ÷ (−25 percent), which is 2.67. Because the cross elasticity of demand for the two is positive the two are substitutes; page 129.

3. The owner can determine how the quantities of burgers and cola he or she sells will change if the price of a nearby pizza place changes the price of its pizza; pages 129-130.

4. The income elasticity of demand for frozen fish cakes is (−5 percent) ÷ (10 percent) = −0.50. The income elasticity is negative and the negative elasticity indicates that frozen fish cakes are an inferior good; page 130.

5. The income elasticity of demand for fresh fish is (15 percent) ÷(10 percent) = 1.50; page 130.

6. The owner of a fresh fish shop can use these two elasticities to predict how sales of fresh and frozen fish change when people's income change. For instance, if the economy in Miami goes into a recession so that people's incomes generally fall, the owner can predict that the quantity of frozen fish demanded will increase and the quantity of fresh fish demanded will decrease. As a result, the owner can stock more frozen fish and less fresh fish; page 131

Efficiency and Fairness of Markets

Chapter 6

1 **Describe the alternative methods of allocating scarce resources and define and explain the features of an efficient allocation.**

Ways of allocating resources include: market price; command; majority rule; contest; first-come, first-served; sharing equally; lottery; personal characteristics; and force. Allocative efficiency occurs when we produce the quantities of goods and services on the *PPF* that people value most highly. Marginal benefit is the benefit that people receive from consuming one more unit of the product; marginal cost is the opportunity cost of producing one more unit of the product. The marginal benefit curve is downward sloping and the marginal cost curve is upward sloping. Allocative efficiency requires producing where the curves intersect, at the quantity that makes the marginal benefit equal the marginal cost.

2 **Distinguish between value and price and define consumer surplus.**

Value is what buyers get and price is what buyers pay. The value is the *marginal benefit,* which is the maximum price that buyers are willing to pay for another unit of the good. The demand curve is the marginal benefit curve. Consumer surplus is the marginal benefit from a good or service in excess of the price paid for it, summed over the quantity consumed.

3 **Distinguish between cost and price and define producer surplus.**

Cost is what a seller gives up to produce a good and price is what a seller receives when the good is sold. The cost of producing one more unit of a good or service is its *marginal cost.* The supply curve is the marginal cost curve. Producer surplus is the price of a good or service in excess of the marginal cost of producing it, summed over the quantity produced.

4 **Evaluate the efficiency of the alternative methods of allocating resources.**

When marginal benefit equals the marginal cost, the efficient quantity is produced. The sum of consumer surplus and producer surplus is maximized at a competitive equilibrium. According to Adam Smith, each participant in a competitive market is "led by an invisible hand" to promote the efficient use of resources. Market failure--underproduction or overproduction relative to the efficient quantity—creates a deadweight loss. Government imposed price and quantity regulations, taxes and subsidies, externalities, public goods, common resources, monopoly, and high transactions costs are obstacles to efficiency. Other means of allocation sometimes are efficient.

5 **Explain the main ideas about fairness and evaluate the fairness of the alternative methods of allocating scarce resources.**

Two views of fairness are: it's not fair if the *rules* aren't fair and it's not fair if the *result* isn't fair. When private property and property rights are protected and exchanges are voluntary is a fair rules approach. The fair results idea of income equality ignores the Big Tradeoff between efficiency and fairness. The Big Tradeoff points out the cost in terms of inefficiency of making income transfers that increase fairness.

CHECKPOINT 6.1

■ **Describe the alternative methods of allocating scarce resources and define and explain the features of an efficient allocation.**

Quick Review

- *Allocation methods* Resources can be allocated by: using the market price; command; majority rule; a contest, first-come, first served; sharing equally; lottery; personal characteristics; and force.
- *Marginal benefit* The benefit that a person receives from consuming one more unit of a good or service.
- *Marginal cost* The opportunity cost of producing one more unit of a good or service.
- *Allocative efficiency* When the quantities of the goods and services produced are those that people value most highly—it is not possible to produce more of a good or service without giving up some of the another good or service that people value more highly. Allocative efficiency occurs when production is at the point where marginal benefit equals marginal cost.

Additional Practice Problems 6.1

1. Why is it necessary to allocate resources?
2. What is the command method of allocating resources?
3. Explain the relationship between production efficiency and allocative efficiency.

Solutions to Additional Practice Problems 6.1

1. Resources are scarce, so not everyone's wants can be fulfilled. Because not everyone can get everything he or she wants, *some* method must be used to determine whether or not resources are to be allocated to fulfilling each specific want.
2. The command method of allocating resources relies upon someone in authority to order how resources shall be allocated. The former Soviet Union and currently North Korea and Cuba are examples of entire economies in which command was (and still is for North Korea and Cuba) the major allocation method.
3. Production efficiency is a situation in it is impossible to produce more of one good or service without producing less of some other good or service—production is at a point on the *PPF*. Allocative efficiency is the most highly valued combination of goods and services on the *PPF*.

■ Self Test 6.1

Fill in the blanks

Because only one person can become chair of General Electric and collect a salary of tens of millions of dollars, this position is allocated in a type of ____ (first-come, first-served; contest; command) allocation scheme. ____ (Production; Allocative) efficiency occurs at each combination of goods and services on the *PPF*. ____ (Production; Allocative) efficiency occurs when the economy produces the most highly valued combination of goods and services on the *PPF*. As more of a good is consumed, its marginal benefit ____ (increases; decreases), and as more of a good is produced, its marginal cost ____ (increases; decreases). Allocative efficiency occurs when the marginal benefit of a good is ____ (greater than; equal to; less than) the marginal cost of the good.

True or false

1. When market prices are used to allocate resources, only the people who are able and willing to pay get the resources.

2. All combinations of goods and services on the production possibilities frontier are combinations of allocative efficiency.

3. The marginal benefit of a good increases as more of the good is consumed.

4. A production point can be allocatively efficient but not be production efficient.

Multiple choice

1. If a landlord will rent an apartment only to married couples over 30 years old, the landlord is allocating resources using a _____ allocation method.
   a. first-come, first-served
   b. market price
   c. contest
   d. personal characteristics
   e. command

2. Allocative efficiency occurs when
   a. the most highly valued goods and services are produced.
   b. all citizens have equal access to goods and services.
   c. the environment is protected at all cost.
   d. goods and services are free.
   e. production takes place at any point on the *PPF*.

3. Marginal benefit equals the
   a. benefit that a person receives from consuming another unit of a good.
   b. additional efficiency from producing another unit of a good.
   c. increase in profit from producing another unit of a good.
   d. cost of producing another unit of a good.
   e. total benefit from consuming all the units of the good or service.

4. In general, the marginal cost curve
   a. has a positive slope.
   b. has a negative slope.
   c. is horizontal.
   d. is vertical.
   e. is U-shaped.

5. Allocative efficiency is achieved when the marginal benefit of a good
   a. exceeds the marginal cost by as much as possible.
   b. exceeds the marginal cost but not by as much as possible.
   c. is less than the marginal cost.
   d. equals the marginal cost.
   e. equals zero.

Complete the graph

■ FIGURE 6.1
Marginal benefit and marginal cost (trucks per tractor)

1. An economy produces only trucks and tractors and Figure 6.1 shows the marginal benefit and marginal cost of tractors. How many tractors are produced at the point of allocative efficiency?

Short answer and numeric questions

1. Suppose the price of a new BMW is $50,000. Which two kinds of people decide not to buy these BMWs? Is it true that when resources are allocated by market price, the rich always consume everything?

2. Only one person can become President of Sony, yet many of Sony's top executives would like that job. What allocation method is typically used to determine who becomes President? How does this allocation method benefit Sony?

3. Along a production possibilities frontier, to produce the first skateboard, 1 pair of roller blades must be forgone. To produce the second skateboard, 2 more pairs of roller blades must be forgone. Is the marginal cost of the second skate board 2 or 3 pairs of roller blades?

4. Why does allocative efficiency require producing where marginal benefit equals marginal cost rather than where marginal benefit exceeds marginal cost?

Additional Exercises (also in MyEconLab Test A)

1. Which method is used to allocate the following scarce resources?

a. Airline tickets on the eve of Thanksgiving
b. Goods at department stores in the January sales
c. Presidency of the Students' Union
d. The first serve in the final at the U.S. Open

Possibility	Bananas (pounds)	Coffee (pounds)
A	80	20
B	60	60
C	40	120
D	20	150

Bananas (pounds)	Willing to give up	Must give up
	(pounds of coffee per pound of bananas)	
20	3	1
40	2	2
60	1	3

2. The first table shows a nation's production possibilities of bananas and coffee. The second table shows the nation's marginal benefit schedule and marginal cost schedule. What is the marginal cost of growing 120 pounds of coffee? Calculate the quantity of coffee produced and the marginal benefit from coffee when the nation uses its resources efficiently.

CHECKPOINT 6.2

■ **Distinguish between value and price and define consumer surplus.**

Quick Review

- *Value* In economics the idea of value is called marginal benefit, which we measure as the maximum price that people are willing to pay for another unit of a good or service.
- *Consumer surplus* Consumer surplus is the marginal benefit from a good or service in excess of the price paid for it, summed over the quantity consumed.

Additional Practice Problems 6.2

1. The figure shows the demand curve for maga-zines and the market price of a magazine. Use the figure to answer the following questions.

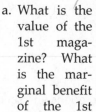

a. What is the value of the 1st magazine? What is the marginal benefit of the 1st magazine? What is the consumer surplus of the 1st magazine?
b. What is the marginal benefit of the 2nd magazine? What is the consumer surplus of the 2nd magazine?
c. What is the total quantity of magazines bought and the consumer surplus?
d. If the price of a magazine rises to $10, what is the quantity bought and what is the consumer surplus?

2. Your friend paid a lawyer $50 for the hour it took the lawyer to write a letter to settle a rent dispute. Your friend wonders if the concepts of value, marginal benefit, and consumer surplus apply not only to goods but also to services, such as the lawyer's letter. What do you tell your friend?

Solutions to Additional Practice Problems 6.2

1a. The value of the 1st maga-zine equals the maximum price a consumer is willing to pay for the magazine. The figure shows that the maximum price for the 1st magazine is $15, so the value of the maga-zine equals $15. The marginal benefit of the magazine is equal to the maximum price the consumer will pay, which is $15. The consumer surplus is equal to the marginal benefit of the 1st magazine ($15) minus the price of the magazine ($5) so the consumer surplus is $10.

1b. The marginal benefit of the magazine is equal to the maximum price the consumer will pay. The figure shows that the maximum price for the 2nd magazine is $10, so the marginal benefit of the magazine equals $5. The consumer surplus is equal to $5.

1c. The quantity bought is 3 magazines because the demand curve shows that the quantity demanded at the price of $5 is 3 magazines. The consumer surplus equals the area of the darkened triangle in the figure. Calculating the area of the consumer surplus triangle, which is equal to one half the base of the triangle multiplied by the height or 1/2 × (3 − 0) × ($20 − $5), which is $22.50.

1d. If the price of a magazine rises to $10, the quantity bought is 2 magazines. The consumer surplus now equals 1/2 × (2 − 0) × ($20 − $10), which is $10.00.

2. All the concepts of value, marginal benefit, and consumer surplus apply to services as well as to goods. In your friend's case, there was some maximum amount your friend was willing to pay the attorney to write the letter. This maximum amount was the value

to your friend of the letter. It is also the marginal benefit of the letter. Presumably your friend got the letter for some amount less than the maximum your friend was willing to pay. The difference between the marginal benefit of the letter and the price paid it is the consumer surplus your friend enjoyed from the letter.

■ Self Test 6.2

Fill in the blanks

The benefit a person receives from consuming one more unit of a good is its ____. The opportunity cost of producing one more unit of a good is its ____. Allocative efficiency is at the quantity where the marginal benefit is ____ (greater than; equal to; less than) marginal cost. The demand curve ____ (is; is not) the marginal benefit curve. The consumer surplus equals the marginal benefit of a good ____ (plus; multiplied by; minus) the price paid for it.

True or false

1. In economics, value and price refer to the same thing.

2. A demand curve is a marginal benefit curve.

3. The consumer surplus from one unit of a good is the marginal benefit from the good minus the price paid for it.

4. Consumer surplus always equals zero because consumers always pay for the goods and services they consume.

Multiple choice

1. Value is
   a. the price we pay for a good.
   b. the cost of resources used to produce a good.
   c. objective so that it is determined by market forces, not preferences.
   d. the marginal benefit we get from consuming another unit of a good or service.
   e. the difference between the price paid for a good and the marginal cost of producing that unit of the good.

2. A marginal benefit curve
   a. is the same as a demand curve.
   b. is the same as a supply curve.
   c. slopes upwards.
   d. is a vertical line at the efficient quantity.
   e. is U-shaped.

3. In general, as the consumption of a good or service increases, the marginal benefit from consuming that good or service
   a. increases.
   b. decreases.
   c. stays the same.
   d. at first increases and then decreases.
   e. at first decreases and then increases.

4. The difference between the marginal benefit from a new pair of shoes and the price of the new pair of shoes is
   a. the consumer surplus from that pair of shoes.
   b. what we get.
   c. what we have to pay.
   d. the price when the marginal benefit is maximized.
   e. the consumer's expenditure on the shoes.

5. Suppose the price of a scooter is $200 and Cora Lee is willing to pay $250. Cora Lee's
   a. consumer surplus from that scooter is $200.
   b. consumer surplus from that scooter is $50.
   c. marginal benefit from that scooter is $200.
   d. consumer surplus from that scooter is $150.
   e. consumer surplus from that scooter is $250.

6. If the price of a pizza is $10 per pizza, the consumer surplus from the first pizza consumed ____ the consumer surplus from the second pizza consumed.
   a. is greater than
   b. equals
   c. is less than
   d. cannot be compared to
   e. None of the above answers is correct because more information is needed about the marginal cost of producing the pizzas to answer the question.

Complete the graph

■ **FIGURE 6.2**

1. Figure 6.2 shows the demand curve for roller blades.
   a. What is the marginal benefit of the 20,000th pair of roller blades?
   b. What is the marginal benefit of the 40,000th pair of roller blades?
   c. If the price of a pair of roller blades is $100, what is the consumer surplus on the 20,000th pair of roller blades?
   d. If the price of a pair of roller blades is $100, what is the quantity of roller blades purchased? What is the amount of the consumer surplus?

■ **FIGURE 6.3**

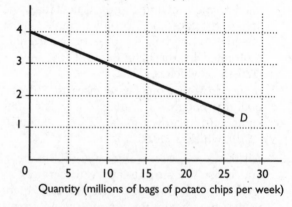

2. Figure 6.3 shows the demand curve for bags of potato chips.

a. What is the maximum price a consumer is willing to pay for the 10 millionth bag of chips?

b. What is the marginal benefit from the 10 millionth bag of chips? What is the relationship between your answer to part (a) and your answer to this part?

c. If the price of a bag of chips equals $2, in Figure 6.3 shade the area that equals the amount of the consumer surplus.

d. If the price of a bag of chips equals $2, what is the amount of consumer surplus?

Short answer and numeric questions

1. What is the relationship between the value of a good, the maximum price a consumer is willing to pay for the good, and the marginal benefit from the good?

2. What is the relationship between the marginal benefit of a slice of pizza, the price paid for the slice, and its consumer surplus?

Price (dollars per tablet)	Quantity (millions of tablets per year)	Consumer surplus (dollars)
500	4	____
400	8	____
300	12	____
200	16	____
100	20	____

3. The table above gives the demand schedule for tablets. Suppose the price of a tablet is $200.

a. Complete the table by calculating the consumer surplus. In the first row, calculate the consumer surplus for the 4 millionth tablet; in the second row, calculate the consumer surplus for the 8 millionth tablet; and so on.

b. As more tablets are purchased, what happens to the consumer surplus of the last unit purchased? Why?

Additional Exercises (also in MyEconLab Test A)

■ FIGURE 6.4

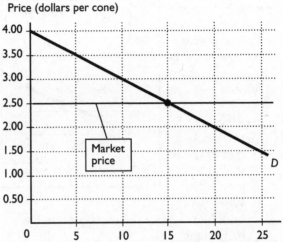
Price (dollars per cone)

Figure 6.4 shows the demand curve for ice cream and the market price of a cone.

1. What is the value of the 15th cone, the willingness to pay for the 5th cone, and the consumer surplus on the 5th cone?

2. How many ice cream cones are bought? Calculate the consumer surplus, the total expenditure on ice cream, and the total benefit from ice cream.

3. If demand for ice cream doubles, what is the change in total expenditure on ice cream and the change in consumer surplus?

CHECKPOINT 6.3

■ **Distinguish between cost and price and define producer surplus.**

Quick Review

- *Cost* Cost is what the seller must give up to produce a good.

- *Producer surplus* The producer surplus equals the price of a good in excess of the marginal cost of producing it, summed over the quantity produced.

Additional Practice Problems 6.3

1. The figure shows the supply curve and the market price of a magazine. Use the figure to answer the following questions.

   a. What is the marginal cost of the 10 millionth magazine?

   b. What is the minimum supply price of the 10 millionth magazine?

   c. What is the producer surplus on the 10 millionth magazine?

   d. What are the quantity of magazines sold and the total producer surplus?

2. Why is the minimum price for which a seller will produce a product equal to the product's marginal cost?

Solutions to Additional Practice Problems 6.3

1a. The marginal cost of the 10 millionth magazine is equal to the minimum supply price of the 10 millionth magazine. The supply curve, which is also the marginal cost curve, shows this price. In the figure, the supply curve shows that the marginal cost of 10 millionth magazine is $2.50.

1b. The minimum supply price of the 10 millionth magazine equals its marginal cost, $2.50.

1c. The producer surplus on the 10 millionth magazine is equal to its market price minus its marginal cost, which is $5 − $2.50 = $2.50.

1d. At the market price of $5, 20 million magazines are sold. The producer surplus equals the area of the grey triangle in the figure. Calculating the area of the triangle as one half the base multiplied by the height, or $1/2 \times (20 \text{ million} − 0) \times (\$5 − \$0)$, the pro-ducer surplus equals $50 million.

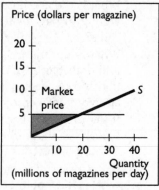

2. A seller is willing to produce a good as long as the price the seller receives covers all the costs of producing the good. So the minimum price for which a seller is willing to produce a unit of the good must be the amount that just equals the cost of the producing that unit. But the cost of producing any unit of a good is its marginal cost, so the minimum supply price equals the good's marginal cost.

■ Self Test 6.3

Fill in the blanks

____ (Price; Cost) is what a seller must give up to produce a good and ____ (price; cost) is what a seller receives when the good is sold. A ____ (demand; supply) curve is a marginal cost curve. A firm receives a producer surplus when price is ____ (greater; less) than marginal cost.

True or false

1. In economics, cost and price are the same thing.

2. The minimum price for which Bobby will grow another pound of rice is 20¢, so the marginal cost of an additional pound of rice is 20¢.

3. A supply curve is a marginal benefit curve.

4. Producer surplus equals the marginal benefit of a good minus the cost of producing it.

Multiple choice

1. Cost
   a. is what the buyer pays to get the good.
   b. is always equal to the marginal benefit for every unit of a good produced.
   c. is what the seller must give up to produce the good.
   d. is greater than market price, which results in a profit for firms.
   e. means the same thing as price.

2. If a firm is willing to supply the 1,000th unit of a good at a price of $23 or more, we know that $23 is the
   a. highest price the seller hopes to realize for this output.
   b. minimum price the seller must receive to produce this unit.
   c. average price of all the prices the seller could charge.
   d. price that sets the marginal benefit equal to the price.
   e. only price for which the seller is willing to sell this unit of the good.

3. A supply curve shows the _____ of producing one more unit of a good or service.
   a. producer surplus
   b. consumer surplus
   c. total benefit
   d. marginal cost
   e. marginal benefit to the producer

4. The producer surplus on a unit of a good is
   a. equal to the marginal benefit from the good minus its price.
   b. equal to the price of the good minus the marginal cost of producing it.
   c. always equal to consumer surplus.
   d. Both answers (a) and (c) are correct.
   e. Both answers (b) and (c) are correct.

5. Suppose you're willing to tutor a student for $10 an hour. The student pays you $15 an hour. What is your producer surplus?
   a. $5 an hour
   b. $10 an hour
   c. $15 an hour
   d. $25 an hour
   e. more than $25 an hour

6. In a figure that shows a supply curve and a demand curve, producer surplus is the area
   a. below the demand curve and above the market price.
   b. below the supply curve and above the market price.
   c. above the demand curve and below the market price.
   d. above the supply curve and below the market price.
   e. between the demand curve and the supply curve.

Complete the graph

■ FIGURE 6.5

Price (dollars per bag of potato chips)

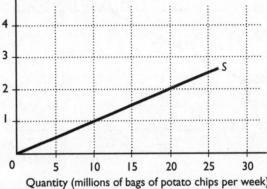

Quantity (millions of bags of potato chips per week)

1. Figure 6.5 shows the supply curve for bags of potato chips.
   a. What is the minimum price for which a supplier is willing to produce the 10 millionth bag of chips?
   b. What is the marginal cost of the 10 millionth bag of chips? What is the relationship between your answer to part (a) and your answer to this part?
   c. If the price of a bag of chips equals $2, in Figure 6.5 shade the area that equals the amount of the producer surplus.
   d. If the price of a bag of chips equals $2, calculate the producer surplus.

Short answer and numeric questions

1. What is the relationship between the minimum price a supplier must receive to produce a slice of pizza and the marginal cost of

the slice of pizza? What is the relationship between the marginal cost curve and the supply curve?

2. What is producer surplus? As the price of a good or service rises and the supply curve does not shift, what happens to the amount of the producer surplus?

Additional Exercises (also in MyEconLab Test A)

■ FIGURE 6.6

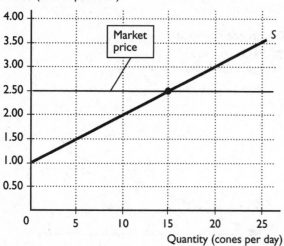
Price (dollars per cone)

Figure 6.6 shows the supply curve of ice cream and the market price of a cone.

1. What is the opportunity cost of the 15th cone, the minimum supply price of the 5th cone, and the producer surplus on the 5th cone?

2. What are the quantity of ice cream cones sold, the producer surplus on ice cream cones, the total revenue from the ice cream cones sold, and the total cost of producing ice cream cones?

3. If the price falls to $2.00 a cone, calculate the change in total revenue and the change in producer surplus?

CHECKPOINT 6.4

■ Evaluate the efficiency of the alternative methods of allocating resources.

Quick Review

- *Efficiency of competitive equilibrium* The condition that marginal benefit equals marginal cost delivers an efficient use of resources. It allocates resources to the activities that create the greatest possible value. Marginal benefit equals marginal cost at a competitive equilibrium, so a competitive equilibrium is efficient.

- *Deadweight loss* The decrease in consumer surplus and producer surplus that results from an inefficient level of production.

Additional Practice Problems 6.4

1. The figure shows the market for paper. Use the figure to answer the following questions.

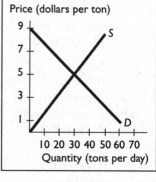
Price (dollars per ton)

   a. What are the equilibrium price and the equilibrium quantity of paper? What is the efficient quantity of paper?

   b. In the market equilibrium, use the figure above to shade the consumer surplus and the producer surplus.

   c. What does the consumer surplus equal? What does the producer surplus equal? What does the total surplus equal?

   d. Is the market for paper efficient? Why or why not? Can the total surplus be any larger at any other level of production?

2. Who benefits from a deadweight loss?

Solutions to Additional Practice Problems 6.4

1a. The equilibrium is shown in the figure and is where the supply and demand curves intersect. The equilibrium price is $5 a ton and the equilibrium quantity is 30 tons a day. The efficient quantity is where the marginal benefit and marginal cost curves intersect. Because the demand curve is the marginal benefit curve and the supply curve is the marginal cost curve, the efficient quantity is 30 tons a day.

1b. The consumer surplus is illustrated in the figure as the area of the top, dark triangle. The producer surplus equals the area of the lower, lighter triangle.

1c. The consumer surplus equals the area of the darker triangle, or 1/2 × (30 tons) × ($4 per ton) = $60, where $4 a ton is the height of the triangle, $9 a ton – $5 a ton. The producer surplus equals the area of the lighter triangle, or 1/2 × (30 tons) × ($5 per ton) = $75, where $5 a ton is the height of the triangle, $5 a ton – $0 a ton. The total surplus equals the sum of the consumer surplus plus the producer surplus, which is $135.

1d. The efficient use of resources occurs when marginal benefit equals marginal cost. The market equilibrium is efficient because the marginal benefit of a ton of paper equals its marginal cost. The sum of the consumer surplus and producer surplus, which equals the total surplus, is at its maximum at the efficient level of production so the total surplus cannot be larger at any other amount of production.

2. No one gains from a deadweight loss created by a market failure. Deadweight loss is a decrease in consumer surplus and producer surplus that results from an inefficient level of production. The deadweight loss is borne by the entire society. It is not a loss for the consumers and a gain for the producer. It is a social loss.

■ Self Test 6.4

Fill in the blanks

Equilibrium in a competitive market ____ (is; is not) efficient. Adam Smith believed that each participant in a competitive market is "led by ____ (an invisible hand; government actions)." A price ____ (ceiling; floor) is a regulation that makes it illegal to charge a price higher than a specified level. ____ (An externality; A public good) is a good or service that is consumed simultaneously by everyone, even if they don't pay for it. Deadweight loss is the decrease in ____ (only consumer surplus; consumer surplus and producer surplus; only producer surplus) that results from an inefficient level of production.

True or false

1. When the demand curve is the marginal benefit curve and the supply curve is the marginal cost curve, the competitive equilibrium is efficient.

2. When the efficient quantity of a good is produced, the consumer surplus is always zero.

3. According to Adam Smith, the invisible hand suggests that competitive markets require government action to ensure that resources are allocated efficiently.

4. Market failure occurs if less than the efficient quantity of a good is produced but producing more than the efficient quantity does not result in market failure.

Multiple choice

1. When a market is efficient the
   a. sum of consumer surplus and producer surplus is maximized.
   b. deadweight gain is maximized.
   c. quantity produced is maximized.
   d. marginal benefit of the last unit produced exceeds the marginal cost by as much as possible.
   e. total benefit equals the total cost.

■ **FIGURE 6.7**

Price (dollars per computer)

Quantity (thousands of computers per week)

2. Figure 6.7 shows the market for computers. What is the equilibrium quantity of computers?
   a. 0 computers per week
   b. 200,000 computers per week
   c. 400,000 computers per week
   d. 600,000 computers per week
   e. more than 600,000 computers per week

3. Figure 6.7 shows the market for computers. What is the efficient quantity of computers?
   a. 0 computers per week
   b. 200,000 computers per week
   c. 400,000 computers per week
   d. 600,000 computers per week
   e. more than 600,000 computers per week

4. Which of the following occurs when a market is efficient?
   a. producers earn the highest income possible
   b. production costs equal total benefit
   c. consumer surplus equals producer surplus
   d. scarce resources are used to produce the goods and services that people value most highly
   e. every consumer has all of the good or service he or she wants.

5. The concept of "the invisible hand" suggests that markets
   a. do not produce the efficient quantity.
   b. are always fair.
   c. produce the efficient quantity.
   d. are unfair though they might be efficient.
   e. allocate resources unfairly and inefficiently.

6. When underproduction occurs,
   a. producers gain more surplus at the expense of consumers.
   b. marginal cost is greater than marginal benefit.
   c. consumer surplus increases to a harmful amount.
   d. there is a deadweight loss that is borne by the entire society.
   e. the deadweight loss harms only consumers.

7. When production moves from the efficient quantity to a point of overproduction,
   a. consumer surplus definitely increases.
   b. the sum of producer surplus and consumer surplus increases.
   c. there is a deadweight loss.
   d. consumers definitely lose and producers definitely gain.
   e. consumers definitely gain and producers definitely lose.

8. Which of the following can result in market failure?
   i.   competition
   ii. an external cost or an external benefit
   iii. a tax
   a. i only.
   b. ii only.
   c. iii only.
   d. ii and iii.
   e. i and iii.

Complete the graph

■ FIGURE 6.8
Price (thousands of dollars per automobile)

1. In Figure 6.8, what is the equilibrium quantity of automobiles? What is the efficient quantity of automobiles? Shade the consumer surplus and the producer surplus and calculate their amounts.

■ FIGURE 6.9
Price (thousands of dollars per automobile)

2. Figure 6.9 is identical to Figure 6.8.
   a. Suppose that 8,000 automobiles are produced. Shade the deadweight loss light grey and calculate its amount.
   b. Suppose that 4,000 automobiles are produced. Shade the deadweight loss dark grey and calculate its amount.

Short answer and numeric questions

1. What is the relationship between a competitive market, efficiency, and the invisible hand?

2. Suppose the demand for cotton clothing increases. What effect does the increase in demand have on the equilibrium quantity and on the efficient quantity?

3. What factors might lead a market failure, that is a market producing an inefficient amount of a good or service?

Additional Exercises (also in MyEconLab Test A)

■ FIGURE 6.10
Price (dollars per cone)

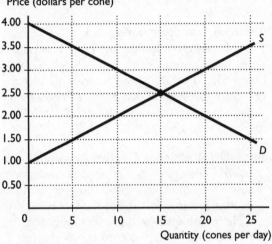

Figure 6.10 shows the market for ice cream cones.

1. At the market equilibrium, what are consumer surplus, producer surplus and total surplus? Is the market for ice cream cones efficient? Why or why not?

2. The government limits the quantity that producers can sell to 10 cones a day. Is the market for ice cream cones efficient? Explain. Calculate the deadweight loss.

3. The government passes a law requiring producers to sell 20 ice cream cones a day. Is the market for ice cream cones efficient? Explain. Calculate the deadweight loss.

CHECKPOINT 6.5

■ **Explain the main ideas about fairness and evaluate the fairness of alternative methods of allocating scarce resources.**

Quick Review

- *Big tradeoff* The big tradeoff is the tradeoff between efficiency and fairness that results when income transfers are made.

Additional Practice Problem 6.5

1. If Bill Gates gives $1,000 to a homeless person, would the transaction be fair? If Mr. Gates is taxed $1,000 by the government and the government gives the $1,000 to the same homeless person, would the transaction be fair? Comment on your answers.

Solution to Additional Practice Problem 6.5

1. If Mr. Gates gives $1,000 to a homeless person, the action is considered fair. The exchange is fair according to the fair rules principle because the exchange is voluntary. And the outcome is fair according to the fair results principle because there is more equality of income. If Mr. Gates is taxed by the government, the outcome is fair according to the fair results principle because there is more equality of income. But the transaction is not fair according to the fair rules principle because the exchange does not occur voluntarily.

■ Self Test 6.5

Fill in the blanks

Two views of fairness are that "it's not fair if the ____ (result; income distribution) isn't fair;" and "it's not fair if the ____ (rules; tradeoffs) aren't fair." According to Robert Nozick, fair-rules ideas require ____ (government intervention; property rights and voluntary exchange).

True or false

1. The principle that "it's not fair if the result isn't fair" can conflict with the principle that "it's not fair if the rules aren't fair."

2. The big tradeoff is the tradeoff between efficiency and happiness.

3. According to the "fair-rules" view of fairness, in times of natural disasters it is fair to force people to make available necessary goods and services at lower than usual prices.

Multiple choice

1. The "fair-rules" view of fairness is based on
   a. income transfers from the rich to the poor.
   b. property rights and voluntary exchange.
   c. efficiency.
   d. the big tradeoff.
   e. allocating resources using majority rule.

2. The idea that unequal incomes is unfair generally uses the ____ principle of fairness.
   a. big tradeoff
   b. involuntary exchange
   c. voluntary exchange
   d. it's not fair if the result isn't fair
   e. it's not fair if the rules aren't fair

3. Which of the following is an example in which "the big tradeoff" can occur?
   a. the government redistributes income from the rich to the poor
   b. Ford increases the price of a pickup truck
   c. a basketball player signs a $5 million contract
   d. a college lowers tuition
   e. the price of personal computers falls year after year

Short answer and numeric questions

1. In the United States, richer people generally pay a larger fraction of their income as taxes than do poorer people. Is this arrangement fair? Answer from a fair-results view and from a fair-rules view.

2. Suppose that during their working lifetimes, Matt and Pat have earned identical incomes as computer programmers. The only difference between the two is that

Matt spent all of his income while Pat saved a large portion of hers. Now that they are retired, Pat's income is substantially higher than Matt's because of Pat's saving. Is it fair for Pat's income to be higher than Matt's? Answer from a fair results and from a fair rules perspective.

3. What is the effect of the big tradeoff in transferring income from people with high incomes to people with low incomes?

4. According to the "fair rules" approach to fairness, is it fair for the government to limit the prices sellers charge for bottled water after a flood destroys a town's water supply? Why or why not?

Additional Exercises (also in MyEconLab Test A)
An earthquake destroys the homes of a quarter of a city's population. People who are lucky enough to own one of the remaining homes offer rooms for rent at the highest amount that people are willing to pay.
1. Who gets to occupy the available rooms? Who receives the consumer surplus and who receives the producer surplus on rooms?

2. Is the allocation of rooms efficient? By what principle of fairness is the allocation fair or unfair

SELF TEST ANSWERS

■ CHECKPOINT 6.1

Fill in the blanks

Because only one person can become chair of General Electric and collect a salary of tens of millions of dollars, this position is allocated in a type of <u>contest</u> allocation scheme. <u>Production</u> efficiency occurs at each combination of goods and services on the *PPF*. <u>Allocative</u> efficiency occurs when the economy produces the most highly valued combination of goods and services on the *PPF*. As more of a good is consumed, its marginal benefit <u>decreases</u>, and as more of a good is produced, its marginal cost <u>increases</u>. Allocative efficiency occurs when the marginal benefit of a good is <u>equal to</u> the marginal cost of the good.

True or false

1. True; page 138
2. False; page 141
3. False; page 142
4. False; page 138

Multiple choice

1. d; page 140
2. a; page 141
3. a; page 142
4. a; page 143
5. d; pages 143-144

Complete the graph

1. Allocative efficiency is the most highly valued combination of goods and services on the *PPF*. It is the combination where marginal cost equals marginal benefit. In Figure 6.1, allocative efficiency is achieved when 30 tractors a week are produced; page 144.

Short answer and numeric questions

1. The people who do not buy these BMWs are the people cannot afford to pay $50,000 for the new BMW and the people who can afford to pay but choose not to pay it. The point that people can decide not to buy a particular good or service shows that the rich do not necessary consume everything; they buy and consume only the goods and services for which they choose to pay the market price; page 138.

2. Sony is using a contest allocation method. Sony benefits from this allocation scheme because all the top executives who want to be President will work extremely hard for Sony in an effort to win the contest; page 139.

3. The marginal cost of the second skate board is 2 pairs roller blades. Marginal cost is the opportunity cost of producing one more unit of a good or service. It is not the cost of all the units produced; pages 142-143.

4. If the marginal benefit from an additional unit of a good or service exceeds its marginal cost, the unit should be produced because its production benefits society more than it costs society to produce. Producing where marginal benefit equals marginal cost insures that *all* units that have a net benefit for society are produced, so this level of production is the point of allocative efficiency; page 144.

Additional Exercises (also in MyEconLab Test A)

1. a. Market price; page 138.
   b. First-Come, First-Serve and Market Price.; pages 140 and 139.
   c. Majority rule; page 139.
   d. Contest; page 139.

2. If 120 pounds of coffee are grown, the first table, which shows the nation's production possibilities, indicates that 40 pounds of bananas are produced. The marginal cost when this many bananas are produced is in the second table, which shows that the marginal cost of another pound of bananas is 2 pounds of coffee per pound of bananas. (This result is from the "Must give up" column because what must be given shows the marginal cost; the "Willing to give up" column shows the marginal benefit.) If the marginal cost of another pound of bananas is 2 pounds of coffee, then the marginal cost of another pound of coffee is 1/2 of a pound of bananas. In other words, to gain another pound of coffee,

the nation must forgo 1/2 of a pound of bananas. Resources are used efficiently when the marginal benefit of a pound of coffee equals the marginal cost of a pound of coffee. When 120 pounds of coffee are grown, 40 pounds of bananas are grown the marginal cost of pound of coffee is 1/2 of a pound of bananas. The table also shows that at this quantity, the marginal benefit of a pound of bananas is 2 pounds of coffee, so the marginal benefit of a pound of coffee is 1/2 of a pound of bananas. Thus when 120 pounds of coffee are produced, the nation is producing the efficient quantity of coffee and the marginal benefit of a pound of coffee is 1/2 of a pound of bananas; pages 143-144 .

■ CHECKPOINT 6.2

Fill in the blanks

The benefit a person receives from consuming one more unit of a good is its <u>marginal benefit</u>. The opportunity cost of producing one more unit of a good is its <u>marginal cost</u>. Allocative efficiency is at the quantity where the marginal benefit is <u>equal to</u> marginal cost. The demand curve <u>is</u> the marginal benefit curve. The consumer surplus equals the marginal benefit of a good <u>minus</u> the price paid for it.

True or false

1. False; page 146
2. True; page 146
3. True; page 147
4. False; page 147

Multiple choice

1. d; page 146
2. a; page 146
3. b; page 146
4. a; page 147
5. b; page 147
6. a; page 147

Complete the graph

1. a. The marginal benefit of the 20,000th pair of roller blades is the maximum price a

consumer is willing to pay for that pair, which is $150; page 146.

b. The marginal benefit of the 40,000th pair of roller blades is the maximum price a consumer is willing to pay for that pair, which is $100; page 146.

c. The consumer surplus is the difference between the marginal benefit, $150, minus the price paid, $100, or $50; page 147.

d. If the price is $100, then 40,000 pairs of roller blades will be purchased. The consumer surplus equals $1/2 \times (\$200 - \$100) \times (40,000 - 0)$, or $40,000,000; page 147.

2. a. The maximum price is $3; page 146.

b. The marginal benefit is $3. The marginal benefit is the maximum price a consumer is willing to pay for another bag of potato chips; page 146.

■ FIGURE 6.11

Price (dollars per bag of potato chips)

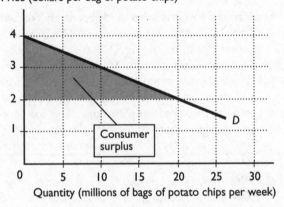

Quantity (millions of bags of potato chips per week)

c. Figure 6.11 shades the area of the consumer surplus; page 147.

d. The consumer surplus equals the area of the shaded triangle in Figure 6.11, which is $1/2 \times (\$4 - \$2) \times 20$ million = $20 million; page 147.

Short answer and numeric questions

1. The value of a good is equal to the maximum price a buyer is willing to pay, which also equals the marginal benefit; page 146.

2. The marginal benefit of the slice of pizza equals the price paid plus the consumer surplus on that slice; page 147.

Price (dollars per tablet)	Quantity (millions of tablets per year)	Consumer surplus (dollars)
500	4	300
400	8	200
300	12	100
200	16	0
100	20	0

3. a. The table above has the consumer surpluses. The consumer surplus is zero for the 20 millionth tablet because when the price is $200, the 20 millionth tablet is not purchased. For the remaining quantities, the consumer surplus is the marginal benefit, which equals the maximum price consumers are willing to pay minus the price; page 147.

   b. The consumer surplus decreases as more tablets are purchased because the value of an additional tablets decreases as more are purchased; page 147.

Additional Exercises (also in MyEconLab Test A)

1. The value of the 15th cone is $2.50. A consumer is willing to pay $3.50 for the 5th cone. The consumer surplus is the difference between the marginal benefit, which is what a consumer is willing to pay for the 5th cone, and the price paid for the cone. The consumer's marginal benefit for the 5th cone is $3.50 and the price is $2.50, so the consumer surplus equals $1.00; pages 146-147.

2. Fifteen cones are bought. The consumer surplus is the triangular area below the demand curve and above the market price. The area of a triangle equals 1/2 × base × height, which is 1/2 × 15 cones × $1.50 per cone = $11.25. The total expenditure on cones is 15 cones × $2.50 per cone, which equals $37.50. The total benefit from the cones is the area under the demand curve, composed of total expenditure of $37.50 plus consumer surplus of $11.25, which equals $48.75; page 147.

3. If demand doubles, the total expenditure increases. At every price consumers now buy double the quantity of cones they had previously purchased, so the total number of cones purchased is 30. The total expenditure

on cones is 30 cones × $2.50 per cone, or $75.00. The vertical intercept does not change (doubling zero is still zero), so the area of the consumer surplus triangle is 1/2 × (30 cones) × ($1.50 per cone)= $22.50; page 147.

■ CHECKPOINT 6.3

Fill in the blanks

Cost is what a seller must give up to produce a good and price is what a seller receives when the good is sold. A supply curve is a marginal cost curve. A firm receives a producer surplus when price is greater than marginal cost.

True or false

1. False; page 149
2. True; page 149
3. False; page 149
4. False; page 150

Multiple choice

1. c; page 149
2. b; page 149
3. d; page 149
4. b; page 150
5. a; page 150
6. d; page 150

Complete the graph

■ FIGURE 6.12

Price (dollars per bag of potato chips)

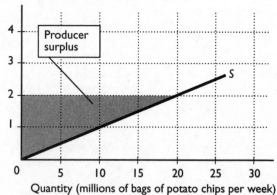

Quantity (millions of bags of potato chips per week)

1. a. As Figure 6.12 shows, the minimum price is $1; page 149.

   b. The marginal cost is $1. The marginal cost of the 10 millionth bag is the minimum price for which a supplier is willing to produce that bag of chips; page 149.

c. Figure 6.12 shades the area of the producer surplus; page 150.

d. The producer surplus equals the area of the shaded triangle in Figure 6.12, so producer surplus is $1/2 \times (\$2 - \$0) \times 20$ million, which equals $20 million; page 150.

Short answer and numeric questions

1. The minimum price for which a firm will produce a slice of pizza equals the marginal cost of producing that slice. It is just worth producing one more slice of pizza if the price for which it can be sold equals its marginal cost. The supply curve tells us this price. So the supply curve is the same as the marginal cost curve; page 149.

2. Producer surplus equals the price of a good or service minus the marginal cost of producing it. As the price of a good or service rises and the supply curve does not shift, the producer surplus increases; page 150.

Additional Exercises (also in MyEconLab Test A)

1. The opportunity cost of the 15th cone is $2.50. The minimum supply price of the 5th cone is $1.50. Producer surplus is the price of a good minus the marginal cost of producing it, which is its opportunity cost. On the 5th cone, the producer surplus is $2.50 − $1.50, which is $1.00; pages 149-150.

2. Fifteen cones are sold. The producer surplus is the triangular area above the supply curve and below the market price. The area of a triangle equals $1/2 \times$ base $\times$ height, which is $1/2 \times 15$ cones $\times \$1.50$ per cone = $11.25. The total revenue from ice cream cones is 15 cones × $2.50 per cone, which equals $37.50. Total cost can be calculated as the area under the supply curve between the y-axis and the quantity of 15 ice cream cones. Alternatively, this area equals total revenue minus producer surplus, $37.50 − $11.25, which is $26.25; page 150.

3. If the price of a cone falls to $2.00 per cone, the number of cones sold decreases to 10. The total revenue from ice cream cones is 10

cones × $2.00 per cone, which equals $20.00. The producer surplus is the triangular area above the supply curve and below the (new) market price. The area of this triangle equals is $1/2 \times 10$ cones $\times \$1.00$ per cone = $5.00. The change in producer surplus is $11.25 − $5.00, which equals $6.25; page 150.

■ CHECKPOINT 6.4

Fill in the blanks

Equilibrium in a competitive market is efficient. Adam Smith believed that each participant in a competitive market is "led by an invisible hand." A price ceiling is a regulation that makes it illegal to charge a price higher than a specified level. A public good is a good or service that is consumed simultaneously by everyone, even if they don't pay for it. Deadweight loss is the decrease in consumer surplus and producer surplus that results from an inefficient level of production.

True or false

1. True; page 152
2. False; page 152
3. False; page 153
4. False; page 155

Multiple choice

1. a; page 153
2. d; page 152
3. d; page 152
4. d; page 152
5. c; page 153
6. d; page 155
7. c; page 155
8. d; page 156

Complete the graph

1. In Figure 6.13 (on the next page) the equilibrium quantity of automobiles is 6,000 a week. The efficient quantity of automobiles is also 6,000 a week because that is the quantity at which the marginal benefit equals the marginal cost. The consumer surplus and producer surplus are the shown in the figure. The consumer surplus is the area of the light

■ **FIGURE 6.13**

Price (thousands of dollars per automobile)

Quantity (thousands of automobiles per week)

grey triangle, which is 1/2 × ($40.00 – $30.00) × (6,000) = $60,000. The producer surplus is the area of the dark grey triangle, which is 1/2 × ($30.00 – $0.00) × (60,000) = $90,000; page 152.

■ **FIGURE 6.14**

Price (thousands of dollars per automobile)

Quantity (thousands of automobiles per week)

2. a. When 8,000 automobiles are produced, there is a deadweight loss from overproduction because for the last 2,000 automobiles, the marginal cost exceeds the marginal benefit. The deadweight loss is the area of the light grey triangle in Figure 6.14, which is 1/2 × ($40.00 – $26.67) × (8,000 – 6,000) = $1,330; page 155.

   b. If 4,000 automobiles are produced, there again is a deadweight loss, this time from underproduction, because automobiles for which the marginal benefit exceeds the marginal cost are not produced. The amount of the deadweight loss is the area

of dark grey triangle in Figure 6.14, which is 1/2 × ($33.33 – $20.00) × (6,000 – 4,000) = $1,330; page 155.

Short answer and numeric questions

1. Adam Smith was the first to suggest that competitive markets send resources to the uses in which they have the highest value so that competitive markets are efficient. Smith said that each participant in a competitive market is "led by an invisible hand to promote an end [the efficient use of resources] which is no part of his intention;" page 153.

2. If the demand for cotton clothing increases, the demand curve for cotton clothing shifts rightward and the equilibrium quantity increases. The demand curve is the marginal benefit curve, so when the demand curve shifts rightward, the marginal benefit curve also shifts rightward. The efficient quantity also increases; page 152.

3. Governments influence markets by setting price and quantity regulations as well as taxes and subsidies, all of which can create inefficiency. Other obstacles to achieving an efficient allocation of resources are externalities, public goods and common resources, monopoly, and high transactions costs; pages 156-157.

Additional Exercises (also in MyEconLab Test A)

1. The equilibrium price of a cone is $2.50 per cone and equilibrium quantity is 15 cones. At the market equilibrium, consumer surplus is $11.25 and the producer surplus is $11.25. The total surplus is $22.50. The market for ice cream cones is efficient because 15 cones are produced and this is the quantity for which the marginal cost equals marginal benefit so that the sum of consumer surplus and producer surplus is a maximum; page 152.

2. If output is limited to 10 cones per day, the market is not efficient; there is market failure. When 10 cones per day are produced, the marginal cost of the 10th cone, $2.00, does not equal the marginal benefit from the 10th cone, $3.00. The market is underproducing.

The deadweight loss is equal to the triangular area between demand and supply curves from 10 cones per day to 15 cones per day. The area of the triangle equals $1/2 \times$ base $\times$ height, which is $1/2 \times 5$ cones $\times \$1.00$ per cone = $\$2.50$; page 155.

3. If the government requires 20 cones to be produced per day, the market is not efficient. When 20 cones are produced, the marginal cost of the 20th cone, $\$3.00$, does not equal marginal benefit from the 10th cone, $\$2.00$. The market is overproducing.

The deadweight loss is equal to the triangular area between the supply and demand curves from 15 cones per day to 20 cones per day. The area of a triangle equals $1/2 \times$ base $\times$ height, which is $1/2 \times 5$ cones $\times \$1.00$ per cone = $\$2.50$; page 155.

■ CHECKPOINT 6.5

Fill in the blanks

Two views of fairness are that "it's not fair if the <u>result</u> isn't fair;" and "it's not fair if the <u>rules</u> aren't fair." According to Robert Nozick, fair-rules ideas require <u>property rights and voluntary exchange</u>.

True or false

1. True; page 159
2. False; page 159
3. False; page 160

Multiple choice

1. b; page 159
2. d; page 159
3. a; page 161

Short answer and numeric questions

1. The tax arrangement is fair from a fair-results view because it leads to a greater equality of income. The tax arrangement is not fair from a fair-results view because the tax is not a voluntary exchange; page 159.

2. From a fair-results view, it is not fair for Pat's income to be substantially higher than Matt's. From a fair-rules view, it is fair because Pat and Matt had the same opportunities; page 159.

3. Income can be transferred from people with high incomes to people with low incomes only by taxing incomes, which discourages work. This tax results in the quantity of labor being less than the efficient quantity. Similarly, taxing income from capital discourages saving, which results in the quantity of capital being less than the efficient quantity. With less labor and less capital than the efficient amounts, the total amount of production is less than the efficient amount. So the greater the amount of income redistribution through income taxes, the greater is the inefficiency and the smaller is the economic pie; page 161.

4. Limiting the price that can be charged is unfair because it compels the seller to help and such compulsion is unfair since the seller is not engaging in a voluntary transaction; page 159.

Additional Exercises (also in MyEconLab Test A)

1. The people who value the rooms the most will occupy the rooms because they will be the people willing to pay the highest price for the rooms.

The consumers who occupy the rooms are the consumers who receive the consumer surplus.

Presuming there is no resale of rooms from one renter to another at a higher rent than the homeowner charges, the homeowners renting the rooms receive the producer surplus. If there is resale, then the reselling renters also receive producer surplus; pages 138 and 152.

2. The outcome is efficient. The outcome is unfair based on the fair-results principle because poor people can't afford to rent a room. So, the rooms will be shared unequally. The outcome is fair based on the fair-rules principle because the homeowners' property rights are enforced and there is voluntary exchange between the homeowners and renters. So the outcome is fair based on the fair-rules idea and unfair based on the fair results idea; page 159.

Government Actions in Markets

Chapter 7

In Chapter 7 we look at the inefficiency that is created when the government imposes a rent ceiling in the housing market, a minimum wage in the labor market, and a price support in an agricultural market.

1 Explain how a price ceiling works and show how a rent ceiling creates a housing shortage, inefficiency, and unfairness.

A price ceiling is an *upper* limit on the price at which a particular good, service, or factor of production may be traded. A rent ceiling is an example of a price ceiling. A rent ceiling set above the equilibrium rent is ineffective. A housing shortage occurs when a rent ceiling is set below the equilibrium rent because the quantity of housing demanded exceeds the quantity of housing supplied. A shortage results in black markets and search activity. A black market is an illegal market that operates alongside a government regulated market and search activity is the time spent looking for someone with whom to do business, increases. A rent ceiling creates a deadweight loss and decreases consumer surplus and producer surplus. Resources are also used in search. Rent ceilings violate the fair-rules view of fairness because they block voluntary exchange and they violate the "fair results" view because housing is generally *not* allocated to the poorest. Rent ceilings exist because of political support from current renters.

2 Explain how a price floor works and show how the minimum wage creates unemployment, inefficiency, and unfairness.

A price floor is a government regulation that sets a *lower* limit on the price at which a particular good, service, or factor of production may be traded. A minimum wage law is an example of a price floor. A minimum wage law is a government regulation that makes hiring labor services for less than a specified wage illegal. When a minimum wage is set above the equilibrium wage rate the quantity of labor supplied exceeds the quantity of labor demanded so that unemployment results. A minimum wage increases job search activity and illegal hiring. The minimum wage creates a deadweight loss. The minimum wage is unfair because it delivers an unfair result and blocks voluntary exchange.

3 Explain how a price support in the market for an agricultural product creates a surplus, inefficiency, and unfairness.

When governments intervene in agricultural markets, they isolate the domestic market from global competition by limiting imports. The government introduces a price floor, which in an agricultural market is called a price support. The price support leads to a surplus, so the government pays the farmers a subsidy by purchasing the surplus to keep the price at the support level. Buyers are worse off because the price rises and the quantity they purchase decreases and they must pay taxes to the government for the subsidy. Farmers are better off but a deadweight loss is created because buyers' losses exceed farmers' gains. Farmers in developing economies are harmed two ways: First, their exports to the domestic nation are limited and, second, the domestic government sells the surplus it has purchased in the rest of the world, thereby lowering the price received by farmers in developing countries.

CHECKPOINT 7.1

■ **Explain how a price ceiling works and show how a rent ceiling creates a housing shortage, inefficiency, and unfairness.**

Quick Review

- *Price ceiling* A government regulation that places an *upper* limit on the price at which a particular good, service, or factor of production may be traded.
- *Rent ceiling* A government regulation that makes it illegal to charge more than a specified rent for housing.
- *Effective rent ceiling* When a rent ceiling is set below the equilibrium rent, the quantity of housing demanded is greater than the equilibrium quantity and the quantity of housing supplied is less than the equilibrium quantity. A housing shortage occurs.

Additional Practice Problems 7.1

1. The figure shows the rental market for apartments in Ocala, Florida.

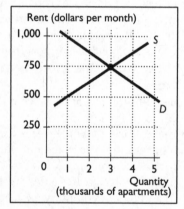

   a. With no government intervention, what is the rent and how many apartments are rented?

   b. If the government imposes a rent ceiling of $500 a month, what is the rent and how many apartments are rented?

   c. With a strictly enforced $500 rent ceiling, why is the housing market inefficient? What does the deadweight loss equal?

   d. With a strictly enforced $500 rent ceiling, is there a shortage or surplus of apartments?

Price (dollars per round of golf)	Quantity demanded	Quantity supplied
	(rounds per week)	
50	2,000	2,800
40	2,300	2,700
30	2,600	2,600
20	2,900	2,500
10	3,200	2,400

2. The table above gives the supply and demand schedules for rounds of golf at a golf course.

   a. What is the equilibrium price and equilibrium quantity of rounds of golf?

   b. Suppose the city government imposes a price ceiling of $40 a round of golf. What will be the price and quantity of rounds of golf? Is there a shortage?

   c. Suppose the city government imposes a price ceiling of $20 a round of golf. What will be the price and quantity of rounds of golf? Is there a shortage?

Solutions to Additional Practice Problems 7.1

1a. In the figure, the equilibrium rent and the equilibrium quantity are determined at the point where the demand curve and the supply curve intersect. The rent is $750 a month and 3,000 apartments are rented.

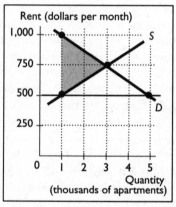

1b. To answer this practice problem remember that a rent ceiling is effective only when it is set below the equilibrium price. The rent ceiling of $500 per month is below the equilibrium rent, so it has an effect. The quantity of apartments rented decreases to 1,000 and the rent is $500.

1c. The market is inefficient because the marginal benefit of the last apartment rented, the 1,000th apartment, exceeds the marginal cost of the apartment. Because the housing market is inefficient a deadweight loss arises. In the figure the deadweight loss is shown by the grey triangle. The amount of the deadweight loss equals the area of the grey triangle. This area is 1/2 × ($1,000 − $500) × (3,000 − 1,000) = $500,000.

1d. There is a shortage of apartments. At the $500 rent ceiling, the quantity of apartments demanded is 5,000 and the quantity supplied is 1,000. So there is a shortage of 4,000 apartments.

2a. The equilibrium price is $30 a round of golf and the equilibrium quantity is 2,600 rounds a week.

2b. The price ceiling is above the equilibrium price, so the price remains at $30 a round and the quantity remains at 2,600 rounds a week. There is no shortage.

2c. The price ceiling is below the equilibrium price. The price falls to $20 a round. The quantity played equals the quantity supplied at $20, which is 2,500 rounds a week. There is a shortage of 400 rounds a week.

■ Self Test 7.1

Fill in the blanks

A price ceiling is the ____ (highest; lowest) price at which it is legal to trade a particular good, service, or factor of production. A rent ceiling is effective if it is set ____ (above; below) the equilibrium rent. A rent ceiling can create a housing ____ (shortage; surplus), which leads to ____ (increased; decreased) search activity. Rent ceilings ____ (can result in; do not result in) inefficiency. The ____ (less; more) inelastic the demand or the supply of housing, the smaller the deadweight loss created by a rent ceiling. Rent ceilings ____ (are; are not) fair.

True or false

1. A rent ceiling always lowers the rent paid.
2. When a rent ceiling is higher than the equilibrium rent, a black market emerges.
3. The opportunity cost of a dorm room is equal to its rent plus the value of the search time spent finding the dorm room.

4. Rent ceilings are efficient because they lower the cost of housing to low-income families.
5. The total loss from a rent ceiling exceeds the deadweight loss.

Multiple choice

1. A price ceiling is a government regulation that makes it illegal to charge a price
   a. below the equilibrium price.
   b. above the equilibrium price.
   c. for a good or service.
   d. above some specified level.
   e. below some specified level.

2. When a price ceiling is set below the equilibrium price, the quantity supplied ____ the quantity demanded and ____ exists.
   a. is less than; a surplus
   b. is less than; a shortage
   c. is greater than; a surplus
   d. is greater than; a shortage
   e. equals; an equilibrium

3. In a housing market with a rent ceiling set below the equilibrium rent,
   a. some people seeking an apartment to rent will not be able to find one.
   b. the total cost of renting an apartment will decrease for all those seeking housing.
   c. some landlords will not be able to find renters to fill available apartments.
   d. search will decrease because renters no longer need to search for less expensive apartments.
   e. None of the above answers are correct because to have an impact the rent ceiling must be set *above* the equilibrium rent.

4. A rent ceiling on housing creates a problem of allocating the housing units because
   a. the demand for housing decreases and the demand curve shifts leftward.
   b. the supply of housing increases and the supply curve shifts rightward.
   c. a shortage of apartments occurs.
   d. a surplus of apartments occurs.
   e. it eliminates search, which is one of the major ways housing units are allocated.

■ **FIGURE 7.1**

Rent (dollars per month)

5. Figure 7.1 shows a housing market. If the government imposes a rent ceiling of $1,000 per month, there will be a
   a. surplus of 2,000 units.
   b. shortage of 2,000 units.
   c. surplus of 4,000 units.
   d. shortage of 1,000 units.
   e. neither a shortage nor a surplus of units.

6. Figure 7.1 shows a housing market. If the government imposes a rent ceiling of $400 per month, there will be a
   a. shortage of 1,000 units.
   b. shortage of 2,000 units.
   c. shortage of 3,000 units.
   d. shortage of 4,000 units.
   e. neither a shortage nor a surplus of units.

7. Figure 7.1 shows a housing market. Of the rent ceilings listed below, the deadweight loss from a rent ceiling is largest when the rent ceiling equals _____ per month.
   a. $1,000
   b. $800
   c. $600
   d. $400
   e. More information is needed to determine which of the rent ceilings has the largest deadweight loss.

8. Rent ceilings
   a. increase search activity.
   b. result in surpluses.
   c. are efficient.
   d. benefit producers.
   e. have no effect if they are set below the equilibrium rent.

9. Suppose that the government imposes a price ceiling on gasoline that is below the equilibrium price. The black market for gasoline is _____ market in which the price _____ the ceiling price.
   a. a legal; exceeds
   b. an illegal; exceeds
   c. a legal; is less than
   d. an illegal; is less than
   e. an illegal; equals

10. A rent ceiling creates a deadweight loss
    a. if it is set below the equilibrium rent.
    b. if it is set equal to the equilibrium rent.
    c. if it set above the equilibrium rent.
    d. if it decreases the taxes the government collects in the housing market.
    e. never, because if it did create a deadweight loss, the government would not impose it.

11. Rent ceilings
    a. eliminate the problem of scarcity.
    b. allocate resources efficiently.
    c. ensure that housing goes to the poor.
    d. benefit renters living in rent-controlled apartments.
    e. benefit landlords because the landlords know what rent to charge their renters.

Complete the graph

■ FIGURE 7.2

Price (dollars per purse)

■ FIGURE 7.3

c. Does the rent ceiling result in a shortage or a surplus of housing? Indicate the shortage or surplus in Figure 7.3.

1. Figure 7.2 shows the market for purses.
   a. What is the equilibrium price and quantity of purses?
   b. Suppose the government imposes a $20 price ceiling. With the price ceiling, what is the quantity of purses demanded and the quantity of purses supplied? What is the shortage? Indicate the shortage in the figure.
   c. The price ceiling creates a deadweight loss. Show the deadweight loss in the figure.

Rent (dollars per month)	Quantity demanded	Quantity supplied
	(housing units per month)	
900	200	350
800	300	300
700	400	250
600	500	200
500	600	150

2. The table above gives the demand and supply schedules for housing in a small town. In Figure 7.3, graph the demand and supply curves. Label the axes.
   a. What is the equilibrium rent and quantity of housing?
   b. Suppose the government imposes a $600 a month rent ceiling. With the rent ceiling, what is the quantity of housing demanded and the quantity of housing supplied?

Short answer and numeric questions

1. What is a price ceiling?

Price (dollars per carton)	Quantity demanded	Quantity supplied
	(cartons per day)	
1.00	200	110
1.25	175	130
1.50	150	150
1.75	125	170
2.00	100	190

2. The table above gives the demand and supply schedules for milk.
   a. What is the market equilibrium in the milk market?
   b. Suppose the government imposes a price ceiling of $1.25 per carton. What is the price of a carton of milk and what quantity is purchased? Is there a shortage or surplus of milk?
   c. Suppose the government imposes a price ceiling of $1.75 per carton. What is the price of a carton of milk and what quantity is purchased? Is there a shortage or surplus of milk?

3. Are rent ceilings efficient?

4. Are rent ceilings fair?

Additional Exercises (also in MyEconLab Test A)

■ FIGURE 7.4

Rent (dollars per month)

[Graph showing a downward-sloping demand line labeled D. Y-axis shows Rent (dollars per month) with values 100, 125, 150, 175. X-axis shows Quantity (rooms) with values 2,000, 2,500, 3,000, 3,500.]

Figure 7.4 shows the demand for on-campus housing at the University of Idaho, in Moscow, Idaho. The college has 2,000 rooms for rent.

1. What is the equilibrium rent and how many rooms are rented? If the college sets a rent ceiling on on-campus housing of $125 a week, how would you describe the on-campus housing market? Would the allocation of housing be efficient? Would it be fair?

2. If the rent ceiling of $125 a week is strictly enforced and there is no black market, who would gain and who would lose?

3. If a black market developed as a result of the $125 a week rent ceiling, what range of rents would be offered for a room? Would the allocation of housing be efficient? Would it be fair? Explain.

CHECKPOINT 7.2

■ Explain how a price floor works and show how the minimum wage creates unemployment, inefficiency, and unfairness.

Quick Review

- *Price floor* A government regulation that places a *lower* limit on the price at which a particular good, service, or factor of production may be traded.

- *Minimum wage law* A government regulation that makes hiring labor services for less than a specified wage illegal.

- *Effective minimum wage law* When the minimum wage is set above the equilibrium wage rate, the quantity of labor demanded is less than the equilibrium quantity and the quantity of labor supplied is greater than the equilibrium quantity. Unemployment occurs.

Additional Practice Problems 7.2

1. The figure shows the market for fast food workers in Ocala, Florida.

   Wage rate (dollars per hour)

   a. What is the equilibrium wage rate and what is the equilibrium quantity of employment?

   b. If Ocala introduces a minimum wage for fast food workers of $10 an hour, how many fast food workers are employed?

   c. With the minimum wage, is there a surplus or a shortage of fast food workers? Indicate the amount of any shortage or surplus in the figure.

   d. Is the minimum wage of $10 an hour efficient? Is it fair?

Price (cents per pound)	Quantity demanded	Quantity supplied
	(tons of sugar per year)	
10	300	225
15	275	275
20	250	325
25	225	375

2. The above table gives the supply and demand schedules for sugar.

   a. What is the equilibrium price and quantity of sugar?

   b. If the government imposes a price floor of

25¢ a pound, what is the quantity demanded and the quantity supplied? Is there a shortage or surplus? How much?

Solutions to Additional Practice Problems 7.2

1a. The equilibrium wage rate and the equilibrium quantity of the workers are determined where the labor demand curve and the labor supply curve intersect. The equilibrium wage rate is $7.50 an hour and the equilibrium quantity of workers is 150.

1b. 50 fast food workers are employed. This amount equals the quantity of labor demanded when the wage rate is $10 an hour.

1c. The minimum wage creates a surplus of workers. At the $10 wage rate, 200 workers are willing to work but firms are willing to hire only 50 workers. There is a surplus of 150 workers, that is, there are 150 workers unemployed. In the figure, the length of the arrow shows the 150 unemployed workers.

1d. The minimum wage of $10 an hour is not efficient because the marginal benefit to restaurants who demand workers exceeds the marginal cost borne by the workers who supply work. A deadweight loss is created. An additional loss arises as unemployed workers search for jobs. The minimum wage is not fair. It violates the "fair-rules" view of fairness because it prevents voluntary exchange. It violates the "fair-results" view of fairness because 100 workers lose their jobs and are made poorer.

2a. The equilibrium price is 15¢ a pound and the equilibrium quantity is 275 tons a year.

2b. The quantity demanded at 25¢ a pound is 225 tons and the quantity supplied is 375 tons. There is a surplus of 150 tons.

■ Self Test 7.2

Fill in the blanks

A minimum wage is a price ____ (ceiling; floor). A price floor is the ____ (highest; lowest) price at which it is legal to trade a particular good, service, or factor of production. If a minimum wage is set above the equilibrium wage rate, the quantity of labor demanded ____ (decreases; increases) and the quantity of labor supplied ____ (decreases; increases). A minimum wage ____ (creates; does not create) unemployment and ____ (decreases; increases) job search activity. An efficient allocation of labor occurs when the marginal ____ (benefit; cost) to firms ____ (equals; is greater than; is less than) the marginal ____ (benefit; cost) borne by workers. The minimum wage is ____ (fair; unfair). Labor unions ____ (do not support; support) the minimum wage.

True or false

1. Firms hire labor, so they determine how much labor to supply in a market.

2. A minimum wage has an impact when it is set above the equilibrium wage rate.

3. A minimum wage law can lead to increased job search activity and illegal hiring.

4. When a minimum wage is set above the equilibrium wage rate, the employee's marginal cost of working exceeds the employer's marginal benefit from hiring labor.

5. A minimum wage is fair because low-income workers receive an increase in take-home pay.

Multiple choice

1. A price floor is
   a. the highest price at which it is legal to trade a particular good, service, or factor of production.
   b. the lowest price at which it is legal to trade a particular good, service, or factor of production.
   c. an illegal price to charge.
   d. the price when the stock market crashes.
   e. the lowest price for which the quantity demanded equals the quantity supplied.

2. To be effective in raising people's wages, a minimum wage must be set
   a. above the equilibrium wage rate.
   b. below the equilibrium wage rate.
   c. equal to the equilibrium wage rate.
   d. below $7.
   e. either above or below the equilibrium wage depending on whether the supply curve of labor shifts rightward or leftward in response to the minimum wage.

3. A minimum wage set above the equilibrium wage rate
   a. increases the quantity of labor services supplied.
   b. decreases the quantity of labor services supplied.
   c. has no effect on the quantity of labor services supplied.
   d. shifts the labor supply curve rightward.
   e. shifts the labor supply curve leftward.

4. Suppose the current equilibrium wage rate for lifeguards in Houston is $7.85 an hour. A minimum wage law that creates a price floor of $8.50 an hour leads to
   a. a surplus of lifeguards in Houston.
   b. a shortage of lifeguards in Houston.
   c. no changes in the lifeguard market.
   d. a change in the quantity of lifeguards supplied but no change in the quantity of lifeguards demanded.
   e. an increase in the number of lifeguards employed.

5. If the minimum wage is above the equilibrium wage rate, then an increase in the minimum wage ____ employment and ____ unemployment.
   a. increases; increases
   b. increases; decreases
   c. decreases; increases
   d. decreases; decreases
   e. does not change; increases

■ **FIGURE 7.5**

Wage rate (dollars per hour)

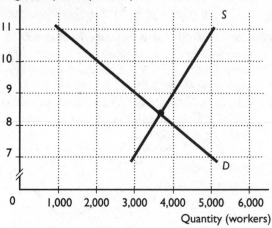

6. Figure 7.5 shows the market for fast food workers in San Francisco. A minimum wage of $11 per hour leads to unemployment of ____ workers.
   a. 1,000
   b. 2,000
   c. 3,000
   d. 4,000
   e. 5,000

7. In Figure 7.5, which of the following minimum wages creates the most unemployment?
   a. $7 an hour
   b. $8 an hour
   c. $9 an hour
   d. $10 an hour
   e. $11 an hour

8. If a minimum wage is introduced that is above the equilibrium wage rate,
   a. the quantity of labor services demanded increases.
   b. job search activity increases.
   c. the supply of labor increases and the supply of labor curve shifts rightward.
   d. unemployment decreases because more workers accept jobs at the higher minimum wage rate.
   e. the quantity of labor supplied decreases because of the increase in unemployment.

9. The minimum wage is set above the equilibrium wage rate. Does the minimum wage create inefficiency?
   a. Yes.
   b. No.
   c. Only if the supply of labor is perfectly inelastic.
   d. Only if the supply of labor is perfectly elastic.
   e. Only if employment exceeds the efficient amount.

10. When the minimum wage is raised, the ____ union labor ____.
   a. demand for; increases
   b. demand for; decreases
   c. supply of; increases
   d. supply of; decreases
   e. demand for; does not change

Complete the graph

Wage rate (dollars per hour)	Quantity demanded	Quantity supplied
	(workers per day)	
6	3,500	2,750
7	3,000	3,000
8	2,500	3,250
9	2,000	3,500
10	1,500	3,750

1. The table above gives the demand and supply schedules for labor in a small town.
   a. In Figure 7.6, at the top of the next column, label the axes. Draw the labor demand and labor supply curves. What is the equilibrium wage rate and employment?
   b. Suppose the government imposes a $6 an hour minimum wage. What is the effect on the wage rate and levels of employment and unemployment?
   c. Suppose the government raises the minimum wage from $6 an hour to $9 an hour. What is the effect on the wage rate and levels of employment and unemployment? Indicate any unemployment.

■ **FIGURE 7.6**

■ **FIGURE 7.7**

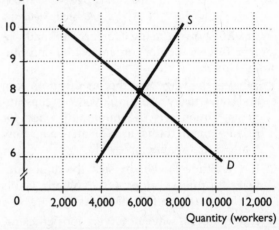

2. Figure 7.7 shows the labor demand and labor supply curves for Rochester, New York. Suppose the city is considering instituting a minimum wage. Indicate the minimum wages that lead to unemployment by darkening the vertical axis for all the minimum wages that create unemployment.

Short answer and numeric questions
1. What is the effect of a minimum wage set below the equilibrium wage rate?
2. How does a minimum wage affect the time needed to find a job?
3. Do all low-wage workers benefit from a minimum wage?

Additional Exercises (also in MyEconLab Test A)

■ **FIGURE 7.8**

Wage rate (dollars per hour)

Figure 7.8 shows a market for private math tutors in College Station organized by the Students' Union.

1. What is the wage rate that math tutors earn and how many are employed? If the Students' Union sets the minimum wage for private math tutors at $20 an hour, how many tutors are unemployed?

2. If the Students' Union sets the minimum wage for private tutors at $12 an hour, is this minimum wage efficient? Is it fair?

3. Is a minimum wage of $20 an hour efficient? Is it fair? If a black market gets going, what wage rate might some tutors earn?

CHECKPOINT 7.3

■ **Explain how a price support in the market for an agricultural product creates a surplus, inefficiency, and unfairness.**

Quick Review

• *Price support* A price support is a price floor in an agricultural market maintained by a government guarantee to buy any surplus output at that price. The price support is the minimum price for which the product may be sold.

Additional Practice Problems 7.3

1. The figure shows the market for sugar.

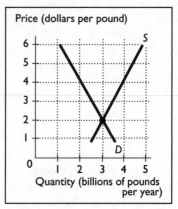

   a. What are the equilibrium price and quantity of sugar?
   b. If the government imposes a price support for sugar at $4 per pound, in the figure above, indicate this price support.
   c. With the price support, how much sugar is produced? How much sugar is purchased by private consumers? How much is purchased by the government?
   d. With the price support, what is the subsidy received by sugar producers?
   e. Are consumers made better off or worse off with the price support?
   f. Without the price support, is the market efficient? With the price support, is the market efficient?

2. With a price support, the government pays a subsidy to farmers by buying part of the crop. Why is this purchase necessary?

Solutions to Additional Practice Problems 7.3

1a. The equilibrium price and the equilibrium quantity of sugar are determined where the demand curve and the supply curve intersect. The figure shows that the equi-

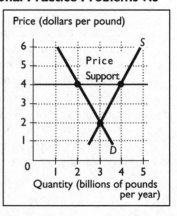

librium price is $2 a pound and the equilibrium quantity is 3 billion pounds a year.

1b. The price support is shown in the figure as the solid line at $4 per pound.

1c. With the price support, the supply curve shows that at $4 per pound, 4 billion pounds of sugar are produced. The demand curve shows that at this price consumers buy 2 billion pounds. The government buys the surplus quantity of sugar, 2 billion pounds.

1d. The government buys 2 billion pounds of sugar at $4 per pound, so the subsidy is 2 billion pounds × $4 per pound, $8 billion.

1e. Consumers are worse off with the price support. With the price support the price they must pay for sugar increases, from $2 per pound to $4 per pound. In response consumers decrease the quantity of sugar they consume from 3 billion pounds to 2 billion pounds.

1f. Without the price support, the market is efficient. With the price support, the market is not efficient.

2. The price support leads to a surplus of the crop. If the government did not buy the surplus, the farmers would not be able to cover their costs because there would be part of the crop left unsold.

■ Self Test 7.3

Fill in the blanks

A price support is a ____ (price ceiling; price floor) in an agricultural market. The government maintains the price support by guaranteeing to ____ (buy; sell) the product at the support price. The government gives a ____ to producers to cover part of the costs of production. When the price support is above the equilibrium price, producers ____ (increase; decrease) the quantity supplied and consumers ____ (increase; decrease) the quantity demanded. Farmers ____ (gain; lose) from a price support and consumers ____ (gain; lose) from a price support. A price support ____ (creates; does not create) inefficiency and a deadweight loss.

True or false

1. In order to have an effective price support, the government isolates the domestic market from the world market by restricting imports.

2. A price support sets the maximum price for which farmers may sell their crop.

3. In order to keep the price of a crop above the equilibrium price and equal to the supported price, the government must buy some of the crop.

4. Because they decrease production, price supports decrease farmers' total revenue.

5. Price supports are efficient because they guarantee production of the good.

Multiple choice

1. Price supports are generally used in
   a. labor markets.
   b. industrial markets.
   c. housing markets.
   d. markets for services.
   e. agricultural markets.

2. To have an effective price support program, the government must
   i. isolate the domestic market from the world market
   ii. pay the farmers a subsidy
   iii. introduce a price floor
   a. i only.
   b. ii only.
   c. iii only.
   d. ii and iii.
   e. i, ii, and iii.

3. A price support directly sets the
   a. amount of production.
   b. subsidy the government must receive from producers.
   c. equilibrium quantity.
   d. lowest price for which the good may be sold.
   e. highest price for which the good may be sold.

4. To keep the price at the level set by the price support, the government must
   a. buy some of the good.
   b. sell some of the good.
   c. receive a subsidy from the producers.
   d. insure that imports are readily available.
   e. be careful to always set the price support below the equilibrium price.

5. With a price support program, who receives a subsidy?
   a. only consumers
   b. only producers
   c. the government
   d. importers
   e. both consumers and producers receive a subsidy

6. When a price support is set above the equilibrium price, producers ____ the quantity supplied and consumers ____ the quantity demanded.
   a. increase; increase
   b. increase; decrease
   c. decrease; increase
   d. decrease; decrease
   e. do not change; do not change

7. Figure 7.9 (in the next column above) shows a price support program in an agricultural market. The amount of the subsidy necessary to keep the price at the price support is
   a. $4.
   b. $32,000.
   c. $8,000.
   d. $16,000.
   e. $24,000.

8. A price support ____ producers and ____ a deadweight loss.
   a. has no effect on; does not create
   b. benefits; creates
   c. harms; creates
   d. benefits; does not create
   e. harms; does not create

■ FIGURE 7.9

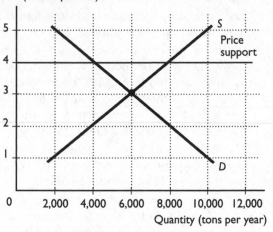

Price (dollars per ton)

Complete the graph

Price (dollars per bushel)	Quantity demanded	Quantity supplied
	(millions of bushels per year)	
3	3,500	2,000
4	3,000	3,000
5	2,500	4,000
6	2,000	5,000
7	1,500	6,000

1. The table gives the demand and supply schedules for wheat.
   a. In Figure 7.10 label the axes. Draw the demand curve and supply curve and indicate the equilibrium price and quantity.

■ FIGURE 7.10

b. Suppose the government imposes a price support of $5 per bushel. What is the effect on the price of wheat, the quantity of wheat produced and the marginal cost of a bushel of wheat? Is there a deadweight loss?

c. With the $5 per bushel price support, how much wheat do consumers buy? What is the subsidy the government must pay to producers?

■ FIGURE 7.11

Price (dollars per ton)

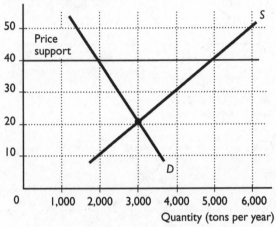

2. Figure 7.11 shows the demand and supply curves for peanuts. There is a price support of $40 per ton of peanuts.

a. At the support price, what is the quantity of peanuts produced? What is the quantity consumers buy? How many tons of peanuts must the government buy? Indicate the amount the government must buy in Figure 7.11.

b. How much is the subsidy paid by the government to producers?

Short answer and numeric questions

1. Why must a price support be set above the equilibrium price in order to have an effect?

2. "A price support program benefits producers and harms consumers. But there is no overall net effect on society." Comment on the above assertion. Is it correct or incorrect?

Additional Exercises (also in MyEconLab Test A)

■ FIGURE 7.12

Price (dollars per pound)

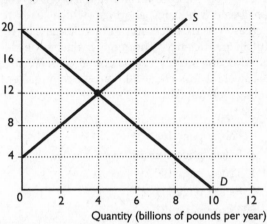

Figure 7.12 shows the market for peanuts. The government introduces a price support for peanuts at $16 per pound.

1. Before the price support is introduced, what are the equilibrium price and quantity of peanuts? Is the market for peanuts efficient?

2. After the government introduces the price support, what is the quantity of peanuts demanded, the quantity produced, and the subsidy received by peanut farmers? Is the peanut market with the price support inefficient?

3. Who gains and who loses from the price support and what is the deadweight loss?

SELF TEST ANSWERS

■ CHECKPOINT 7.1

Fill in the blanks

A price ceiling is the <u>highest</u> price at which it is legal to trade a particular good, service, or factor of production. A rent ceiling is effective if it is set <u>below</u> the equilibrium rent. A rent ceiling can create a housing <u>shortage</u>, which leads to <u>increased</u> search activity. Rent ceilings <u>can result in</u> inefficiency. The <u>more</u> inelastic the demand or the supply of housing, the smaller the deadweight loss created by a rent ceiling. Rent ceilings <u>are not</u> fair.

True or false

1. False; page 168
2. False; pages 168-169
3. True; page 170
4. False; page 171
5. True; page 171

Multiple choice

1. d; page 168
2. b; pages 169
3. a; page 169
4. c; page 169
5. e; page 168
6. d; pages 168-169
7. d; page 171
8. a; page 170
9. b; page 169
10. a; page 171
11. d; page 172

Complete the graph

1. a. The equilibrium price is $30 per purse and the equilibrium quantity is 3,000 purses.
   b. The quantity of purses demanded is 4,000, the quantity of purses supplied is 2,000, and the shortage equals 2,000 purses. In Figure 7.13, the shortage equals the length of the double-headed arrow; page 169.
   c. The deadweight loss is shown in the figure; page 171.
2. a. Figure 7.14 shows the demand curve and supply curve. The equilibrium rent is $800

■ FIGURE 7.13

Price (dollars per purse)

■ FIGURE 7.14

Rent (dollars per month)

a month and the quantity is 300 housing units a month.
   b. The quantity of housing demanded is 500 units a month; the quantity supplied is 200 units a month; page 169.
   c. The shortage of 300 units a month is indicated by the arrow; page 169.

Short answer and numeric questions

1. A price ceiling is the highest price at which it is legal to trade a particular good, service, or factor of production; page 168.
2. a. The equilibrium price is $1.50 a carton and the quantity is 150 cartons a day.

b. The price is $1.25 a carton and 130 cartons a day are purchased. There is a shortage of 45 cartons a day; page 169.

c. The price ceiling is above the equilibrium price, and is ineffective. The price is $1.50 a carton, 150 cartons a day are purchased, and there is neither a shortage nor a surplus; page 168.

3. Rent ceilings can create a deadweight loss and therefore are not efficient; page 173.

4. Rent ceilings are not fair. They violate both the fair-results view and fair-rules view of fairness; page 172.

Additional Exercises (also in MyEconLab Test A)

1. The equilibrium rent is $150 a week and the equilibrium quantity is 2,000 rooms rented. At a rent ceiling of $125 a week, the quantity of rooms demanded is 2,500 and there is a shortage of 500 rooms on campus. The allocation remains efficient because the supply of rooms is perfectly inelastic. As a result, the quantity of rooms rented with the rent ceiling remains 2,000 so that there is no deadweight loss from underproduction. The allocation is not fair because it prevents voluntary exchange and does not necessarily reallocate housing to the poorest students; pages 168, 171-172.

2. The gainers from the ceiling are those students who get the cheaper apartments on campus. The losers include those students who are unable to rent on campus at the $125 ceiling. The university also loses because it charges a lower rent; pages 171-172.

3. If a black market develops, rents will range from $125 a week to $150 a week. The highest rent that someone would offer is $150 a week. This rent equals the willingness of someone to pay for the 2,000th room. This market is efficient because the supply is perfectly inelastic, so 2,000 rooms are rented, the same as the efficient equilibrium quantity with no rent ceiling. (Generally a black market is inefficient because marginal benefit exceeds marginal cost and a deadweight loss arises.) A black market is not fair because it

does not provide rooms to the students who are most in need; pages 169-170, 172.

■ CHECKPOINT 7.2

Fill in the blanks

A minimum wage is a price <u>floor</u>. A price floor is the <u>lowest</u> price at which it is legal to trade a particular good, service, or factor of production. If a minimum wage is set above the equilibrium wage rate, the quantity of labor demanded <u>decreases</u> and the quantity of labor supplied <u>increases</u>. A minimum wage <u>creates</u> unemployment and <u>increases</u> job search activity. An efficient allocation of labor occurs when the marginal <u>benefit</u> to firms <u>equals</u> the marginal <u>cost</u> borne by workers. The minimum wage is <u>unfair</u>. Labor unions <u>support</u> the minimum wage.

True or false

1. False; page 174
2. True; page 175
3. True; page 176
4. False; page 178
5. False; page 179

Multiple choice

1. b; page 174
2. a; page 175
3. a; page 175
4. a; page 175
5. c; page 175
6. d; page 175
7. e; page 175
8. b; page 176
9. a; page 178
10. a; page 179

Complete the graph

1. a. Figure 7.15 (on the next page) shows the demand and supply curves. The equilibrium wage rate is $7 an hour and the equilibrium employment is 3,000 workers a day.

b. The $6 minimum wage is below the equilibrium wage and has no effect; page 175.

■ **FIGURE 7.15**

Wage rate (dollars per hour)

c. The $9 minimum wage raises the wage rate to $9. Employment decreases to 2,000 workers. The number of workers looking for work is 3,500. Unemployment equals 3,500 − 2,000, which is 1,500 people. The amount of unemployment is shown by the arrow in Figure 7.15; pages 175.

■ **FIGURE 7.16**

Wage rate (dollars per hour)

2. In order to have an effect in the market, the minimum wage must be set above the equilibrium wage. As Figure 7.16 shows, any minimum wage above $8 per hour creates unemployment; page 175.

Short answer and numeric questions

1. A minimum wage set below the equilibrium wage rate has no effect on the wage rate or

amount of employment; page 175.

2. By decreasing the quantity of labor demanded and creating unemployment, a minimum wage increases the time spent searching for a job; page 176.

3. A minimum wage harms low-wage workers who lose their jobs or cannot find jobs because of the minimum wage; page 178.

Additional Exercises (also in MyEconLab Test A)

1. The equilibrium wage rate is $15 an hour and the equilibrium quantity is 100 tutors. At a minimum wage of $20 an hour, only 50 tutors are hired and 150 people want to work as tutors. 100 tutors are unemployed; pages 174-176.

2. A $12 an hour minimum wage has no effect because it is below the equilibrium wage. The equilibrium wage rate remains at $15 an hour and the equilibrium quantity remains at 100. No tutors are unemployed. The $12 an hour minimum wage is efficient because it has no effect on the market equilibrium. According to the "fair results" view, it is unfair because some students have different income than other students. According to the "fair rules" view, it is fair as a competitive equilibrium; pages 178-179.

3. The minimum wage rate of $20 is inefficient because marginal benefit exceeds the marginal cost and there is a deadweight loss. The outcome is unfair. It benefits only the tutors who get the jobs and the unemployed tutors earn nothing. Students are unable to hire the tutors they want. If a black market develops and some tutors charge below the minimum wage, the supply curve shows that some are willing to tutor for $10 (or slightly more) an hour; pages 176, 178.

■ **CHECKPOINT 7.3**

Fill in the blanks

A price support is a <u>price floor</u> in an agricultural market. The government maintains the price support by guaranteeing to <u>buy</u> the product at the support price. The government gives a <u>sub-</u>

sidy to producers to cover part of the costs of production. When the price support is above the equilibrium price, producers <u>increase</u> the quantity supplied and consumers <u>decrease</u> the quantity demanded. Farmers <u>gain</u> from a price support and consumers <u>lose</u> from a price support. A price support <u>creates</u> inefficiency and a deadweight loss.

True or false

1. True; page 181
2. False; page 181
3. True; page 182
4. False; page 183
5. False; page 183

Multiple choice

1. e; page 181
2. e; page 181
3. d; page 181
4. a; page 182
5. b; page 182
6. b; page 182
7. d; page 182
8. b; page 183

Complete the graph

■ FIGURE 7.17

Price (dollars per bushel)

1. a. Figure 7.17 shows the demand and supply curves. The equilibrium price is $4 a bush-

el and the equilibrium quantity is 3,000 million bushels a year.

b. The $5 per bushel price support is illustrated in the figure. This price support raises the price of wheat to $5 per bushel. The quantity of wheat produced increases to 4,000 million bushels per year and the marginal cost of the last bushel of wheat produced increases to $5. There is a deadweight loss because the marginal cost exceeds the marginal benefit; pages 182-183.

c. With the price support, consumers buy only 2,500 million bushels per year. There is a surplus of 1,500 million bushels (4,000 million bushels produced minus $2,500 million purchased by consumers) that the government must buy. The government pays a subsidy of $5 per bushel × 1,500 million bushels, which is $7.5 billion; page 182.

■ FIGURE 7.18

Price (dollars per ton)

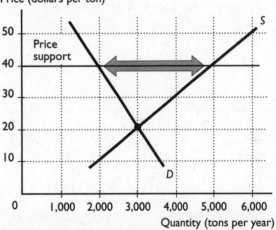

2. a. Figure 7.18 shows that at the support price of $40 per ton, 5,000 tons are produced and consumers buy 2,000 tons. The government must buy the surplus, 3,000 tons. The amount the government must buy is equal to the length of the arrow in Figure 7.15; page 182.

b. To buy the surplus, the government pays a subsidy to producers of $40 per ton × 3,000 tons, which is $120,000; page 182.

Short answer and numeric questions

1. If a price support is set below the equilibrium price, it does not make the equilibrium price illegal and so is ineffective. If a price support is set above the equilibrium price, it makes the equilibrium price illegal and is effective; pages 181-182.

2. The first assertion is correct: a price support program increases producer surplus (which benefits producers) and decreases consumer surplus (which harms consumers). But the second assertion is incorrect. There is a net effect on society because a deadweight loss is created, which harms society; page 183.

Additional Exercises (also in MyEconLab Test A)

1. The equilibrium price is $12 a pound and the equilibrium quantity is 4 billion pounds a year. If this price is the same as the world price, the market is efficient because marginal benefit equals marginal cost.

2. The price support of $16 per pound leads to a quantity demanded of 2 billion pounds of peanuts and a quantity produced of 6 billion pounds of peanuts. There is surplus of 4 billion pounds of peanuts. With the price support of $16 per pound, the government must buy the 4 billion pound surplus, so the total subsidy paid to peanut farmers is $16 per pound multiplied by 4 billion pounds, or $64 billion.

The market with the price support is inefficient because marginal cost exceeds marginal benefit. There is overproduction and a deadweight loss is created; pages 181-182.

3. Consumers lose because they must pay a higher price for a reduced quantity. Producers gain. Taxpayers lose because they must pay $64 billion in subsidies to suppliers. The deadweight loss is equal to 1/2 × 2 billion pounds of peanuts × ($16 per pound − $8 per pound), or $8 billion; pages 182-183.

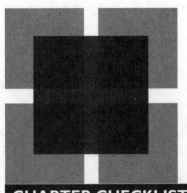

Chapter 8

Taxes

In Chapter 8 we study how taxes affect markets, who actually pays the tax, the effect of an income tax and a Social Security tax, and review ideas about the fairness of taxes.

1 Explain how taxes change prices and quantities, are shared by buyers and sellers, and create inefficiency.

Taxes raise the price paid by buyers, lower the price received by sellers, and decrease the quantity of the good. Tax incidence is the division of the burden of a tax between the buyers and the sellers; generally sellers and buyers both pay part of a tax. The incidence of a tax depends on the elasticities of demand and supply and *not* upon whom, the buyers or sellers, the government levies the tax. For a given elasticity of supply, buyers pay a larger share of the tax the more inelastic the demand for the good. Buyers pay the entire tax when demand is perfectly inelastic or supply is perfectly elastic. Similarly, for a given elasticity of demand, sellers pay a larger share of the tax the more inelastic the supply of the good. Sellers pay the entire tax when demand is perfectly elastic or supply is perfectly inelastic. The excess burden of a tax is the amount by which the burden of a tax exceeds the tax revenue received by the government—the deadweight loss from a tax. The more inelastic the demand or supply, the smaller the excess burden of the tax, that is, the smaller the deadweight loss from the tax.

2 Explain how income taxes and Social Security taxes change wage rates and employment, are shared by employers and workers, and create inefficiency.

The marginal tax rate is the percentage of an additional dollar that is paid in tax; the average tax rate is the percentage of income that is paid in tax. With a progressive tax, the average tax rate rises as income increases; with a proportional tax, the average tax rate is constant at all income levels; with a regressive tax, the average tax rate decreases as income increases. A tax on labor income decreases employment and creates a deadweight loss. Both the employer and the worker pay part of the tax. A tax on capital income decreases the quantity of capital and creates a deadweight loss. The supply of capital is highly elastic. If the supply of capital is perfectly elastic, then the demanders, that is, firms, pay the entire tax. A tax on land or other unique resource does not decrease the quantity and creates no deadweight loss because supply is perfectly inelastic. The entire burden of the tax falls on the owner of the resource. Social Security tax laws are written so that both workers and employers pay equal shares but the incidence *actually* depends on the elasticities of the demand for labor and the supply of labor.

3 Review ideas about the fairness of the tax system.

The benefits principle is the proposition that people should pay taxes equal to the benefits received from public services. This taxing principle means that those who benefit the most pay the most. The ability-to-pay principle is the proposition that people should pay taxes according to how easily they can bear the burden. For fairness, the ability-to-pay principle compares people along vertical and horizontal dimensions. The fairness and efficiency of taxes can conflict, leading to the big tradeoff.

CHECKPOINT 8.1

■ **Explain how taxes change prices and quantities, are shared by buyers and sellers, and create inefficiency.**

Quick Review

• *Effect of a sales tax on the supply curve* A sales tax decreases the supply of the good and the supply curve shifts leftward. The vertical distance between the supply curve without the tax and the supply curve with the tax equals the amount of the tax.

• *Tax incidence and elasticities of demand and supply* For a given elasticity of supply, the more inelastic the demand, the larger the share of a tax paid by the buyer. And, for a given elasticity of demand, the more inelastic the supply, the larger the share of a tax paid by the seller.

Additional Practice Problem 8.1

1. The figure illustrates the initial equilibrium in the markets for Coke and Pepsi. The price of a 2 liter bottle of a Coke and a Pepsi are the same, $1.50, and the quantity of each are the same, 12 million bottles a week. The supply of Coke is identical to the supply of Pepsi and both are given by supply curve *S* in the figure. However, as shown in the figure with the demand curve *Dc* for Coke and *Dp* for Pepsi, the demand for Coke is more elastic than the demand for Pepsi. The government now imposes a $1 per bottle sales tax on Coke and Pepsi.

a. Does the price paid by consumers for a Coke rise by more than, less than, or the same amount as the price paid for a Pepsi?

b. Do the consumers of Coke pay more of the tax than do consumers of Pepsi? Do the producers of Coke pay more of the tax than do the producers of Pepsi?

c. Does the quantity of Coke decrease by more, less, or the same amount as the quantity of Pepsi?

d. Does the government collect more, less, or the same amount of tax revenue from the tax on Coke as it does from the tax on Pepsi?

e. Is the deadweight loss from the tax on Coke larger, smaller, or the same amount as the deadweight loss from the tax on Pepsi?

Solution to Additional Practice Problem 8.1

1a. A tax is like an increase in the suppliers' costs, so a tax decreases the supply and shifts the supply curve leftward.
The vertical distance between the

supply curve with the tax and the supply curve without the tax is equal to the amount of the tax, $1 per bottle in this problem. The figure shows this effect, with the supply curves for Coke and Pepsi both shifting to the curve labeled *S+tax*. The demand for Coke is more elastic, so the price paid by consumers for a Coke rises only to $1.75, a 25¢ increase. The demand for Pepsi is less elastic, so the price paid by consumers for a Pepsi rises to $2.25, a 75¢ increase.

1b. The demand for Coke is more elastic, so consumers pay less of the tax imposed on Coke. The price paid by consumers for a Coke rises 25¢, so consumers pay 25¢ of this tax and producers pay the remaining 75¢. The demand for Pepsi is more inelastic, so consumers pay more of the tax imposed on Pepsi.

The price paid by consumers for a Pepsi rises 75¢, so consumers pay 75¢ of this tax and producers pay 25¢.

1c. The quantity of Coke decreases by more than the quantity of Pepsi because the demand for Coke is more elastic than the demand for Pepsi. In the figure, the equilibrium quantity of Coke decreases to 6 million bottles per week and the equilibrium quantity of Pepsi decreases only to 10 million bottles per week.

1d. The total amount of tax revenue equals the tax multiplied by the quantity sold. Because the decrease in the quantity of Coke sold is greater than the decrease in the quantity of Pepsi sold, less Coke than Pepsi is sold after the tax is imposed so the government collects less tax revenue from the tax on Coke.

1e. Because the decrease in the quantity of Coke is greater than the decrease in the quantity of Pepsi, the deadweight loss of the tax is greater in the market for Coke than that for Pepsi.

■ Self Test 8.1

Fill in the blanks

The tax ____ (elasticity; incidence) is the division of the burden of a tax between the buyer and the seller. A tax is like ____ (a decrease; an increase) in suppliers' costs. For a given elasticity of supply, the buyer pays a larger share of the tax the more ____ (elastic; inelastic) is the demand for the good. If the supply is perfectly ____ (elastic; inelastic), the seller pays the entire tax. Taxes ____ (create; do not create) a deadweight loss. The excess burden of a tax is the ____ (deadweight loss; surplus) from the tax and is larger the ____ (more; less) elastic the demand for the good being taxed.

True or false

1. When the government imposes a tax on the sale of a good, the burden of the tax falls entirely on the buyer.

2. A tax on fast-food meals does not create a deadweight loss because the elasticity of supply of fast-food meals equals 1.0.

3. The excess burden of a tax is the deadweight loss from the tax.

4. For a given elasticity of supply, the more inelastic the demand for a good, the smaller the share of the tax paid by the buyer.

5. When the government taxes a good that has a perfectly elastic supply, the buyer pays the entire tax.

Multiple choice

1. Tax incidence refers to
   a. how government taxes are spent by the government.
   b. the incidences of tax revolts by the tax payers.
   c. the amount of a tax minus its burden.
   d. the division of the burden of a tax between the buyers and the sellers.
   e. tax revenue minus excess burden.

2. Neither the supply of nor demand for a good is perfectly elastic or perfectly inelastic. So imposing a tax on the good results in a ____ in the price paid by buyers and ____ in the equilibrium quantity.
   a. rise; an increase
   b. rise; a decrease
   c. fall; an increase
   d. fall; a decrease
   e. rise; no change

3. Neither the supply of nor demand for a good is perfectly elastic or perfectly inelastic. So imposing a tax on the good results in a ____ in the price received by sellers and a ____ in the price paid by buyers.
   a. rise; rise
   b. rise; fall
   c. fall; rise
   d. fall; fall
   e. no change; rise

4. A sales tax imposed on tires ____ consumer surplus and ____ producer surplus.
   a. increases; increases
   b. increases; decreases
   c. decreases; increases
   d. decreases; decreases
   e. does not change; does not change

■ **FIGURE 8.1**
Price (dollars per pizza)

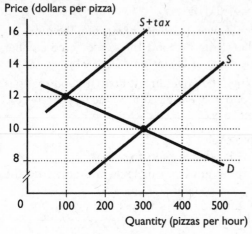

Quantity (pizzas per hour)

5. Figure 8.1 shows the market for delivered pizza. The government has imposed a tax of ____ per pizza.
   a. $6
   b. $8
   c. $10
   d. $12
   e. $16

6. In Figure 8.1, before the tax was imposed consumers paid ____ for a pizza and after the tax is imposed consumers pay ____ for a pizza.
   a. $10; $16
   b. $12; $16
   c. $10; $12
   d. $12; $16
   e. $10; $6

7. In Figure 8.1, the division of the tax is that consumers pay ____ of the tax and suppliers pay ____ of the tax.
   a. $6; $0
   b. $3; $3
   c. $0; $6
   d. $4; $2
   e. $2; $4

8. The deadweight loss from a tax is called the
   a. marginal benefit of the tax.
   b. marginal cost of the tax.
   c. excess burden of the tax.
   d. net gain from taxation.
   e. net loss from taxation.

9. A sales tax creates a deadweight loss because
   a. there is some paperwork opportunity cost of sellers paying the sales tax.
   b. demand and supply both decrease.
   c. less is produced and consumed.
   d. citizens value government goods less than private goods.
   e. the government spends the tax revenue it collects.

10. To determine who bears the greater share of a tax, we compare the
   a. number of buyers to the number of sellers.
   b. elasticity of supply to the elasticity of demand.
   c. size of the tax to the price of the good.
   d. government tax revenue to the revenue collected by the suppliers.
   e. pre-tax quantity to the post-tax quantity.

11. Suppose the demand for barley is perfectly inelastic. The supply curve of barley is upward sloping. If a tax is imposed on barley,
   a. barley sellers pay the entire tax.
   b. barley buyers pay the entire tax.
   c. the government pays the entire tax.
   d. the tax is split evenly between barley buyers and sellers.
   e. who pays the tax depends on whether the government imposes the tax on barley sellers or on barley buyers.

Complete the graph

■ **FIGURE 8.2**

1. The supply curve and the demand curve for pizza slices are shown in Figure 8.2. The price is in dollars per slice and the quantity is pizza slices per day. Label the axes.
   a. What is the equilibrium price and quantity of pizza slices?
   b. Suppose the government imposes a sales tax of $4 a slice of pizza. In Figure 8.2, draw the new supply curve after the tax is imposed.
   c. After the tax is imposed, what is the price paid by buyers for a slice of pizza? What is the price received by sellers for a slice of pizza? What is the incidence of the tax?
   d. In Figure 8.2, darken the area of the deadweight loss from the tax.

2. The supply curve and the demand curve for pizza slices are again shown in Figure 8.3. The price is in dollars per slice and the quantity is pizza slices per day. Once again, label the axes.
   a. Suppose the government imposes a tax on buyers of $4 a slice of pizza. In Figure 8.3, draw the new demand curve after the tax is imposed.
   b. After the tax is imposed, what is the price paid by buyers for a slice of pizza? What is the price received by sellers for a slice of pizza? What is the incidence of the tax?

■ **FIGURE 8.3**

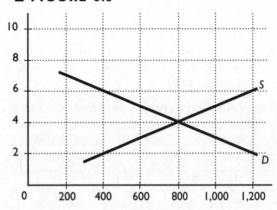

   c. How do the prices paid and the tax incidence in this question compare to those in question 1? What general principle does your answer uncover?

Short answer and numeric questions

Price (dollars per golf ball)	Quantity demanded (golf balls)	Before-tax quantity supplied (golf balls)	After-tax quantity supplied (golf balls)
0.50	1,100	600	0
1.00	1,000	620	0
1.50	900	680	0
2.00	700	700	0
2.50	600	850	____
3.00	300	950	
3.50	60	1,180	680

1. The above table gives the monthly demand and supply schedules for golf balls at the College Hills Golf Shop. With no tax, what is the equilibrium price and quantity? Suppose a $2 per ball tax is imposed.
   a. Complete the last column of the table.
   b. What is the equilibrium price and quantity after the tax is imposed?
   c. How much of the tax is paid by the buyer? How much is paid by the seller?
   d. How much tax revenue does the government collect?

2. The government decides to tax high blood pressure medicine. The supply by drug companies is elastic; the demand by patients is inelastic. Do the drug companies

bear the entire tax burden? Is there much deadweight loss from this tax?

3. What is the relationship between the deadweight loss from a tax and the excess burden of a tax? Why does a tax create a deadweight loss?

Additional Exercises (also in MyEconLab Test A)

With the increased popularity of cell phones, the government imposes a tax of $20 a cell phone and a tax of 10¢ a call made on a cell phone. Suppose that the supply of cell phones is elastic, the demand for cell phones is inelastic, the supply of calls is perfectly elastic, and the demand for calls is elastic. Use this information to answer exercises 1 and 2.

1. Does the buyer or the seller pay more of the tax on a phone? Who pays more of the tax on a call? Would the taxes reduce the number of cell phones bought and the number of calls made from cell phones?

2. Which tax would raise more revenue for the government? Why? Which tax do you think would have the greater excess burden? Why?

3. The supply of apartments in New York City is inelastic, and the demand for apartments is elastic. The city introduces a tax on apartment rentals. Explain why the landlord would pay more of the tax than the renter would pay and why the government would collect a large revenue from this tax.

CHECKPOINT 8.2

■ **Explain how income taxes and Social Security taxes change wage rates and employment, are shared by employers and workers, and create inefficiency.**

Quick Review

- *Progressive tax* A tax is progressive if the average tax rate increases as income increases.
- *Proportional tax* A tax is proportional if the average tax rate remains constant at

all income levels.

- *Regressive tax* A tax is regressive if the average tax rate decreases as income increases.

Additional Practice Problems 8.2

1. The supply of capital is perfectly elastic. The income from capital is the interest received. If a tax is imposed on the income from capital, who pays the tax: the firms who demand capital or the suppliers of capital? Explain your answer.

2. The supply of land is perfectly inelastic. The income from land is rent. If a tax is imposed on the income from land, who pays the tax: the demanders of land or the suppliers? Explain your answer.

3. In Hong Kong, the marginal tax rates on salaries ranges from 2 percent to 20 percent with a maximum average tax of 15 percent, which is reached on incomes of about $59,000. Compare the tax rates in Hong Kong with the U.S. federal tax rate. In which country is the personal income tax (tax on salaries) more progressive? Why?

Solutions to Additional Practice Problems 8.2

1. Because the supply of capital is perfectly elastic, the suppliers pay none of the tax. The entire tax is paid by the demanders. Supply being perfectly elastic means that the suppliers have a huge number of options where to supply their capital, with all the options paying the same interest rate. If one of these options imposes a tax, suppliers will not supply any capital there unless the interest rate rises to compensate them fully for the tax. When the interest rate rises by the full amount of the tax, suppliers pay none of the tax. The interest rate must rise by the full amount of the tax because that is the only way that the return from supplying capital to this option equals the return from supplying capital to all the other options.

2. Because the supply of land is perfectly inelastic, the suppliers pay all of the tax. The demanders pay none of the tax. Supply being perfectly inelastic means that suppliers have

no other choice but to supply their land. Demanders determine the maximum price they are willing to pay for this quantity of land and that is the price. If a tax is imposed on land, demanders will not pay any of the tax because they are already paying the maximum price they are wiling to pay. So suppliers pay the entire tax.

3. The personal income tax in the United States is more progressive because the average tax rate increases to higher levels in the United States. Hong Kong's marginal tax rates are lower than U.S. marginal tax rates, so Hong Kong's average tax rate remains lower than the U.S. average tax rate.

■ Self Test 8.2

Fill in the blanks

The percentage of an additional dollar that is paid in tax is _____ (a progressive tax; a marginal tax; an average tax) rate. A tax is regressive if the average tax rate _____ (increases; decreases) as income increases. A tax on labor income _____ (creates; does not create) a deadweight loss. If the supply of capital is perfectly elastic, a tax on capital income is paid entirely by the _____ (firms; suppliers of capital) and the tax _____ (creates; does not create) a deadweight loss. If the supply of land is perfectly _____ (inelastic; elastic), a tax on income from land is paid entirely by the landowners and the tax _____ (creates; does not create) a deadweight loss. A Social Security tax imposed on workers and a Social Security tax imposed on firms both _____ (raise; lower) the wage rate that employees receive and _____ (increase; decrease) employment.

True or false

1. When Hank earns an additional dollar, he pays 30 cents in additional tax. Hank's marginal tax rate is 30 percent.

2. If the average tax rate increases as income increases, the tax is a progressive tax.

3. Sam has $40,000 of taxable income and pays $4,000 income tax. Bert has $50,000 of taxable income and pays $4,500 income tax. Sam and Bert live in a country with a progressive income tax.

4. An income tax on labor creates a deadweight loss.

5. If the supply of capital is perfectly elastic, a tax on capital income decreases the demand for capital and decreases the interest rate.

Multiple choice

1. The percentage of an additional dollar of income that is paid in tax is the
   a. sales tax.
   b. excise tax.
   c. marginal tax rate.
   d. personal income tax.
   e. regressive tax.

2. If the average tax rate is constant as income increases, then the tax is called
   a. regressive.
   b. progressive.
   c. proportional.
   d. an average tax.
   e. efficient.

3. A tax on labor income
   a. increases the quantity employed because the demand for labor increases.
   b. decreases the quantity employed because the supply of labor decreases.
   c. increases the quantity employed because the supply of labor increases.
   d. decreases the quantity employed because the demand for labor increases.
   e. does not change the quantity employed because people must have jobs in order to earn any income.

4. The incidence of an income tax on labor income is generally that the tax is
   a. paid only by workers.
   b. paid only by employers.
   c. shared equally between workers and employers.
   d. shared but not necessarily equally between workers and employers.
   e. funded by the deadweight loss.

5. When governments tax capital income, the equilibrium quantity of capital
   a. increases because of the international mobility of capital.
   b. does not change because the supply of capital is perfectly elastic.
   c. decreases.
   d. does not change because the supply of capital is perfectly inelastic.
   e. might increase or decrease depending on whether the demand for capital is inelastic or elastic.

6. If the supply of capital is perfectly elastic, the incidence of a tax on capital income is
   a. paid entirely by the suppliers of capital.
   b. paid entirely by firms that demand capital.
   c. shared between firms that demand capital and the suppliers of capital.
   d. shared but not equally between firms that demand capital and the suppliers of capital.
   e. unknown.

■ FIGURE 8.4

Interest rate (percent per year)

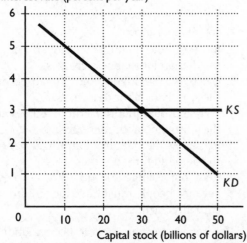

Capital stock (billions of dollars)

7. Figure 8.4 shows the capital market. If the government imposes a 2 percent tax on capital income, the interest rate ____.
   a. stays at 3 percent.
   b. rises to 4 percent.
   c. rises to 5 percent.
   d. falls to 2 percent.
   e. falls to 1 percent.

8. Figure 8.4 shows the capital market. If the government imposes a 2 percent tax on capital income, the equilibrium quantity of capital becomes
   a. $10 billion.
   b. $20 billion.
   c. $30 billion.
   d. $40 billion.
   e. $50 billion.

9. A tax on income from land in Montana is borne entirely by landowners because the
   a. demand for land is perfectly inelastic.
   b. supply of land is perfectly inelastic.
   c. supply of land is perfectly elastic.
   d. demand for land is perfectly elastic.
   e. deadweight loss from the tax would otherwise be infinite.

10. When a social security tax is imposed on workers, employment ____ and when a social security tax is imposed on employers, employment ____.
    a. increases; increases
    b. increases; decreases
    c. decreases; increases
    d. decreases; decreases
    e. decreases; does not change

Complete the graph

■ FIGURE 8.5

Wage rate (dollars per hour)

Quantity of labor (hours per week)

1. Figure 8.5 shows the labor market.
   a. Label the curves. What is the equilibrium wage rate and quantity of labor?

b. Suppose the government imposes an income tax of $4 an hour on labor income. Illustrate the effect of this tax in the figure.

c. After the tax is imposed, what is the wage rate paid by firms and what is the amount received by households?

d. If a deadweight loss is created, shade its area. If a deadweight loss is not created, explain why not.

■ FIGURE 8.6

Rent (dollars per acre per year)

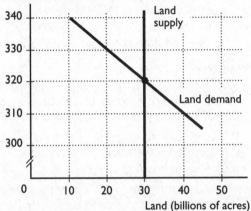

2. Figure 8.6 shows the market for land.

a. What is the equilibrium rent and quantity of land?

b. If the government imposes a tax on land income of $10 an acre, what is the new equilibrium rent paid by renters? What is the amount of rent kept by landowners? What is the equilibrium quantity of land?

c. If a deadweight loss is created, shade its area. If a deadweight loss is not created, explain why not.

3. Figure 8.7 (at the top of the next column) has a labor supply curve and labor demand curve. The initial equilibrium wage rate is $32.50 an hour. The government imposes a $3 an hour Social Security tax on firms.

a. In the figure, show the effect of this tax. What is the wage that workers receive before the tax and after the tax?

b. Even though the Social Security tax has been imposed on the firms, how is the burden of the tax split?

■ FIGURE 8.7

Wage rate (dollars per hour)

Quantity (thousands of workers)

Short answer and numeric questions

1. Why is the supply of capital highly elastic? Who pays the tax on capital income if the supply of capital is perfectly elastic?

2. The government mandates that half of a Social Security tax has to be paid by the employer and the other half has to be paid by the worker. Does this law mean that the burden of the tax is shared equally by the employer and worker?

Additional Exercises (also in MyEconLab Test A)

1. California taxes personal incomes, and in 2004, there were six tax brackets that ranged from 1.0 percent on a taxable income of $6,146 to 8.3 percent on taxable incomes above $40,345. California has an 8.84 percent corporate income tax. California has a 7.25 percent sales tax. Other taxes are 18 cents a gallon on gasoline, 87 cents a pack on cigarettes, and $0.20 per gallon on beer and wine. Property taxes vary across the counties and range from 1 percent to 2 percent of property values.

a. Classify California's taxes into progressive, proportional, and regressive taxes.

b. Which of California's taxes creates the biggest excess burden? Explain.

CHECKPOINT 8.3

■ **Review ideas about the fairness of the tax system.**

Quick Review

- *Benefits principle* People should pay taxes equal to the benefits they receive from public services.
- *Ability-to-pay principle* People should pay taxes according to how easily they can bear the burden.

Additional Practice Problem 8.3

1. "The only fair taxes are user fees, such as toll roads. The gas tax is fair because the funds raised go for road maintenance. All government-provided services need to be funded through user fees. To pay for parks, we need to charge entrance fees. The cost of garbage collection must be based on how much garbage the household creates. Any tax except a user fee is unfair and must be abolished!" Comment on the fairness principle being used. Is it possible for *all* government programs to be funded through user fees?

Solution to Additional Practice Problem 8.3

1. The speaker is advocating the benefits principle of taxation, which is the proposition that people should pay taxes equal to the benefits they receive from public services. Although user fees have merit, it is not possible to fund all government programs through user fees. First, for public goods such as national defense, everyone consumes the same amount. It is impossible to determine how much any particular person benefits and therefore not possible to determine the proper fee. Second, some programs are designed to redistribute income to poorer people. It would be ludicrous to tax welfare recipients an amount equal to the benefits they received, which is the case under a user-fee arrangement.

■ **Self Test 8.3**

Fill in the blanks

The ____ (ability-to-pay; benefits) principle is the proposition that people should pay taxes equal to the benefits they receive from public services. Imposing a higher sales tax on the purchase of jewelry than on food is fair according to the ____ (ability-to-pay; benefit) principle. ____ (Horizontal; Vertical) equity requires that taxpayers with the same ability to pay do pay the same taxes. In the United States, the marriage tax problem is that a couple who both work pay often ____ (more; less) taxes when they are married than when they are single.

True or false

1. The benefits principle asserts that those people who are harmed by the deadweight loss of a tax should not pay the tax.

2. If the revenue from gasoline taxes is used to pay for road repairs, the tax reflects the ability-to-pay principle.

3. The U.S. income tax, which uses progressive income taxes, can be considered fair based on the principle of vertical equity.

4. Both vertical and horizontal equity can be achieved and the marriage tax problem eliminated if married couples are taxed as two single persons.

5. The taxes with the largest deadweight loss are taxes on capital income, and the people who pay these taxes generally have the greatest ability to pay taxes.

Multiple choice

1. Which of the following taxes best illustrates the benefits principle of taxation?
   a. sales tax on clothing used to fund food stamps
   b. state income tax used to fund state universities
   c. medicare tax imposed on all workers used to fund medical care for the elderly
   d. gasoline tax used to fund road repairs
   e. federal income tax used to fund NASA spending

2. The proposition that people should pay taxes according to how easily they can bear the burden is the ____ principle
   a. regressive tax
   b. benefits
   c. ability-to-pay
   d. fairness
   e. incidence of fairness

3. The government once imposed a luxury tax on very expensive jewelry. This tax followed the ____ principle.
   a. benefits
   b. ability-to-pay
   c. vertical equity
   d. horizontal equity
   e. fair-tax incidence

4. The proposition that taxpayers with the same ability to pay should pay the same taxes is called
   a. the benefits principle.
   b. the ability-to-pay imperative.
   c. vertical equity.
   d. horizontal equity.
   e. fair-tax incidence principle.

5. Vertical equity implies that
   i. tax rates should be equal for all tax payers.
   ii. people with higher incomes should pay more in taxes.
   iii. people with higher incomes should pay a lower average tax rate.
   a. i only.
   b. ii only.
   c. iii only.
   d. i and ii.
   e. ii and iii.

6. Joan's income is $60,000 and she pays $6,000 in taxes. Juan's income is $40,000 and he pays $7,000 in taxes. This situation violates
   a. the benefits principle.
   b. the big tradeoff.
   c. vertical equity.
   d. horizontal equity.
   e. the fair-tax incidence principle.

7. Because the U.S. income tax is a progressive tax, taxing married couples as two single persons can violate
   a. the benefits principle.
   b. the ability-to-pay imperative.
   c. vertical equity.
   d. horizontal equity.
   e. the government's need for more revenue.

8. Compared to taxes on labor income, taxes on capital income generate ____ deadweight loss and are paid by people who generally have the ____ ability to pay.
   a. a larger; most
   b. a larger; least
   c. a smaller; most
   d. a smaller; least
   e. no; least

Short answer and numeric questions

1. There are a variety of welfare programs, such as food stamps, designed to boost the income of poor families. Does it make sense to raise the tax revenue necessary to fund these programs by using the benefits principle of taxation?

2. What is the marriage tax problem? If a married couple is taxed as two single individuals, what problem is created?

Additional Exercises (also in MyEconLab Test A)

1. In Canada, the marginal income tax rates range from 22 percent to 40 percent. Does Canada place greater weight on the ability-to-pay principle than does the United States? Does Canada place a greater weight on efficiency and a smaller weight on fairness than does the United States?

SELF TEST ANSWERS

■ CHECKPOINT 8.1

Fill in the blanks

The tax <u>incidence</u> is the division of the burden of a tax between the buyer and the seller. A tax is like <u>an increase</u> in suppliers' costs. For a given elasticity of supply, the buyer pays a larger share of the tax the more <u>inelastic</u> is the demand for the good. If the supply is perfectly <u>inelastic</u>, the seller pays the entire tax. Taxes <u>create</u> a deadweight loss. The excess burden of a tax is the <u>deadweight loss</u> from the tax and is larger the <u>more</u> elastic the demand for the good being taxed.

True or false

1. False; pages 190-191
2. False; page 192
3. True; page 192
4. False; page 193
5. True; page 194

Multiple choice

1. d; page 190
2. b; page 191
3. c; page 191
4. d; page 192
5. a; page 191
6. c; page 191
7. e; page 191
8. c; page 192
9. c; page 192
10. b; page 193
11. b; page 193

Complete the graph

1. The axes are labeled in Figure 8.8.
   a. The price is $4 a slice and the quantity is 800 slices a day; page 191.
   b. Figure 8.8 shows the supply curve after the tax is imposed; page 191.
   c. Buyers pay $6 a slice; sellers receive $2 a slice. The tax is split equally; page 191.
   d. The deadweight loss is the grey triangle in Figure 8.8; page 192.

■ FIGURE 8.8

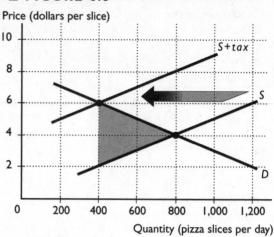

Price (dollars per slice)

Quantity (pizza slices per day)

■ FIGURE 8.9

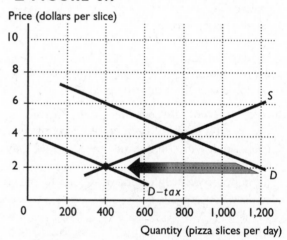

Price (dollars per slice)

Quantity (pizza slices per day)

2. The axes are labeled in Figure 8.9.
   a. Figure 8.9 shows the demand curve after the tax is imposed; page 191.
   b. Buyers pay $6 a slice; sellers receive $2 a slice. The tax is split equally; page 191.
   c. The price paid and the tax incidence is the same in problem 1, when the tax is imposed on sellers, and in problem 2, when the tax is imposed on buyers. The general principle is that the tax incidence depends on the elasticity of demand and the elasticity of supply, not on who sends the tax to the government; pages 191, 193.

Short answer and numeric questions

1. The equilibrium price is $2.00 a golf ball and the equilibrium quantity is 700 golf balls.

Price (dollars per golf ball)	After-tax quantity supplied (golf balls per month)
2.50	600
3.00	620

a. The completed supply schedule is in the table above; page 190.

b. $2.50 a golf ball and 600 golf balls; page 191.

c. The buyer pays $0.50 of the tax. The seller pays $1.50 of the tax; page 191.

d. The tax revenue is $2 a ball × 600 balls, which is $1,200; page 190.

2. The burden of the tax will fall mainly upon buyers, not the drug companies, because demand is inelastic and supply is elastic. Because the demand is inelastic, the decrease in the quantity will not be large and so the deadweight loss from the tax is small; page 193.

3. The excess burden of a tax is the same as the deadweight loss. The deadweight loss arises because the tax leads to less of the good or service being produced and consumed; page 192.

Additional Exercises (also in MyEconLab Test A)

1. Because the demand for cell phones is inelastic and the supply of cell phones is elastic, the buyer pays more of the tax on phones. Because the demand for calls is elastic and the supply is perfectly elastic, the buyer pays *all* of the tax on calls. The taxes decrease the number of cell phones. First, the tax on cell phones directly decreases the equilibrium quantity. Second, the tax on cell phone calls increases the price of cell phone calls, which are a complement to cell phones. The rise in the price of a complement decreases the demand for cell phones, further decreasing the equilibrium quantity of cell phones. The taxes decrease the number of cell phone calls. First, the tax on cell phone calls directly decreases the equilibrium quantity. Second, the tax on cell phones increases the price of cell phones, which are a complement to cell phone calls. The rise in the price of a complement decreases the demand for cell phone calls, further decreasing the equilibrium quantity of cell phone calls; pages 193-194.

2. The tax on cell phones raises more revenue for the government because the decrease in the equilibrium quantity of cell phones is less than the decrease in the quantity of cell phone calls. The tax on cell phones is paid only partly by the buyers, so the price does not rise by the full amount of the tax. And, the demand for cell phones is inelastic, so the higher price of a cell phone decreases the quantity by a relatively small proportion. The tax on cell phone calls is totally paid by the buyers, so the price rises by the full amount of the tax. And, the demand for cell phone calls is elastic, so the (much) higher price of a cell phone call decreases the quantity by a relatively large proportion. The excess burden is greatest on cell phone calls because both the rise in price and the decrease in quantity are greater for cell phone calls than for cell phones; pages 193-194.

3. The landlords pay a greater share of the tax because the supply of apartments is inelastic and the demand for apartments is elastic. The government will collect a large revenue from the tax because the equilibrium quantity does not decrease by much since the supply is inelastic. Even though the tax means that the suppliers receive less, with an inelastic supply the quantity supplied does not decrease substantially; page 194.

■ CHECKPOINT 8.2

Fill in the blanks

The percentage of an additional dollar that is paid in tax is a marginal tax rate. A tax is regressive if the average tax rate decreases as income increases. A tax on labor income creates a deadweight loss. If the supply of capital is perfectly elastic, a tax on capital income is paid entirely by the firms and the tax creates a deadweight loss. If the supply of land is perfectly <u>inelastic</u>, a tax on income from land is paid entirely by the landowners and the tax <u>does not create</u> a deadweight loss. A Social Security tax imposed on workers and a Social Security tax imposed on firms both <u>lower</u> the wage rate that employees receive and <u>decrease</u> employment.

True or false

1. True; page 197
2. True; page 197
3. False; page 197
4. True; page 198
5. False; page 199

Multiple choice

1. c; page 197
2. c; page 197
3. b; page 198
4. d; page 198
5. c; page 198
6. b; page 198
7. c; page 198
8. a; page 198
9. b; page 199
10. d; pages 200-201

Complete the graph

■ **FIGURE 8.10**

Wage rate (dollars per hour)

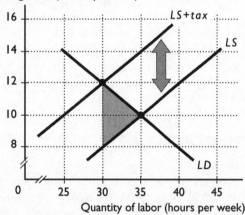

1. a. The curves are labeled *LD* and *LS* in Figure 8.10. The equilibrium wage rate is $10 an hour and the equilibrium quantity of labor is 35 hours a week; page 198.

b. The income tax decreases the supply of labor services. The labor supply curve shifts leftward from *LS* to *LS + tax*. The vertical distance between the two supply curves, indicated by the arrow, is equal to the $4 tax; page 198.

c. Firms pay a wage rate of $12 an hour; workers receive a wage rate of $8 an hour; page 198.

d. The deadweight loss is the grey triangle in Figure 8.10; page 198.

2. a. The equilibrium rent is $320 an acre per year and the equilibrium quantity of land is 30 billion acres; page 199.

b. After the tax, renters pay $320 an acre and landowners keep $310 an acre. The equilibrium quantity of land is 30 billion acres, the same as before the tax was imposed; page 199.

c. There is no deadweight loss created because the equilibrium quantity does not change. The amount produced remains the efficient quantity; page 199.

■ **FIGURE 8.11**

Wage rate (dollars per hour)

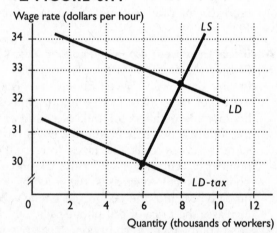

Quantity (thousands of workers)

3. a. Figure 8.11 shows the effect of the tax. Because the tax is imposed on firms, the tax decreases the demand for labor services and shifts the labor demand curve leftward. The vertical distance between the initial supply curve, *LD*, and the new supply curve, *LD + tax*, is the amount of the

tax, $3 an hour. The workers received $32.50 per hour before the tax and $30.00 after the tax; page 202.

b. Even though the tax is imposed on firms, the workers pay $2.50 of the $3.00 Social Security tax and the firms pay $0.50; page 202.

Short answer and numeric questions

1. Because capital is internationally mobile, its supply is highly (perhaps perfectly) elastic. If the supply of capital is perfectly elastic, firms pay the entire tax on capital income; page 199.

2. The burden of the Social Security tax is determined by the elasticity of supply and the elasticity of demand of labor, not by the law splitting the tax. If the demand for labor is more elastic than supply, the burden falls more on the worker and less on the employer. The government can legislate how the tax is collected, but cannot legislate the division of the tax's burden; pages 202-203.

Additional Exercises (also in MyEconLab Test A)

1. a. California's personal income tax is progressive; its corporate income tax is proportional; its sales tax and taxes on cigarettes and liquor are regressive. California's property taxes are progressive if the counties with higher property tax rates also have higher property values; page 197.

b. For two reasons, the tax that has the largest excess burden is probably the personal income tax. First, it has the highest marginal tax rate. Second, it is the largest tax, accounting for much more revenue than any of the other taxes. As a result, it probably has a large effect on the equilibrium quantity of labor and therefore a large excess burden; page 198.

■ CHECKPOINT 8.3

Fill in the blanks

The benefits principle is the proposition that people should pay taxes equal to the benefits they receive from public services. Imposing a higher sales tax on the purchase of jewelry than on food is fair according to the ability-to-pay principle. Horizontal equity requires that taxpayers with the same ability to pay do pay the same taxes. In the United States, the marriage tax problem is that a couple who both work often pay more taxes when they are married than when they are single.

True or false

1. False; page 206
2. False; page 206
3. True; page 207
4. False; pages 207-208
5. True; page 208

Multiple choice

1. d; page 206
2. c; page 206
3. b; page 206
4. d; page 206
5. b; page 207
6. c; page 207
7. d; page 207
8. a; page 208

Short answer and numeric questions

1. If the taxes necessary to fund the various welfare programs, such as food stamps, were assessed using the benefits principle of taxation, poor families would be required to pay the tax because they are the ones who benefit from the programs. But this outcome would defeat the purpose of the programs, which are designed to increase these families' incomes. The benefits principle of taxation does not work for government programs designed to increase the incomes of the poor; page 206.

2. The marriage tax problem is that a working couple pays more taxes if they are married than if they are single. Taxing the couple as single taxpayers violates horizontal equity because then two married couples with the same total income could pay different taxes depending on how much each partner earned; pages 207-208.

Additional Exercises (also in MyEconLab Test A)
1. The lowest marginal tax rate in Canada is higher than the lowest marginal tax rate in the United States. The highest marginal tax rates are almost the same. Because the tax rate is higher in Canada than in the United States, Canada places more weight on the ability-to-pay principle. Because the Canadian tax rate exceeds the U.S. tax rate, Canada places less weight on efficiency and more weight on fairness than does the United States; pages 206-208.

Global Markets in Action

Chapter **9**

1   Explain how markets work with international trade.

The goods and services that we buy from people in other countries are our imports and those we sell to people in other countries are our exports. Comparative advantage enables countries to gain from trade. A nation has a comparative advantage in producing a good if it can produce that good at a lower opportunity cost than another country. In this case, the domestic no-trade price is lower than the world price so with international trade the country exports this good. However if the domestic no-trade price is higher than the world price, with international trade the country imports the good.

2   Identify the gains from international trade and its winners and losers.

International trade lowers the prices of the goods and services imported into the country. The lower prices for imported goods mean that consumers gain additional consumer surplus from imports but the lower prices also mean that producers lose producer surplus. The gain to consumers, however, exceeds the loss to producers. International trade raises the prices of the goods and services exported from the country The higher prices for exported goods mean that producers gain additional producer surplus from exports but the higher prices also mean that consumers lose consumer surplus. The gain to producers, however, exceeds the loss to consumers.

3   Explain the effects of international trade barriers.

A tariff is a tax imposed on a good when it is imported. A tariff raises the domestic price of the good and reduces imports of it. A tariff increases domestic production of the good, decreases domestic consumption, and yields revenue for the government. It decreases consumer surplus, increases producer surplus and creates a deadweight loss. An import quota is a quantitative restriction on the import of a good that limits the maximum quantity of a good that may be imported in a given period of time. Voluntary export restraints are like an import quota given to exporters of the good. Import quotas and voluntary export restraints (VER) reduce imports, decrease domestic consumption, and increase domestic production. Both decrease consumer surplus, increase producer surplus, and create a deadweight loss. A subsidy is a payment by the government to a producer. Some countries subsidize products which are then exported. Export subsidies increase domestic production of the good but create deadweight losses.

4   Explain and evaluate arguments used to justify restricting international trade.

The three main arguments for protection and restriction of trade are the national security argument, the infant-industry argument, and the dumping argument. Each of these arguments is flawed. Other flawed arguments for protection are that protection saves jobs, allows us to compete with cheap foreign labor, brings diversity and stability, and penalizes lax environmental standards. Tariffs are imposed in some nations to gain revenue for the government. More generally, trade is restricted because of rent seeking from those who benefit from trade restrictions.

CHECKPOINT 9.1

■ Explain how markets work with international trade.

Quick Review

- *Imports* The goods and services that firms in one country buy from people and firms in other countries.
- *Exports* The goods and services that people and firms in one country sell to firms in other countries.
- *Comparative advantage* A nation has a comparative advantage in a good when its opportunity cost of producing the good is lower than any other nation's opportunity cost of producing the good.

Additional Practice Problem 9.1

1. The figure shows the market for CPU chips in the United States with no international trade. The world price for a CPU chip is $150.

Price (dollars per CPU chip)

   a. Does the United States have a comparative advantage in producing CPU chips? How can you tell?
   b. If international trade is allowed, will the United States import or export CPU chips?
   c. Will the quantity of CPU chips produced in the United States increase or decrease? By how much?
   d. Will the quantity of CPU chips consumed in the United States increase or decrease? By how much?
   e. How many CPU chips will the United States import or export?

Solution to Additional Practice Problem 9.1

1a. Because the price of a CPU chip in the United States is lower than the world price, the United States has a comparative advantage in producing CPU chips.

1b. Because the United States has a comparative advantage in producing CPU chips, the United States will export CPU chips.

1c. With international trade, the price of a CPU chip in the United States will be $150. At this price, the supply curve shows that the quantity of chips produced will equal 20 million per year. With no international trade, the equilibrium quantity of CPU chips produced is 15 million, so international trade leads to 5 million more chips being produced.

1d. With international trade, the price of a CPU chip in the United States will be $150. At this price, the demand curve shows that the quantity of chips demanded will equal 10 million per year. With no international trade, the equilibrium quantity of CPU chips consumed is 15 million, so international trade leads to 5 million fewer chips being consumed.

1e. The quantity of CPU chips exported equals the difference between the quantity of CPU chips produced, 20 million per year, and the quantity consumed, 10 million per year. So the United States will export 20 million CPU chips – 10 million CPU chips, which is 10 million CPU chips.

■ Self Test 9.1

Fill in the blanks

Global international trade accounts for about ____ (27; 50; 67) percent of global production. If a country can produce a good at a lower opportunity cost than any other country, the country has ____ (an export advantage; a comparative advantage) in the production of that good. The United States will export a good if its price in the United States with no international trade is ____ (lower; higher) than its world price. If the United States imports a good, then U.S. production of the good ____ (increases; decreases) and U.S. consumption of the good ____ (increases; decreases).

True or false

1. The United States is the world's largest international trader.

2. If a nation can produce a service at a lower opportunity cost than any other nation, the nation has a national comparative advantage in producing that service.

3. If the price of a good in the United States with no international trade is higher than the world price, then with international trade the United States will export that good.

4. As a result of international trade, the U.S. production of goods exported from the United States increases and the U.S. production of goods imported into the United States decreases.

Multiple choice

1. Goods and services that we buy from people and firms in other countries are called our
   a. imports.
   b. exports.
   c. inputs.
   d. raw materials.
   e. obligations.

2. If the United States exports planes to Brazil and imports ethanol from Brazil, the price received by U.S. producers of planes ____ and the price received by Brazilian producers of ethanol ____.
   a. does not change; does not change
   b. rises; rises
   c. rises; falls
   d. falls; rises
   e. falls; falls

3. When Italy buys Boeing jets, the price Italy pays is ____ if it produced its own jets and the price Boeing receives is ____ than it could receive from an additional U.S. buyer.
   a. lower than; lower
   b. higher than; higher
   c. lower than; higher
   d. higher than; lower
   e. the same as; higher

4. A nation will import a good if its no-trade, domestic
   a. price is equal to the world price.
   b. price is less than the world price.
   c. price is greater than the world price.
   d. quantity is less than the world quantity.
   e. quantity is greater than the world quantity.

5. When a good is imported, the domestic production of it ____ and the domestic consumption of it ____.
   a. increases; increases
   b. increases; decreases
   c. decreases; increases
   d. decreases; decreases
   e. increases; does not change

6. The United States exports a good if its no-trade U.S. price is ____ its world price. With international trade, U.S. production of the good ____ compared to the level of no-trade production.
   a. higher than; does not change
   b. higher than; increases
   c. lower than; increases
   d. the same as; increases
   e. the same as; does not change

Complete the graph

■ **FIGURE 9.1**

Price (dollars per bushel)

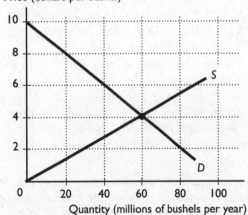

Quantity (millions of bushels per year)

1. Figure 9.1 shows the U.S. demand and supply curves for wheat.
   a. In the absence of international trade, what

is the price of a bushel of wheat in the United States?

b. If the world price of a bushel of wheat is $6 a bushel, will the United States import or export wheat? Above what world price for wheat will the United States export wheat? Below what world price for wheat will the United States import wheat?

Short answer and numeric questions

1. French cheese is flown to the United States abroad a United Airlines plane. Classify these transactions from the vantage point of the United States and from the vantage point of France.

Price (dollars per ton)	Quantity supplied (tons per year)	Quantity demanded (tons per year)
400	38	58
500	42	52
600	46	46
700	50	40
800	54	34
900	58	28

2. The table above has the U.S. demand and supply schedules for potatoes.

a. If there is no international trade, what is the equilibrium price and quantity of potatoes?

b. If the world price of potatoes is $800 a ton, what is the quantity supplied and the quantity demanded in the United States? Does the United States import or export potatoes? What quantity?

c. If the world price of potatoes rises to $900 a ton, what are the quantity supplied and the quantity demanded in the United States? Does the United States import or export potatoes? What quantity?

d. Would the United States ever import potatoes?

3. How does international trade affect the domestic production and domestic consumption of goods imported into the country?

Additional Exercises (also in MyEconLab Test A)

1. Suppose that the world price of bananas is 18 U.S. cents a pound and that when Australia does not trade bananas internationally, their equilibrium price in Australia is 12 U.S. cents a pound. If Australia opens up to international trade, does it export or import bananas? Explain how the price of bananas in Australia changes. How does the quantity of bananas consumed in Australia change? How does the quantity of bananas grown in Australia change?

2. Both the United States and Canada produce lumber and wine. Canada exports lumber and imports wine. The United States imports lumber and exports wine. If the United States and Canada did not trade internationally, compare the equilibrium prices of lumber and wine in the two countries with the world prices of lumber and wine. Compare the quantities of lumber that Americans buy with and without international trade, and compare the quantities of wine that Canadians buy with and without international trade. Also compare the quantities of lumber that Americans produce with and without international trade, and compare the quantities of wine that Canadians produce with and without international trade.

CHECKPOINT 9.2

■ Identify the gains from international trade and its winners and losers.

Quick Review

- *Consumer surplus* Consumer surplus is the marginal benefit from a good or service minus the price paid for it, summed over the quantity consumed.

- *Producer surplus* The producer surplus of a good equals the price of a good minus the marginal cost of producing it summed over the quantity produced.

Additional Practice Problem 9.2

1. The figure shows the U.S. market for CPU chips with no international trade. The world price for a CPU chip is $150.

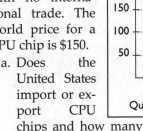

Price (dollars per CPU chip)

a. Does the United States import or export CPU chips and how many chips are imported or exported?

b. In the United States, tell who gains and who loses from the international trade and explain why they gain or lose. In the figure show the gains, the losses, and the net gain or net loss.

Solution to Additional Practice Problem 9.2

1a. The United States exports 15 million CPU chips per year. (20 million are produced in the United States and 5 million are consumed in the United States.)

1b. Producers of CPU chips gain and consumers of CPU chips lose. The gains and loses are in the figure. Producers gain because the price of a CPU chip with international trade is higher than the price without international trade, so the producer surplus increases. The increase in producer surplus is equal to the sum of the area of the dark grey triangle and the light grey trapezoid. Consumers lose for precisely the same reason producers gain: The price of a CPU chip is higher with international trade than without international trade, so the consumer surplus decreases. The decrease in consumer surplus is equal to

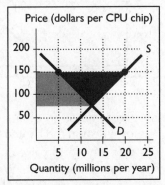

the area of the light grey trapezoid. On net, the economy gains from international trade. The increase in producer surplus is larger than the decrease in consumer surplus, as shown in the figure by the area of the dark grey triangle.

■ Self Test 9.2

Fill in the blanks

Imports ____ (decrease; increase) the producer surplus of domestic producers of the product and also ____ (decrease; increase) the consumer surplus of domestic consumers of the product. The consumer surplus from a good that would be exported is larger ____ (with; without) international trade and the consumer surplus from a good that would be imported is larger ____ (with; without) international trade. On net, society ____ (gains; loses) from international trade because the total surplus ____ (increases; decreases) with international trade.

True or false

1. International trade harms the nation.

2. Imports increase consumer surplus and decrease producer surplus.

3. The nation's total surplus increases when goods are exported.

4. Everyone in a nation gains from exports.

Multiple choice

1. International trade is definitely in the social interest if
   a. consumer surplus increases.
   b. producer surplus increases.
   c. consumer surplus does not decrease.
   d. producer surplus does not decrease.
   e. total surplus increases.

2. Imports ____ consumer surplus, ____ producer surplus, and ____ total surplus
   a. decrease; decrease; decrease
   b. increase; increase; increase
   c. increase; decrease; decrease
   d. increase; decrease; increase
   e. decrease; increase; increase

3. When a country imports a good, the ____ in consumer surplus is ____ the ____ in producer surplus.
   a. decrease; larger than; increase
   b. decrease; smaller than; increase
   c. increase; smaller than; decrease
   d. increase; equal to; decrease
   e. increase; larger than; decrease

4. When a country exports a good, the country's producer surplus ____, consumer surplus ____, and the country ____ from the trade.
   a. increases; increases; gains
   b. decreases; increases; gains
   c. increases; decreases; gains
   d. decreases; decreases; loses
   e. increases; decreases; loses

5. Which of the following is correct?
   i.   U.S. total surplus decreases when the United States exports a good.
   ii. U.S. total surplus decreases when the United States imports a good.
   iii. U.S. total surplus increases when the United States imports a good and when the United States exports a good.
   a. i only.
   b. iii only.
   c. i and ii.
   d. ii only.
   e. None of the above because the U.S. total surplus does not change as a result of trade.

Complete the graph
1. Figure 9.2 (at the top of the next column) shows the supply of and demand for sugar in the United States.
   a. If the world price of sugar is 10¢ a pound, draw the world price line in the figure. What is the quantity consumed in the United States, the quantity produced in the United States, and the quantity imported?
   b. Show the changes in consumer surplus, producer surplus, and total surplus once the United States imports sugar.

■ **FIGURE 9.2**
Price (cents per pound)

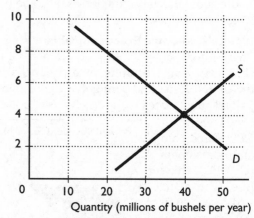

Quantity (millions of pounds per month)

■ **FIGURE 9.3**
Price (dollars per bushel)

Quantity (millions of bushels per year)

2. Figure 9.3 shows the supply of and demand for wheat in the United States.
   a. If the world price of wheat is $6 a bushel, draw the world price line in the figure. What is the quantity consumed in the United States, the quantity produced in the United States, and the quantity exported?
   b. Show the changes in consumer surplus, producer surplus, and total surplus once the United States exports wheat.

Short answer and numeric questions
1. How are the gains from international trade measured?

2. Why do consumers gain from imports?

3. Suppose the U.S. price of sugar without any international trade is 30¢ a pound. If the United States then allows international trade, when would the U.S. gain be the largest: when the international price is 20¢ a pound or when the international price is 10¢ a pound? Explain your answer.

4. Why doesn't everyone in a nation gain from exporting a good?

Additional Exercises (also in MyEconLab Test A)

The United States does not trade with Cuba. The price of a fine cigar is $20 in the United States and $2 in Cuba. The price of a basic car is $10,000 in the United States and $25,000 in Cuba. The world price of a fine cigar is $10 and the world price of a basic car is $15,000. Suppose that the two countries began to trade.

1. What would Cuba import and export? Who, in Cuba, would gain and who would lose from trade with the United States? Would Cuba gain from international trade? Draw graphs to illustrate your answer.

2. What would the United States import and export? Who in the United States would gain who would lose from trade with Cuba? Would the United States gain from international trade? Draw graphs to illustrate your answer.

CHECKPOINT 9.3

■ **Explain the effects of international trade barriers.**

Quick Review

- *Tariff* A tariff is a tax imposed on a good when it is imported.
- *Import Quota* An import quota is a quantitative restriction on the import of a good that limits the maximum quantity of a good that may be imported in a given period.

Additional Practice Problems 9.3

Price (dollars per ton of plywood)	U.S. quantity supplied (tons per month)	U.S. quantity demanded (tons per month)
1,000	600	1,400
750	500	1,600
500	300	1,800
250	100	2,000

1. The table above shows the U.S. supply and demand schedules for plywood. The United States also can buy plywood from Canada at the world price of $500 per ton.

   a. If there are no tariffs or other barriers to trade, what is the price of a ton of plywood in the United States? How much plywood is produced in the United States and how much is consumed? How much plywood is imported from Canada?

   b. Suppose that the United States imposes a $250 per ton tariff on all plywood imported into the country. What now is the price of a ton of plywood in the United States? How much plywood is produced in the United States and how much is consumed? How much plywood is imported from Canada?

   c. Who has gained from the tariff and who has lost?

2. For many years Japan conducted extremely slow, detailed, and costly safety inspections of *all* U.S. cars imported into Japan. In terms of trade, what was the effect of this inspection? How did the inspection affect the price and quantity of cars in Japan?

Solutions to Additional Practice Problems 9.3

1a. With no tariffs or nontariff barriers, the price of a ton of plywood is equal to the world price, $500 per ton. At this price, 300 tons per month are produced in the United States and 1,800 tons per month are consumed. The difference between the quantity consumed and the quantity produced, which is 1,500 tons per month, is imported from Canada.

1b. If a $250 per ton tariff is imposed, the price in the United States rises to $750 per ton. At this price, 500 tons per month are produced in the United States and 1,600 tons per month are consumed. The difference between the quantity consumed and the quantity produced, which is 1,100 tons per month, is imported from Canada.

1c. Gainers from the tariff are U.S. producers of plywood, who have a higher price for plywood and therefore increase their production, and the U.S. government, which gains tariff revenue. Losers are U.S. consumers, who consume less plywood with the tariff, and Canadian producers of plywood, who wind up exporting less plywood to the United States.

2. Japan's safety inspection (which has since been eliminated) was an example of a barrier to trade. It served a role similar to tariffs, import quotas, and VERs. The safety inspection added to the cost of selling cars in Japan. It raised the price of U.S. produced cars in Japan and decreased the quantity of U.S. cars sold. The Japanese government, however, received no tariff revenue.

■ Self Test 9.3

Fill in the blanks

A tax on a good that is imposed when the good is imported is ____ (an import quota; a tariff) and a specified maximum amount of a good that may be imported in a given period of time is ____ (an import quota; a tariff). A tariff ____ (raises; lowers) the price paid by domestic consumers, ____ (increases; decreases) the quantity produced by domestic producers, and ____ (creates; does not create) a deadweight loss. An import quota ____ (raises; lowers) the price paid by domestic consumers and ____ (increases; decreases) the quantity produced by domestic producers.

True or false

1. If the United States imposes a tariff, the price paid by U.S. consumers does not change.

2. If a country imposes a tariff on rice imports, domestic production of rice will increase and domestic consumption of rice will decrease.

3. A tariff increases the gains from trade for the exporting country.

4. An import quota on imports of a particular good specifies the minimum quantity of that good that can be imported in a given period.

Multiple choice

1. A tax imposed on a good when it is imported is called
   a. an import tax quota.
   b. a VER.
   c. a tariff.
   d. a sanction.
   e. a border tax.

2. The average U.S. tariff was highest in the
   a. 1930s.
   b. 1940s.
   c. 1970s.
   d. 1980s.
   e. 1990s.

3. Suppose the world price of a shirt is $10. If the United States imposes a tariff of $5 a shirt, then the price of a shirt in the
   a. United States falls to $5.
   b. United States rises to $15.
   c. world falls to $5.
   d. world rises to $5.
   e. world rises to $15.

4. When a tariff is imposed on a good, the ____ increases.
   a. domestic quantity purchased
   b. domestic quantity produced
   c. quantity imported
   d. quantity exported
   e. world price

5. When a tariff is imposed on a good, domestic consumers of the good ____ and domestic producers of the good ____.
   a. win; lose
   b. lose; win
   c. win; win
   d. lose; lose
   e. lose; neither win nor lose

6. Which of the following parties benefits from an import quota but not from a tariff?
   a. the domestic government
   b. domestic producers
   c. domestic consumers
   d. the person with the right to import the good
   e. the foreign government

Complete the graph

■ FIGURE 9.4

Price (cents per pound)

Quantity (millions of pounds per month)

1. Figure 9.4 shows the supply of and demand for sugar in the United States.
   a. If the world price of sugar is 10¢ a pound, draw the world price line in the figure. What is the quantity consumed in the United States, the quantity produced in the United States, and the quantity imported?
   b. Suppose the government imposes a 5¢ a pound tariff on sugar. Show the effect of the tariff in Figure 9.4. After the tariff, what is the quantity consumed in the United States, the quantity produced in the United States, and the quantity imported?
   c. Who wins and who loses from this tariff?

Short answer and numeric questions

Price (dollars per ton of steel)	U.S. quantity supplied (tons per month)	U.S. quantity demanded (tons per month)
1,000	20,000	20,000
750	17,000	22,000
500	14,000	24,000
250	11,000	26,000

1. The table above gives the U.S. supply and the U.S. demand schedules for steel. Suppose the world price of steel is $500 per ton.
   a. If there are no barriers to trade, what is the price of steel in the United States, the quantity of steel consumed in the United States, the quantity produced in the United States, and the quantity imported into the United States?
   b. If the U.S. government imposes a tariff of $250 per ton of steel, what is the price of steel in the United States, the quantity of steel consumed in the United States, the quantity produced in the United States, and the quantity imported into the United States?
   c. Instead of a tariff, if the U.S. government imposes an import quota of 5,000 tons of steel per month, what is the price of steel in the United States, the quantity of steel consumed in the United States, the quantity produced in the United States, and the quantity imported into the United States?
   d. Comparing your answers to parts (b) and (c), are U.S. consumers better off with the tariff or the import quota? Are U.S. producers better off with the tariff or the import quota?

2. Suppose the U.S. government imposes a tariff on sugar. How does the tariff affect the price of sugar, U.S. sugar consumers, and U.S. sugar producers?

3. Suppose the U.S. government imposes an import quota on sugar. How does the import quota affect the price of sugar, U.S. sugar consumers, and U.S. sugar producers?

4. Why do consumers lose from a tariff?

Additional Exercises (also in MyEconLab Test A)

Suppose that in response to huge job losses in the U.S. textile industry, Congress imposes a 100 percent tariff on imports of textiles from China. Use this formation to answer exercises 1 and 2.

1. Explain how the tariff on textiles will change the price of textiles, the quantity of textiles imported, and the quantity of textiles produced in the United States.

2. Explain how the U.S. and Chinese gains from trade will change. Who in the United States will lose and who will gain?

3. With free international trade between Australia and the United States, Australia would export beef to the United States. But the United States imposes an import quota on Australia beef. Explain how this import quota influences the price that U.S. consumers pay for beef, the quantity of beef produced in the United States, and the U.S. and Australian gains from trade. Who in the United States gains from the import quota on beef imports and who loses?

CHECKPOINT 9.4

■ **Explain and evaluate arguments used to justify restricting international trade.**

Quick Review

- *Rent seeking* Lobbying and other political activity that seeks to capture the gains from trade.

Additional Practice Problems 9.4

1. Pork is a popular food in China. China has occasionally limited U.S. exports of pork to China, most recently when swine flu was in the news. What argument might China make to limit imports of pork? Who in China would lose from this restriction of trade? Who would gain?

2. The United States has, from time to time, limited imports of lumber from Canada. What is the argument that the United States has used to

justify this import quota? Who wins from this restriction? Who loses?

3. In each of the first two Practice Problems, identify who is rent seeking.

Solutions to Additional Practice Problems 9.4

1. The primary argument China has made involves the health of Chinese consumers. In particular, China argues that it must prohibit pork imports from the United States because Chinese consumers might catch swine flu from it. This argument is scientifically flawed because swine flu is not transmitted through pork products. The losers from the Chinese limitations are Chinese consumers who must pay a higher price for the pork they buy. The gainers are the Chinese pork farmers and processors who enjoy a higher price for pork.

2. In past decades, the United States asserted that the lumber industry was needed because it played a major role in national defense. With the use of more exotic materials in defense armaments, the national defense argument has passed into history. More recently, the United States has set import quotas and tariffs allegedly for environmental reasons and allegedly because the Canadian government was subsidizing the production of lumber. Both of these arguments are probably not the true reason for the restrictions. The import quotas and tariffs are the result of political lobbying by lumber producers and lumber workers. The winners from the import quotas and tariffs are the lumber producers and lumber workers. The losers are all U.S. lumber consumers.

3. Rent seeking is lobbying and other political activity that seeks to capture the gains from trade. In Practice Problem 1, the Chinese producers of pork are rent seeking. In Practice Problem 2, the U.S. lumber producers and U.S. lumber workers are rent seeking. It is important to keep in mind that free trade promotes prosperity for all countries. Protection reduces the potential gains from trade

■ Self Test 9.4

Fill in the blanks

The assertion that it is necessary to protect a new industry to enable it to grow into a mature industry that can compete in world markets is the ____ (infant-industry; maturing-industry) argument. Dumping occurs when ____ (U.S. jobs are lost to cheap foreign labor; a foreign firm sells its exports at a lower price than its cost of production). Protection ____ (is; is not) necessary to bring diversity and stability to our economy. Protection ____ (is; is not) necessary to penalize countries with lax environmental standards. The major reason why international trade is restricted is because ____ (foreign countries protect their industries; of rent seeking).

True or false

1. The national security argument is the only valid argument for protection.
2. Dumping by a foreign producer is easy to detect.
3. Protection saves U.S. jobs at no cost.
4. International trade is an attractive source for tax collection in developing countries

Multiple choice

1. The national security argument is used by those who assert they want to
   a. increase imports as a way of strengthening their country.
   b. increase exports as a way of earning money to strengthen their country.
   c. limit imports that compete with domestic producers important for national defense.
   d. limit exports to control the flow of technology to third world nations.
   e. limit all imports.

2. The argument that it is necessary to protect a new industry to enable it to grow into a mature industry that can compete in world markets is the
   a. national security argument.
   b. diversity argument.
   c. infant-industry argument.
   d. environmental protection argument.
   e. national youth protection argument.

3. ____ occurs when a foreign firm sells its exports at a lower price than its cost of production.
   a. Dumping
   b. The trickle-down effect
   c. Rent seeking
   d. Tariff avoidance
   e. Nontariff barrier protection

4. The United States
   a. needs tariffs to allow us to compete with cheap foreign labor.
   b. does not need tariffs to allow us to compete with cheap foreign labor.
   c. should not trade with countries that have cheap labor.
   d. will not benefit from trade with countries that have cheap labor.
   e. avoids trading with countries that have cheap labor.

5. Why do governments in less-developed nations impose tariffs?
   a. The government gains revenue from the tariff.
   b. The government's low-paid workers are protected from high-paid foreign workers.
   c. The nation's total income is increased.
   d. The national security of the country definitely is improved.
   e. The government helps diversify its economy.

6. What is a major reason international trade is restricted in developed countries?
   a. rent seeking
   b. to allow competition with cheap foreign labor
   c. to save jobs
   d. to prevent dumping
   e. for national security

Short answer and numeric questions

1. What is the dumping argument for protection? What is its flaw?
2. How do you respond to a speaker who says that we need to limit auto imports from Japan in order to save U.S. jobs?

3. Why is it incorrect to assert that trade with countries that have lax environmental standards needs to be restricted?

4. The Eye on Your Life discusses the role international trade plays in your life. Suppose you get a job working for Frito Lay, the maker of corn chips (and other snacks). Frito Lay is a big user of corn. Corn can also be used to produce ethanol and increasingly more ethanol is being used as a replacement (or additive) fuel for gasoline. Currently the U.S. government places a hefty tariff on ethanol imported from Brazil. As a representative of Frito Lay, would you be in favor of this tariff? Explain your answer.

Additional Exercises (also in MyEconLab Test A)

1. Venezuelan president Hugo Chavez opposes the creation of a Free Trade Area of the Americas (FTAA). Why? Who does he think will gain and lose? Do you think he is correct?

2. Hong Kong has never restricted trade. What gains has Hong Kong reaped by unilaterally adopting free trade with all nations? Is there any argument for restricted trade that might have benefited Hong Kong?

SELF TEST ANSWERS

■ CHECKPOINT 9.1

Fill in the blanks

Global international trade accounts for about <u>27</u> percent of global production. If a country can produce a good at a lower opportunity cost than any other country, the country has <u>a comparative advantage</u> in the production of that good. The United States will export a good if its price in the United States with no international trade is <u>lower</u> than its world price. If the United States imports a good, then U.S. production of the good <u>decreases</u> and U.S. consumption of the good <u>increases</u>.

True or false

1. True; page 214
2. True; page 214
3. False; pages 216-217
4. True; page 216

Multiple choice

1. a; page 214
2. b; page 214
3. c; page 214
4. c; page 216
5. c; page 216
6. c; page 217

Complete the graph

1. a. In the absence of international trade, the equilibrium price of a bushel of wheat in the United States is $4; pages 216-217.

   b. If the world price of a bushel of wheat is $6 a bushel, the United States will export wheat because the world price exceeds the no-trade price. If the price of wheat exceeds $4 a bushel, the United States will export wheat. If the price of wheat is less than $4 a bushel, the United States will import wheat; pages 216-217.

Short answer and numeric questions

1. From the U.S. vantage, the cheese is an imported good and the air transportation is an exported service. From the French vantage, the cheese is an exported good and the air transportation is an imported service; page 214.

2. a. In the absence of international trade, the equilibrium price is $600 a ton and the equilibrium quantity is 46 tons; pages 216-217.

   b. In the United States, the quantity supplied is 54 tons and the quantity demanded is 34 tons. The United States exports 20 tons of potatoes; page 217.

   c. In the United States, the quantity supplied is 58 tons and the quantity demanded is 28 tons. The United States exports 30 tons of potatoes; page 217.

   d. The United States would import potatoes if the world price is less than $600 a ton; page 216.

3. International trade lowers the domestic price of imported goods. The lower price increases the quantity domestic demanders consume and decreases the quantity domestic suppliers produce; page 216.

Additional Exercises (also in MyEconLab Test A)

1. With no international trade, the price in Australia is less than that in the world, so Australia has a comparative advantage in producing bananas. As a result, if Australia opens up to international trade, it will export bananas. With international trade, the price of bananas in Australia rises. The higher price leads to a decrease in the quantity of bananas consumed in Australia. The higher price also leads to an increase in the quantity of bananas grown in Australia; page 217.

2. Canada exports wood, so Canada has a comparative advantage in producing wood. If Canada did not trade internationally, the price of wood in Canada would be less than the world price. Canada imports wine, so Canada does *not* have a comparative advantage in producing wine. If Canada did not trade internationally, the price of wine in Canada would be higher than the world price. The United States exports wine, so the

United States has a comparative advantage in producing wine. If the United States did not trade internationally, the price of wine in the United States would be less than the world price. The United States imports wood, so the United States does *not* have a comparative advantage in producing wood. If the United States did not trade internationally, the price of wood in the United States would be higher than the world price.

With international trade, Americans buy more wood because the price of wood is lower in the United States with international trade than it would be without international trade. With international trade, Canadians buy more wine because the price of wine is lower in Canada with international trade than it would be without international trade.

With international trade, the quantity of wood produced in the United States is less than it would be without international trade because international trade lowers the price of wood in the United States. With international trade, the quantity of wine produced in Canada is less than it would be without international trade because international trade lowers the price of wine in Canada; pages 216-217.

■ CHECKPOINT 9.2

Fill in the blanks

Imports <u>decrease</u> the producer surplus of domestic producers of the product and also <u>increase</u> the consumer surplus of domestic consumers of the product. The consumer surplus from a good that would be exported is larger <u>without</u> international trade and the consumer surplus from a good that would be imported is larger <u>with</u> international trade. On net, society <u>gains</u> from international trade because the total surplus <u>increases</u> with international trade.

True or false

1. False; pages 220-221
2. True; page 220
3. True; page 221
4. False; page 221

Multiple choice

1. e; page 219
2. d; page 220
3. e; page 220
4. c; page 221
5. b; pages 220-221

Complete the graph

■ FIGURE 9.5

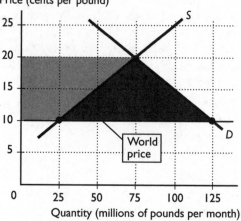

Price (cents per pound)

Quantity (millions of pounds per month)

1. a. Figure 9.5 shows the world price line. At this price, 125 million pounds of sugar per month are consumed in the United States and 25 million pounds of sugar are produced in the United States. The difference, 100 million pounds of sugar per month, is imported into the United States; page 220.

   b. Consumer surplus increases. The increase in consumer surplus is equal to the sum of the area of the lighter grey trapezoid plus the area of the dark grey triangle in Figure 9.5. The producer surplus decreases. The decrease is equal to the area of the light grey trapezoid. On net, total surplus increases. The net increase is equal to the area of the dark grey triangle; page 220.

2. a. Figure 9.6 shows the world price line. At this price, 30 million bushels of wheat per year are consumed in the United States and 50 million bushels of wheat are produced in the United States. The difference, 20 million bushels of wheat per year, is exported from the United States; page 221.

■ **FIGURE 9.6**
Price (dollars per bushel)

b. Consumer surplus decreases. The decrease in consumer surplus is equal to the area of the lighter grey trapezoid in Figure 9.6. The producer surplus increases. The increase is equal to the sum of the area of the light grey trapezoid plus the area of the dark grey triangle. On net, total surplus increases. The increase is equal to the area of the dark grey triangle; page 221.

Short answer and numeric questions

1. The gains from international trade are measured as increases in consumer surplus or in producer surplus. The net gain from international trade is measured as the gain in the total surplus; page 219.

2. Consumers gain from imports because international trade lowers the prices of imported goods and services. Consumer surplus increases because the price is lower and because the lower price leads consumers to buy more of the good or service; page 220.

3. Consumers are the group that gains from imports. Consumers gain because international trade lowers the prices of imported goods and services, which then increases their consumer surplus. The increase in consumer surplus will be larger the lower the price. So the United States gains more if the international price of sugar is 10¢ a pound rather than 20¢ a pound; page 220.

4. When a good is exported, its domestic price rises. Producers gain from the higher price but consumers lose. (The gain to the producers, however, is larger than the loss to consumers.) So not everyone gains when a good is exported because consumers of that good lose; page 221.

Additional Exercises (also in MyEconLab Test A)

■ **FIGURE 9.7**
Price (thousands of dollars per car)

1. Cuba would import cars and export cigars. Producers of cigars and consumers of cars would gain from international trade. Producers of cars and consumers of cigars would lose from international trade.

With the world price of a car of $15,000, Figure 9.7 shows the situation in Cuba in the market for cars. Producers of cars lose producer surplus equal to the lighter gray area. Consumers of cars gain this gray area as additional consumer surplus *and* they also gain the dark grey area as still more consumer surplus. So the net gain for the Cuban economy is the dark grey area.

With the world price of a cigar of $10, Figure 9.8 (on the next page) shows the situation in Cuba in the market for cigars. Consumers of cigars lose consumer surplus equal to the lighter grey area. Producers of cigars gain this gray area as additional producer surplus *and*

■ **FIGURE 9.8**
Price (dollars per cigar)

Quantity of cigars (millions of cigars per year)

■ **FIGURE 9.9**
Price (dollars per cigar)

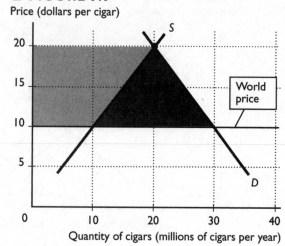

Quantity of cigars (millions of cigars per year)

■ **FIGURE 9.10**
Price (thousands of dollars per car)

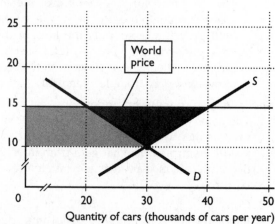

Quantity of cars (thousands of cars per year)

they also gain the dark grey area as still more producer surplus. So the net gain for the Cuban economy is the dark grey area.

The Cuban economy, overall, would gain from international trade; pages 220-221.

2. The United States would import cigars and export cars. Producers of cars and consumers of cigars would gain from international trade. Producers of cigars and consumers of cars would lose from international trade.

With the world price of a cigar of $10, Figure 9.9 shows the situation in the United States in the market for cigars. Producers of cigars lose producer surplus equal to the lighter gray area. Consumers of cigars gain this gray area as additional consumer surplus *and* they also gain the dark grey area as still more consumer surplus. So the net gain for the U.S. economy is the dark grey area.

With the world price of a car of $15,000, Figure 9.10 shows the situation in the United States in the market for cars. Consumers of cars lose consumer surplus equal to the lighter gray area. Producers of cars gain this gray area as additional producer surplus *and* they also gain the dark grey area as still more producer surplus. So the net gain for the U.S. economy is the dark grey area. The U.S. economy would gain from this international trade; pages 220-221.

■ **CHECKPOINT 9.3**

Fill in the blanks

A tax on a good that is imposed when the good is imported is a <u>tariff</u> and a specified maximum amount of a good that may be imported is called <u>an import quota</u>. A tariff <u>raises</u> the price paid by domestic consumers, <u>increases</u> the quantity produced by domestic producers, and <u>creates</u> a deadweight loss. An import quota <u>raises</u> the price paid by domestic consumers and <u>increases</u> the quantity produced by domestic producers.

True or false

1. False; page 224
2. True; page 224
3. False; page 226
4. False; page 227

Multiple choice

1. c; page 223
2. a; page 223
3. b; page 224
4. b; page 224
5. b; pages 225-226
6. d; page 227

Complete the graph

■ **FIGURE 9.11**

Price (cents per pound)

Quantity (millions of pounds per month)

1. a. The world price line is shown in Figure 9.11. 125 million pounds of sugar are consumed in the United States, 25 million pounds are produced in the United States, and 100 million pounds are imported into the United States; page 224.

   b. The tariff increases the domestic price, as shown in the figure. The quantity consumed in the United States decreases to 100 million pounds, the quantity produced in the United States increases to 50 million pounds, and the amount imported decreases to 50 million pounds; page 224.

   c. Consumers lose because consumer surplus decreases. Producers gain because producer surplus increases. The govern-

ment also gains because it raises revenue from the tariff; page 226.

Short answer and numeric questions

1. a. The price is the world price, $500 per ton. At this price, the quantity consumed in the United States is 24,000 tons per month, the quantity produced in the United States is 14,000 tons per month, and the quantity imported is the difference, 10,000 tons per month; page 224.

   b. With a $250 per ton tariff, the price is $750 per ton. At this price, the quantity consumed in the United States is 22,000 tons per month, the quantity produced in the United States is 17,000 tons per month, and the quantity imported is the difference, 5,000 tons per month; page 224.

   c. With an import quota of 5,000 tons per month, the total supply schedule equals the U.S. supply schedule plus an additional 5,000 tons per month. The price of steel is $750 per ton because this is the price that sets the U.S. quantity demanded (22,000 tons) equal to the U.S. quantity supplied (17,000 tons) plus the quantity that can be imported (5,000 tons). At this price, the quantity consumed in the United States is 22,000 tons per month and the quantity produced in the United States is 17,000 tons per month; page 227.

   d. U.S. consumers are no better off or worse off with the tariff or the import quota because both raise the price to $750 per ton and decrease the quantity consumed to 22,000 tons. U.S. producers are no better off or worse off with the tariff or the import quota because both raise the price to $750 per ton and increase the quantity produced to 17,000 tons; page 227.

2. The tariff raises the price of sugar. U.S. sugar consumers decrease the quantity they purchase and U.S. sugar producers increase the quantity they produce; pages 224-226.

3. The import quota has the same effects as the tariff in the previous question. The import quota raises the price of sugar. U.S. sugar

consumers decrease the quantity purchased and U.S. sugar producers increase the quantity produced; page 227.

4. Consumers lose from a tariff because the tariff raises the price they pay and the quantity bought decreases. The tariff makes people pay more than the opportunity cost of the good. Society also loses because the tariff creates a deadweight loss; page 226.

Additional Exercises (also in MyEconLab Test A)

1. Higher tariffs increase the price U.S. consumers pay for textiles imported from China. Because the price of Chinese imported textiles rises, the quantity imported decreases. The quantity of textiles produced in the United States increases; page 224.

2. This trade restriction means that the U.S. and Chinese gains from trade definitely decrease. Textile workers and owners of textile firms will gain from the higher price. Textile consumers will lose from the higher price; pages 225-226.

3. By restricting the amount of beef imported into the United States, the import quota raises the price of beef to U.S. consumers. The quantity of beef produced in the United States increases. The U.S. and Australian gains from trade are reduced by the U.S. import quota. U.S. beef producers and their workers gain from the import quota on beef. In addition, the importers who have the right to import beef gain. U.S. consumers lose from the higher price of beef; pages 227-228.

■ CHECKPOINT 9.4

Fill in the blanks

The assertion that it is necessary to protect a new industry to enable it to grow into a mature industry that can compete in world markets is the infant-industry argument. Dumping occurs when a foreign firm sells its exports at a lower price than its cost of production. Protection is not necessary to bring diversity and stability to our economy. Protection is not necessary to penalize countries with lax environmental stand-

ards. The major reason why international trade is restricted is because of rent seeking.

True or false

1. False; page 231
2. False; page 232
3. False; page 233
4. True; page 234

Multiple choice

1. c; page 231
2. c; page 231
3. a; page 232
4. b; page 233
5. a; page 234
6. a; page 235

Short answer and numeric questions

1. Dumping occurs when a foreign firm sells its exports at a lower price than its cost of production. The dumping argument is flawed for the following reasons. First, it is virtually impossible to detect dumping because it is hard to determine a firm's costs and the fair market price. Second, it is hard to think of a good that is produced by a global natural monopoly. Third, if a firm truly was a global natural monopoly, the best way to deal with it would be by regulation; page 232.

2. Saving jobs is one of the oldest arguments in favor of protection. It is also incorrect. Protecting a particular industry will likely save jobs in that industry but will cost many other jobs in other industries. The cost to consumers of saving a job is many times the wage rate of the job saved; page 233.

3. The assertion that trade with developing countries that have lax environmental standards should be restricted to "punish" the developing nation for its lower standards is weak. Everyone wants a clean environment, but not every country can afford to devote resources toward this goal. The rich nations can afford this expenditure of resources, but for many poor nations protecting the environment takes second place to more pressing problems such as feeding their people. These

nations must develop and grow economically in order to be able to afford to protect their environment. One important way to help these poorer nations grow is by trading with them. Through trade these nations' incomes increase and with this increase also increases their ability and willingness to protect the environment; page 234.

4. The tariff on ethanol imported from Brazil severely limits the quantity of ethanol that can be imported and, by so doing, keeps the price of ethanol high in the United States. The high price for ethanol increases the demand for U.S. corn to be processed into ethanol. The higher demand for corn means that the tariff on ethanol keeps the price of corn in the United States higher than it would be in the absence of the tariff. As a representative of Frito Lay, your interest lies in lowering the price of corn. So you would be in favor of lowering or eliminating entirely this tariff; page 224.

Additional Exercises (also in MyEconLab Test A)

1. Mr. Chavez argues against the Free Trade Area of the Americas because he thinks that poor workers in nations such as Venezuela and other countries will be harmed by the trade. He also worries that U.S. firms will come to dominate markets in other countries. He is likely incorrect on both counts. First, poor workers in Venezuela will benefit from increased trade with the United States because the trade will increase the demand for their labor and thereby lead to higher wage rates. Second, it is unlikely U.S. firms will be able to dominate markets in other countries because to do so U.S. firms would need some sort of cost advantage over their foreign rivals, which is unlikely; pages 232-234.

2. Hong Kong has one of the most successful economies in the world as a result of adopting unilateral free trade. Both its exports and imports increased a result. There really isn't any argument for restricted free trade that might have benefited Hong Kong; page 235.

Externalities

Chapter 10

An externality is a cost or benefit that arises from production and that falls on someone other than its producer or a cost or benefit that arises from consumption and that falls on someone other than the consumer. A negative externality imposes an external cost and a positive externality provides an external benefit. Externalities in an unregulated market lead to inefficiency and create a deadweight loss.

1 **Explain why negative externalities lead to inefficient overproduction and how property rights, pollution charges, and taxes can achieve a more efficient outcome.**

Marginal private cost (MC) is the cost of producing an additional unit of a good or service that is borne by the producer of that good or service. Marginal external cost is the cost of producing an additional unit of a good or service that falls on people other than the producer. Marginal social cost (MSC), the marginal cost incurred by society, is the sum of marginal private cost and marginal external cost. Producers take account only of marginal private cost and overproduce when there is a marginal external cost. Sometimes it is possible to reduce the inefficiency arising from an externality by establishing a property right where one does not currently exist. The Coase theorem is the proposition that if property rights exist, only a small number of parties are involved, and transactions costs are low, then private transactions are efficient and the outcome is not affected by who is assigned the property right. When property rights cannot be assigned, the three main methods that governments can use to cope with externalities are pollution limits (a quantity limit on pollution), pollution charges or taxes (a fee equal to the marginal external cost of the pollution that producers must pay), and marketable pollution permits, also called cap-and-trade (firms are issued permits that allow a certain amount of pollution; the permits can be bought and sold).

2 **Explain why positive externalities lead to inefficient underproduction and how public provision, subsidies, and vouchers can achieve a more efficient outcome.**

Marginal private benefit (MB) is the benefit from an additional unit of a good or service that the consumer of that good or service receives. Marginal external benefit is the benefit from an additional unit of a good or service that people other than the consumer of the good or service enjoy. Marginal social benefit (MSB), the marginal benefit enjoyed by society, is the sum of marginal private benefit and marginal external benefit. External benefits from education arise because better-educated people are better citizens, commit fewer crimes, and support social activities. When people make decisions about how much schooling to obtain, they neglect its external benefit. The result is that if education were provided only by private schools that charged full-cost tuition, we would produce too few graduates. Three devices that governments can use to overcome the inefficiency created by external benefits are public provision, subsidies (payments to the producers by the government), and vouchers.

CHECKPOINT 10.1

■ **Explain why negative externalities lead to inefficient overproduction and how property rights, pollution charges, and taxes can achieve a more efficient outcome.**

Quick Review

- *Marginal external cost* The cost of producing an additional unit of a good or service that falls on people other than the producer.
- *Efficiency* Efficiency is achieved when the marginal social benefit equals the marginal social cost.
- *Coase theorem* If property rights exist, only a small number of parties are involved, and transactions costs are low, then private transactions are efficient and the outcome is not affected by who is assigned the property right.

Additional Practice Problems 10.1

1. The figure illustrates the unregulated market for paper. When factories produce paper, they also create air pollution. The cost of the pollution is $1,500 per ton. The pollution is a marginal external cost.

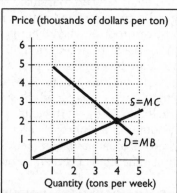

a. What is the quantity of paper produced in an unregulated market? What is the price of a ton of paper?

b. Draw the marginal social cost curve in the figure. What is the efficient quantity of paper to produce?

c. If the government imposed a tax on the firms, what must the tax equal to have the efficient quantity of paper produced? With this tax imposed, what is the equilibrium price of a ton of paper?

2. Two factories each emit 10 tons of the pollutant sulfur dioxide a week. The cost to eliminate a ton of sulfur dioxide to Factory A is $4 and the cost to Factory B is $2. The government wants to eliminate 10 tons of sulfur dioxide a week.

a. If the government requires that Firm A decrease emissions by 10 tons a week, what is the cost of eliminating the pollution?

b. If the government requires that Firm B decrease emissions by 10 tons a week, what is the cost of the eliminating the pollution?

c. If the government gives each firm 5 marketable permits, each permit allowing 1 ton of pollution, what will occur?

Solutions to Additional Practice Problems 10.1

1a. The equilibrium is determined by the intersection of the demand and supply curves. So the equilibrium quantity is 4 tons of paper per week and the equilibrium price is $2,000 per ton.

1b. The figure shows the marginal social cost curve, labeled *MSC*. At 1 ton of paper this curve lies $1,500 above the supply curve; at 2

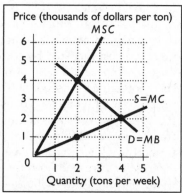

tons of paper it lies $3,000 above the supply curve; and so on. The efficient quantity is where the marginal social cost equals the marginal benefit, which the figure shows, is 2 tons of paper.

1c. To lead to efficiency, the tax must equal the marginal external cost. So the tax should be $1,500 per ton. At the efficient quantity of 2 tons, the tax is $3,000. With this tax, the equilibrium price is $4,000 per ton of paper.

2a. The cost for Firm A to decrease emissions is $4 a ton multiplied by 10 tons, which is $40 a week.

2b. The cost for Firm B to decrease emissions is $2 a ton multiplied by 10 tons, which is $20 a week.

2c. Firm A is willing to buy permits from Firm B for any price less than $4 per permit; Firm B is willing to sell permits to Firm A for any price greater than $2 per permit. The two companies will settle on a price and Firm A will buy 5 permits from Firm B. Only Firm B will decrease its pollution and incur a cost of $20 a week.

■ Self Test 10.1

Fill in the blanks

Marginal social cost equals marginal private cost ____ (minus; plus) marginal external cost. A pollution externality creates an ____ (efficient; inefficient) equilibrium. According to the Coase theorem, if property rights exist, then private transactions are efficient and the outcome ____ (is; is not) affected by who is assigned the property right. By setting the pollution tax rate equal to the marginal ____ (external; private; social) cost, firms behave in the same way as they would if they bore the cost of the externality directly.

True or false

1. All externalities are negative.

2. Smoking on a plane creates a negative externality.

3. Marginal social cost equals marginal private cost minus marginal external cost.

4. Copper mining creates land pollution. If the copper mining industry is unregulated, then the quantity of copper mined is less than the efficient quantity.

5. The Coase theorem concludes that if property rights to a polluted river are assigned to the polluter, the quantity of pollution will increase.

6. Pollution charges require the government to set the price for a unit of pollution.

7. By issuing marketable permits, the government sets the price for each unit of pollution produced.

8. If the government imposes a pollution tax on lead mining equal to its marginal external cost, the quantity of lead mined will be the efficient quantity.

Multiple choice

1. Which of the following best describes an externality?
   a. something that is external to the economy
   b. a sales tax on a good in addition to the market price
   c. an effect of a transaction felt by someone other than the consumer or producer
   d. anything produced in other countries
   e. a change from what is normal

2. Pollution is an example of a ____ externality.
   a. negative production
   b. positive production
   c. negative consumption
   d. positive consumption
   e. Coasian

3. Which of the following is an example of an external cost?
   i. second-hand smoke
   ii. sulfur emitting from a smoke stack
   iii. garbage on the roadside
   a. i only.
   b. ii only.
   c. iii only.
   d. ii and iii.
   e. i, ii, and iii.

4. The cost of producing one more unit of a good or service that is borne by the producer of that good or service
   a. always equals the benefit the consumer derives from that good or service.
   b. equals the cost borne by people other than the producer.
   c. is the marginal private cost.
   d. is the external cost.
   e. is the marginal social cost.

5. The cost of producing an additional unit of a good or service that falls on people other than the producer is
   a. the marginal cost.
   b. represented by the demand curve.
   c. represented by the supply curve.
   d. the marginal external cost.
   e. the marginal social cost.

6. The marginal cost of production that is borne by the entire society is the marginal
   a. private cost.
   b. social cost.
   c. external cost.
   d. public cost.
   e. user cost.

7. If the marginal private cost of producing one kilowatt of power in California is 8¢ and the marginal social cost of each kilowatt is 13¢, then the marginal external cost equals ____ a kilowatt.
   a. 8¢
   b. 13¢
   c. 5¢
   d. 0¢
   e. 21¢

8. When the production of a good has a marginal external cost, which of the following will occur in an unregulated market?
   i. Overproduction relative to the efficient level will occur
   ii. The market price will be less than the marginal social cost at the equilibrium quantity
   iii. A deadweight loss will occur
   a. i only.
   b. ii only.
   c. iii only.
   d. i and ii.
   e. i, ii, and iii.

■ **FIGURE 10.1**

9. Figure 10.1 shows the market for a good with an external cost. The external cost equals ____.
   a. $5
   b. $10
   c. $15
   d. $20
   e. $25

10. Figure 10.1 shows the market for a good with an external cost. If the market is unregulated, the equilibrium quantity is ____ tons per year.
    a. 0
    b. 100
    c. 200
    d. 300
    e. 400

11. Figure 10.1 shows the market for a good with an external cost. The efficient quantity is ____ tons per year.
    a. 0
    b. 100
    c. 200
    d. 300
    e. 400

12. The Coase theorem is the proposition that if property rights exist, a small number of people are involved, and transactions costs are low, then private transactions are
    a. inefficient.
    b. efficient.
    c. inequitable.
    d. illegal.
    e. unnecessary.

13. If a polluting producers are required to pay a pollution charge or a pollution tax, what is the effect on the supply and demand curves for the product?
    a. The quantity supplied along the supply curve will increase.
    b. The demand curve shifts leftward.
    c. The supply curve shifts rightward.
    d. The supply curve shifts leftward.
    e. *Both* the supply curve and the demand curve shift leftward.

14. A marketable pollution permit
    a. allows firms to pollute all they want without any cost.
    b. allows firms to buy additional rights to pollute from the government.
    c. eliminates pollution by setting the price of pollution permits above the marginal cost of polluting.
    d. allows firms to buy and sell the right to pollute from other firms.
    e. is the Coase solution to pollution.

15. If we compare air pollution today to air pollution in 1980, we see that
    a. pollution of all forms has increased.
    b. pollution of all forms has been reduced.
    c. pollution of most types has been decreased.
    d. pollution from lead has increased.
    e. pollution of most types has not changed.

Complete the graph

Quantity (megawatts per day)	Marginal private cost (dollars)	Marginal social cost (dollars)	Marginal benefit (dollars)
1	5	10	50
2	10	20	40
3	15	30	30
4	20	40	20

1. The table above shows the marginal private cost, marginal social cost, and marginal benefit schedules for generating electricity.
    a. In Figure 10.2, label the axes and then plot the marginal private cost curve, the marginal social cost curve, and the marginal benefit curve.

■ **FIGURE 10.2**

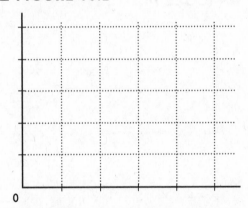

    b. How much electricity will an unregulated market produce? What is the marginal external cost at this amount of production?
    c. What is the efficient amount of electricity? Illustrate the deadweight loss resulting from the unregulated market equilibrium.
    d. At the efficient quantity of electricity, what is the marginal external cost? If the government imposes a pollution tax on producing electricity, in order to eliminate the deadweight loss, what should be the amount of tax? How much electricity is generated and what is its price?

Quantity (tons per day)	Marginal private cost (dollars)	Marginal benefit (dollars)
1	200	600
2	300	500
3	400	400
4	500	300

2. The table above shows the marginal private cost and marginal benefit schedules for producing PBDE, a chemical flame retardant. Suppose that there is an external cost of $100 per ton of PBDE produced.

a. In Figure 10.3, label the axes and then plot the marginal private cost curve, the marginal social cost curve, and the marginal benefit curve.

■ **FIGURE 10.3**

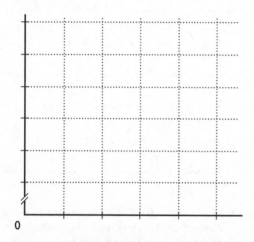

0

b. How much PBDE will an unregulated market produce? What is the equilibrium price? What is the amount of the marginal external cost at the equilibrium quantity of production?

c. What is the efficient amount of PBDE? At the efficient quantity, what is the amount of the marginal external cost?

d. If the government set an pollution charge for producing PBDE, what must the charge equal to lead to the efficient quantity of PBDE?

Short answer and numeric questions

1. If the marginal social cost curve lies above the marginal private cost curve, is there an external cost or benefit from production of the good or service?

Quantity (tons of pesticide per day)	Marginal private cost (dollars per ton)	Marginal external cost (dollars per ton)	Marginal social cost (dollars per ton)
1	100	___	130
2	120	40	___
3	___	60	210
4	190	___	280
5	240	120	___

2. The table above shows the costs of producing pesticide. Complete the table.

3. According to the Coase theorem, when are private transactions efficient?

4. The production of fertilizer creates water pollution. How do pollution charges and pollution taxes result in an efficient quantity of production? What information must the government possess to use pollution charges and pollution taxes effectively?

5. What is a marketable permit? What advantage do marketable permits have over the government assigning each firm a limit on how much it can pollute?

CHECKPOINT 10.2

■ **Explain why positive externalities lead to inefficient underproduction and how public provision, subsidies, and vouchers can achieve a more efficient outcome.**

Quick Review

- *Marginal external benefit* The benefit from an additional unit of a good or service that people other than the consumer of the good or service enjoy.

Additional Practice Problems 10.2

1. The figure shows the marginal private benefit, marginal social benefit, and marginal cost of college education.

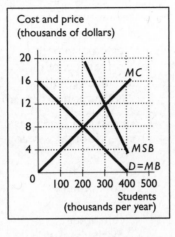

   a. What does the marginal external benefit equal when there are 300,000 students per year?

   b. If colleges are private and government has no involvement in college education, how many people will undertake a college education and what will be the tuition?

   c. What is the efficient number of students?

   d. If the government decides to provide public colleges, what tuition will these colleges charge to achieve the efficient number of students? What is the marginal cost of educating this many students? Why is it justified to charge a tuition that is less than the marginal cost?

2. A vaccine for chicken pox was recently developed. The company that developed the vaccine, Merck Incorporated, was required to submit a document comparing the costs and benefits of vaccinating children. The government would approve the drug only if the benefit of vaccination exceeded the cost. The producer reports that the marginal cost of a dose of vaccine is $80. The marginal benefit to the child being vaccinated is estimated to be $30 and an additional marginal benefit to the child's parents is estimated at $60.

   a. How much is the marginal private benefit and the marginal external benefit?

   b. Based on these data, should the government have approved the vaccine?

Solutions to Additional Practice Problems 10.2

1a. The marginal external benefit equals the vertical distance between the marginal social benefit curve, *MSB*, and the marginal private benefit curve, *MB*. In the figure the difference is $8,000, so the marginal external benefit equals $8,000.

1b. If the government has no involvement, the equilibrium tuition and number of students is determined by the equilibrium between supply and demand. The supply curve is the marginal private cost curve, $S = MC$, and the demand curve is the marginal private benefit curve, *MB*. The figure shows that the equilibrium tuition equals $8,000 a year and the equilibrium enrollment is 200,000 students a year.

1c. The efficient number of students is 300,000 because this the quantity at which the marginal cost equals the marginal social benefit.

1d. The demand curve, which is the same as the marginal private benefit curve, shows that tuition must be $4,000 in order for 300,000 students to attend college. The marginal cost of educating 300,000 students is $12,000 students per year. It is justified to charge a tuition that is less than the marginal cost because education has external benefits so that society as well as the student benefits from the college education.

2a. The marginal private benefit is the benefit to the child being vaccinated and is $30. The marginal external benefit is the benefit to the child's parents and is $60.

2b. Based on the data that were submitted, the government should have approved the vaccine. The marginal social benefit equals the marginal private benefit to the child of $30 plus the marginal external benefit to the parent of $60, which is $90. The marginal social benefit from the vaccine is greater than the marginal cost.

■ Self Test 10.2

Fill in the blanks

Marginal ____ (social; external) benefit is the benefit enjoyed by society from one more unit of a good or service. If the government leaves education to the private market, ____ (overproduction; underproduction) occurs. A payment that the government makes to private producers to cover part of the costs of production is ____ (a subsidy; public provision).

True or false

1. The marginal private benefit from a good or service must exceed the marginal external benefit.

2. The expanded job opportunities from a college degree are a marginal private benefit enjoyed by college graduates.

3. A flu vaccination has an external benefit, so the marginal private benefit curve for flu vaccinations lies above the marginal social benefit curve for flu vaccinations.

4. An unregulated market underproduces products with external benefits, such as education.

5. A public community college is an example of public provision of a good that has an external benefit.

6. To overcome the inefficiency in the market for a good with an external benefit, the government can either tax or subsidize the good.

7. Vouchers can help overcome the inefficiency created by a good with an external cost but not the inefficiency created by a good with an external benefit.

Multiple choice

1. The benefit the consumer of a good or service receives is the
   a. social benefit.
   b. external benefit.
   c. private benefit.
   d. public benefit.
   e. consumption benefit.

2. An external benefit is a benefit from a good or service that someone other than the ____ receives.
   a. seller of the good or service
   b. government
   c. foreign sector
   d. consumer
   e. market maker

3. When Ronald takes another economics class, other people in society benefit. The benefit to these other people is called the marginal ____ benefit of the class.
   a. social
   b. private
   c. external
   d. opportunity
   e. extra

4. Marginal social benefit equals
   a. marginal external benefit.
   b. marginal private benefit.
   c. marginal private benefit minus marginal external benefit.
   d. marginal private benefit plus marginal external benefit
   e. marginal external benefit minus marginal private benefit.

5. If an external benefit is present, then the
   a. marginal private benefit curve lies above the marginal private cost curve.
   b. marginal social benefit curve lies above the marginal private benefit curve.
   c. marginal social cost curve lies above the marginal private benefit curve.
   d. marginal social benefit is equal to the marginal social cost.
   e. marginal social benefit curve is the same as the marginal private benefit curve.

6. In an unregulated market with an external benefit, the
   a. quantity produced is greater than the efficient quantity.
   b. price charged is too high for efficiency.
   c. quantity produced is less than the efficient quantity.
   d. producer is causing pollution but not paying for it.
   e. government can impose a tax to restore the efficient amount of production.

■ **FIGURE 10.4**

Price (dollars per shot)

Quantity (millions of shots per year)

7. Figure 10.4 shows the market for flu vaccination, which has ____.
   a. only external costs
   b. only external benefits
   c. both external costs and external benefits
   d. neither external costs nor external benefits
   e. might have external benefits or external costs, but more information is needed

8. Figure 10.4 shows the market for flu vaccination. If the market is unregulated, the equilibrium quantity of vaccinations is ____ shots per year.
   a. 0
   b. 50 million
   c. 75 million
   d. 100 million
   e. 125 million

9. Figure 10.4 shows the market for flu vaccination. The efficient quantity of vaccinations is ____ shots per year.
   a. 0
   b. 50 million
   c. 75 million
   d. 100 million
   e. 125 million

10. If all education in the United States were provided by private, tuition-charging schools,
    a. too much education would be consumed.
    b. too little education would be consumed.
    c. the efficient level of education would be provided.
    d. the government would provide *both* students and schools with vouchers.
    e. education would no longer have an external benefit.

11. Which of the following is a method used by government to cope with the situation in which production of a good creates an external benefit?
    a. removing property rights
    b. paying subsidies
    c. issuing marketable permits
    d. running a lottery
    e. imposing a Coasian tax

12. If tuition at a college is $30,000 and the external benefit of graduating from this college is $10,000, then
    i. in the absence of any government intervention, the number of students graduating is less than the efficient number
    ii. the government could increase the number of graduates by giving the college a $10,000 subsidy per student
    iii. the government could increase the number of graduates by giving the students $10,000 vouchers
    a. i only.
    b. i and ii.
    c. i and iii.
    d. ii and iii.
    e. i, ii, and iii.

13. Which of the following is an example of a voucher?
    a. the postal service
    b. police services
    c. social security
    d. food stamps
    e. a tax on gasoline

Complete the graph

■ **FIGURE 10.5**

Price (dollars per pound of honey)

Quantity (tons of honey per year)

1. Figure 10.5 illustrates the market for honey.
   a. Label the curves in the figure.
   b. Based on Figure 10.5, does the production of honey create an external cost? An external benefit?
   c. What is the efficient quantity of honey? What is the quantity that will be produced in an unregulated market?
   d. Shade the area that equals the deadweight loss in an unregulated market.

Short answer and numeric questions

Quantity (millions of students per year)	Marginal private cost (thousands of dollars per student)	Marginal private benefit (thousands of dollars per student)	Marginal social benefit (thousands of dollars per student)
10	10	25	34
20	12	20	29
30	15	15	24
40	19	10	19
50	24	5	14

1. The table above shows the benefits and costs of a college education.
   a. Based on the table, what is the amount of the marginal external benefit?
   b. If the market for education was left unregulated, what would be the number of students educated per year?
   c. What is the efficient number of students educated per year?
   d. Would a subsidy or a tax be the proper government policy to make the market for education more efficient? What must the subsidy or tax equal to have the efficient number of students being educated?

2. Is efficiency guaranteed when production is such that the marginal private benefit equals the marginal private cost? Or does efficiency require that the marginal social benefit equal the marginal social cost?

3. Most elementary schools require that children be vaccinated before allowing the child to attend school. Can this policy be justified using economic analysis?

4. What is a voucher? How do vouchers work? Why is a voucher a proper policy to deal with the inefficiency created by a good or service that has an external benefit?

SELF TEST ANSWERS

■ CHECKPOINT 10.1

Fill in the blanks

Marginal social cost equals marginal private cost <u>plus</u> marginal external cost. A pollution externality creates an <u>inefficient</u> equilibrium. According to the Coase theorem, if property rights exist, then private transactions are efficient and the outcome <u>is not</u> affected by who is assigned the property right. By setting the pollution tax rate equal to the marginal <u>external</u> cost, firms behave in the same way as they would if they bore the cost of the externality directly.

True or false

1. False; page 242
2. True; page 243
3. False; page 244
4. False; page 246
5. False; page 248
6. True; pages 249-250
7. False; page 250
8. True; page 250

Multiple choice

1. c; page 242
2. a; page 242
3. e; pages 242-243
4. c; page 244
5. d; page 244
6. b; page 244
7. c; page 244
8. e; page 246
9. b; page 245
10. c; page 246
11. b; page 246
12. b; page 248
13. d; page 250
14. d; page 250
15. c; page 251

Complete the graph

1. a. Figure 10.6 shows the *MSC*, *MC*, and *MB* curves; page 246.

■ FIGURE 10.6

Price (dollars per megawatt)

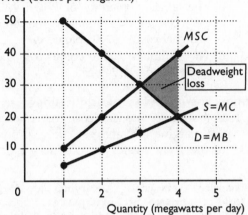

b. An unregulated market produces 4 megawatts of electricity a day. The marginal external cost at this production is $20 per megawatt; page 246.
c. The efficient amount of electricity is 3 megawatts a day. The deadweight loss is illustrated in the figure; page 246.
d. At the efficient quantity of electricity, the marginal external cost is $15 a megawatt. The tax is $15 a megawatt. With the tax, 3 megawatts of electricity are produced. The price is $30 per megawatt; pages 249-250.

■ FIGURE 10.7

Price (dollars per ton)

2. a. Figure 10.7 shows the *MSC*, *MC*, and *MB* curves; page 246.

b. An unregulated market produces 3 tons of PBDE a day. At this quantity the marginal external cost is $300; page 246.

c. The efficient quantity of PBDE is 2 tons per day. At this quantity the marginal external cost is $200; page 246.

d. The pollution charge equals $100 per ton of PBDE; pages 249-250.

Short answer and numeric questions

1. If the marginal social cost curve lies above the marginal private cost curve, production of the good creates an external cost; page 245.

Quantity (tons of pesticide per day)	Marginal private cost (dollars per ton)	Marginal external cost (dollars per ton)	Marginal social cost (dollars per ton)
1	100	<u>30</u>	130
2	120	40	<u>160</u>
3	<u>150</u>	60	210
4	190	<u>90</u>	280
5	240	120	<u>360</u>

2. The completed table is above; page 244.

3. According to the Coase theorem, if property rights are assigned, the number of people involved is small, and transactions costs are low, then private transactions are efficient; page 248.

4. Pollution charges and pollution taxes are designed to charge polluting firms the cost of their pollution. By forcing firms to pay this cost, the firms' marginal private cost becomes equal to the marginal social cost. To use pollution charges or pollution taxes to overcome the problem of pollution, the government must know the marginal external cost at different levels of output; pages 249-250.

5. A marketable permit is a government-issued permit given to firms that allows the company to pollute up to the limit of the permit. Permits can be bought and sold amongst firms. The advantage marketable permits have over assigning each firm a limit for its pollution is the incentive it gives firms. When firms are assigned a limit, the price ex-

ceeds their marginal private so each firm has an incentive to increase its production past its limit. The government must monitor firms' compliance, which can be difficult and costly. Marketable permits, however, give the firms an incentive to increase its producer surplus by developing new, low-cost technology to limit pollution and thereby be able to sell its pollution permits; page 250.

■ CHECKPOINT 10.2

Fill in the blanks

Marginal <u>social</u> benefit is the benefit enjoyed by society from one more unit of a good or service. If the government leaves education to the private market, <u>underproduction</u> occurs. A payment that the government makes to private producers to cover part of the costs of production is <u>a subsidy</u>.

True or false

1. False; page 254
2. True; page 254
3. False; page 254
4. True; page 255
5. True; page 256
6. False; page 256
7. False; page 258

Multiple choice

1. c; page 254
2. d; page 254
3. c; page 254
4. d; page 254
5. b; page 254
6. c; page 255
7. b; page 255
8. c; page 255
9. d; page 255
10. b; page 255
11. b; page 256
12. e; pages 255-258
13. d; page 258

Complete the graph

■ **FIGURE 10.8**

Price (dollars per pound of honey)

1. a. Figure 10.8 labels the curves; page 255.
   b. The production of honey has an external benefit but no external cost; page 255.
   c. The efficient quantity of honey is 300 tons, a year, at the intersection of the *MSB* curve and the *S = MC* curve. In an unregulated market, the equilibrium quantity is 200 tons a year, at the intersection of the *D = MB* curve and the *S = MC* curve; page 255.
   d. Figure 10.8 shades the deadweight loss; page 255.

Short answer and numeric questions

1. a. The marginal external benefit equals the difference between the marginal social benefit and the marginal private benefit, so it is $9,000 per student; page 254.
   b. The competitive equilibrium is where the marginal private cost (which determines the supply) equals the marginal private benefit (which determines the demand),

so the equilibrium number of students is 30 million per year; page 255.
   c. The efficient quantity is produced when the marginal social benefit equals the marginal cost, so the efficient amount is 40 million students per year; page 255.
   d. A subsidy would be a proper government policy. The subsidy would equal $9,000 per student, the amount of the marginal external benefit at the efficient quantity; page 257.

2. Efficiency is not guaranteed when production sets the marginal private benefit equal to the marginal cost. The efficient quantity is produced when the marginal social benefit equals marginal cost; page 255.

3. Vaccination protects not only the child who is vaccinated, but also makes it less likely for classmates to catch the disease. So a vaccination has an external benefit. Although at some number of vaccinations, the marginal cost of a vaccination is greater than the marginal private benefit of a vaccination, because the marginal social benefit exceeds the marginal private benefit the market will provide too few vaccinations. The market might be efficient when vaccination is required; page 255.

4. A voucher is a token that the government gives to households which they can use to buy specified goods or services. Vouchers increase the demand for the product and shift the demand curve (which is the same as the marginal private benefit curve, or *MB* curve) rightward, closer to the marginal social benefit curve. Vouchers reduce the inefficiency created by a good or service with an external benefit; page 258.

Public Goods and Common Resources

Chapter 11

1 **Distinguish among private goods, public goods, and common resources.**

An excludable good, service, or resource is one that it is possible to prevent someone from enjoying its benefits; a nonexcludable good, service, or resource is one that it is impossible to prevent someone from enjoying its benefits. A rival good, service, or resource is one for which its use by one person decreases the quantity available for someone else; a nonrival good, service, or resource is one for which its use by one person does not decrease the quantity available to someone else. A private good is excludable and rival. A public good can be consumed simultaneously by everyone and from which no one can be excluded. A public good is nonexcludable and nonrival. A common resource is a resource that is nonexcludable and rival. A natural monopoly is excludable and nonrival.

2 **Explain the free-rider problem and how public provision might help to overcome it and deliver an efficient quantity of pubic goods.**

Public goods create a free-rider problem, a person who enjoys the benefits of a good or service without paying for it. The economy's marginal social benefit curve for a public good is the vertical sum of the individual marginal benefit curves. The efficient quantity of a public good is the quantity that sets marginal social benefit equal to marginal social cost. Because of the free-rider problem, public goods are under-provided by private firms so public provision of public goods might lead efficiency. The tendency for political parties to propose identical policies in order to appeal to the maximum number of voters is an example of the principle of minimum differentiation. Rational ignorance is the decision not to acquire information because the marginal cost of doing so exceeds the expected marginal benefit. Rational ignorance, combined with the bureaucratic desire to maximize budgets, can lead to inefficient overprovision of public goods.

3 **Explain the tragedy of the commons and review its possible solutions.**

Common resources suffer from the tragedy of the commons, which is the absence of incentives to prevent the overuse and depletion of a commonly owned resource. Fish are an example of a common resource. The marginal private cost of fishing is the additional cost incurred to catch additional fish. Fishers, however, create an external cost because each boat makes it more costly for other fishers to catch fish so $MSC > MC$. The marginal social benefit is the same as the marginal private benefit. Efficiency occurs when the marginal social benefit from a resource equals its marginal social cost. But the marginal private cost is less than the marginal social cost, so in an unregulated market overuse of the resource occurs. The government can bring about an efficient use of the common resource by assigning property rights to the resource; by setting a production quota on the amount of the resource that can be used; or by creating a program of individual transferable quotas (ITQ). An individual transferable quota is a production limit that the owner can transfer to someone else.

CHECKPOINT 11.1

■ **Distinguish among private goods, public goods, and common resources.**

Quick Review

- *Public good* A public good is nonrival and nonexcludable.
- *Private good* A private good is rival and excludable.
- *Common resource* A common resource is rival and nonexcludable.

Additional Practice Problem 11.1

1. It's a balmy, pleasant Sunday afternoon on a fall day on Long Island, where the U.S. Open Tennis Men's Singles Finals are being played. A variety of goods and services are being consumed. Classify each of the list of goods and services as rival, nonrival, excludable, and nonexcludable. State if they are a public good, a private good, or a common resource.

   a. U.S. Lawn Tennis Association membership
   b. tennis lessons
   c. racquets
   d. watching the Men's Singles Championship
   e. a pleasant, sunny afternoon
   f. sunset seen over Fire Island
   g. shrimp eaten at a tailgate party

Solution to Additional Practice Problem 11.1

1a. Membership in the U.S. Lawn Tennis Association is nonrival and excludable.

1b. Tennis lessons are rival and excludable and are a private good.

1c. Racquets are rival and excludable and hence are a private good.

1d. Watching the Men's Singles Championship is excludable. Whether it is rival depends on whether the match is a sell out. If it is a sell out, then watching the championship is rival and it is a private good; in the event that it is not sold out and seats remain available, it is nonrival.

1e. The pleasant afternoon is nonrival and nonexcludable and so is a public good.

1f. The sunset is nonrival and nonexcludable and so is a public good.

1g. The shrimp are rival and excludable and so are a private good.

■ Self Test 11.1

Fill in the blanks

A good is ____ (rival; nonrival; excludable) if it is possible to prevent someone from enjoying its benefits. A good is ____ (rival; nonrival; excludable) if its use by one person does not decrease the quantity available for someone else. A good that is nonrival and nonexcludable is a ____ (private; public; common) good and a good that is rival and excludable is a ____ (private; public; common) good. A common resource is ____ (rival; nonrival) and ____ (excludable; nonexcludable).

True or false

1. A good is nonexcludable if it is impossible to prevent someone from benefiting from it.
2. A private good is nonrival and nonexcludable.
3. A taco from Taco Bell is a public good.
4. A common resource is nonrival and excludable.
5. Fish in the ocean are rival and nonexcludable.

Multiple choice

1. The fact that Heidi's enjoyment of a sunset on Saint Simon's Island does not preclude Mounette from enjoying the same sunset is an example of
   a. a good that is nonrival.
   b. a good that is excludable.
   c. a private good.
   d. the rival nature of consumption.
   e. a common resource.

2. When use of a good decreases the quantity available for someone else, the good is
   a. rival.
   b. nonrival.
   c. excludable.
   d. nonexcludable.
   e. a public good.

3. A private good is ____ and ____.
   a. rival; excludable
   b. rival; nonexcludable
   c. nonrival; excludable
   d. nonrival; nonexcludable
   e. scarce; expensive

4. If I order a pizza and invite my neighbors to eat it, the pizza is
   a. a private good.
   b. a common resource.
   c. a public good because many people ate it.
   d. either a common resource or a public good depending on whether it is over-used.
   e. produced by a natural monopoly.

5. A public good is ____ and ____.
   a. rival; excludable
   b. rival; nonexcludable
   c. nonrival; excludable
   d. nonrival; nonexcludable
   e. cheap; available

6. A public good
   a. can only be consumed by one person at a time.
   b. can be consumed simultaneously by many people.
   c. is any good provided by a company owned by a member of the public.
   d. is any good provided by government.
   e. is both rival and excludable.

7. Which of the following is the best example of a public good?
   a. national defense
   b. a Ford Thunderbird
   c. Yosemite national park
   d. a Mountain Dew
   e. a satellite radio

8. Which of the following is the best example of a common resource?
   a. national defense
   b. a Ford Thunderbird
   c. Yosemite national park
   d. a can of Mountain Dew
   e. a cable television network

Short answer and numeric questions

1. What does it mean for a good to be nonexcludable? Nonrival?

2. Goods can be excludable or nonexcludable, rival or nonrival. Using these criteria, what is a public good, a private good, and a common resource?

CHECKPOINT 11.2

■ **Explain the free-rider problem and how public provision might help to overcome it and deliver an efficient quantity of public goods.**

Quick Review
- *Free rider* A free rider enjoys the benefits of a good or service without paying for the good or service.

Additional Practice Problems 11.2

Quantity (square miles per day)	Abe's marginal benefit (dollars per day)	Bee's marginal benefit (dollars per day)	Kris's marginal benefit (dollars per day)
1	20	20	30
2	35	35	50
3	48	42	60
4	60	45	65
5	70	47	68

1. A (small) city that is exactly 5 square miles in size has three people in it, Abe, Bee, and Kris. The table above gives the marginal benefit of each from a mosquito control program.
   a. Is mosquito spraying a public good or a private good? Explain your answer.
   b. Calculate the marginal social benefit for spraying 1, 2, 3, 4, and 5 square miles a day.

c. If the marginal cost of spraying was constant at $150 for a square mile, what it is the efficient number of miles that should be sprayed?

d. How many square miles would the bureau head of the city's mosquito control project lobby the city commissioners to spray?

2. How do rational ignorance and bureaucrats' goal of budget maximization combine to lead to inefficient overprovision of public goods?

Solutions to Additional Practice Problems 11.2

1a. Mosquito spraying is a public good because it's both nonrival—everyone can simultaneously enjoy not being bitten—and nonexcludable—even if one of the residents does not pay, the mosquitoes still do not bite that resident.

1b. The marginal social benefit is equal to the sum of the benefits of all the residents for each quantity. So the marginal social benefit for spraying 1 square mile is equal to $20 + $20 +$30 = $70. The rest of the answers in the table are calculated similarly.

Quantity (square miles per day)	Marginal social benefit (dollars per day)
1	70
2	120
3	150
4	170
5	185

1c. The marginal social cost equals the marginal social benefit when 3 square miles are sprayed, so 3 square miles is the efficient quantity of spraying.

1d. The head of the city's mosquito control commission wants to maximize the budget of the commission, so the head will lobby to spray 5 square miles.

2. If voters knew the marginal social benefit and marginal social cost of a public good, they could elect politicians who would deliver the efficient quantity. But voters generally are rationally ignorant about the marginal social benefit and marginal social cost of most public goods. So bureaucrats, who want to increase their budget, and special interest groups, such as the producers of a public good, lobby politi-cians to provide more than the efficient amount of public goods. Politicians accede to the lobbying because they know that (rationally ignorant) voters will not realize that too much of the public good is provided.

■ Self Test 11.2

Fill in the blanks

A person who enjoys the benefit of a good or service without paying for it is a ____. The marginal social benefit curve for a public good is the ____ (horizontal; vertical) sum of the individual marginal benefit curves. The efficient quantity of a public good is the quantity at which the marginal benefit ____ the marginal cost. ____ (Rational ignorance; The principle of minimum differentiation) is the decision to not acquire information because the marginal cost of doing so exceeds the expected marginal benefit. Bureaucrats try to ____ (maximize; minimize) their budgets.

True or false

1. Beth is a free rider when she is protected by the nation's military but does not pay anything for the protection.

2. The marginal social benefit curve for a public good slopes downward.

3. The efficient quantity of a public good is the quantity at which marginal social benefit equals marginal social cost.

4. A private firm would produce too much of a public good.

5. Rational ignorance can lead to the provision of more than the efficient amount of a public good.

Multiple choice

1. When someone enjoys the benefit of a good or service but does not pay for it, that person
   a. is a free range consumer.
   b. is a free rider.
   c. receives no marginal benefit from the good.
   d. must be consuming an excludable good
   e. is contributing to the tragedy of the commons.

2. The marginal social benefit of a public good is the
   a. sum of the marginal benefits of all the individuals at each quantity.
   b. marginal benefit of the individual person who places the lowest value on the good, multiplied by the number of people in the economy.
   c. marginal benefit of the individual person who places the highest value on the good, multiplied by the number of people in the economy.
   d. benefit of the last person's consumption.
   e. average of the marginal benefits of all the individuals at each quantity.

3. The marginal social benefit curve of a public good
   a. slopes downward.
   b. slopes upward.
   c. is vertical.
   d. is horizontal.
   e. is U-shaped.

4. Sue and Mark are the only two members of a community. Sue's marginal benefit from one lighthouse is $2,000 and Mark's marginal benefit is $1,000. If the marginal social cost of one lighthouse is $2,500 and if a lighthouse is a public good, then for efficiency the lighthouse should
   a. be built but only Sue should be allowed to use it.
   b. be built but only Mark should be allowed to use it.
   c. be built and both Sue and Mark should be allowed to use it.
   d. not be built because its marginal cost exceeds Sue's marginal benefit.
   e. not be built because its marginal cost exceeds both Sue's and Mark's marginal benefit.

5. The efficient quantity of a public good is
   a. the quantity produced by private firms.
   b. the quantity at which the marginal social benefit equals the marginal social cost.
   c. impossible to determine because each person's marginal benefit is different.
   d. the quantity at which the marginal social benefit exceeds the marginal social cost by as much as possible.
   e. where the demand curve and supply curve of the good intersects.

6. The efficient quantity of a public good can't be produced by private firms because
   a. only government has the necessary resources.
   b. it is impossible to determine the efficient amount.
   c. consumers have an incentive to free ride and not pay for their share of the good.
   d. private firms aren't large enough.
   e. the price would be too high if private firms produced the goods.

7. If the two political parties propose similar or identical policies, they are following the principle of
   a. rational ignorance.
   b. inefficient overprovision.
   c. free riding.
   d. minimum differentiation.
   e. the commons.

8. ____ is the decision not to acquire information because the marginal cost of doing so exceeds expected marginal benefit.
   a. Rational ignorance
   b. The principle of minimum differentiation
   c. A free rider
   d. Consumer ignorance
   e. The tragedy of the commons

9. Government bureaucracies over-provide public goods and grow larger because of their goal of ____ combined with ____ of the voters.
   a. budget maximization; rational ignorance
   b. budget minimization; irrational intelligence
   c. budget maximization; minimum differentiation
   d. budget maximization; irrational exuberance
   e. minimum differentiation; budget maximization

Complete the graph

Quantity (lighthouses)	Marginal benefit, Firm A (dollars)	Marginal benefit, Firm B (dollars)	Marginal benefit, Firm C (dollars)
1	50,000	50,000	50,000
2	45,000	45,000	45,000
3	40,000	40,000	40,000
4	35,000	35,000	35,000

1. Three shipping firms serve the west coast of a nation. The table has the firms' marginal benefit schedules for lighthouses. Lighthouses are a public good and the marginal social cost of constructing a lighthouse is constant at $120,000.

   a. Complete the table below. Then graph the economy's marginal social benefit and marginal social cost curves in Figure 11.1.

Quantity (lighthouses)	Marginal social benefit, (dollars per lighthouse)
1	
2	
3	
4	

   b. What is the efficient number of lighthouses to build?

   c. If all three firms agree to split the cost of building lighthouses equally, how much would each firm pay per lighthouse and how many lighthouses will be built?

   d. Suppose that one firm decides to free ride and not pay for the construction of any lighthouses. How much would each of the two other firms pay per lighthouse and how many lighthouses will be built?

■ FIGURE 11.1

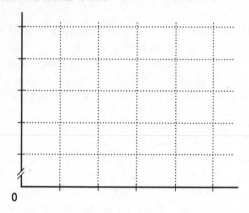

0

   e. In the situation described in part (d), how might government action overcome the problem?

Short answer and numeric questions

1. What is a free rider? Why is free riding not a problem for private goods?

2. A very small (!) nation has 10 citizens. Each resident has a $10 marginal benefit from 1 unit of a private good. In addition, each has a $10 marginal benefit from 1 unit of a public good. What is one combination of marginal social benefit and quantity on the economy's marginal social benefit curve for the private good and what is one combination on the economy's marginal social benefit curve for the public good? Explain the difference.

3. How does free riding affect the private provision of a public good? How does rational ignorance affect the public provision of a public good?

4. The Eye on Your Life in the book explains how MP3 files have a free rider problem. One of the most common instances of free riding amongst students comes when a group of students are assigned to complete a project. Explain how free riding can occur in this situation. Occasionally instructors grade a group project by basing each student's grade, in part, on the group member's evaluations of each other. Explain how this technique can overcome the free rider problem.

CHECKPOINT 11.3

■ **Explain the tragedy of the commons and review its possible solutions.**

Quick Review

- *Tragedy of the commons* The absence of incentives to prevent the overuse and depletion of a commonly owned resource.
- *Marginal private cost* The cost incurred by an individual from using a resource.
- *Marginal social cost* The cost incurred by society when an individual uses a resource.

Additional Practice Problem 11.3

1. Cod in the ocean are a common resource. The figure shows the marginal private cost, marginal social cost, and marginal social benefit of fishing.

a. What is the marginal external cost when 2 tons of cod are caught? Why is there an external cost from catching cod?

b. If fishing is unregulated, what will be the quantity of cod caught?

c. What is the efficient quantity of cod?

d. Is cod fishing subject to the tragedy of commons?

Solution to Additional Practice Problem 11.3

1a. The marginal external cost at any quantity is equal to the difference between the marginal social cost and the marginal private cost. At 2 tons of cod, the marginal external cost is $100 per ton. Cod fishing is subject to this external cost because it is a common resource. As a new boat starts to fish, by catching some of the fish stock, the new boat makes it more

difficult, and therefore more costly, for the boats already fishing to catch fish. The increase in the other boats' costs is the external cost created by the new boat's catch of fish.

1b. The equilibrium quantity is determined by where the marginal private cost curve (the supply curve) and marginal social benefit curve (the demand curve) cross, or 4 tons of fish.

1c. The efficient quantity is determined by where the marginal social cost curve and marginal social benefit curve cross, or 3 tons of fish.

1d. Similar to other common resources, cod fishing is subject to the tragedy of commons because the equilibrium quantity of cod caught exceeds the efficient quantity of cod.

■ Self Test 11.3

Fill in the blanks

The tragedy of the commons is the absence of incentives to prevent the ____ (overuse; under use) of a commonly owned resource. The marginal private cost of an additional fishing boat is the ____ (marginal cost incurred by the boat's owner; marginal cost incurred by society).. The marginal private cost curve for a common resource lies ____ (above; below) the marginal social cost curve. To use a common resource efficiently, establishing property rights ____ (is; is not) a potential solution. The price of an individual transferable quota equals the marginal social ____ (benefit; cost) of the resource at the efficient quantity ____ (plus; minus) the marginal cost of using the resource.

True or false

1. The tragedy of the commons is the absence of incentives that prevent the overuse and depletion of a commonly owned resource.

2. The efficient use of a common resource occurs when the marginal private benefit equals the marginal private cost.

3. At the efficient level of use, the marginal private cost of a common resource exceeds the marginal social cost.

4. Property rights and production quotas are potential solutions to the tragedy of the commons.

Multiple choice

1. The tragedy of the commons is the absence of incentives to
   a. correctly measure the marginal benefit.
   b. prevent under use of the common resource.
   c. prevent overuse and depletion of the common resource.
   d. discover the resource.
   e. prevent the free-rider problem.

2. For a common resource such as fish, the marginal private benefit ____ the marginal social benefit and the marginal private cost ____ the marginal social cost.
   a. equals; is less than
   b. is greater than; equals
   c. equals; equals
   d. is less than; is less than
   e. is greater than; is greater than

3. For a common resource, the marginal private cost curve ____ and the marginal social cost curve ____.
   a. slopes upward; slopes upward
   b. slopes upward; slopes downward
   c. slopes downward; slopes upward
   d. slopes downward; slopes downward
   e. is vertical; is horizontal

4. For a common resource, the equilibrium with no government intervention is such that ____ equals ____ cost.
   a. marginal private benefit; marginal social cost
   b. marginal social benefit; marginal private cost
   c. marginal social benefit; marginal social cost
   d. marginal external benefit; marginal external cost
   e. marginal social benefit; marginal external cost

5. For a common resource, efficiency requires that the ____ equals the ____.
   a. marginal private benefit; marginal private cost
   b. marginal social benefit; marginal private cost
   c. marginal social benefit; marginal social cost
   d. marginal external benefit; marginal external cost
   e. marginal social benefit; marginal external cost

■ **FIGURE 11.2**

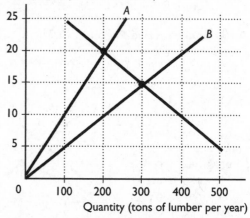

Price (dollars per ton of lumber)

6. Figure 11.2 shows a market for logging in a tropical rainforest, which is a common resource. In the figure, curve *A* is the ____ and curve *B* is the ____.
   a. *MSC; MC*
   b. *MSB; MB*
   c. *MB; MSB*
   d. *MC; MSC*
   e. *MC; MB*

7. Figure 11.2 shows a market for logging in a tropical rainforest, which is a common resource. The efficient quantity of timber is ____ and if the market is unregulated, the equilibrium quantity of timber is ____.
   a. 0 tons; 500 tons
   b. 0 tons; 300 tons
   c. 300 tons; 200 tons
   d. 300 tons; 0 tons
   e. 200 tons; 300 tons

8. Which of the following is *not* a potential solution to the tragedy of the commons?
   a. Subsidizing use of the resource
   b. Setting a production quota
   c. Granting individual transferable quotas
   d. Establish property rights to the resource
   e. None of the above are correct because they are all potential solutions to the tragedy of the commons.

9. If the government assigns private property rights to a common resource, then the
   a. resource is under-utilized.
   b. marginal private cost becomes equal to the marginal social cost.
   c. government needs to set a quota to achieve efficiency.
   d. resource becomes subject to the free riding problem.
   e. resource cannot be utilized.

10. The market price of an individual transferable quota is equal to the
    a. marginal private benefit.
    b. marginal social benefit.
    c. marginal private benefit minus the marginal private cost.
    d. marginal social benefit minus the marginal cost.
    e. marginal private benefit plus the marginal cost.

Complete the graph

■ **FIGURE 11.3**

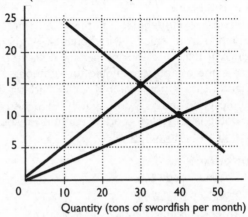

Price (thousands of dollars per ton of swordfish)

1. Figure 11.3 shows the marginal social cost, marginal private cost, and marginal social benefit curves for swordfish, a common resource. Label each curve.
   a. What is the equilibrium catch and what is the efficient catch?
   b. If the government sets a quota, what quota achieves the efficient outcome?
   c. If the government issues individual transferable quotas (ITQ), each good for one ton of swordfish, how many ITQs does the government issue? What is the market price of an ITQ?

Short answer and numeric questions

1. What is the tragedy of the commons and why does it occur? Give an example of how the tragedy of the commons affects the world's fisheries.

2. For a common resource, why does the marginal private cost not equal the marginal social cost? Which is smaller?

3. Shrimp are now farmed in ponds belonging to individual owners. Is this shrimp farming subject to the tragedy of the commons? Why or why not?

SELF TEST ANSWERS

■ CHECKPOINT 11.1

Fill in the blanks

A good is <u>excludable</u> if it is possible to prevent someone from enjoying its benefits. A good is <u>nonrival</u> if its use by one person does not decrease the quantity available for someone else. A good that is nonrival and nonexcludable is a <u>public</u> good and a good that is rival and excludable is a <u>private</u> good. A common resource is <u>rival</u> and <u>nonexcludable</u>.

True or false

1. True; page 266
2. False; page 266
3. False; pages 266-267
4. False; page 267
5. True; page 267

Multiple choice

1. a; page 266
2. a; page 266
3. a; pages 266-267
4. a; page 266
5. d; page 267
6. b; page 267
7. a; page 267
8. c; page 267

Short answer and numeric questions

1. A good is nonexcludable if it is impossible (or extremely costly) to prevent someone from benefiting from it. For example, the national defense provided by a fighter plane benefits everyone and so is nonexcludable. A good is nonrival if its use by one person does not decrease the quantity available for someone else. For example, the national defense provided by a fighter plane to you does not decrease the amount of defense it provides to your neighbor and so is nonrival; page 266.

2. A public good is nonrival and nonexcludable. A private good is rival and excludable. A common resource is rival and nonexcludable; pages 266-267.

■ CHECKPOINT 11.2

Fill in the blanks

A person who enjoys the benefit of a good or service without paying for it is a <u>free rider</u>. The marginal social benefit curve for a public good is the <u>vertical</u> sum of the individual marginal benefit curves. The efficient quantity of a public good is the quantity at which the marginal benefit <u>equals</u> the marginal cost. <u>Rational ignorance</u> is the decision to not acquire information because the marginal cost of doing so exceeds the expected marginal benefit. Bureaucrats try to <u>maximize</u> their budgets.

True or false

1. True; page 269
2. True; pages 270-271
3. True; page 272
4. False; page 272
5. True; pages 274-275

Multiple choice

1. b; page 269
2. a; pages 270-271
3. a; page 271
4. c; page 272
5. b; page 272
6. c; page 272
7. d; page 274
8. a; pages 274-275
9. a; page 275

Complete the graph

Quantity (lighthouses)	Marginal social benefit (dollars)
1	150,000
2	135,000
3	120,000
4	105,000

1. a. The complete table is above and the completed figure is Figure 11.4 (on the next page); pages 270-271.

■ FIGURE 11.4

Marginal social benefit and marginal social cost
(thousands of dollars per lighthouse)

b. The efficient number of lighthouses to build is 3; page 272.

c. Each firm pays $40,000 per lighthouse and three lighthouses are built; page 272.

d. If one firm free rides, the other firms would need to pay $60,000 a lighthouse. No lighthouses would be built because $60,000 exceeds each firm's marginal benefit from any lighthouse; page 272.

e. The government could tax each firm $40,000 per lighthouse and use the tax revenue to build three lighthouses; pages 273-274.

Short answer and numeric questions

1. A free rider is a person who enjoys the benefits of a good or service without paying for it. Free riding is not a problem for private goods because private goods are excludable; page 269.

2. For the private good, one combination on the economy's marginal social benefit curve is: $10 marginal social benefit and 10 units. For the public good, one combination is: $100 marginal social benefit and 1 unit. The difference occurs because for the rival private good, all residents need their own unit of the good in order to consume it, whereas for the nonrival public good, each citizen will consume the same unit. So to obtain the economy's marginal social benefit curve for a pri-

vate good, we sum the quantities demanded at each price. To obtain the economy's marginal social benefit curve for a public good, we sum the marginal benefits of all individuals at each quantity; pages 270-271.

3. Because everyone can consume the same quantity of a public good and no one can be excluded from enjoying its benefits, no one has an incentive to pay for it. Everyone has an incentive to free ride. Because of the free-rider problem, the market would provide too small a quantity of a public good.

   Bureaucrats who maximize their budgets and voters who work in the industry exert a larger influence on public policy than voters who are rationally ignorant. This set of circumstances leads to overprovision; pages 272 and 275.

4. The free rider problem in student groups is that a student might try to avoid all work and rely on the other students to complete the assignment. The grading technique in which group members assign grades to other members can overcome this free rider problem because each of the other group members can assign the free rider a grade of F. In order to avoid this grade, the potential free rider now is given the incentive to work and not free ride.

■ CHECKPOINT 11.3

Fill in the blanks

The tragedy of the commons is the absence of incentives to prevent the <u>overuse</u> of a commonly owned resource. The marginal private cost of an additional fishing boat is the <u>marginal cost incurred by the boat's owner</u>. The marginal private cost curve for a common resource lies <u>below</u> the marginal social cost curve. To use a common resource efficiently, establishing property rights <u>is</u> a potential solution. The price of an individual transferable quota equals the marginal social <u>benefit</u> of the resource at the efficient quantity <u>minus</u> the marginal cost of using the resource.

True or false

1. True; page 278
2. False; pages 280-281
3. False; page 281
4. True; page 282

Multiple choice

1. c; page 278
2. a; pages 279-281
3. a; page 281
4. b; page 281
5. c; page 281
6. a; page 281
7. e; page 281
8. a; page 282
9. b; page 282
10. d; page 285

Complete the graph

■ **FIGURE 11.5**

Price (thousands of dollars per ton of swordfish)

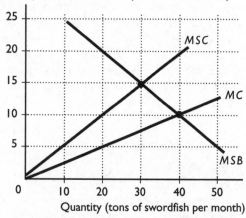

Quantity (tons of swordfish per month)

1. Figure 11.5 labels the curves.; page 281.
   a. The equilibrium catch is determined by the intersection of the marginal cost curve, *MC*, and the marginal social benefit curve, *MSB*, so the equilibrium catch is 40 tons of swordfish. The efficient catch is determined by the intersection of the marginal social cost curve and the marginal social benefit curve, so the efficient catch is 30 tons of swordfish per month; page 281.

   b. If the government sets the quota at the efficient quantity, the quota for the catch is 30 tons of swordfish per month; pages 283-284.

   c. The efficient catch is 30 tons per month, so the government would issue 30 ITQs, each good for one ton per month. The market price of an individual transferable quota (ITQ) equals the marginal social benefit (which will equal the price) minus the marginal cost at the quota level of fish. The government issues ITQs for 30 tons, so the market price of an ITQ is $15,000, the marginal social benefit, minus $7,500, the marginal private cost, which equals a market price of $7,500; pages 284-285.

Short answer and numeric questions

1. The tragedy of the commons is that there is no incentive to prevent the overuse and depletion of a commonly used resource. For example, as a new boat fishes a common resource fishing ground, the quantity of fish that the other boats can catch in an hour decreases. Their catch decreases because the new boat lands some of the fish that the other boats would have caught, which means that the initial boats' marginal cost of catching fish increases. But no individual boat owner takes account of the increase in the costs of the other boats because this is an external cost to the boat owner. Each owner is concerned with his or her costs and what he or she catches. Additional boats continue to fish until their marginal private benefit equals their marginal private cost of fishing. Each boat considers only its marginal private cost and ignores the external cost. With this many boats fishing, marginal private cost is greater than marginal social benefit and the fish stock is depleted; pages 278-280.

2. The marginal private cost of using a common resource does not equal the marginal social cost because the marginal private cost does not take account of the effect that using the resource has on others. As a common resource is used more intensively, each addi-

tional person's use increases everyone else's cost of using the resource. For instance, one person pumping water from an underground water pool—a common resource—decreases the total amount of water available and thereby increases the other users' costs of pumping water. Marginal private cost ignores the increase in other people's costs. The marginal social cost takes account of *both* the added cost to the new user (the marginal private cost) *and* the increase in everyone else's costs. So the marginal social cost exceeds the marginal private cost; pages 279-280.

3. The farmed shrimp are not subject to the tragedy of the commons because the shrimp are no longer a common resource. Because the shrimp belong to an individual farmer, the shrimp are now excludable; that is, the individual farmer decides what to do with his or her shrimp. Effectively the tragedy of the commons has been overcome because the farmer has the property right to the shrimp; pages 282-283.

Markets with Private Information

Chapter 12

1 Describe the lemons problem and explain how the used-car market solves it.

In some markets, either the buyer or seller might have some relevant information that the other side lacks. This information is called private information. Asymmetric information is a situation in which the person on one side of a transaction has private information about things that are relevant to the transaction. The used car market is one with private information: The sellers *but not the buyers*, know if the car they are selling is a lemon. This market is subject to adverse selection, the tendency for people to enter into transactions that bring them benefits from their private information and impose costs on the uninformed party. In the used car market, adverse selection can result in only lemons being sold. The used car market overcomes this problem using signals, when an informed person takes an action that sends information to uninformed people. Warranties are an example of a signal that can allow the used car market to operate efficiently. Without warranties, the outcome will be a pooling equilibrium: when an uninformed person cannot determine quality so only lemons are traded. With warranties, the outcome will be a separating equilibrium: when the messages signaled provide full information to a previously uninformed party so that both lemons and good cars trade, with different prices.

2 Describe the asymmetric information problems in the insurance market and explain how they are solved.

People buy insurance to reduce risk. Insurance works by pooling a large number of risks so that the total number of adverse outcomes is relatively certain. The company uses the payments from all policy holders to compensate the few that suffer losses. But there is asymmetric information in the insurance market because the policy holders have private information. The asymmetric information creates two problems, moral hazard (an incentive after making an agreement to behave in a way that imposes costs on the other party to the agreement, for example an insured driver driving more aggressively) and adverse selection (for example, risky drivers are more inclined to buy insurance). Insurance companies use screens, when an uninformed person creates an incentive for an informed person to reveal relevant private information. Offering no-claim bonuses and policies with high deductibles screen drivers and create a separating equilibrium because safe drivers will prefer these policies.

3 Explain the information problems and other economic problems in health-care markets.

Health-care markets suffer from asymmetric information (adverse selection means less healthy people are more inclined to buy insurance; moral hazard means that insured people are less careful); from a missing insurance market (people with a pre-existing health issue cannot buy insurance); and from public-health externalities (vaccination and treatment help prevent disease from spreading). The U.S. health system is higher cost and less efficient than health-care systems in other rich nations.

CHECKPOINT 12.1

■ **Describe the lemons problem and explain how the used-car market solves it.**

Quick Review

- *Private information* Information relevant to a transaction possessed by some market participants but not all.

- *Asymmetric information* A situation in which either the buyers or sellers have private information.

- *Adverse selection* The tendency for people to enter into transactions that bring them benefits from their private information.

- *Signal* When an informed person takes an action that sends information to uninformed persons.

Additional Practice Problems 12.1

1. What role does private information and adverse selection play in the fact that salespeople are often paid a commission that depends on their sales rather than a flat salary?

2. Suppose a teacher has an announced policy of giving all students a grade of A regardless of their effort or test scores. What sort of students will enroll in this instructor's class? How does this policy affect hard-working students in the class?

3. Which is preferable: a pooling equilibrium in the used car market or a separating equilibrium in the used car market? Why?

Solutions to Additional Practice Problems 12.1

1. Salespeople can either work hard to make sales or take it easy by shirking on the job. If a company offered its salespeople a flat salary, it would tend to attract salespeople who do not want to work hard. In other words, it would adversely select lazy salespeople. To overcome this adverse selection problem, most companies offer their salespeople a commission that depends on their sales.

2. This class will have a severe adverse selection problem: Largely lazy students who do not study and do not work hard will enroll in this class. The instructor's policy harms hard-working students in the class. A student's GPA sends a signal to potential employers and other schools about the student's ability to work hard and learn new material. Without this signal, these abilities remain the student's private information. By giving everyone in the class an A, this instructor degrades the information provided by his or her grade and makes it more difficult for hard working students to convey this information to others.

3. The separating equilibrium is preferable. In the pooling equilibrium, the price of a used car is low and only lemons are sold. Buyers who would prefer to pay a higher price to buy a good car cannot do so. There is a deadweight loss from the over-supply of lemons and the under-supply of good used cars. In the separating equilibrium, there are two prices: A low price for lemons and a higher price for good used cars. The deadweight losses are eliminated.

■ Self Test 12.1

Fill in the blanks

In the used car market, ____ (buyers; sellers; neither buyers nor sellers) have private information about the quality of the used car being sold. Adverse selection in the used car market with signals means that only ____ (good cars; lemons) are offered for sale. In the used car market, a warranty acts as a ____. If there are no signals in the used car market, too ____ (many; few) good used cars are sold. Signals that allow buyers to distinguish between good used cars and lemons result in a ____ (pooling; separating) equilibrium. In the used car market with a pooling equilibrium, there ____ (is one price; are two prices) for used cars and ____ (only lemons; both lemons and good cars) are sold. In the used car market with a separating equilibrium, there ____ (is one price; are two prices) for used cars and ____ (only lemons; both lemons and good cars) are sold.

True or false

1. Asymmetric information means that either the buyer or seller has private information.

2. Adverse selection occurs when one person enters into a contract with private information that will enable him or her to increase his or her benefits at the cost of decreasing the other party's benefits.

3. In the used car market, a warranty is an example of a signal.

4. In the used car market, warranties can lead to an equilibrium in which good cars have higher prices than lemons do.

5. In a pooling equilibrium, the price of a good used car is the same as the price of a lemon.

Multiple choice

1. Asymmetric information means that
   a. the buyer *must* have information that the seller does not have.
   b. the seller *must* have information that the buyer does not have.
   c. either the buyer has information that the seller does not have *or* the seller has information that the buyer does not have.
   d. the buyer and seller have the same information.
   e. None of the above are correct.

2. The lemons problem in the used car market is that
   a. the price of a lemon is too high.
   b. the price of a lemon is too low.
   c. no lemons are bought or sold.
   d. only lemons are bought and sold.
   e. Both answers a and d are correct.

3. The fact that people who know they are risky drivers are more likely to buy auto insurance reflects
   a. adverse selection.
   b. moral hazard.
   c. a separating equilibrium.
   d. signaling.
   e. the lemons problem.

4. JCPenney guarantees to refund a customer's money if the customer returns poorly made clothing. This guarantee is an example of
   a. the adverse selection problem.
   b. the moral hazard problem.
   c. the cost of risk.
   d. signaling.
   e. a lemon problem.

5. If buyers cannot assess the quality of used cars and there are no warranties,
   a. only lemons are sold.
   b. only good used cars are sold.
   c. good cars are sold at a higher price than bad cars.
   d. there is no adverse selection problem.
   e. lemons and good cars sell for the same price.

6. In the used car market, with a pooling equilibrium the price of a lemon is ____ the price of a good used car and with a separating equilibrium the price of a lemon is ____ the price of a good used car.
   a. less than; equal to
   b. equal to; less than
   c. equal to; more than
   d. more than; more than
   e. equal to; equal to

Short answer and numeric questions

1. What is the lemons problem? What role does asymmetric information play in the lemons problem?

2. Explain the relationship between asymmetric information and adverse selection.

3. How does signaling affect the equilibrium in a market with asymmetric information?

4. How does a pooling equilibrium differ from a separating equilibrium? Which is more efficient?

CHECKPOINT 12.2

■ **Describe the asymmetric information problems in the insurance market and explain how they are solved.**

Quick Review

- *Moral hazard* The tendency for a person with private information to use it in ways that impose costs on an uninformed party with whom they have made an agreement.
- *Screening* When an uninformed person creates an incentive for an informed person to reveal relevant private information.

Additional Practice Problem 12.2

1. How do insurance companies "pool risks?" Can insurance make people better off?

Solutions to Additional Practice Problem 12.2

1. Insurance companies pool risks by insuring many people and thereby sharing risk. Take auto insurance. In any given year, an individual driver might or might not have an accident. There is significant uncertainty for the driver. But if the insurance company insures many drivers, while the company cannot predict *which* driver *will* have an accident, the company can forecast *how many* drivers will have accidents. The company can set its premium at a level that allows it to pay the amount it expects to pay and be reasonably certain that this amount is what it will pay.

   Insurance decreases the risks that the buyer faces and this effect makes people better off. Once again, take auto insurance. Without insurance, the buyer faces the risk of an accident which would decrease his or her wealth significantly. By purchasing insurance, the buyer eliminates the risk of a large fall in wealth from an accident by replacing it with a small, certain fall in wealth from the insurance premium. This decrease in risk can make the buyer better off.

■ Self Test 12.2

Fill in the blanks

Insurance reduces the risk that people face by ____ (totally eliminating; pooling) the risks of many individuals. In a pooling equilibrium, careful and aggressive drivers pay ____ (the same rate; different rates) for auto insurance. In the market for auto insurance, moral hazard ____ (occurs; does not occur) and adverse selection ____ (occurs; does not occur). Screening is used to create a ____ (pooling; separating) equilibrium.

True or false

1. Buying insurance reduces the purchasers' risk.
2. Insurance companies pool risks.
3. If Kevin buys auto insurance, Kevin has decreased the risk that he will have an auto accident.
4. Adverse selection means that people who are at greater risk are more likely to buy insurance.
5. The number of traffic tickets a driver has accumulated is an example of a signal.
6. Aggressive drivers will buy insurance with a high deductible and low premium.

Multiple choice

1. In the United States, of all types of insurance, people spend the most on ____ insurance.
   a. auto
   b. property and casualty
   c. life
   d. health
   e. hurricane

2. Insurance companies
   a. pool risk and enable everyone to share the costs of bad outcomes.
   b. never can earn a profit because they accept risk.
   c. eliminate the risk of a bad outcome.
   d. know who will have a bad outcome.
   e. are risk averse.

3. When Sam makes an agreement and then behaves after the agreement in a way to increase his benefits and harm the other party to the agreement, Sam is illustrating
   a. signaling.
   b. adverse selection.
   c. moral hazard.
   d. the cost of contracting.
   e. a pooling equilibrium.

4. Ben is an aggressive driver so he is more likely to buy auto insurance. This situation illustrates the idea of
   a. moral hazard.
   b. adverse selection.
   c. the lemons problem.
   d. inefficiency.
   e. a separating equilibrium.

5. If you have private information that you are a riskier driver than your record indicates, you are likely to buy from your insurance company a policy that has a ____ deductible and a ____ premium.
   a. high; high
   b. high; low
   c. low; high
   d. low; low
   e. None of the above answers are correct because private information has no effect in the market for auto insurance.

6. Screening
   a. leads to a pooling equilibrium in the insurance market.
   b. means an uninformed person passes knowledge to an informed person.
   c. makes no-claim bonuses unnecessary.
   d. explains why insurance companies offer low-premium, high-deductible policies and high-premium, low-deductible policies.
   e. makes the insurance market inefficient.

Short answer and numeric questions

1. The risk of an auto accident is always present, so how does auto insurance increase a driver's well-being?

2. Which of the following are examples of adverse selection and which are examples of moral hazard?
   a. A skier takes additional risks once she has health insurance.
   b. A baseball player takes more days off for minor injuries after signing a long-term contract.
   c. A person who is a poor credit risk is more likely to use pay-day advance loans.
   d. A student who is likely to work little in a class signs up for a section that has extensive group work rather than a section that is graded solely on the basis of exams.
   e. A lazy used car salesperson applies for a job with a car dealership where the pay is a fixed amount rather than based on sales.
   f. A realtor shows a house for sale only once a month rather than once a week as was verbally promised before the sales contract was signed.

3. Igor owns a pet bat. Sadly, this species has a 20 percent annual probability of dying. Igor buys insurance from the All Bat Insurance Company, which will pay Igor in case his bat dies. Suppose that Igor knew his bat was already sickly and had a higher than normal chance of dying but All Bat did not know this, and so charged Igor the premium that applies to healthy bats. Who expects to gain more than usual from this policy? What does this situation illustrate?

4. Larry and Harry have private information about their safety as drivers. Larry is a safe driver; he never speeds and comes to a full stop at every red light. Harry believes that speed limit signs are the minimum speed and that yellow lights mean full speed ahead.
   a. If you owned an automobile insurance company and had to charge everyone the same rate, who do you want to insure?
   b. You want to sell insurance to safe drivers, like Larry, for $500 a year and to risky drivers, like Harry, for $1,500 a year. If you cannot determine who is safe and who is risky, you offer both Larry and

Harry insurance for $1,000 a year with no deductible. Is Harry likely to buy the insurance? Is Larry? Does Larry's decision depend on whether he can convince another insurance company that he is a safe driver?

c. Suppose that you decide to sell two types of insurance policies: one costs $1,300 a year and has a $100 deductible and the other costs $300 a year and has a $1,500 deductible. Which type of insurance is Harry most likely to buy? Larry? Why?

d. What do your answers to part (c) tell you about the role played by deductibles?

CHECKPOINT 12.3

■ Explain the information problems and other economic problems in health-care markets.

Quick Review

- *Moral hazard in the health-care market* Once incurred, a person has less incentive to adopt a healthy life style.

- *Adverse selection in the health-care market* The healthiest people are less likely to buy health insurance.

Additional Practice Problem 12.3

1. How does the health-care system in the United States compare to health-care systems in other major countries?

Solutions to Additional Practice Problem 12.3

1. The health-care system in the United States is unique compared to that in other major countries. All other major countries have a comprehensive national health-care system in which everyone is insured by a government-funded national insurance program. Health-care services are provided by private physicians, clinics, and so on but are paid for by the government. Patient care is allocated by urgency of need, so there are frequently long-waiting lists for treatment. In some nations people are permitted to buy private in-

surance and private health care. But in a few countries, no one is allowed to buy private insurance or private treatment.

The United States has no comprehensive national health-care system and has no government-funded national insurance program. In the United States, people choose whether to buy health insurance. Treatment is allocated by price; those who can pay the price receive treatment.

■ Self Test 12.3

Fill in the blanks

Adverse selection and moral hazard ____ (are; are not) present in the market for health insurance. In the United States, private insurance companies ____ (sell; do not sell) health insurance to anyone with pre-existing health problems. Some aspects of public-health ____ (are; are not) subject to the free-rider problem and other aspects ____ (have; do not have) positive externalities. The Obama Affordable Care Act ____ (addresses; does not address) the problem of people who have pre-existing health problems and ____ (address; does not address) the problem of over-expenditure on health care.

True or false

1. The market for health-care insurance is characterized by the absence of asymmetric information.

2. Health Maintenance Organizations help address the moral hazard problem in the market for health-care services.

3. The total expenditure by Medicaid and Medicare is determined by the decisions of Congress.

4. Vaccination against disease has a positive externality.

5. Most major nations do not have comprehensive national health-care systems.

6. The expenditure per person in the United States on health care is larger than in other major nations.

7. The Obama Affordable Care Act addresses the issue of over-expenditure on health care.

Multiple choice

1. Which of the following is *not* a problem in health-care markets?
   a. hospitals are not trying to maximize their profit
   b. asymmetric information
   c. public-health externalities
   d. a missing insurance market
   e. None of the above answers are correct; that is, all the answers are problems in health-care markets.

2. Moral hazard in the market for health-care services leads
   a. patients to adopt healthy life styles.
   b. to a separating equilibrium.
   c. to all people buying health insurance
   d. to healthy people not buying health insurance.
   e. to providers over treating patients.

3. The missing insurance market is the insurance market for
   a. young healthy people.
   b. infectious diseases.
   c. people who have pre-existing health problems.
   d. people in Health Maintenance Organizations.
   e. vaccinations.

4. Vaccination against infectious diseases ___, so private markets will provide ____ efficient quantity of vaccination.
   a. is a public good; less than the
   b. is a public good; the
   c. leads to adverse selection; less than the
   d. has a positive externality; less than the
   e. has a positive externality; the

5. Compared to other major nations, the United States spends ____ on health care and achieves ____ efficiency.
   a. less; greater
   b. more; about the same
   c. less; less
   d. more; less
   e. about the same amount; less

Short answer and numeric questions

1. What is the missing insurance market in health care?

2. Describe the public-health externalities. Do they mean that health care would be over-provided or under-provided by private markets?

3. How can health care be under-provided in the United States yet face a problem of over-expenditure?

4. The Eye on Your Life discusses the role grades and a college education play in signaling your ability. Signals also play a role in assigning grades. Frequently instructors who assign group projects base some of the grade on grades each group participant assigns to the other participants. Using the concepts discussed in this chapter, explain why instructors use this method rather than assign everyone in the project the same grade.

SELF TEST ANSWERS

■ CHECKPOINT 12.1

Fill in the blanks

In the used car market, <u>sellers</u> have private information about the quality of the used car being sold. Adverse selection in the used car market with signals means that only <u>lemons</u> are offered for sale. In the used car market, a warranty acts as a <u>signal</u>. If there are no signals in the used car market, too <u>few</u> good used cars are sold. Signals that allow buyers to distinguish between good used cars and lemons result in a <u>separating</u> equilibrium. In the used car market with a pooling equilibrium, there <u>is one price</u> for used cars and <u>only lemons</u> are sold. In the used car market with a separating equilibrium, there <u>are two prices</u> for used cars and <u>both lemons and good cars</u> are sold.

True or false

1. True; page 292
2. True; page 295
3. True; page 296
4. True   page 297
5. True; page 297

Multiple choice

1. c; page 292
2. d; pages 294-295
3. a; page 295
4. d; page 296
5. a; pages 294-295, 297
6. b; page 297

Short answer and numeric questions

1. The lemons problem is an issue that arises in the used car market from asymmetric information. Sellers of used cars have private information about the quality of the car they are selling. If buyers cannot determine the quality of the car, they realize that owners of lemons are more likely to sell their car than owners of good used cars. In this case buyers will be willing to pay only a low price, the price they are willing to pay for a lemon. Sellers of good cars cannot receive the higher price their car is worth, so they are unwilling to sell their (good) used cars. Hence only lemons are bought and sold; pages 292-295.

2. Adverse selection is one of the issues asymmetric information creates. Adverse selection is the tendency for people to enter into transactions when their private information indicates to them that they will receive additional benefits than the other party expected. For instance, people who have private information that they are more prone to illness than the typical person are more likely to buy health insurance; page 295.

3. Signaling can change the equilibrium from a pooling equilibrium to a separating equilibrium. In a pooling equilibrium, buyers cannot tell the difference between a high-quality item and a low-quality item. Both will trade for the same price which means that mainly (or only) low-quality items will trade. Signaling enables buyers to tell a high-quality item from a low-quality item and leads to a separating equilibrium: High-quality items sell for a higher price and low-quality items sell for a lower price. Both high- and low-quality items are traded; pages 296-297.

4. In a pooling equilibrium, high-quality items sell for the same price as low-quality items, so generally only low-quality items are traded. In a separating equilibrium, high-quality items sell for a higher price than low-quality items, so both high-and low-quality items are traded. The pooling equilibrium has a deadweight loss because too many low-quality items are traded and too few high-quality items are traded. The separating equilibrium does not have a deadweight loss; page 297.

■ CHECKPOINT 12.2

Fill in the blanks

Insurance reduces the risk that people face by <u>pooling</u> the risks of many individuals. In a pooling equilibrium, careful and aggressive drivers pay <u>the same rate</u> for auto insurance. In the market for auto insurance, moral hazard <u>occurs</u> and adverse selection <u>occurs</u>. Screening is used to create a <u>separating</u> equilibrium.

True or false

1. True; page 300
2. True; page 300
3. False; page 300
4. True; page 301
5. True; page 302
6. False; page 302

Multiple choice

1. d; page 299
2. a; page 300
3. c; page 301
4. b; page 301
5. c; page 302
6. d; pages 302-303

Short answer and numeric questions

1 While the risk of an auto accident is always present, auto insurance removes the financial risk. Auto insurance means that the driver no longer faces the possibility of a large loss because if the driver has an accident, the insurance company reimburses the driver. However the driver must pay the insurance company its premium, so the driver has traded the risky possibility of a large loss for the certain case of a small loss. By reducing the driver's financial risk, the driver is made better off; pages 299-300.

2 a. Moral hazard; because the skier is changing behavior after the health insurance was purchased; page 301.

b. Moral hazard, because the ball player's behavior is changing after the contract was signed; page 301.

c. Adverse selection, because the pay-day loan company is attracting poor credit risks; page 301.

d. Adverse selection, because the class section based on group work is attracting lazy students; page 301.

e. Adverse selection, because the car dealership is attracting lazy salespeople; page 301.

f. Moral hazard, because the realtor's behavior is changing after the contract was signed; page 301.

3. Igor expects to gain more from the policy because the probability of his bat dying exceeds the normal probability. Thus the probability that All Bat will need to pay off on the policy exceeds normal. This situation illustrates the adverse selection problem: The people who most want to buy bat insurance are those who have sickly bats; page 301.

4. a. You most want to sell insurance to Larry because you expect that his policy will be more profitable than Harry's policy; pages 300-303.

b. Harry is likely to buy the policy. If Harry does not buy the policy, he expects to pay $1,500 a year for his accidents. If he buys the policy, he pays only $1,000, a saving to Harry of $500. Larry may or may not buy a policy. If he is very risk averse and cannot obtain a lower price from another company, he will buy your insurance. But, if he is only a little risk averse, he may decide to do without insurance. If another company can recognize him as a safe driver, it will therefore offer him a less expensive policy. Larry then will buy from your competitor; pages 302-303.

c. Harry probably will buy the first policy; Larry likely will buy the second. From Harry's standpoint, the second policy is more expensive than the first. Harry, the risky driver, is likely to have an accident and thereby incur the $1,500 deductible. Larry realizes that he is unlikely to have an accident and is not likely to have to pay the deductible. Larry is more likely to opt for the second policy because, if he has no accident, he pays only $300 rather than $1,300 for his insurance; pages 302-303.

d. Insurance companies use deductibles to separate risky and safe drivers. Safe drivers prefer a low premium and high deductible because they realize that they are not likely to have an accident and be forced to pay the deductible. Risky drivers prefer a high premium and low deductible because they know that an accident is probable and they do not want to be hit with a high deductible payment. High-risk drivers know that they are accident prone and they are willing to pay higher premiums for nearly full coverage, but low-risk drivers know that they seldom have accidents and they will choose lower premiums with lower coverage; page 302.

■ CHECKPOINT 12.3

Fill in the blanks

Adverse selection and moral hazard <u>are</u> present in the market for health insurance. In the United States, private insurance companies <u>do not sell</u> health insurance to anyone with pre-existing health problems. Some aspects of public health <u>are</u> subject to the free-rider problem and other aspects <u>have</u> positive externalities. The Obama Affordable Care Act <u>addresses</u> the problem of people who have pre-existing health problems and <u>does not address</u> the problem of over-expenditure on health care.

True or false

1. False; page 305
2. True; page 306
3. False; page 306
4. True; page 307
5. False; page 307
6. True; page 308
7. False; page 309

Multiple choice

1. a; page 305
2. e; pages 305-306
3. c; page 306
4. d; page 307
5. d; page 308

Short answer and numeric questions

1. The missing insurance market is the market for insurance for people who have pre-existing medical conditions. These people can either get no insurance or else get insurance that excludes their pre-existing condition. Hence the people with the greatest want for health insurance are often unable to obtain it; page 306.

2. There are two public health externalities. The first is that the control of infectious diseases is often a public good. For example, public sanitation, which helps control infectious diseases, is a public good and so is provided by the government to avoid the free-rider problem. The second externality arises from vaccination against infectious diseases, which has a positive externality. If a person is vaccinated, that person enjoys a gain from the vaccination but so, too, do his or her friends who become less likely to catch the disease; page 307.

3. Medicare and Medicaid are government programs that cover health care for the aged and those too poor to buy health insurance. Even with these programs, health care in the United States is under provided because there are still millions of people without health-care insurance. Over-expenditure remains a problem, however, because insurance means that patients do not bear the full cost of their treatment. For instance, the total expenditure made under the Medicare and Medicaid programs is determined by the patients and not set by governmental decisions; pages 306, 309.

4. The group members have private information about each member's contribution, that is, who worked hard and who shirked. The instructor would like to know this private information, so the instructor allows the group members to signal this information by the grades they assign the other members. By acquiring this information, the instructor helps overcome the moral hazard created by the group members' incentives to not work and count on the other members to carry the load.

Consumer Choice and Demand

Chapter 13

CHAPTER CHECKLIST

Chapter 13 presents a model of consumer choice based on marginal utility. We use marginal utility theory to derive a demand curve and explain the paradox of value.

1 Calculate and graph a budget line that shows the limits to a person's consumption possibilities.

The budget line describes the limits to a consumer's consumption possibilities. A consumer can afford any combination on the budget line and inside it, but cannot afford any combination outside the budget line. When the price of a good changes, the slope of the budget line changes. A relative price is the price of one good in terms of another good—an opportunity cost. It equals the price of one good divided by the price of another good. The slope of the budget line equals the relative price of the good on the x-axis. An increase in the budget shifts the budget line rightward, and a decrease shifts the budget line leftward. An increase in the price of the good measured along the horizontal axis rotates the budget line inward around the vertical intercept and a decrease in the price rotates the budget line outward.

2 Explain marginal utility theory and use it to derive a consumer's demand curve.

Utility is the benefit or satisfaction a person gets from the consumption of a good or service. Total utility is the total benefit that a person gets from the consumption of a good or service; marginal utility is the change in total utility that results from a one-unit increase in the quantity of a good consumed. As more of a good is consumed, its total utility increases but its marginal utility decreases. A consumer maximizes total utility when he or she allocates his or her entire available budget and makes the marginal utility per dollar the same for all goods. The marginal utility per dollar is the marginal utility from the good relative to the price of the good. It equals the marginal utility divided by the price. If the price of a good falls, the marginal utility per dollar for that good rises at the current consumption level and the consumer buys more of that good. So when the price of a good falls, there is an increase in the quantity demanded and a movement down along the demand curve.

3 Use marginal utility theory to explain the paradox of value: why water is vital but cheap while diamonds are relatively useless but expensive.

The paradox of value is that water, which is essential to life, is cheap, while diamonds, which are relatively useless, are expensive. We solve this puzzle by distinguishing between total utility and marginal utility. The total utility from water is enormous. But we use so much water that its marginal utility is a small value. The total utility from diamonds is small. But we have few diamonds so their marginal utility is high. Diamonds have a high price and a high marginal utility while water has a low price and a low marginal utility. When the (high) marginal utility of diamonds is divided by the (high) price of a diamond, the result equals the (low) marginal utility of water divided by the (low) price of water so the marginal utility per dollar of diamonds equals that of water. Water is cheap but provides a large consumer surplus; diamonds are expensive but provide a small consumer surplus.

CHECKPOINT 13.1

- ■ **Calculate and graph a budget line that shows the limits to a person's consumption possibilities.**

Quick Review

- • *Budget line* A line that describes the limits to consumption choices and that depends on a consumer's budget and the prices of goods and services.

Additional Practice Problems 13.1

1. Mark, a chemistry major at Cal State East Bay, dines by himself at the local Olive Garden. He has $30 per week to spend. Pizza is $15 and a salad is $5.

   a. List the combinations of pizza and salads he can buy.

   b. Graph Mark's budget line in the figure to the right.

   c. What is the opportunity cost of a pizza?

   d. What is the relative price of a pizza?

2. Sue is a student at Chabot Junior College. She has a budget of $240 that she will spend on purses and/or shoes. The price of a purse is $40 and the price of a pair of shoes is $60.

   a. Draw a graph of Sue's budget line in the figure to the right.

   b. If purses rise in price to $60, in the figure show what happens to Sue's budget line.

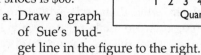

Solutions to Additional Practice Problems 13.1

1a. The combinations of pizza and salads that Mark can afford are listed in the table. To construct this table, select the combinations of pizza and salad that spend all of Mark's $30 budget.

Pizza	Salads
0	6
1	3
2	0

1b. The figure shows Mark's budget line. The maximum number of pizzas he can buy is 2; the maximum number of salads he can buy is 6.

1c. The slope of the budget line is the opportunity cost of a pizza. The slope is (6 salads) ÷ (2 pizzas), which equals 3 salads per pizza. So consuming 1 pizza means Mark forgoes 3 salads.

1d. The opportunity cost of a pizza is also its relative price. The relative price of a pizza is 3 salads per pizza.

2a. The figure shows Sue's budget line as the grey line. The maximum number of purses Sue can buy is 6, where the budget line intersects the *x*-axis, and the maximum number of shoes Sue can buy is 4, where the budget line intersects the *y*-axis.

2b. When the price of a purse rises, the maximum number of purses that can be purchased decreases to 4 but the maximum number of shoes is unchanged. The budget line rotates inward as shown in the figure by the dark budget line.

■ Self Test 13.1

Fill in the blanks

A ____ shows the limits to consumption possibilities. The budget line becomes ____ (less steep; steeper) when the price of the good measured on the x-axis increases and everything else remains the same. The slope of the budget line is equal to a ____ price. When a consumer's budget increases, the budget line shifts ____ (inward; outward).

True or false

1. Dian's budget line shows the limits to what Dian can consume.

2. When Stan's budget increases, his budget line shifts outward.

3. A fall in the price of the good measured along the x-axis, all other things remaining the same, rotates the budget line inward.

4. The slope of the budget line measures the opportunity cost of one more unit of the good plotted on the x-axis.

5. The price of one good plus the price of another good equals the relative price.

Multiple choice

1. A budget line shows the
   a. limits to production possibilities.
   b. limits to production opportunities.
   c. the slope of the demand curve.
   d. limits to consumption possibilities.
   e. way the demand curve shifts if the consumer's budget changes.

2. A budget line
   a. represents combinations of goods a consumer desires.
   b. marks the boundary between what a consumer can afford and cannot afford.
   c. has a positive slope.
   d. is the same as the production possibilities frontier.
   e. is the same as a demand curve.

3. Linda has $10 a month to spend on ice cream cones and chocolate bars. If the price of an ice cream cone is $2 a cone and the price of a chocolate bar is $1 a bar, which of the following is a point on Linda's budget line?
   a. 4 cones and 0 chocolate bars
   b. 1 cone and 8 chocolate bars
   c. 3 cones and 1 chocolate bar
   d. 5 cones and 10 chocolate bars
   e. 0 cones and 0 chocolate bars

4. If a consumer's budget increases, the budget line
   a. rotates outward and its slope changes.
   b. rotates inward and its slope changes.
   c. shifts outward and its slope does not change.
   d. shifts inward and its slope does not change.
   e. does not change.

5. Reb buys fishing lures and steaks. If his budget increases, the maximum number of fishing lures he can purchase ____ and the maximum number of steaks he can purchase ____.
   a. increases; increases
   b. increases; decreases
   c. decreases; increases
   d. decreases; decreases
   e. does not change; does not change

6. If a budget line rotates inward and becomes steeper, then the
   a. consumer's budget decreased.
   b. consumer's budget increased.
   c. price of one of the goods decreased.
   d. price of one of the goods increased.
   e. price of both of the goods must have decreased.

■ **FIGURE 13.1**

Quantity (movies per month)

Quantity (hours playing paintball per month)

7. ____ will change Bobby's budget line as shown by the change from the gray budget line to the black budget line in Figure 13.1.
   a. An increase in Bobby's budget
   b. A decrease in Bobby's budget
   c. A fall in the price of playing paintball
   d. A rise in the price playing paintball
   e. A rise in the price of a movie

8. If the budget line rotates inward and becomes steeper, there is a
   a. higher opportunity cost of the good measured on the x-axis.
   b. lower opportunity cost of the good measured on the x-axis.
   c. larger budget.
   d. higher price for the good measured on the y-axis.
   e. lower price for the good measured on the x-axis.

9. A relative price is the
   a. price of a substitute.
   b. price of a related good.
   c. price of one good divided by the price of another.
   d. absolute price of a good.
   e. price of one good multiplied by the price of another.

Complete the graph

■ **FIGURE 13.2**

Quantity (magazines per week)

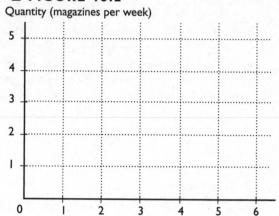

Quantity (hamburgers per week)

1. Jack buys two things: magazines, which have a price of $3 each, and hamburgers, which have a price of $4 each. Jack's income is $12.
   a. In Figure 13.2, draw Jack's budget line.
   b. What does the slope of the budget line equal? What is the interpretation of this slope?
   c. Can Jack buy 2 magazines and 1 hamburger? Can he buy 2 magazines and 3 hamburgers?
   d. Suppose the price of a hamburger falls to $2. In Figure 13.2, draw Jack's new budget line.
   e. What does the slope of the new budget line equal? How does the slope compare to your answer to part (b)?
   f. Can Jack now buy 2 magazines and 1 hamburger? Can he now buy 2 magazines and 3 hamburgers?

Short answer and numeric questions

1. How is a budget line similar to a production possibilities frontier? How is it dissimilar?

2. If a consumer's budget increases, what happens to his or her budget line? Does its slope change?

3. What does the slope of a budget line equal?

4. What is the relationship between the relative price of a good and its opportunity cost?

Additional Exercises (also in MyEconLab Test A)

Jenny's burger and salad budget is $36 a week. The price of a burger is $3, and the price of a salad is $2.

1. List the combinations of burgers and salads that Jenny can afford.

2. Draw a graph of Jenny's budget line with the quantity of burgers plotted on the x-axis. Describe how Jenny's budget line changes if, other things remaining the same, the following changes occur one at a time:
   a. The price of a salad rises.
   b. Jenny's burger and salad budget decreases.

3. How does the relative price of a salad change if the price of a salad falls to $1? Explain your answer.

CHECKPOINT 13.2

■ **Explain marginal utility theory and use it to derive a consumer's demand curve.**

Quick Review

- *Marginal utility* The change in total utility that results from a one-unit increase in the quantity of a good consumed.

- *Marginal utility per dollar* The increase in total utility that comes from the last dollar spent on the good.

Additional Practice Problems 13.2

Orange juice		Cookies	
Quantity per week	Total utility	Quantity per week	Total utility
0	0	0	0
1	20	1	60
2	32	2	100
3	40	3	120
4	44	4	130
5	46	5	145

1. The table above shows Tommy's total utility from orange juice and cookies.

a. Calculate Tommy's marginal utility schedule from orange juice and from cookies by completing the table below.

Orange juice		Cookies	
Quantity per week	Marginal utility	Quantity per week	Marginal utility
0	XX	0	XX
1	___	1	___
2	___	2	___
3	___	3	___
4	___	4	___
5	___	5	___

b. If the price of a carton of orange juice is $2, what is Tommy's marginal utility per dollar for orange juice when Tommy buys 2 cartons of orange juice a week?

c. If the price of a box of cookies is $4, what is Tommy's marginal utility per dollar for cookies when Tommy buys 3 boxes of cookies a week?

d. If Tommy's budget for orange juice and cookies is $10 per week and orange juice is $2 per carton and cookies are $4 per box, what combination of orange juice and cookies will Tommy buy? Why does Tommy buy this combination? What is his total utility?

e. Tommy could afford to buy 5 cartons of orange juice a week. Why does he not buy 5 cartons?

2. If Jenny is allocating her entire available budget on movies and popcorn, explain the rule she follows to maximize her total utility.

Solutions to Additional Practice Problems 13.2

Orange juice		Cookies	
Quantity per week	Marginal utility	Quantity per week	Marginal utility
0	XX	0	XX
1	20	1	60
2	12	2	40
3	8	3	20
4	4	4	10
5	2	5	5

1a. The completed table is above. Marginal utility equals the change in total utility from a one-unit increase in the quantity of the good consumed. So the marginal utility of the second box of cookies equals 100 – 60, which is 40.

1b. The marginal utility per dollar is 12 ÷ $2 = 6.

1c. The marginal utility per dollar is 20 ÷ $4 = 5.

1d. Tommy buys 2 boxes of cookies and 1 carton of orange juice. This combination allocates his entire budget and the marginal utility per dollar for orange juice, 10, equals the marginal utility per dollar for cookies, 10. This combination gives Tommy total utility of 120.

1e. Tommy does not buy 5 cartons of orange juice because his total utility would be only 46, well less than his total utility from the utility-maximizing combination derived in the answer to part (d).

2. If the marginal utility per dollar from movies exceeds the marginal utility per dollar from popcorn, then Jenny sees more movies and buys less popcorn because this action increases her total utility; if the marginal utility per dollar from popcorn exceeds the marginal utility per dollar from movies, Jenny buys more popcorn and sees fewer movies because this action increases her total utility. More generally, if the marginal gain from an action exceeds the marginal loss, take the action. Jenny is maximizing her total utility when the marginal utility per dollar from movies equals the marginal utility per dollar from popcorn.

■ Self Test 13.2

Fill in the blanks

The total benefit a person gets from the consumption of a good or service is ____ (marginal; total) utility. The change in total utility that results from a one-unit increase in the consumption of a good or service is ____ (marginal; elastic) utility. As the quantity of a good consumed increases, total utility ____ (increases; decreases) and marginal utility ____ (increases; decreases). The marginal utility per dollar equals the marginal utility of a good ____ (multiplied; divided) by the price of the good. When total utility is maximized, the marginal utility per dollar ____ (equals 1; is equal) for all goods. Marginal utility theory implies that, other things remaining the same, the ____ (higher; lower) the price of a good, the smaller is the quantity demanded of that good.

True or false

1. As Katie consumes more sushi, her total utility from sushi increases.

2. As Katie consumes more sushi, her marginal utility from sushi increases.

3. Bobby maximizes his utility whenever he allocates his entire available budget.

4. Tommy is allocating his entire available budget. If Tommy's marginal utility per dollar for tacos is 8 and the marginal utility per dollar from burritos is 10, then Tommy is NOT maximizing his total utility.

5. Marginal utility theory implies that other things remaining the same, the higher the price of a good, the greater is the quantity demanded of that good.

Multiple choice

1. In economics, utility
   a. always decreases as income increases.
   b. equals opportunity cost.
   c. is an index of satisfaction.
   d. is measured by the same units as relative price.
   e. and relative price are the same thing.

2. Marginal utility is the
   a. change in total utility that results from a one-unit increase in the quantity of a good consumed.
   b. total benefit from the consumption of a good or service.
   c. quantity of a good a consumer prefers.
   d. average utility per unit consumed.
   e. change in total utility that results from a one dollar increase in the price of a good consumed.

3. Sushi costs $3 per piece. Cynthia's total utility after eating one piece is 30 and her total utility after eating 2 pieces is 51, so her marginal utility from the second piece is
   a. 17.
   b. 10.
   c. 51.
   d. 7.
   e. 21.

4. As Shaniq drinks additional cups of tea at breakfast, Shaniq's
   a. marginal utility from tea decreases.
   b. total utility from tea increases.
   c. total utility from tea decreases.
   d. Both answers (a) and (b) are correct.
   e. Both answers (b) and (c) are correct.

5. Marginal utility per dollar is calculated by ____ the price of the good.
   a. multiplying the marginal utility from a good by
   b. dividing the marginal utility from a good by
   c. multiplying the total utility from a good by
   d. dividing the total utility from a good by
   e. averaging the marginal utility from the good with

6. Sushi costs $3 per piece. Cynthia's total utility after eating one piece is 30 and her total utility after eating 2 pieces is 51, so her marginal utility per dollar from the second piece is
   a. 17.
   b. 10.
   c. 51.
   d. 7.
   e. 21.

7. When Chris maximizes his total utility, then his entire available budget is allocated in such a way that the
   a. marginal utility from all goods is equal.
   b. marginal utility per dollar is equal for all goods.
   c. marginal utility is as large as possible for goods.
   d. marginal utility will start decreasing if it consumes fewer goods.
   e. quantities consumed of each good are equal.

8. Suppose that Misty likes pizza and hotdogs. If her marginal utility per dollar from pizza is 6 and from hotdogs is 5, Misty
   a. is maximizing her total utility.
   b. could increase her total utility by buying more hotdogs and less pizza.
   c. could increase her total utility by buying more pizza and fewer hotdogs.
   d. is maximizing her marginal utility.
   e. must obtain more income in order to reach her consumer equilibrium.

9. You can use marginal utility theory to find the demand curve by changing
   a. only the price of one good.
   b. only income.
   c. the utility schedule.
   d. only the prices of both goods.
   e. income and the prices of both goods.

10. Suppose that Hank consumes only Mountain Dew and pizza. If Hank's total utility from all amounts of both Mountain Dew and pizza double from what they were before, then Hank's demand for
    a. both goods must double.
    b. one of the goods must double.
    c. both goods must decrease by one-half.
    d. one of the goods must decrease by one-half.
    e. neither good changes.

Complete the graph

Quantity (slices per day)	Total utility, pizza	Marginal utility, pizza	Quantity (cans per day)	Total utility, soda	Marginal utility, soda
0	0		0	0	
1	45		1	25	
2	85	___	2	45	___
3	120	___	3	60	___
4	150	___	4	70	___
5	175	___	5	75	___
6	195	___	6	76	___

1. Bertha consumes only soda and pizza. The table above gives Bertha's total utility from soda and pizza slices.

  a. Complete the marginal utility columns of the table.

  b. The price of a can of soda is $1 and the price of a slice of pizza is $2. If Bertha's budget is $6, how many cans of soda and slices of pizza will she consume?

  c. Suppose the price of a slice of pizza rises to $3, while the price of a can of soda and Bertha's budget does not change. Now how many cans of soda and slices of pizza will she consume?

■ **FIGURE 13.3**

  d. What are two points on Bertha's demand curve for slices of pizza? Assuming her demand curve is a straight line, label the axes and then draw her demand curve in Figure 13.3.

Short answer and numeric questions

Quantity (bottles of Aquafina per day)	Total utility	Marginal utility
0	0	
1	25	
2	45	___
3	60	___
4	70	___
5	75	___
6	76	___

1. Carlos drinks Aquafina bottled water. The table above gives his total utility from this water. Calculate his marginal utility.

Quantity (tacos per week)	Marginal utility	Quantity (hamburgers per week)	Marginal utility
0	0	0	0
1	50	1	80
2	40	2	40
3	30	3	20
4	20	4	10
5	10	5	5

2. Lisa eats tacos and hamburgers. The quantities and marginal utilities from each are in the table above. Lisa's budget is $8.

  a. If the price of taco is $1 and the price of a hamburger is $2, what quantity of tacos and hamburgers will Lisa purchase?

  b. If the price of a taco rises to $2 while neither Lisa's income nor the price of a hamburger change, what quantity of tacos and hamburgers will Lisa purchase?

  c. How does Lisa respond to a change in the price of a taco?

3. What does it mean to "allocate the entire available budget?" How does saving fit into the picture?

4. What is marginal analysis? Why is making the marginal utility per dollar necessary for a consumer to maximize his or her utility?

Additional Exercises (also in MyEconLab Test A)

The table on the next page shows Wanda's total utility for juice and pasta. The price of a can of juice is $1, the price of a dish of pasta is $4, and Wanda has $11 a week to spend.

Juice		Pasta	
Cans per week	Total utility	Dishes per week	Total utility
0	0	0	0
1	22	1	64
2	40	2	120
3	54	3	168
4	60	4	208
5	62	5	240
6	62	6	264

1. Calculate Wanda's marginal utility and marginal utility per dollar from pasta when she buys 3 dishes a week. Calculate Wanda's marginal utility and marginal utility per dollar from juice when she buys 2 cans a week.

2. If Wanda buys 2 cans of juice and 2 dishes of pasta a week, is she maximizing her total utility? If Wanda is not maximizing her total utility, explain how she must adjust her consumption of juice and pasta to do so.

CHECKPOINT 13.3

■ **Use marginal utility theory to explain the paradox of value: why water is vital but cheap while diamonds are relatively useless but expensive.**

Quick Review

- *The paradox of value* Why is water, which is essential to life, cheap, but diamonds, which are useless compared to water, expensive?

Additional Practice Problem 13.3

1. Anthony buys 30,000 gallons of water a month. His marginal utility from a gallon of water is 100 units. The price of a gallon of water is $0.001. Anthony also buys 4 boxes of Krispy Kreme doughnuts a month. He pays $5 for a box. Anthony is maximizing his utility.

    a. What is the marginal utility from a box of Krispy Kreme doughnuts?

    b. Why does Anthony receive a lower marginal utility from his consumption of water?

Solution to Additional Practice Problem 13.3

1a. Because Anthony is maximizing his utility, the marginal utility per dollar he spends on water equals the marginal utility per dollar he spends on doughnuts. The marginal utility per dollar for water equals 100 units ÷ $0.001 = 100,000. So the marginal utility of a box of doughnuts divided by the price of a box of doughnuts ($5) must equal 100,000. In terms of a formula, $MU ÷ 5 = 100,000$, so the marginal utility of a box of doughnuts equals $5 \times 100,000$, which is 500,000.

1b. Anthony buys 30,000 gallons of water a month and (only) 4 boxes of doughnuts a month. As the quantity of a good consumed increases, the marginal utility decreases. Because Anthony is consuming much more water than doughnuts, his total utility from water is almost surely greater than his total utility from doughnuts, but his marginal utility from water is much less than his marginal utility from doughnuts.

■ Self Test 13.3

Fill in the blanks

Marginal benefit is the maximum price a consumer is willing to pay for an extra unit of a good or service when ____. The paradox of value is resolved by noting that diamonds have a high price, a ____ (high; low) total utility, and a ____ (high; low) marginal utility. Water provides ____ (more; less) consumer surplus than diamonds.

True or false

1. Susan's demand curve for curry shows the quantity of curry she demands at each price when her total utility is maximized.

2. Marginal benefit is the maximum price a consumer is willing to pay for an extra unit of a good or service when total utility is maximized.

3. The paradox of value is that water, which is essential to life, is plentiful, while dia-

monds, which are not essential to life, are much less plentiful.

4. The paradox of value is solved by noting that the total utility from water is small while the marginal utility from water is large.

5. The consumer surplus from water is greater than the consumer surplus from diamonds.

Multiple choice

1. At all points on a demand curve, the
   i. consumer's budget has been allocated to maximize total utility.
   ii. quantity is the quantity demanded at each price when total utility is maximized.
   iii. price represents the marginal benefit the consumer gets from an extra unit of a good.
   a. i only.
   b. ii only.
   c. i and ii.
   d. i and iii.
   e. i, ii, and iii.

2. As more of a good is consumed, the marginal utility of an additional unit ____, so consumers are willing to pay ____ for an additional unit.
   a. decreases; less
   b. increases; less
   c. decreases; more
   d. increases; more
   e. does not change; less

3. The paradox of value refers to the
   a. utility maximizing rule.
   b. fact that water is vital but cheap while diamonds are relatively useless but expensive.
   c. fact that consumers have different preferences and utility schedules.
   d. law of demand.
   e. issue of why the consumer surplus from water equals the consumer surplus from diamonds.

4. One reason why water is cheap compared to diamonds is because the
   a. marginal utility of water is enormous.
   b. marginal utility of water is small.
   c. total utility of water is enormous.
   d. total utility of water is small.
   e. total utility of water and diamonds must be equal but the marginal utility of water is much lower than the marginal utility of diamonds.

5. In the paradox of value between expensive diamonds and inexpensive water, we see that
   a. the consumer surpluses are very high for both goods.
   b. diamonds have a low consumer surplus while water has a high consumer surplus.
   c. diamonds have a high consumer surplus while water has a low consumer surplus.
   d. the consumer surpluses are very low for both goods.
   e. the consumer surpluses for the two goods cannot be compared.

Complete the graph

■ **FIGURE 13.4**

Price (dollars per thousand gallons)

1. Figure 13.4 shows the market for water. Indicate the equilibrium price and then shade in the area of the consumer surplus.

■ **FIGURE 13.5**

Price (thousands of dollars per carat)

2. Figure 13.5 shows the market for rubies. Indicate the equilibrium price and then shade in the area of the consumer surplus.

3. Based on Figures 13.4 and 13.5, is there more consumer surplus for water or rubies? Which is larger: the marginal utility of a gallon of water or a carat of rubies?

Short answer and numeric questions

1. Bobby consumes potato chips and Gatorade and is maximizing his utility. His marginal utility from the last bag of chips he eats is 40 and his marginal utility from the last bottle of Gatorade he drinks is 60. The price of a bag of chips is $2. What must be the price of a bottle of Gatorade?

2. Does the price Bianca is willing to pay for another purse depend on her total utility from purses or her marginal utility? Explain your answer.

3. What is the paradox of value and what is its solution?

Additional Exercises (also in MyEconLab Test A)

1. Which good is more valuable to you: water or your economics text?

SELF TEST ANSWERS

■ CHECKPOINT 13.1

Fill in the blanks

A <u>budget line</u> shows the limits to consumption possibilities. The budget line becomes <u>steeper</u> when the price of the good measured on the x-axis increases and everything else remains the same. The slope of the budget line is equal to a <u>relative</u> price. When a consumer's budget increases, the budget line shifts <u>outward</u>.

True or false

1. True; page 316
2. True; page 317
3. False; page 318
4. True; page 319
5. False; page 320

Multiple choice

1. d; page 316
2. b; page 316
3. b; page 316
4. c; page 317
5. a; page 317
6. d; page 318
7. c; page 318
8. a; page 320
9. c; page 320

Complete the graph

1. a. The budget line in Figure 13.6 labeled "hamburgers $4" is Jack's budget line; page 316.
   b. The slope of the budget line equals (−4 magazines/3 hamburgers), which is −1 1/3 of a magazine per hamburger. The slope is the opportunity cost of a hamburger, which is the relative price of a hamburger; page 319.
   c. Jack can buy 2 magazines and 1 hamburger. Jack cannot buy 2 magazines and 3 hamburgers because that combination is outside his budget line; page 316.
   d. The new budget line is in Figure 13.6, labeled "Hamburgers $2"; page 316.

■ FIGURE 13.6

Quantity (magazines per week)

Budget line, hamburgers $4

Budget line, hamburgers $2

Quantity (hamburgers per week)

e. The slope of the new budget line is −2/3 of a magazine per hamburger. Compared to the slope in part (b), the opportunity cost of a hamburger is lower when its price falls; page 320.

f. Jack can buy 2 magazines and 1 hamburger. Jack also can buy 2 magazines and 3 hamburgers because that combination is now on his budget line; page 316.

Short answer and numeric questions

1. A budget line is similar to the production possibilities frontier. Both curves show a limit to what is feasible. The *PPF* is a technological limit that does not depend on prices. But the budget line does depend on prices. Consumption possibilities change when prices or the available budget change; page 316.

2. The budget line shifts outward. Its slope does not change; page 317.

3. The slope of the budget line equals the opportunity cost and the relative price of the good measured along the x-axis; page 319.

4. The relative price is the price of one good in terms of another good. The relative price is an opportunity cost. It equals the price of one good divided by the price of another good; page 320.

Additional Exercises (also in MyEconLab Test A)

1. The affordable combinations of burgers and salad, all of which spend the $36 in Jenny's budget, are:

   - 0 burgers and 18 salads
   - 2 burgers and 15 salads
   - 4 burgers and 12 salads
   - 6 burgers and 9 salads
   - 8 burgers and 6 salads
   - 10 burgers and 3 salads
   - 12 burgers and 0 salads

■ **FIGURE 13.7**

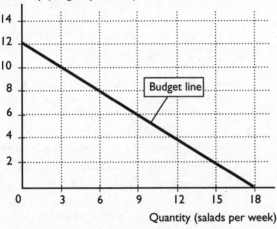

Quantity (burgers per week)

2. Figure 13.7 shows Jenny's budget line.

   a. If the price of a salad rises, the budget line rotates inward and becomes steeper. The vertical intercept stays the same (12 burgers) but the horizontal intercept decreases.

   b. If Jenny's burger and salad budget decreases, the budget line shifts inward and its slope does not change; page 318.

3. The relative price of a salad is the opportunity cost of a salad—the number of burgers that Jenny must forgo to get 1 salad. The relative price of a salad equals the price of a salad divided by the price of a burger, which is $1 a salad ÷ $3 a burger = 1/3 of a burger for a salad. Hence the fall in the (money) price of a salad together with no change in the (money) price of a burger leads to a fall

in the relative price of a salad; pages 319-320.

■ **CHECKPOINT 13.2**

Fill in the blanks

The total benefit a person gets from the consumption of a good or service is <u>total</u> utility. The change in total utility that results from a one-unit increase in the consumption of a good or service is <u>marginal</u> utility. As the quantity of a good consumed increases, total utility <u>increases</u> and marginal utility <u>decreases</u>. The marginal utility per dollar equals the marginal utility of a good <u>divided</u> by the price of the good. When total utility is maximized, the marginal utility per dollar <u>is equal</u> for all goods. Marginal utility theory implies that, other things remaining the same, the <u>higher</u> the price of a good, the smaller is the quantity demanded of that good.

True or false

1. True; page 322
2. False; page 322
3. False; page 324
4. True; pages 324-325
5. False; page 327

Multiple choice

1. c; page 322
2. a; page 322
3. e; page 322
4. d; page 322
5. b; page 324
6. d; page 324
7. b; page 324
8. c; page 326
9. a; page 327
10. e; page 327

Complete the graph

Pizza			Soda		
Quantity (slices per day)	Total utility, pizza	Marginal utility, pizza	Quantity (cans per day)	Total utility, soda	Marginal utility, soda
0	0		0	0	
1	45	45	1	25	25
2	85	40	2	45	20
3	120	35	3	60	15
4	150	30	4	70	10
5	175	25	5	75	5
6	195	20	6	76	1

1. a. The completed table is above; page 299.

   b. Bertha will consume 2 cans of soda and 2 slices of pizza. This combination allocates all her budget and equalizes the marginal utility per dollar from soda and pizza at 20 units; page 326.

   c. Bertha will now consume 3 cans of soda and 1 slice of pizza. This combination allocates all of her budget and equalizes the marginal utility per dollar from soda and pizza at 15 units; page 326.

■ **FIGURE 13.8**

Price (dollars per slice of pizza)

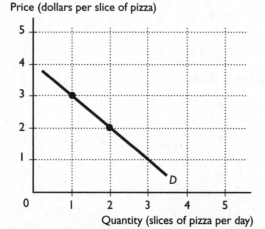

Quantity (slices of pizza per day)

   d. One point on her demand curve is $2 and 2 slices of pizza; another point is $3 and 1 slice of pizza. Figure 13.8 shows Bertha's demand curve; page 327.

Short answer and numeric questions

Quantity (bottles of Aquafina per day)	Total utility	Marginal utility
0	0	
1	25	25
2	45	20
3	60	15
4	70	10
5	75	5
6	76	1

1. The completed table is above; page 322.

2. a. Lisa will buy 4 tacos and 2 hamburgers because this combination allocates her entire budget and sets the marginal utility per dollar from tacos equal to the marginal utility per dollar from hamburgers; page 326.

   b. Lisa will buy 2 tacos and 2 hamburgers because this combination allocates all her budget and equalizes the marginal utility per dollar from tacos and hamburgers at 20 units; page 326.

   c. When the price of a taco rises, the quantity of tacos demanded decreases; page 327.

3. To "allocate the entire available budget" means that we use the entire available budget. Using the entire budget doesn't mean not saving anything. The available budget is the amount available after choosing how much to save; page 324.

4. Marginal analysis compares the marginal gain from having more of one good with the marginal loss from having less of another good. The "equalize the marginal utility per dollar" rule is the result of marginal analysis. Suppose the marginal utility per dollar for a blouse exceeds that of a dollar for a purse. Marginal analysis indicates that the consumer can increase her total utility by spending a dollar less on purses and spending a dollar more on blouses because the gain in utility from the dollar spent on blouses exceeds the loss in utility from the dollar reduction on purses; page 326.

Additional Exercises (also in MyEconLab Test A)

1. The total utility of the third dish of pasta is 168 units and the total utility of the second dish of pasta is 120 units. The change in total utility equals the marginal utility, so the marginal utility is (168 units) − (120 units) = 48 units. The marginal utility per dollar from pasta when Wanda has 3 dishes of pasta a week is 48 units ÷ $4 = 12 units per dollar.

   The total utility of the second can of juice is 40 units and the total utility of the first can of juice is 22 units. The change in total utility equals the marginal utility, so the marginal utility is (40 units) − (22 units) = 18 units. The marginal utility per dollar from juice when Wanda has 2 cans of juice a week 18 units ÷ $1 = 18 units per dollar on the 2nd can of juice; pages 322, 324.

2. Wanda is not maximizing her utility. She is not allocating all of her budget and the marginal utility per dollar from juice, 18 units per dollar, does not equal the marginal utility per dollar from pasta, 14 units per dollar. To maximize her utility, Wanda should buy 1 more can of juice so that she consumes 3 cans of juice and 2 dishes of pasta. This combination allocates all of her budget and sets the marginal utility per dollar from juice equal to the marginal utility per dollar from pasta—14 units per dollar; pages 324, 326.

■ CHECKPOINT 13.3

Fill in the blanks

Marginal benefit is the maximum price a consumer is willing to pay for an extra unit of a good or service when <u>total utility is maximized</u>. The paradox of value is resolved by noting that diamonds have a high price, a <u>low</u> total utility, and a <u>high</u> marginal utility. Water provides <u>more</u> consumer surplus than diamonds.

True or false

1. True; page 329
2. True; page 329
3. False; page 329
4. False; page 329
5. True; page 330

Multiple choice

1. e; page 329
2. a; page 329
3. b; page 329
4. b; page 329
5. b; page 330

Complete the graph

■ FIGURE 13.9

1. The equilibrium price is $5 per thousand gallons of water. The consumer surplus is the gray triangle in Figure 13.9; page 330.

■ FIGURE 13.10

2. The equilibrium price is $20,000 a carat. Figure 13.10 shows the consumer surplus; page 330.

3. There is more consumer surplus for water than rubies. Because the price of a carat of rubies is much greater than the price of a gallon of water, it must be the case that the marginal utility of a carat of rubies is much greater than the marginal utility of a gallon of water; page 330.

Short answer and numeric questions

1. Bobby maximizes his total utility by consuming the combination of chips and Gatorade such that the marginal utility per dollar for chips equals the marginal utility per dollar for Gatorade. The marginal utility from the last bag of chips is 40 and the price of a bag of chips is $2, so the marginal utility per dollar is 40 ÷ $2 = 20. Because the marginal utility of the Gatorade is 60, the price is $3 to make the marginal utility per dollar equal to 20; page 329.

2. The price Bianca is willing to pay for another purse depends on her marginal utility. Bianca maximizes her total utility by making her marginal utility per dollar equal for all goods. If her marginal utility from an additional purse is high, she is willing to pay a high price for the purse; page 329.

3. The paradox of value is that water, which is essential for life, is cheap while diamonds are relatively useless but expensive. The solution to the paradox is that people consume a lot of water, so the marginal utility of an additional gallon of water is very low. People consume only a few diamonds, so the marginal utility of an additional diamond is quite high. A household maximizes its total when the marginal utility per dollar is equal for all goods. So water has a low marginal utility and a low price and diamonds have a high marginal utility and a high price; page 329.

Additional Exercises (also in MyEconLab Test A)

1. On the margin, the economics book is more valuable. The marginal utility from the economics book exceeds the marginal utility from another gallon of water. But, the total utility from the economics book is *much* less than the total utility from water. An economist can live without an economics book but not even an economist can live without water!; page 329.

Appendix: Indifference Curves

Chapter 13

The appendix uses indifference curves and budget lines to derive a demand curve.

1 Indifference curves

An indifference curve is a line that shows combinations of goods among which a consumer is indifferent. All combinations above the indifference curve are preferred to those on the indifference curve and all combinations on the indifference curve are preferred to those below the indifference curve. The marginal rate of substitution, *MRS*, is the rate at which the consumer will give up the good y (the good measured on the y-axis) to get more of the good x (the good measured on the x-axis) and at the same time remain on the same indifference curve. The magnitude of the slope of the indifference curve equals the marginal rate of substitution. The marginal rate of substitution diminishes as the consumer moves along an indifference curve, increasing consumption of the good measured on the x-axis and decreasing consumption of the good measured on the y-axis. The consumer equilibrium is at the best affordable point: the consumer is on the budget line and is on the highest attainable indifference curve. At this point the marginal rate of substitution equals the relative price of the two goods. We can use the indifference curve model to derive a consumer's demand curve.

CHECKPOINT 1

■ **Indifference curves.**

Additional Practice Problems 1

1. Figure A13.1 shows one of Maria's indifference curves between ice cream cones and milkshakes. Lightly shade combinations of cones and milkshakes that are more preferred to those on the indifference curve. More heavily shade combinations that are less preferred to those on the indifference curve.

2. In Figure A13.1, what is Maria's marginal rate of substitution when she is consuming 4 ice cream cones and 2 milkshakes?

■ **FIGURE A13.1**

■ **FIGURE A13.2**

Milkshakes (number per week)

3. Figure A13.2 shows Maria's budget line and several of her indifference curves.

a. What is Maria's best affordable point?

b. If Maria consumed 3 milkshakes and 2 ice creams, how would her marginal rate of substitution between cones and shakes compare to the relative price of cones and shakes?

Solutions to Additional Practice Problems I

■ **FIGURE A13.3**

Milkshakes (number per week)

1. Figure A13.3 shows that all combinations above the indifference curve are more preferred to those on it and all combinations below the indifference curve are less preferred to those on it.

2. Maria's marginal rate of substitution equals the magnitude of the slope of the indifference curve. Use the straight line that goes

through the combination of 4 ice cream cones and 2 milkshakes and touches the indifference curve at only that point. The magnitude of the slope of this line is 1/2 of a milkshake per ice cream cone, so Maria's marginal rate of substitution is 1/2 of a milkshake per ice cream cone. This marginal rate of substitution means that when Maria is consuming 4 ice cream cones and 2 milkshakes, she is willing to give up only 1/2 of a milkshake in order to get another ice cream cone.

■ **FIGURE A13.4**

Milkshakes (number per week)

3a. Figure A13.4 shows Maria's best affordable point. This point is on Maria's budget line and also on the highest attainable indifference curve, I_3. At this point, Maria's marginal rate of substitution between cones and shakes equals the relative price of cones and shakes.

3b. If Maria consumed 3 milkshakes and 2 ice cream cones, she would be on indifference curve I_3. The slope of this indifference curve at that point equals Maria's marginal rate of substitution. So Maria's marginal rate of substitution between cones and shakes at this consumption possibility is greater than the relative price of cones and shakes.

■ **Self Test I**

Fill in the blanks

An ____ is a curve that shows combinations of goods among which a consumer is indifferent. A consumer prefers being on a ____ (lower;

higher) indifference curve. The magnitude of the slope of an indifference curve equals the ____. If an indifference curve is steep, the marginal rate of substitution is ____ (high; low). The best affordable point occurs at the point on the budget line where the magnitude of the slope of the budget line ____ (is greater than; equals; is less than) the marginal rate of substitution.

True or false

1. A consumer is indifferent among combinations of goods that are on his or her indifference curve.

2. A consumer is indifferent among combinations on different indifference curves.

3. The marginal rate of substitution is the rate at which a person will give up the good measured on the *y*-axis to get more of the good measured on the *x*-axis and at the same time remain indifferent.

4. The only requirement for a consumer to be at his best affordable point is that the consumer be on the budget line.

5. Along a demand curve that is derived using indifference curves, the quantity of the good demanded increases when the price rises.

Multiple choice

1. An indifference curve is a line that shows combinations of goods among which a consumer
   a. prefers one over the other.
   b. places no value on any of the items.
   c. can afford to buy all the combinations.
   d. is indifferent.
   e. believes that all combinations have the same marginal rate of substitution.

2. What is the difference between a budget line and an indifference curve?
   a. One is measured in dollars while the other is measured in units of goods.
   b. One shows what is possible while the other shows what is preferred.
   c. One shows a positive relationship and the other shows a negative relationship.
   d. The budget line is bowed in toward the origin and the indifference curves are linear.
   e. There is no difference.

3. In a preference map, consumption combinations on higher indifference curves
   a. always cost more than any combination on a lower indifference curve.
   b. always are preferred to combinations on lower indifference curves.
   c. always cost less than any combination on a lower indifference curve.
   d. always are less preferred than combinations on lower indifference curves.
   e. are sometimes more preferred, sometimes less preferred, and sometimes equally preferred than any combination on a lower indifference curve.

4. The marginal rate of substitution for the good on the horizontal axis is
   a. the consumer surplus.
   b. the same as the consumer's budget line.
   c. equal to the magnitude of the slope of the indifference curve.
   d. equal to the magnitude of the slope of the consumer surplus curve.
   e. equal to 1.0 if the indifference curves are linear.

■ **FIGURE A13.5**

Slices of pizza (quantity per week)

Tacos (quantity per week)

5. When the consumer whose indifference curve is illustrated in the figure above is consuming 3 slices of pizza and 3 tacos per week, the marginal rate of substitution is _____ of pizza per taco
   a. 3 slices
   b. 9 slices
   c. 0 slices
   d. 1 slice
   e. More information is needed about the consumer's budget line to determine the marginal rate of substitution.

6. When the consumer whose indifference curve is illustrated in the figure above is consuming 1½ slices of pizza and 6 tacos per week, the marginal rate of substitution is _____ of pizza per taco
   a. 6 slices
   b. 1½ of a slice
   c. 1/4 of a slice
   d. 1 slice
   e. More information is needed about the consumer's budget line to determine the marginal rate of substitution.

7. When the consumer whose indifference curve is illustrated in the figure consumes more tacos, the marginal rate of substitution is of slices of pizza for tacos
   a. stays the same.
   b. increases.
   c. decreases.
   d. changes randomly.
   e. More information is needed about the consumer's budget line to determine how the marginal rate of substitution changes.

8. At her best affordable point, Kris
   i.   is on her budget line.
   ii. is on the highest attainable indifference curve.
   iii. has a marginal rate of substitution equal to the relative price of the goods.
   a. i only.
   b. ii only.
   c. iii only.
   d. i, and ii.
   e. i, ii, and iii.

9. When Bo is at his best affordable consumption point, his marginal rate of substitution is
   a. greater than the relative price.
   b. equal to the relative price.
   c. less than the relative price.
   d. equal to one.
   e. maximized.

10. To derive a demand curve using the indifference curve model, you must change the
   a. consumer's preferences.
   b. consumer's income.
   c. price of one good, holding the price of the other good and income constant.
   d. price of both goods simultaneously but by different amounts.
   e. price of both goods simultaneously but by the same percentage.

Complete the graph

■ FIGURE A13.6

Movies (number per month)

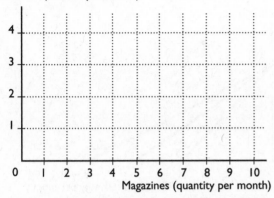

Magazines (quantity per month)

1. For entertainment, Laura goes to the movies and buys magazines. Laura devotes a monthly budget of $24 per month for entertainment. The price of a movie is $8 and the price of a magazine is $4.

   a. In Figure A13.6, draw Laura's budget line and label it BL_1.

   b. Suppose magazines rise in price to $6. Draw Laura's new budget line in Figure A13.6 and label it BL_2.

   c. Finally suppose that magazines fall in price to $3. Draw Laura's new budget line in Figure A13.6 and label it BL_3.

■ FIGURE A13.7

Movies (number per month)

DVDs (quantity per month)

2. Brent goes to the movies and buys DVDs. Figure A13.7 shows two of his indifference curves.

   a. Initially, the price of a movie is $10 and the price of a DVD is also $10. Brent's income is $40 per month. Draw Brent's budget line in Figure A13.7. How many DVDs does Brent buy per month?

   b. DVDs fall in price to $5. Brent's income remains at $40 and the price of a movie remains at $10. Draw Brent's new budget line in Figure A13.7. How many DVDs does Brent now buy per month?

■ FIGURE A13.8

Price (dollars per DVD)

Quantity (DVDs per month)

   c. You have two points on Brent's demand curve for DVDs. What are these two points? Assuming Brent's demand curve is linear, plot these points in Figure A13.8 and draw his demand curve. How does a fall in the price of a DVD affect the quantity of DVDs Brent buys?

Short answer and numeric questions

1. What is the defining characteristic of the points on an indifference curve?

2. If Alberto's marginal rate of substitution between shirts and pants is 2 shirts per pair of pants, what does this number mean? As Alberto obtains more pants, what happens to his marginal rate of substitution?

3. What is the difference between an indifference curve and a demand curve?

SELF TEST ANSWERS

■ CHECKPOINT 1

Fill in the blanks

An <u>indifference curve</u> is a curve that shows combinations of goods among which a consumer is indifferent. A consumer prefers being on a <u>higher</u> indifference curve. The magnitude of the slope of an indifference curve equals the <u>marginal rate of substitution</u>. If an indifference curve is steep, the marginal rate of substitution is <u>high</u>. The best affordable point occurs at the point on the budget line where the magnitude of the slope of the budget line <u>equals</u> the marginal rate of substitution.

True or false

1. True; page 337
2. False; page 337
3. True; page 338
4. False; page 339
5. False; page 341

Multiple choice

1. d; page 337
2. b; page 337
3. b; page 337
4. c; page 338
5. d; page 339
6. c; page 339
7. c; page 338
8. e; page 339
9. b; page 340
10. c; page 341

Complete the graph

1. a. Figure A13.9 shows the budget line; page 316.
   b. Figure A13.9 shows the budget line; page 318.
   c. Figure A13.9 shows the budget line; page 318.

■ **FIGURE A13.9**

■ **FIGURE A13.10**

2. a. Figure A13.10 shows the original budget line when DVDs are $10. Brent buys 2 DVDs a month; page 340.
   b. Figure A13.10 shows the new budget line after DVDs have fallen in price. Brent now buys 4 DVDs a month; page 340.

■ **FIGURE A13.11**

Price (dollars per DVD)

c. One point on Brent's demand curve is from part (a). When the price of a DVD rental is $10, the quantity of DVDs Brent buys is 2 a month. The other point is from part (b). When the price of a DVD is $5, Brent buys 4 DVDs a month. Figure A13.11 plots these two points and draws Brent's demand curve. A fall in the price of a DVD increases the quantity of DVDs Brent buys; page 341.

Short answer and numeric questions

1. The defining characteristic of points on an indifference curve is that the consumer is indifferent about which combination he or she consumes. Of all the possible combinations on an indifference curve, the consumer does not care which combination he or she receives; page 337.

2. The marginal rate of 2 shirts per pair of pants means that Alberto is willing to give up 2 shirts in order to get another pair of pants. As Alberto obtains more pants, his marginal rate of substitution decreases; page 338.

3. An indifference curve and a demand curve are quite different. An indifference curve shows combinations of goods among which a consumer is indifferent. A demand curve shows the relationship between the price of a good and the quantity demanded. An indifference curve, along with a budget line, can be used to derive a demand curve. Hence the demand curve is properly viewed as a result of the consumer's indifference curve (and budget line); pages 337 and 341.

Production and Cost

Chapter 14

1 Explain and distinguish between the economic and accounting measures of a firm's cost of production and profit.

A firm's goal is to maximize its profit. The highest-valued alternative forgone is the opportunity cost of a firm's production. An explicit cost is paid in money. An implicit cost is incurred when a firm uses a factor of production but does not make a direct money payment for its use. The return to entrepreneurship is normal profit. A normal profit is part of the firm's costs because it compensates the entrepreneur for not running another business. Total cost is the sum of explicit costs and implicit costs, so it is the opportunity cost of production. A firm's economic profit equals total revenue minus total cost.

2 Explain the relationship between a firm's output and labor employed in the short run.

The short run is the time frame in which the quantities of some resources are fixed; the long run is the time frame in which the quantities of all resources can be varied. Marginal product is the change in total product that results from a one-unit increase in the quantity of labor employed. As firms hire labor, initially increasing marginal returns occur but eventually decreasing marginal returns set in. Average product is total product divided by the quantity of an input. When marginal product exceeds the average product, the average product curve slopes upward and average product increases as more labor is employed. And when marginal product is less than average product, the average product curve slopes downward and average product decreases as more labor is employed.

3 Explain the relationship between a firm's output and costs in the short run.

Fixed costs are paid to fixed factors of production; variable costs are paid to variable factors of production. Total cost is the sum of total fixed cost and total variable cost. Marginal cost is the change in total cost that results from a one-unit increase in total product. Average total cost is the sum of average fixed cost and average variable cost. The U-shape of the average total cost curve arises from the influence of two opposing forces: spreading total fixed cost over a larger output and decreasing marginal returns. The marginal cost curve intersects the average variable cost and average total cost curves at their minimum points. The average cost curve and the marginal cost curve shift when technology changes or when the price of a factor of production changes.

4 Derive and explain a firm's long-run average cost curve.

In the long run, all costs are variable. When a firm changes its plant size, it might experience economies of scale, diseconomies of scale, or constant returns to scale. The long-run average cost curve shows the lowest average total cost at which it is possible to produce each output when the firm has had sufficient time to change both its plant size and labor employed. The long-run average cost curve slopes downward with economies of scale and upward with diseconomies of scale.

CHECKPOINT 14.1

■ **Explain and distinguish between the economic and accounting measures of a firm's cost of production and profit.**

Quick Review

- *Explicit cost* A cost paid in money.
- *Implicit cost* A cost incurred by using a factor of production but for which no direct money payment is made.
- *Economic profit* Total revenue minus total opportunity cost.

Additional Practice Problem 14.1

1. Gary manufactures toy gliders made of balsa wood. Each week, Gary pays $200 in wages, buys balsa wood for $400, pays $50 to lease saws and sanders, and pays $150 in rent for the workspace. To fund his operations, Gary withdrew his life's savings, $162,500, from his savings account at the bank, which paid interest of $250 a week. The normal profit for a glider company is $250 a week. Gary sells $1,500 worth of gliders a week.

   a. How much are the weekly explicit costs?

   b. How much are the weekly implicit costs?

   c. What does an accountant compute for the weekly profit?

   d. What does an economist compute for the weekly economic profit?

Solution to Additional Practice Problem 14.1

1a. The explicit costs are the wages, the balsa wood, the leased saws and sanders, and rent. The weekly explicit costs are $200 + $400 + $50 + $150, which equal $800.

1b. The implicit costs are the forgone interest and the normal profit. The weekly implicit costs are $250 + $250, which equal $500.

1c. Accountants calculate profit as total revenue minus explicit costs, which is $1,500 − $800 = $700.

1d. Economic profit is total revenue minus total cost. Total cost is the sum of explicit and implicit costs. So Gary's total cost is $800 + $500, which is $1,300. Gary's economic profit equals $1,500 − $1,300, which is $200.

■ **Self Test 14.1**

Fill in the blanks

The firm's goal is to maximize its ____ (growth; market share; profit). A cost paid in money is an ____ (explicit; implicit) cost; a cost incurred when a firm uses a factor of production for which it does not make a direct money payment is an ____ (explicit; implicit) cost. The return to entrepreneurship is ____ (normal; economic) profit and ____ (is; is not) part of the firm's opportunity cost. A firm's total revenue minus total opportunity cost is ____ (normal; economic) profit.

True or false

1. The firm's goal is to maximize profit.

2. An accountant measures profit as total revenue minus opportunity cost.

3. All of a firm's costs must be paid in money.

4. If a firm earns an economic profit, the return to the entrepreneur exceeds normal profit.

Multiple choice

1. The paramount goal of a firm is to
   a. maximize profit.
   b. maximize sales.
   c. maximize total revenue.
   d. minimize its costs.
   e. force its competitors into bankruptcy.

2. For a business, opportunity cost measures
   a. only the cost of labor and materials.
   b. only the implicit costs of the business.
   c. the cost of all the factors of production the firm employs.
   d. only the explicit costs the firm must pay.
   e. all of the firm's costs including its normal profit *and* its economic profit.

3. Costs paid in money to hire a resource is
   a. normal profit.
   b. an implicit cost.
   c. an explicit cost.
   d. an alternative-use cost.
   e. economic profit.

4. Which of the following is an example of an implicit cost?
   a. wages paid to employees
   b. interest paid to a bank on a building loan
   c. the cost of using capital an owner donates to the business
   d. dollars paid to a supplier for materials used in production
   e. liability insurance payments made only once a year

5. The opportunity cost of a firm using its own capital is .
   a. economic depreciation.
   b. self ownership depreciation.
   c. economic loss.
   d. normal loss.
   e. capital loss.

6. The difference between a firm's total revenue and its total cost is its ____ profit.
   a. explicit
   b. normal
   c. economic
   d. accounting
   e. excess

Short answer and numeric questions

1. What is likely to happen to a firm that does not maximize profit?

2. Bobby quits his job as a veterinarian to open a model train store. Bobby made $80,000 a year as a veterinarian. The first year his train store is open, Bobby pays a helper $26,000. He also pays $24,000 in rent, $10,000 in utilities, and buys $200,000 of model trains. Bobby had a good year because he sold all of his model trains for $300,000. Bobby's normal profit is $30,000.
   a. What would an accountant calculate as Bobby's profit?
   b. What is Bobby's total opportunity cost? What is his economic profit?

3. Why are wages a cost to a business? Why is a normal profit a cost to a business?

Additional Exercises (also in MyEconLab Test A)

1. In 2009, Toni taught music and earned $20,000. She also earned $4,000 by renting out her basement. On January 1, 2010, she quit teaching, stopped renting out her basement, and began to use it as the office for her new Web site design business. She took $2,000 from her savings account to buy a computer. During 2010, she paid $1,500 for the lease of a Web server and $1,750 for high-speed Internet service. She received a total revenue from Web site designing of $45,000 and earned interest at 5 percent a year on her savings account balance. Normal profit is $55,000 a year. At the end of 2010 Toni could have sold her computer for $500. Calculate Toni's explicit costs, implicit costs, and economic profit in 2010.

CHECKPOINT 14.2

■ **Explain the relationship between a firm's output and labor employed in the short run.**

Quick Review

• *Marginal product* The change in total product that results from a one-unit increase in the quantity of labor employed.
• *Formula for the marginal product* The marginal product equals:
Change in total product÷change in quantity of labor

Additional Practice Problems 14.2

1. Bobby runs a cat grooming service. Bobby hires students to groom the cats. The table to the right shows how many cats Bobby's service can groom when Bobby changes the number of students he hires.

Labor (students per day)	Total product (cats groomed per day)
0	0
1	5
2	12
3	18
4	22
5	25

Labor (students per day)	Average product (cats groomed per day)	Marginal product (cats groomed per day)
1	___	___
2	___	___
3	___	___
4	___	___
5	___	___

a. Complete the table above.

b. Draw Bobby's average product curve and his marginal product curve. When does the marginal product equals the average product?

2. The first five members of the men's basketball squad are each 6 feet tall. A sixth player, whose height is 7 feet, is added. Has the average height increased or decreased with the addition of this player? A seventh player, whose height is 5 feet, is added. What happens to the team's average height? An eighth player, whose height is 6 feet, is added. What is the effect on the average height? What is the general rule about how the marginal player's height changes the average height of the team?

Solutions to Additional Practice Problems 14.2

Labor (students per day)	Average product (cats groomed per day)	Marginal product (cats groomed per day)
		5.0
1	5.0	
		7.0
2	6.0	
		6.0
3	6.0	
		4.0
4	5.5	
		3.0
5	5.0	

1a. The completed table is above. The average product equals total product ÷ total labor and the marginal product equals change in total product ÷ change in quantity of labor.

1b. The figure is to the right. The marginal product equals the average product when the average product is at its maximum. Both equal 6 cats groomed per day.

2. The 7-foot player is above the average height, so adding him to the team increases the average height. The 5-foot player is below the average height, so adding him decreases the average height. When the 6-foot player is added, the team's average height equals 6 feet, so his addition has no effect on the average height. The general rule is that when a marginal value lies above the average, the average rises. When the marginal value is below the average, the average falls. And when the marginal value equals the average, the average does not change.

■ **Self Test 14.2**

Fill in the blanks

The time frame in which the quantities of some resources are fixed is the ____ (long; market; short) run and the time frame in which the quantities of *all* resources can be varied is the (long; market; short) ____ run. Marginal product equals ____ (total product; the change in total product) divided by the ____ (quantity of labor; increase in the quantity of labor). Average product equals the ____ (total product; change in total product) divided by the ____ (quantity of labor; change in quantity of labor). When the marginal product of an additional worker is less than the marginal product of the previous worker, the firm experiences decreasing ____ (marginal; fixed) returns. The law of decreasing returns states that as a firm uses more of a ____ (fixed; variable) input, with a given quantity of ____ (fixed; variable) inputs, the marginal product of the ____ (fixed; variable) input eventually decreases. If the marginal product exceeds the average product, the average product curve slopes ____ (downward; upward).

True or false

1. In the short run, the firm's fixed inputs cannot be changed.

2. Points on and below the total product curve are efficient.

3. Most production processes initially have decreasing marginal returns followed eventually by increasing marginal returns.

4. When the marginal product of labor exceeds the average product of labor, the average product curve is downward sloping.

Multiple choice

1. The short run is a time period during which
   a. some of the firm's resources are fixed.
   b. all of the firm's resources are fixed.
   c. all of the firm's resources are variable.
   d. the fixed cost equals zero.
   e. the firm cannot increase its output.

2. In the short run, firms can increase output
   a. only by increasing the size of their plant.
   b. only by decreasing the size of their plant.
   c. only by increasing the amount of labor used.
   d. only by decreasing the amount of labor used.
   e. either increasing the amount of labor used or increasing the size of their plant.

3. Which of the following is correct?
   a. The short run for a firm can be longer than the long run for the same firm.
   b. The short run is the same for all firms.
   c. The long run is the time frame in which the quantities of all resources can be varied.
   d. The long run is the time frame in which all resources are fixed.
   e. The long run does not exist for some firms.

4. Marginal product equals
   a. the total product produced by a certain amount of labor.
   b. the change in total product that results from a one-unit increase in the quantity of labor employed.
   c. total product divided by the total quantity of labor.
   d. the amount of labor needed to produce an increase in production.
   e. total product minus the quantity of labor.

5. If 5 workers can wash 30 cars a day and 6 workers can wash 33 cars a day, then the marginal product of the 6th worker equals
   a. 30 cars a day.
   b. 33 cars a day.
   c. 5 cars a day.
   d. 5.5 cars a day.
   e. 3 cars a day.

6. Increasing marginal returns occur when the
   a. average product of an additional worker is less than the average product of the previous worker.
   b. marginal product of an additional worker exceeds the marginal product of the previous worker.
   c. marginal product of labor is less than the average product of labor.
   d. total output of the firm is at its maximum.
   e. total product curve is horizontal.

7. If 25 workers can pick 100 flats of strawberries an hour, then average product is
   a. 100 flats an hour.
   b. 125 flats an hour.
   c. 75 flats an hour.
   d. 4 flats an hour.
   e. More information is needed about how many flats 24 workers can pick.

Complete the graph

Quantity of labor (workers)	Total product (turkeys per day)	Average product (turkeys per worker)	Marginal product (turkeys per worker)
0	0	xx	
			100
1	100	100	
			____
2	300	____	
			____
3	450	____	
			30
4	____	____	
			____
5	____	100	

1. The table gives the total product schedule at Al's Turkey Town Farm.

   a. Complete this table. (The marginal product is entered midway between rows to emphasize that it is the result of changing inputs, that is, moving from one row to the next.)

   b. In Figure 14.1 label the axes and plot the marginal product (*MP*) and average product (*AP*) curves. (Plot the *MP* curve midway between the quantities of labor.) Where do the two curves intersect?

   c. When the *MP* curve is above the *AP* curve, is the *AP* curve rising or falling? When the *MP* curve is below the *AP* curve, is the *AP* curve rising or falling?

Short answer and numeric questions

1. What is the difference between the short run and the long run?

2. Pizza Hut opens a new store nearby. As the owner adds workers, what happens to their marginal product? Why?

3. What is the law of decreasing returns?

4. If the marginal product of a new worker exceeds the average product, what happens to the average product?

■ **FIGURE 14.1**

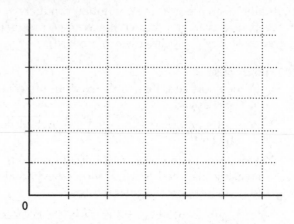

Additional Exercises (also in MyEconLab Test A)

Lizzie hires students in the summer to paint houses. The table sets out her total product schedule.

Labor (students)	Total product (houses painted per week)
0	0
1	2
2	5
3	9
4	12
5	14
6	15

1. Calculate the marginal product of the fourth student and the average product of four students.

2. Over what numbers of students does marginal product decrease?

3. When marginal product decreases, is average product greater than, less than, or equal to marginal product?

CHECKPOINT 14.3

■ **Explain the relationship between a firm's output and costs in the short run.**

Quick Review

• *Total cost* The cost of all the factors of production used by a firm. Total cost equals the sum of total fixed cost and total variable cost.

- *Marginal cost* The cost that arises from a one-unit increase in output.
- *Average total cost* Total cost per unit of output, which equals average fixed cost plus average variable cost as well as total cost divided by output.

Additional Practice Problems 14.3

Labor	Output	TC	MC	TC	MC
0	0	__		__	
			__		__
1	1	__		__	
			__		__
2	5	__		__	
			__		__
3	9	__		__	
			__		__
4	12	__		__	
			__		__
5	14	__		__	
			__		__
6	15	__		__	

1. Pearl owns a company that produces pools. Pearl has total fixed cost of $2,000 a month and pays each of her workers $2,500 a month. The table above shows the number of pools Pearl's company can produce in a month.

   a. Complete the left side of the table.

   b. Suppose that the wage Pearl pays her workers increases to $3,000 a month. Complete the right side of the table.

   c. What was the effect of the wage hike on Pearl's marginal cost?

2. In the figure to the right is an *ATC* curve. In this figure sketch an *AVC* curve and a *MC* curve. Tell what relationships these curves must obey so that they are drawn correctly.

Solutions to Additional Practice Problems 14.3

Labor	Output	TC	MC	TC	MC
0	0	2,000		2,000	
			2,500		3,000
1	1	4,500		5,000	
			625		750
2	5	7,000		8,000	
			625		750
3	9	9,500		11,000	
			833		1,000
4	12	12,000		14,000	
			1,250		1,500
5	14	14,500		17,000	
			2,500		3,000
6	15	17,000		20,000	

1a. The completed table is above. Total cost, *TC*, equals the sum of total fixed cost and total variable cost. For example, when Pearl hires 6 workers, total cost is ($2,000) + (6 × $2,500), which is $17,000. Marginal cost equals the change in the total cost divided by the change in output. For example, when output increases from 14 to 15 pools, marginal cost is ($17,000 − $14,500) ÷ (15 − 14), which is $2,500.

1b. The completed table is above.

1c. The increase in the wage rate increased Pearl's marginal cost at every level of output.

2. The completed figure is to the right. To be drawn correctly, there are three requirements: First, the *AVC* curve must reach its minimum at a lower level of output than does the *ATC* curve. Second, the vertical distance between the *ATC* and *AVC* curves must decrease as output increases. Finally the *MC* curve must go through the minimum points on both the *AVC* and *ATC* curves.

■ Self Test 14.3

Fill in the blanks

Total cost equals total fixed cost _____ (plus; minus; times) total variable cost. _____ (Marginal; Average) cost is the change in total cost that results from a one-unit increase in output. Average total cost equals average fixed cost _____ (plus; minus; times) average variable cost. The average total cost curve is _____ (S-shaped; U-shaped). When the firm hires the quantity of labor so that the marginal product is at its maximum, marginal cost is at its _____ (maximum; minimum).

True or false

1. In the short run, total fixed cost does not change when the firm changes its output.

2. Marginal cost is always less than average total cost.

3. The average total cost curve is U-shaped.

4. An increase in the wage rate shifts the marginal cost curve upward.

Multiple choice

1. Total cost is equal to the sum of
   a. total revenue and total cost.
   b. total variable cost and total product.
   c. total variable cost and total fixed cost.
   d. total fixed cost and total product.
   e. the marginal cost plus the total fixed cost plus the total variable cost.

2. Total fixed cost is the cost of
   a. labor.
   b. production.
   c. a firm's fixed factors of production.
   d. only implicit factors of production.
   e. only explicit factors of production.

3. Jay set up a hot dog stand near the business district. His total variable cost includes the
   a. annual insurance for the hot dog stand.
   b. cost of buying the hot dog stand.
   c. cost of the hot dogs and condiments.
   d. interest he pays on the funds he borrowed to pay for advertising.
   e. revenue he gets when he sells his first hot dog each day.

4. Marginal cost is equal to
   a. the total cost of a firm's production.
   b. total cost minus fixed cost.
   c. a cost that is not related to the quantity produced.
   d. the change in total cost that results from a one-unit increase in output.
   e. the change in fixed cost that results from a one-unit increase in output.

5. To produce 10 shirts, the total cost is $80; to produce 11 shirts, the total cost is $99. The marginal cost of the 11th shirt is equal to
   a. $8.
   b. $9.
   c. $80.
   d. $99.
   e. $19.

6. Average total cost equals
   a. marginal cost divided by output.
   b. average fixed cost plus average variable cost.
   c. total fixed cost plus total variable cost.
   d. marginal cost plus opportunity cost.
   e. marginal cost multiplied by the quantity of output.

7. To produce 10 shirts, the total cost is $80; to produce 11 shirts, the total cost is $99. The average total cost of the 11th shirt is equal to
   a. $8.
   b. $9.
   c. $80.
   d. $99.
   e. $19.

8. One of the major reasons for the U-shaped average total cost curve is the fact that
   a. there are increasing returns to labor regardless of the number of workers employed.
   b. there eventually are decreasing returns to labor as more workers are employed.
   c. prices fall as output increases.
   d. the average fixed cost increases as more output is produced.
   e. the variable cost decreases as more output is produced.

Complete the graph

Labor	Output	TC	ATC	MC
0	0	___	xx	
				___
1	10	___	___	
				___
2	25	___	___	
				___
3	35	___	___	
				___
4	40	___	___	
				___
5	43	___	___	
				___
6	45	___	___	

Labor	Output	TC	ATC	MC
0	0	___	xx	
				___
1	10	___	___	
				___
2	25	___	___	
				___
3	35	___	___	
				___
4	40	___	___	
				___
5	43	___	___	
				___
6	45	___	___	

■ **FIGURE 14.2**

■ **FIGURE 14.3**

Total cost (dollars per unit)

Output (units per hour)

1. Sue hires workers to produce subs at Sue's Super Supper Sub Shop. Sue pays her workers $10 an hour and has fixed costs of $30 an hour. The table above shows Sue's total product schedule.
   a. Complete the table above.
   b. Using the completed table, plot Sue's *ATC* and *MC* curves in figure 14.2. (Plot the *MC*s midway between the quantities.)
   c. Sue's rent increases so her fixed cost rises to $75 an hour. Complete the table above in the next column and then plot Sue's new *ATC* and *MC* curves in Figure 14.2.
   d. How does the increase in fixed cost change Sue's average total cost curve? Her marginal cost curve?
2. Label the cost curves in Figure 14.3.

Short answer and numeric questions

1. If a firm closes and produces nothing, does it still have any costs?
2. What is the difference between marginal cost and average total cost?
3. Why is the average total cost curve U-shaped?
4. Where does the marginal cost curve intersect the average variable cost and average total cost curves?
5. What two factors shift the cost curves?

Additional Exercises (also in MyEconLab Test A)

Lizzie hires students at $250 a week to paint houses. She leases equipment that costs her $500 a week. The table on the next page shows her total product schedule.

1. What is Lizzie's total cost, average total cost,

and marginal cost if she paints 12 houses a week?

Labor (students)	Total product (houses painted per week)
0	0
1	2
2	5
3	9
4	12
5	14
6	15

2. At what output is Lizzie's average total cost a minimum?

3. Explain why the gap between total cost and total variable cost is the same at all output amounts.

CHECKPOINT 14.4

■ **Derive and explain a firm's long-run average cost curve.**

Quick Review

* *Long-run average cost curve* The long-run average cost curve shows the lowest average cost at which it is possible to produce each output when the firm has had sufficient time to adjust its labor force and its plant.

Additional Practice Problem 14.4

1. The figure shows three average total cost curves for A1 Sewing, a company that sells sewing machines. The company can use three different sized stores, which account for the different cost curves.

a. Which average cost curve occurs when A-1 uses the smallest store? The largest store?

b. Indicate A1's long-run average cost curve, *LRAC* in the figure.

c. If A1 plans to sell 6 sewing machines per day, what sized store will A1 use?

d. Over what range of output does A1 Sewing have economies of scale? Diseconomies of scale?

2. Describe economies of scale and diseconomies of scale along a long-run average total cost curve.

Solutions to Additional Practice Problems 14.4

1a. When A1 uses the smallest store, its plant size is the smallest and so its average total cost curve is ATC_1 in the figure. When A1 uses the largest store, its plant size is the largest and so its average total cost curve is ATC_2 in the figure.

1b. The long-run average cost curve is the curve that shows the lowest average total cost to produce each output. In the figure to the right, the *LRAC* curve is the darkened

parts of the three average total cost curves.

1c. If A1 plans to sell 6 sewing machines, it will use the middle sized store because that is the store that gives it the lowest average total cost when selling 6 sewing machines a day.

1d. A1 has economies of scale when selling from 0 to 6 sewing machines per day. It has diseconomies of scale when it sells more than 6 sewing machines per day.

2. When economies of scale are present, the *LRAC* curve slopes downward. When the *LRAC* curve is horizontal, constant returns to scale are present. And when the *LRAC* curve slopes upward, diseconomies of scale are present.

■ Self Test 14.4

Fill in the blanks

In the long run, a firm ____ (can; cannot) vary its quantity of labor and ____ (can; cannot) vary its quantity of capital. Economies of scale occur if, when a firm increases its plant size and labor employed by the same percentage, the firm's average total cost ____ (increases; decreases). When the firm has ____ (economies; diseconomies) of scale, its long-run average cost curve slopes upward.

True or false

1. All costs are fixed in the long run.

2. When a firm increases its plant size and labor, greater specialization of capital and labor can lead to economies of scale.

3. Constant returns to scale occur when the firm increases its output and its average total cost remains the same.

Multiple choice

■ FIGURE 14.4

Average total cost (dollars per unit)

Output (units per day)

1. Figure 14.4 shows four of a firm's *ATC* curves. If the firm produces 2,000 units per day, it will use the plant size with
   a. *ATC₁*.
   b. *ATC₂*.
   c. *ATC₃*.
   d. *ATC₄*.
   e. either *ATC₁* or *ATC₄*.

2. Economies of scale definitely occur whenever a firm's technology is such that when the firm increases its output, its
   a. marginal cost falls.
   b. total cost falls.
   c. marginal product of labor increases.
   d. average total cost falls.
   e. marginal product of labor decreases.

3. The main source of economies of scale is
   a. better management.
   b. constant returns to plant size.
   c. specialization.
   d. long-run cost curves eventually slope up.
   e. increases in the labor force not matched by increases in the plant size.

4. Diseconomies of scale can occur as a result of which of the following?
   a. increasing marginal returns as the firm increases its size
   b. lower total fixed cost as the firm increases its size
   c. management difficulties as the firm increases its size
   d. greater specialization of labor and capital as the firm increases its size
   e. increases in the labor force not matched by increases in the plant

5. In the long run, constant returns to scale necessarily occur when the firm increases its production and the firm's
   a. total cost increases.
   b. total cost does not change.
   c. average total cost increases.
   d. average total cost does not change.
   e. production increases by more than does the firm's total cost.

6. A firm's long-run average cost curve shows the ____ average cost at which it is possible to produce each output when the firm has had ____ time to change both its labor force and its plant.
   a. highest; sufficient
   b. lowest; sufficient
   c. lowest; insufficient
   d. highest insufficient
   e. average; sufficient

7. Economies of scale and diseconomies of scale explain
   a. cost behavior in the short run.
   b. profit maximization in the long run.
   c. the U-shape of the long-run cost curve.
   d. the U-shape of the short-run cost curves.
   e. the U-shape of the marginal cost curves.

Complete the graph

■ **FIGURE 14.5**

1. In Figure 14.5, darken the firm's long-run average total cost curve. Show over which range of output the firm has economies of scale and over which range of output the firm has diseconomies of scale.

Short answer and numeric questions
1. Describe how a long-run average cost curve is constructed.

2. What are economies of scale? What leads to economies of scale?

Additional Exercises (also in MyEconLab Test A)
Lizzie hires students at $50 a day to paint houses. She leases equipment that costs her $100 a day. Suppose that Lizzie doubles the number of students she hires and doubles the amount of equipment that she leases. Lizzie experiences diseconomies of scale.

1. Explain how Lizzie's average total cost curve with one unit of equipment differs from that when she uses double the amount of equipment.

2. Explain what might be the source of Lizzie's diseconomies of scale.

SELF TEST ANSWERS

■ CHECKPOINT 14.1

Fill in the blanks

The firm's goal is to maximize its <u>profit</u>. A cost paid in money is an <u>explicit</u> cost; a cost incurred when a firm uses a factor of production for which it does not make a direct money payment is an <u>implicit</u> cost. The return to entrepreneurship is <u>normal</u> profit and <u>is</u> part of the firm's opportunity cost. A firm's total revenue minus total opportunity cost is <u>economic</u> profit.

True or false

1. True; page 344
2. False; page 344
3. False; page 345
4. True; pages 345-346

Multiple choice

1. a; page 344
2. c; page 344
3. c; page 345
4. c; page 345
5. a; page 345
6. c; page 345

Short answer and numeric questions

1. A firm that does not seek to maximize profit is either driven out of business or bought by firms that do seek that goal; page 344.
2. a. An accountant calculates profit as total revenue minus explicit costs. Bobby's explicit costs are $26,000 + $24,000 + $10,000 + $200,000, which equals $260,000. The accountant calculates profit as $300,000 − $260,000, which is $40,000; page 344.

   b. Bobby's opportunity cost is the sum of his explicit costs and his implicit costs. Bobby's explicit costs are $260,000. His implicit costs are the sum of his income forgone as a veterinarian, $80,000, and normal profit, $30,000. So Bobby's implicit costs are $110,000. His total opportunity cost is $260,000 + $110,000, which is $370,000. Bobby's economic profit is his total revenue minus his opportunity cost, which is

$300,000 − $370,000 = −$70,000. Bobby incurs an economic loss; pages 345-346.

3. Wages are a cost because they are paid to hire a factor of production, labor. A normal profit is a cost because it is paid to obtain the use of another factor of production, entrepreneurship; page 345.

Additional Exercises (also in MyEconLab Test A)

1. Explicit costs are the $1,500 for the lease of a Web server and $1,750 for high-speed Internet service. The total explicit costs are $3,250.

   Implicit costs are the $20,000 in wages forgone, $4,000 in rent forgone, $100 in forgone interest payments on the savings, $55,000 in normal profit, and $1,500 in economic depreciation for the computer. The total implicit costs are $80,600.

   The economic profit equals total revenue minus total opportunity costs, which is $45,000 − ($3,250 + $80,600) = −$38,850. Toni incurred an economic loss of $38,850 for the year; pages 345-346.

■ CHECKPOINT 14.2

Fill in the blanks

The time frame in which the quantities of some resources are fixed is the <u>short</u> run and the time frame in which the quantities of *all* resources can be varied is the <u>long</u> run. Marginal product equals <u>the change in total product</u> divided by the <u>increase in the quantity of labor</u>. Average product equals the <u>total product</u> divided by the <u>quantity of labor</u>. When the marginal product of an additional worker is less than the marginal product of the previous worker, the firm has experienced decreasing <u>marginal</u> returns. The law of decreasing returns states that as a firm uses more of a <u>variable</u> input, with a given quantity of <u>fixed</u> inputs, the marginal product of the <u>variable</u> input eventually decreases. If the marginal product exceeds the average product, the average product curve slopes <u>upward</u>.

True or false
1. True; page 348
2. False; page 350
3. False; page 350
4. False; pages 352-353

Multiple choice
1. a; page 348
2. c; page 348
3. c; page 348
4. b; pages 350-351
5. e; pages 350-351
6. b; page 350
7. d; page 352

Complete the graph
1. a. The completed table is below; pages 349-352.

Quantity of labor	Total product (turkeys per day)	Average product (turkeys per worker)	Marginal product (turkeys per worker)
0	0	xx	
			100
1	100	100	
			200
2	300	150	
			150
3	450	150	
			30
4	480	120	
			20
5	500	100	

b. Figure 14.6 plots the *MP* and *AP* curves. The curves intersect where the *AP* curve is at its maximum; page 352.

c. When the *MP* curve is above the *AP* curve, the *AP* curve is rising. When the *MP* curve is below the *AP* curve, the *AP* curve is falling; pages 352-353.

Short answer and numeric questions
1. The short run is the time frame in which the quantities of some resources (the plant) are fixed. The long run is the time frame in which the quantities of *all* resources can be changed; page 348.

2. As Pizza Hut initially adds workers, the mar-

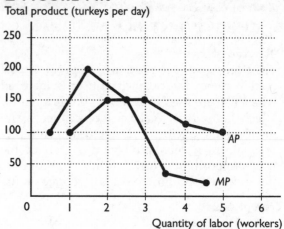

■ FIGURE 14.6

Total product (turkeys per day)

Quantity of labor (workers)

ginal product of each additional worker exceeds the marginal product of the previous worker. The marginal product increases because the workers can specialize. Some workers can make the pizzas and others can deliver them. As more workers are added, eventually the marginal product of each additional worker is less than the marginal product of the previous worker. The marginal product decreases because more workers are using the same equipment, so there is less productive work for each new worker; page 350.

3. The law of decreasing returns states that as a firm uses more of a variable input, with a given quantity of fixed inputs, the marginal product of the variable input eventually decreases; page 352.

4. If the marginal product of a worker exceeds the average product, then hiring the worker will increase the average product; page 353.

Additional Exercises (also in MyEconLab Test A)
1. The marginal product of the fourth student is the change in total product that results from hiring the fourth student. The total product with 3 students is 9 houses painted a week and the total product with 4 students is 12 houses painted a week. The marginal product of the fourth student is 12 houses painted a week minus 9 houses painted a week, or 3 houses painted a week. The average product

equals total product divided by the number of students. When 4 students are hired, average product is 12 houses painted a week divided by 4 students, which equals 3 houses painted a week; pages 350-352.

2. The marginal product decreases between 4 and 6 students; pages 351-352.

3. When the marginal product, though decreasing, exceeds the average product the average product increases as more workers are hired. Eventually as the marginal product decreases it becomes less than the average product. When the marginal product is less than the average product, the average product decreases as more workers are hired; pages 352-353.

■ CHECKPOINT 14.3

Fill in the blanks

Total cost equals total fixed cost plus total variable cost. Marginal cost is the change in total cost that results from a one-unit increase in output. Average total cost equals average fixed cost plus average variable cost. The average total cost curve is U-shaped. When the firm hires the quantity of labor so that the marginal product is at its maximum, marginal cost is at its minimum.

True or false

1. True; page 355
2. False; page 358
3. True; page 358
4. True; page 361

Multiple choice

1. c; page 355
2. c; page 355
3. c; page 355
4. d; page 356
5. e; page 356
6. b; page 357
7 b; page 357
8. b; page 359

Complete the graph

Labor	Output	TC	ATC	MC
0	0	30	xx	
				1.00
1	10	40	4.00	
				0.67
2	25	50	2.00	
				1.00
3	35	60	1.71	
				2.00
4	40	70	1.75	
				3.33
5	43	80	1.86	
				5.00
6	45	90	2.00	

■ FIGURE 14.7

Average and marginal cost (dollars per sub)

1. a. The completed table is above; page 355.
   b. Figure 14.7 plots the curves as ATC_0 and MC.

Labor	Output	TC	ATC	MC
0	0	75	xx	
				1.00
1	10	85	8.50	
				0.67
2	25	95	3.80	
				1.00
3	35	105	3.00	
				2.00
4	40	115	2.88	
				3.33
5	43	125	2.91	
				5.00
6	45	135	3.00	

c. The completed table after the change in costs is above and Figure 14.7 (on the next page) plots the new curves as ATC_1 and MC; page 357.

■ FIGURE 14.8

Total cost (dollars per unit)

d. The average cost curve shifts upward; the marginal cost curve does not change; page 360.

2. The labeled figure, Figure 14.8, is above; page 356.

Short answer and numeric questions

1. Yes, even a closed firm might still have fixed costs. So even if zero output is produced, the firm might have (fixed) costs such as interest payments on a loan or rent on a lease that has not expired; page 355

2. Marginal cost is the change in total cost that results from a one-unit increase in output. Average total cost is total cost per unit of output, which equals average fixed cost plus average variable cost; pages 356-357.

3. When output increases, the firm spreads its total fixed cost over a larger output and its average fixed cost decreases—its average fixed cost curve slopes downward.

   Decreasing marginal returns means that as output increases, ever larger amounts of labor are needed to produce an additional unit of output. So average variable cost eventually increases, and the *AVC* curve eventually slopes upward.

   Initially as output increases, both average fixed cost and average variable cost decrease, so average total cost decreases and the *ATC* curve slopes downward. But as output increases further and decreasing marginal re-

turns set in, average variable cost begins to increase. Eventually, average variable cost increases more quickly than average fixed cost decreases, so average total cost increases and the *ATC* curve slopes upward; page 359.

4. The marginal cost curve intersects the average variable cost curve and the average total cost curve at the point where they are the minimum; page 358.

5. Cost curves shift if there is a change in technology or a change in the price of a factor of production; pages 360-361.

Additional Exercises (also in MyEconLab Test A)

1. When Lizzie paints 12 houses a week, she must hire 4 students. These 4 students create a variable cost of $1,000. Lizzie has fixed costs of $500, so her total cost for painting 12 houses a week is $1,500. Here average total cost is equal to $1,500 ÷ 12 houses, which is $125. Her marginal cost equals the change in total cost divided by the change in the number of houses painted. Going from 9 to 12 houses, the total cost when 9 houses are painted is $1,250 so the change in total cost is $250. The change in the number of houses painted is 3. So the marginal cost is $250 ÷ 3, which is $83.33. Going from 12 to 14, the total cost when 14 houses are painted is $1,750 so the change in total cost is $250. The change in the number of houses is painted is 2. So the marginal cost is $250 ÷ 2, which is $125.00. So averaging these two marginal costs numbers, Lizzie's marginal cost of painting the 12th house is $104.17; pages 355-357.

2. Lizzie's average total cost is at its minimum when she paints 12 or 14 houses a week. At these output levels, her average total cost is $125; page 355.

3. The difference between the total cost and total variable cost is equal to total fixed cost because total cost equals total variable cost plus total fixed cost. Since total fixed cost does not change as output changes, the gap is the same at all outputs; page 356.

■ CHECKPOINT 14.4

Fill in the blanks

In the long run, a firm <u>can</u> vary its quantity of labor and <u>can</u> vary its quantity of capital. Economies of scale occur if, when a firm increases its plant size and labor employed by the same percentage, the firm's average total cost <u>decreases</u>. When the firm has <u>diseconomies</u> of scale, its long-run average cost curve slopes upward.

True or false

1. False; page 363
2. True; page 363
3. True; page 364

Multiple choice

1. c; pages 364-365
2. d; page 363
3. c; page 363
4. c; page 364
5. d; page 364
6. b page 364
7. c; pages 364-365

Complete the graph

■ FIGURE 14.9

Average total cost (dollars per unit)

1. Figure 14.9 darkens the firm's long-run average total cost curve. As indicated by the dotted line, the firm has economies of scale at all output levels less than 3,000 and has diseconomies of scale at all output levels greater than 3,000; pages 364-365.

Short answer and numeric questions

1. A long-run average cost curve is a curve that shows the lowest average total cost at which it is possible to produce each output when the firm has had sufficient time to change both its plant size and labor employed. Suppose a newspaper publisher can operate with four different plant sizes. The segment of each of the four average total cost curves for which that plant has the lowest average total cost is the scallop-shaped curve that is the long-run average cost curve; page 364.

2. Economies of scale is a feature of the firm's technology so that in the long run when output increases the firm's average total cost falls. The main source of economies of scale is greater specialization of both labor and capital (specialization of capital is a source of economies of scale because in the long run the firm can change the amount it uses of both labor and capital); page 363.

Additional Exercises (also in MyEconLab Test A)

1. At low levels of production, Lizzie's average total cost curve with one unit of equipment lies below her average total cost curve with two units of equipment. At higher levels of production, however, Lizzie's average total cost curve with one unit of equipment lies above her average total cost curve with two units of equipment; pages 363-364.

2. The source of her diseconomies of scale could be management problems when she hires more students and leases more equipment. Trying to organize more equipment and more students across different houses in different areas of the town requires more communication and coordination. If she is unable to manage the larger firm as efficiently as she was able to manage the small firm, she has diseconomies of scale; page 364.

Perfect Competition

Chapter 15

In Chapter 15 we study perfect competition, the market in which firms face the maximum amount of competition.

1 Explain a perfectly competitive firm's profit-maximizing choices and derive its supply curve.

Perfect competition exists when: many firms sell an identical product to many buyers; there are no restrictions on entry into (or exit from) the market; established firms have no advantage over new firms; and sellers and buyers are well informed about prices. A firm in perfect competition is a price taker—it cannot influence the price of its product. The *market* demand curve is downward sloping. But a perfectly competitive firm faces a perfectly elastic demand so the *firm's* demand curve is horizontal. Marginal revenue, *MR*, is the change in total revenue that results from a one-unit increase in the quantity sold. In perfect competition, marginal revenue equals price. A firm maximizes its profit by producing the quantity of output at which total revenue exceeds total cost by the largest amount. Another way to find the profit-maximizing output is to use marginal analysis. A firm maximizes its profit by producing the quantity of output at which marginal revenue equals marginal cost. If a firm shuts down, it incurs a loss equal to its total fixed cost. The shutdown point is the price that equals the minimum average variable cost. A firm's supply curve is its marginal cost curve above minimum average variable cost.

2 Explain how output, price, and profit are determined in the short run.

The market supply curve in the short run shows the quantity supplied at each price by a fixed number of firms. Market demand and market supply determine the market price and quantity bought and sold. Each firm takes the price as given and produces its profit-maximizing output. When price equals the average total cost, a firm makes zero economic profit, that is, its owners earn a normal profit. The firm makes an economic profit when price exceeds average total cost and incurs an economic loss when price is less than average total cost.

3 Explain how output, price, and profit are determined in the long run and explain why perfect competition is efficient.

Economic profit is an incentive for new firms to enter a market, but as they do so, the price falls and the economic profit of each existing firm decreases. Economic loss is an incentive for firms to exit a market, and as they do so the price rises and the economic loss of each remaining firm decreases. In the long run, a firm makes zero economic profit and there is no entry or exit. In a market undergoing technological change, firms that adopt the new technology make an economic profit. Firms that stick with the old technology incur economic losses. They either exit the market or switch to the new technology. Competition eliminates economic profit in the long run. Perfect competition is efficient because in a perfectly competitive market the market demand curve is the same as the marginal benefit curve and the market supply curve is the same as the (market's) marginal cost curve.

CHECKPOINT 15.1

■ Explain a perfectly competitive firm's profit-maximizing choices and derive its supply curve.

Quick Review

- *MC = MR* Profit is maximized when production is such that marginal cost equals marginal revenue.

- *A firm's short-run supply curve* At prices less than its minimum average variable cost, the firm shuts down. At prices above the minimum average variable cost, the firm's supply curve is the marginal cost curve.

- *Shutdown point* The price at which price equals the minimum average variable cost.

Additional Practice Problem 15.1

1. Patricia is a perfectly competitive wheat farmer. Her average variable cost curve and her marginal cost are shown in the figure.

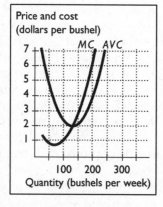

Price and cost (dollars per bushel)

MC AVC

Quantity (bushels per week)

a. If the price of a bushel of wheat is $6 per bushel, how much wheat will Patricia produce?

b. If the price of a bushel of wheat falls to $4 per bushel, how much wheat will Patricia produce?

c. What are two points on Patricia's supply curve?

d. What is the lowest price for which Patricia will produce wheat rather than shut down?

e. Suppose that when the price of a bushel of wheat is $6, Patricia produces a quantity of wheat such that her marginal revenue is greater than marginal cost. Explain why she is not maximizing her profit.

Solutions to Additional Practice Problem 15.1

1a. When the price of a bushel of wheat is $6 per bushel, Patricia's marginal revenue curve is shown in the figure as MR_1. To maximize her profit, Patricia produces 200 bushels of wheat, the quantity at which marginal revenue equals marginal cost.

Price and cost (dollars per bushel)

MC AVC

MR₁

MR₂

Quantity (bushels per week)

1b. If the price of wheat falls to $3 per bushel, Patricia's marginal revenue curve is shown in the figure as MR_2. She decreases the quantity of wheat she produces to 150 bushels per week because that is the quantity at which marginal revenue equals marginal cost.

1c. One point on Patricia's supply curve is a price of $6 and 200 bushels. Another point is a price of $3 and a quantity of 150 bushels.

1d. The lowest price for which Patricia produces rather than shuts down is the price equal to her minimum average variable cost. The figure shows that this price is equal to $2 per bushel.

1e. If marginal revenue exceeds marginal cost, then the extra revenue from selling one more bushel of wheat exceeds the extra cost incurred to produce it. So if Patricia produces one more bushel of wheat, the marginal revenue that she receives from selling that bushel is greater than the cost to produce that bushel and this bushel increases her profit. To maximize profit, Patricia must increase her output until she reaches the point where the marginal revenue equals the marginal cost.

■ Self Test 15.1

Fill in the blanks

The conditions that define perfect competition arise when the market demand for the product is ____ (large; small) relative to the output of a single producer. A perfectly competitive firm faces a perfectly ____ (elastic; inelastic) demand. The change in total revenue that results from a one-unit increase in the quantity sold is the marginal ____ (cost; price; revenue). When a perfectly competitive firm maximizes profit, marginal revenue equals ____ (average variable; marginal) cost. When a firm shuts down, it incurs a loss equal to its total ____ (variable; fixed) cost. A firm will shut down if price is less than minimum ____ (marginal; average total; average variable) cost. A perfectly competitive firm's supply curve is its marginal ____ (cost; revenue) curve above the minimum ____ (average total; average variable) cost.

True or false

1. A perfectly competitive market has many firms.

2. A firm in perfect competition is a price taker.

3. When a perfectly competitive firm is maximizing its profit, the vertical difference between the firm's marginal revenue curve and its marginal cost curve is as large as possible.

4. Stan's U-Pick blueberry farm, a perfectly competitive firm, will shut down if its total revenue is less than its total cost.

5. A perfectly competitive firm's short-run supply curve is its average total cost above minimum average variable cost.

Multiple choice

1. The four market types are
   a. perfect competition, imperfect competition, monopoly, and oligopoly.
   b. oligopoly, monopsony, monopoly, and imperfect competition.
   c. perfect competition, monopoly, monopolistic competition, and oligopoly.
   d. oligopoly, oligopolistic competition, monopoly, and perfect competition.
   e. perfect competition, imperfect competition, monopoly, and duopoly.

2. A requirement of perfect competition is that
   i. many firms sell an identical product to many buyers.
   ii. there are no restrictions on entry into (or exit from) the market, and established firms have no advantage over new firms.
   iii. sellers and buyers are well informed about prices.
   a. i only.
   b. i and ii.
   c. iii only.
   d. i and iii.
   e. i, ii, and iii.

3. A perfectly competitive firm is a price taker because
   a. many other firms produce the same product.
   b. only one firm produces the product.
   c. many firms produce a slightly differentiated product.
   d. a few firms compete.
   e. it faces a vertical demand curve.

4. The demand curve faced by a perfectly competitive firm is
   a. horizontal.
   b. vertical.
   c. downward sloping.
   d. upward sloping.
   e. U-shaped.

5. For a perfectly competitive corn grower in Nebraska, the marginal revenue curve is
   a. downward sloping.
   b. the same as its demand curve.
   c. upward sloping.
   d. U-shaped.
   e. vertical at the profit maximizing quantity of production.

6. A perfectly competitive firm maximizes its profit by producing at the point where
   a. total revenue equals total cost.
   b. marginal revenue is equal to marginal cost.
   c. total revenue is equal to marginal revenue.
   d. total cost is at its minimum.
   e. total revenue is at its maximum.

■ **FIGURE 15.1**
Price and cost (dollars per shirt)

7. Figure 15.1 shows cost curves for Wring Around the Collar, a perfectly competitive dry cleaner. If the price of dry cleaning a shirt is $20 per shirt, the firm will dry clean _____ shirts per hour.
   a. 0
   b. between 1 and 49
   c. 50
   d. 60
   e. 61 or more.

8. In Figure 15.1, if the price of dry cleaning a shirt is $10 per shirt, the firm will dry clear _____ shirts per hour.
   a. 0
   b. between 1 and 49
   c. 50
   d. 60
   e. 61 or more.

9. Based on Figure 15.1, the lowest price for which the company might remain open is
   a. $25 per shirt.
   b. $20 per shirt.
   c. $15 per shirt.
   d. $10 per shirt.
   e. $5 per shirt.

10. If the market price is lower than a perfectly competitive firm's average total cost, the firm will
    a. immediately shut down.
    b. continue to produce if the price exceeds the average fixed cost.
    c. continue to produce if the price exceeds the average variable cost.
    d. shut down if the price exceeds the average fixed cost.
    e. shut down if the price is less than the average fixed cost.

11. One part of a perfectly competitive trout farm's supply curve is its
    a. marginal cost curve below the shutdown point.
    b. entire marginal cost curve.
    c. marginal cost curve above the shutdown point.
    d. average variable cost curve above the shutdown point.
    e. marginal revenue curve above the demand curve.

Complete the graph

■ **FIGURE 15.2**
Price and cost (dollars per unit)

1. Figure 15.2 shows a perfectly competitive firm's cost curves.
   a. Label the curves.
   b. If the market price is $8, what is the firm's equilibrium output and price?

c. If the market price is $4, what is the firm's equilibrium output and price?

d. What is the firm's shutdown price?

e. Darken the firm's supply curve.

Short answer and numeric questions

1. What are the conditions that define perfect competition?

2. What is a "price taker?" Why are perfectly competitive firms price takers?

3. What is the difference between a perfectly competitive firm's demand curve and the market demand curve?

4. Willy, a perfectly competitive wheat farmer, can sell 999 bushels of wheat for $3 per bushel or 1,000 bushels for $3 per bushel. What is Willy's marginal revenue and total revenue if he sells 1,000 bushels of wheat?

Quantity (hogs)	Total cost (dollars)	Total revenue (dollars)	Economic profit (dollars)
0	300	___	___
1	350	___	___
2	425	___	___
3	575	___	___
4	825	___	___
5	1,200	___	___

5. Peter owns Peter's Porkers, a small hog farm. The above table gives Peter's total cost schedule. Peter is in a perfectly competitive market and can sell each hog for $200.

a. Complete the table.

b. What is Peter's profit-maximizing number of hogs and what price will Peter set?

c. When Peter increases his production from 2 hogs to 3 hogs, what is the marginal cost? Is the third hog profitable for Peter?

d. When Peter increases his production from 3 hogs to 4 hogs, what is the marginal cost? Is the fourth hog profitable for Peter?

e. What is the marginal cost of the third hog?

6. When will a firm temporarily shut down?

Additional Exercises (also in MyEconLab Test A)

Paula is an asparagus farmer, and the world asparagus market is perfectly competitive. The market price is $15 a bundle. Paula sells 800 bundles a week and her marginal cost is $18 a bundle.

1. Is Paula maximizing profit? Explain your answer.

2. The price falls to $12 a bundle, and Paula cuts her output to 500 bundles a week. Her average variable cost and marginal cost fall to $12 a bundle. Is Paula maximizing profit? Is she making an economic profit or a loss?

3. What is one point on Paula's supply curve?

CHECKPOINT 15.2

■ **Explain how output, price, and profit are determined in the short run.**

Quick Review

- *Economic profit* If the market price exceeds the average total cost, the firm makes an economic profit.
- *Economic loss* If the market price is less than the average total cost, the firm incurs an economic loss.

Additional Practice Problem 15.2

Quantity (roses per week)	Average total cost	Marginal cost
	(dollars per rose)	
100	2.00	1.50
200	1.50	1.50
300	1.67	2.50
400	2.00	5.00

1. Growing roses is a perfectly competitive industry. There are 100 rose growers and all have the same cost curves. The above table gives the costs of one of the growers, Rosita's Roses. The market demand schedule for roses is in the table to the right.

Price (dollars per rose)	Quantity (roses per week)
1.00	50,000
1.50	45,000
2.00	40,000
2.50	30,000
3.00	20,000

a. Plot the market supply curve and the market demand curve in the figure.

b. What is the equilibrium price of a rose?

c. How many roses does Rosita produce? What is her economic profit or loss?

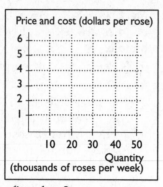

Price and cost (dollars per rose)

Solution to Additional Practice Problem 15.2

1a. The market demand curve and market supply curve are plotted in the figure. The quantity supplied in the market at any price is the sum of the quantities supplied by each firm at that price. Because each firm is identical, the market quantity supplied is 100 times the quantity supplied by any one firm. The firm's supply curve is its marginal cost curve above the minimum average variable cost. For instance, when the price is $2.50 a rose, Rosita's marginal cost schedule shows she will supply 300 roses a week. So the quantity supplied in the market equals $100 \times$ (300 roses a week), which is 30,000 roses a week.

Price and cost (dollars per rose)

1b. The figure shows that the equilibrium market price of a rose is $2.50.

1c. In the short run, a firm can make an economic profit or incur an economic loss. A firm makes an economic profit when price exceeds average total cost and incurs an economic loss when price is less than average total cost. In the case at hand, Rosita produces 300 roses. Rosita makes an economic profit. Rosita's economic profit per rose equals the price of a rose minus the average total cost, which is $2.50 − $1.67 = $0.83. She pro-

duces 300 roses, a week so her total economic profit is (300 roses a week) × ($0.83) = $249 a week.

■ Self Test 15.2

Fill in the blanks

In a perfectly competitive industry, the quantity supplied in the market at any price is ____ (determined by the market demand curve; equal to the sum of the quantities supplied by all firms at that price). A firm makes an economic profit when price exceeds ____ (marginal revenue; average total cost). A firm ____ (can; cannot) incur an economic loss in the short run.

True or false

1. The market supply curve in the short run shows the quantity supplied at each price by a fixed number of firms.

2. Market supply in a perfectly competitive market is perfectly elastic at all prices.

3. A perfectly competitive firm makes an economic profit if price equals average total cost.

4. In a perfectly competitive industry, a firm's economic profit is equal to price minus marginal revenue multiplied by quantity.

5. A perfectly competitive firm has an economic loss if price is less than the marginal cost.

Multiple choice

1. If the market supply curve and market demand curve for a good intersect at 600,000 units and there are 10,000 identical firms in the market, then each firm is producing
   a. 600,000 units.
   b. 60,000,000,000 units.
   c. 60,000 units.
   d. 60 units.
   e. 10,000 units.

2. In the short run, a perfectly competitive firm
   a. must make an economic profit.
   b. must incur an economic loss.
   c. must make zero economic profit.
   d. might make an economic profit, an economic loss, or zero economic profit.
   e. None of the above answers is correct.

3. A perfectly competitive firm definitely makes an economic profit in the short run if price is
   a. equal to marginal cost.
   b. equal to average total cost.
   c. greater than average total cost.
   d. greater than marginal cost.
   e. greater than average variable cost.

4. If a perfectly competitive firm is maximizing its profit and is making an economic profit, which of the following is correct?
   i. price equals marginal revenue
   ii. marginal revenue equals marginal cost
   iii. price is greater than average total cost
   a. i only.
   b. i and ii only.
   c. ii and iii only.
   d. i and iii only.
   e. i, ii, and iii.

■ **FIGURE 15.3**

Price and cost (dollars per unit)

5. Figure 15.3 shows the marginal revenue and cost curves for a perfectly competitive firm. The firm
   a. is incurring an economic loss.
   b. will shut down and will incur an economic loss.
   c. will shut down and will make zero economic profit.
   d. is making zero economic profit.
   e. is making an economic profit.

6. The market for watermelons in Alabama is perfectly competitive. A watermelon producer making zero economic profit could make an economic profit if the
   a. average total cost of selling watermelons does not change.
   b. average total cost of selling watermelons falls.
   c. average total cost of selling watermelons rises.
   d. marginal cost of selling watermelons does not change.
   e. marginal cost of selling watermelons rises.

7. Juan's Software Service Company is in a perfectly competitive market. Juan's total fixed cost is $25,000, average variable cost for 1,000 service calls is $45, and marginal revenue is $75. Juan's makes 1,000 service calls a month. What is his economic profit?
   a. $5,000
   b. $25,000
   c. $45,000
   d. $75,000.
   e. $50,000

8. If a perfectly competitive firm finds that price is less than its *ATC*, then the firm
   a. will raise its price to increase its economic profit.
   b. will lower its price to increase its economic profit.
   c. is making an economic profit.
   d. is incurring an economic loss.
   e. is making zero economic profit.

9. A perfectly competitive furniture-rental firm in Phoenix incurs an economic loss if the average total cost of each rental is
   a. greater than the price of each rental.
   b. less than the marginal cost of each rental.
   c. equal to the marginal revenue of each rental.
   d. equal to the price of each rental.
   e. greater than the average variable cost of each rental.

Complete the graph

■ FIGURE 15.4

Price and cost (dollars per lawn)

1. Moe's Mowers is a perfectly competitive lawn mowing company. Moe's costs and marginal revenue are illustrated in Figure 15.4.

   a. How many lawns does Moe's mow?

   b. Is Moe's making an economic profit or incurring an economic loss? Darken the area that shows the economic profit or loss. What is the amount of economic profit or loss?

■ FIGURE 15.5

Price and cost (dollars per lawn)

2. Larry's Lawns is (another) perfectly competitive lawn mowing company in another city. Larry's costs and marginal revenue are illustrated in Figure 15.5.

   a. How many lawns does Larry's mow?

   b. Is Larry's making an economic profit or incurring an economic loss? Darken the area that shows the economic profit or loss. In the short run, will Larry's remain open or shut down?

Short answer and numeric questions

1. In a perfectly competitive market, how is the market supply calculated?

2. If price is less than average total cost, is the firm making an economic profit or incurring an economic loss?

Additional Exercises (also in MyEconLab Test A)

Tom's Tattoos is a tattooing business in a perfectly competitive market in Miami. The price of a tattoo is $20. The table shows Tom's total costs.

Quantity (tattoos per hour)	Total cost (dollars per hour)
0	30
1	50
2	65
3	75
4	90
5	110
6	140

1. How many tattoos an hour does Tom's Tattoos sell? What is Tom's Tattoos' economic profit in the short run?

2. If the market price of a tattoo falls to $15, how many tattoos an hour does Tom's Tattoos sell? What is Tom's Tattoos' economic profit in the short run?

3. At what market price will Tom's Tattoos shut down? If Tom's Tattoos shuts down temporarily, what is its economic loss?

CHECKPOINT 15.3

■ Explain how output, price, and profit are determined in the long run and explain why perfect competition is efficient.

Quick Review

- *Entry* Economic profit is an incentive for new firms to enter a market, but as they do so, the price falls and the economic profit of each existing firm decreases.

- *Exit* Economic loss is an incentive for firms to exit a market, but as they do so, the price rises and the economic loss of each remaining firm decreases.

Additional Practice Problem 15.3

Quantity (roses per week)	Average total cost (dollars)	Marginal cost (dollars)
100	2.00	1.50
200	1.50	1.50
300	1.67	2.50
400	2.00	5.00

1. Growing roses is a perfectly competitive industry. Initially there are 100 rose growers and all have the same cost curves. The above table gives the costs of one of the growers, Rosita's Roses. The table to the right has the market demand schedule for roses. The price for a rose initially is $2.50.

Price (dollars per rose)	Quantity (roses per week)
1.00	50,000
1.50	45,000
2.00	40,000
2.50	30,000
3.00	20,000

a. Plot Rosita's marginal cost curve and her marginal revenue curve in the figure to the right. Is Rosita making an economic profit or is Rosita incurring an economic loss?

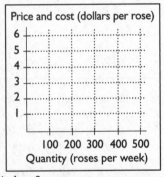

Price and cost (dollars per rose)

Quantity (roses per week)

b. As time passes, what takes place in the market?

c. What will be the long-run price of a rose? What will be Rosita's profit in the long run? In the long run, how many growers will be in the market?

Solutions to Additional Practice Problem 15.3

1a. The figure shows Rosita's marginal cost curve and marginal revenue curve. The figure shows that she is producing 300 roses a week. Rosita is making an economic profit because the price of a rose, $2.50, exceeds her average total cost of producing 300 roses, $1.67.

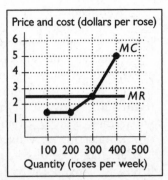

Price and cost (dollars per rose)

Quantity (roses per week)

1b. A perfectly competitive firm makes zero economic profit in the long run. A firm will not incur an economic loss in the long run because it will shut down. And a perfectly competitive firm cannot make an economic profit in the long run because the presence of an economic profit attracts entry, which drives down the price and eliminates economic profit. Competitive firms cannot prevent entry into their market and so they cannot protect any economic profit.

In the case of the rose growers, rose growers are making an economic profit, so more rose growers enter the market. The supply of roses increases and the market supply curve shifts rightward. The equilibrium price of a rose falls and the market equilibrium quantity increases.

1c. The long-run price of a rose will be $1.50 because that is the minimum average total cost. At that price, all rose growers, including Rosita, make zero economic profit. Indeed, the fact that they are making zero economic profit is what removes the incentive for further firms to enter the industry. When the price of a rose is $1.50, the demand schedule shows that the quantity demanded is 45,000 roses. At a price of $1.50, each grower produces 200 roses. There will be 225 growers, each producing 200 roses.

■ Self Test 15.3

Fill in the blanks

In the long run, a perfectly competitive firm _____ (can; cannot) make an economic profit,

_____ (can; cannot) incur an economic loss, and _____ (can; cannot) make zero economic profit. In the long run, a perfectly competitive firm _____ (produces; does not produce) at minimum average total cost. Entry into an industry shifts the market _____ (demand; supply) curve _____ (rightward; leftward). Firms exit an industry when they are _____ (making zero economic profit; incurring an economic loss). A technological change results in perfectly competitive firms _____ (temporarily; permanently) making an economic profit.

True or false

1. When the price equals average total cost, the firm makes zero economic profit.

2. Entry into a perfectly competitive market lowers the price.

3. In the long run, firms respond to an economic loss by exiting a perfectly competitive market.

4. New technology shifts a firm's cost curves upward and the market supply curve leftward.

5. Perfect competition is efficient because the efficient quantity is produced.

Multiple choice

1. In the long run, new firms enter a perfectly competitive market when
   a. normal profit is greater than zero.
   b. economic profit is equal to zero.
   c. normal profit is equal to zero.
   d. economic profit is greater than zero.
   e. the existing firms are weak because they are incurring economic losses.

2. If perfectly competitive firms are making an economic profit, the economic profit
   a. attracts entry by more firms, which lowers the price.
   b. can be made both in the short run and the long run.
   c. is greater than the price.
   d. leads to a decrease in market demand.
   e. generally leads firms to exit as they seek higher profit in other markets.

3. If perfectly competitive firms are making an economic profit, then
   a. the market is in its long-run equilibrium.
   b. new firms enter the market and the economic profit of the firms already in the market decreases.
   c. new firms enter the market and the economic profit of the firms already in the market increases.
   d. firms exit the market and the economic profit of the surviving firms in the market decreases.
   e. firms exit the market and the economic profit of the surviving firms in the market increases.

4. Firms exit a competitive market when they incur an economic loss. In the long run, this exit means that the economic losses of the surviving firms
   a. increase.
   b. decrease until they equal zero.
   c. decrease until economic profits are made.
   d. do not change.
   e. might change but more information is needed about what happens to the price of the good as the firms exit.

5. If firms in a perfectly competitive market incur economic losses, then as time passes firms _____ and the market _____.
   a. enter; demand curve shifts leftward
   b. enter; supply curve shifts rightward
   c. exit; demand curve shifts leftward
   d. exit; supply curve shifts rightward
   e. exit; supply curve shifts leftward

6. As a result of firms leaving the perfectly competitive frozen yogurt market in the early 2000s, the market
   a. supply curve shifted leftward.
   b. supply curve did not change.
   c. demand curve shifted rightward.
   d. supply curve shifted rightward.
   e. demand curve shifted rightward.

7. In the long run, a firm in a perfectly competitive market will
   a. make zero economic profit, so that its owners earn a normal profit.
   b. make zero normal profit but its owners will make an economic profit.
   c. remove all competitors and become a monopolistically competitive firm.
   d. incur a normal loss but will make a positive economic profit.
   e. remove all competitors and become a monopoly.

8. Technological change brings a ____ to firms that adopt the new technology.
   a. permanent economic profit
   b. temporary economic profit
   c. permanent economic loss
   d. temporary economic loss
   e. None of the above answers is correct.

Complete the graph

■ FIGURE 15.6
Price and cost (dollars per unit)

1. In Figure 15.6, suppose that the price of the good is $20. Show the long-run equilibrium for a perfectly competitive firm that produces 150 units per week.

2. Figure 15.7 shows cost curves for two firms in an industry undergoing technological change. Firm 1 uses the old technology and has an average total cost curve ATC_1 and marginal cost curve MC_1. Firm 2 uses the new technology and has an average total cost

■ FIGURE 15.7
Price and cost (dollars per unit)

curve ATC_2 and marginal cost curve MC_2. Initially the price of the product was $6.

a. At the price of $6, do firm 1 and firm 2 make an economic profit, zero economic profit, or incur economic loss?

b. As more firms adopt the new technology, what happens to market supply and price? Do firms 1 and 2 make an economic profit, zero economic profit, or incur an economic loss?

c. In the long run, what will be the new price? Will firm 1 make an economic profit, zero economic profit, or incur an economic loss? Will firm 2 make an economic profit, zero economic profit, or incur an economic loss?

Short answer and numeric questions

1. Why are perfectly competitive firms unable to make an economic profit in the long run? Why won't they incur an economic loss in the long run?

2. Is perfect competition efficient?

3. The Eye on Your Life discusses how competition benefits you by leading to the production of the vast array of goods and services you consume. Competition also benefits you by affecting the prices you pay for goods and services. The market for home delivered pizza is extremely competitive. How does

this competition affect the price you pay for home delivered pizza?

Additional Exercises (also in MyEconLab Test A)

Tom's Tattoos is a tattooing business in a perfectly competitive market in Miami. The table shows Tom's total costs.

Quantity (tattoos per hour)	Total cost (dollars per hour)
0	30
1	50
2	65
3	75
4	90
5	110
6	140

1. If the market price is $20 a tattoo, what is Tom's economic profit in the short run? Do new firms enter or existing firms exit the industry in the long run?

2. In the long run, what is the price of a tattoo, how many tattoos per hour does Tom sell, and what is Tom's economic profit?

3. If an advance in tattoo technology lowers the fixed cost of tattooing to $10 an hour, how does the price and quantity change in the short run and in the long run? Does the number of firms producing tattoos increase, decrease, or remain the same?

SELF TEST ANSWERS

■ CHECKPOINT 15.1

Fill in the blanks

The conditions that define perfect competition arise when the market demand for the product is <u>large</u> relative to the output of a single producer. A perfectly competitive firm faces a perfectly <u>elastic</u> demand. The change in total revenue that results from a one-unit increase in the quantity sold is the marginal <u>revenue</u>. When a perfectly competitive firm maximizes profit, marginal revenue equals <u>marginal</u> cost. When a firm shuts down, it incurs a loss equal to its total <u>fixed</u> cost. A firm will shut down if price is less than minimum <u>average variable</u> cost. A perfectly competitive firm's supply curve is its marginal <u>cost</u> curve above the minimum <u>average variable</u> cost.

True or false

1. True; page 372
2. True; page 373
3. False; page 376
4. False; page 377
5. False; pages 378-379

Multiple choice

1. c; page 372
2. e; page 372
3. a; page 373
4. a; page 374
5. b; page 374
6. b; page 376
7. e; page 376
8. d; page 376
9. e; pages 377-378
10. c; pages 377-378
11. c; pages 378-379

Complete the graph

1. a. Figure 15.8 labels the curves; page 378.
   b. Output is 35 units and the price is $8; page 376.
   c. Output is 30 units and the price is $4; page 376.

■ FIGURE 15.8

Price and cost (dollars per unit)

Output (units per hour)

d. The shutdown price is $2; pages 377-378.
e. The firm's supply curve is darkened in Figure 15.8; page 379.

Short answer and numeric questions

1. Perfect competition exists when many firms sell an identical product to many buyers; there are no restrictions on entry into (or exit from) the market; established firms have no advantage over new firms; and sellers and buyers are well informed about prices; page 372.

2. A price taker is a firm that cannot influence the price of the good or service it produces. Perfectly competitive firms are price takers because there are many competing firms selling an identical product. Any individual firm is such a small part of the market that its actions cannot affect the price; page 373.

3. A perfectly competitive firm's demand is perfectly elastic because all sellers produce goods that are perfect substitutes. So the firm's demand curve is horizontal. The market demand curve is downward sloping; page 374.

4. Willy's marginal revenue equals the price of a bushel of wheat, which is $3. His total revenue equals price multiplied by quantity, which is $3,000; page 375.

Quantity (hogs)	Total cost (dollars)	Total revenue (dollars)	Economic profit (dollars)
0	300	0	−300
1	350	200	−150
2	425	400	−25
3	575	600	25
4	825	800	−25
5	1,200	1,000	−200

5. a. The completed table is above; page 375.

   b. The profit-maximizing number of hogs is 3. Peter charges $200 a hog; page 375.

   c. The marginal cost is the change in total cost that results from producing the third hog. So marginal cost is $150. This is a profitable hog because the marginal revenue from the hog exceeds its marginal cost; page 376.

   d. The marginal cost is $250. This hog is not profitable; page 376.

   e. The marginal cost of the third hog is $200, which is the average of the marginal cost of increasing production from 2 to 3 hogs and of increasing production from 3 to 4 hogs. The marginal cost of the third hog equals the marginal revenue so 3 hogs is the profit-maximizing output; page 376.

6. If a firm shuts down, it incurs an economic loss equal to total fixed cost. If the firm produces some output, it incurs an economic loss equal to total fixed cost plus total variable cost minus total revenue. If total revenue exceeds total variable cost, the firm's economic loss is less than total fixed cost. It pays the firm to produce. But if total revenue is less than total variable cost, the firm's economic loss exceeds total fixed cost. The firm shuts down; pages 377-378.

Additional Exercises (also in MyEconLab Test A)

1. The market is perfectly competitive, so Paula's marginal revenue equals the price, $15 a box. Paula is not maximizing profit because marginal cost ($18) is greater than marginal revenue ($15). She should decrease her production until marginal cost falls to $15 because then her marginal cost equals her marginal revenue and she would maximize her profit; page 376.

2. If the price is $12 a box, Paula's marginal revenue is $12 a box. Paula is maximizing profit by selling 500 boxes a week because marginal cost equals the marginal revenue. Paula is incurring an economic loss if she has any fixed costs because in that case price is less than average total cost; pages 376-377.

3. One point on Paula's supply curve is a price of $12 and quantity of 500 boxes a week. The combination of a price of $15 and quantity of 800 boxes a week is *not* on Paula's supply curve because at that combination she is not maximizing her profit. So this combination is only temporary because Paula will change her production in order to maximize her profit; pages 378-379.

■ CHECKPOINT 15.2

Fill in the blanks

In a perfectly competitive industry, the market supply at any price is equal to the sum of the quantities supplied by all firms at that price. A perfectly competitive firm makes an economic profit if the price exceeds average total cost. A firm can incur an economic loss in the short run.

True or false

1. True; page 381
2. False; page 381
3. False; page 382
4. False; page 383
5. False; page 384

Multiple choice

1. d; page 381
2. d; pages 382-384
3. c; page 383
4. e; page 383
5. e; page 383
6. c; page 383
7. a; page 383
8. d; page 384
9. a; page 384

Complete the graph

■ FIGURE 15.9

Price and cost (dollars per lawn)

Output (lawns per week)

1. a. Moe mows 105 lawns per week because that is the quantity at which marginal revenue equals marginal cost; page 376.

   b. Moe makes an economic profit. Figure 15.9 illustrates the economic profit. The economic profit per lawn equals price minus average total cost, which is $30 − $20 = $10 per lawn. The quantity is 105 lawns, so the total economic profit equals ($10 per lawn) × (105 lawns), which is $1,050 a week; page 383.

■ FIGURE 15.10

Price and cost (dollars per lawn)

Output (lawns per week)

2. a. Larry mows 90 lawns per day because that is the quantity at which marginal revenue equals marginal cost; page 386.

   b. Larry has an economic loss. Figure 15.10 illustrates the economic loss as the darkened rectangle. Even though he has an economic loss, Larry remains open in the short run because the price exceeds his average variable cost; page 384.

Short answer and numeric questions

1. The market supply in the short run is the quantity supplied at each price by a fixed number of firms. The quantity supplied at a given price is the sum of the quantities supplied by all firms at that price. For example, if there are 100 firms in the geranium market and each produces 50 geraniums when the price is $3, then the quantity supplied in the market at $3 is 5,000 geraniums; page 381.

2. The firm incurs an economic loss. If the price is less than average total cost, the firm incurs an economic loss on each unit produced and so has an overall economic loss; page 384.

Additional Exercises (also in MyEconLab Test A)

1. If the market price is $20 a tattoo, the marginal revenue is $20 a tattoo. The marginal cost of the fifth tattoo is the total cost of 5 tattoos minus the total cost of 4 tattoos, which is $110 − $90 = $20. So, Tom sells 5 tattoos an hour because the marginal cost of the fifth tattoo, $20, equals the marginal revenue.

   The average total cost of a tattoo equals the total cost divided by the quantity of tattoos, or $110 ÷ 5 tattoos = $22 a tattoo. The price of a tattoo is $20 a tattoo, so Tom makes an economic "profit" of $20 minus $22, which is −$2 a tattoo. Tom sells 5 tattoos an hour, so his total economic "profit" equals −$2 × 5 tattoos, which is −$10. Tom incurs an economic loss of $10 an hour; pages 376, 384.

2. If the market price falls to $15 a tattoo, the marginal revenue is $15 a tattoo. If Tom remains open, the marginal cost of the fourth tattoo is the total cost of 4 tattoos minus the total cost of 3 tattoos, which is $90 − $75 =

$15. So, Tom sells 4 tattoos an hour because the marginal cost of the fourth tattoo, $15, equals the marginal revenue. Alternatively, Tom might shut down and produce 0 because the price, $15, is the same as the minimum average variable cost.

If Tom remains open, the average total cost of a tattoo equals the total cost divided by the quantity of tattoos, which is $90 ÷ 4 tattoos = $22.50 a tattoo. The price of a tattoo is $15, so Tom makes an economic "profit" of $15.00 minus $22.50, which is –$7.50 a tattoo. Tom sells 4 tattoos an hour, so his total economic "profit" equals –$7.50 × 4 tattoos, which is –$30. Tom incurs an economic loss of $30 an hour. Alternatively, if Tom shuts down, then Tom's economic loss equals his fixed cost, $30. Tom's loss is the same regardless of whether he remains open or shuts down; pages 376- 377, 384.

3. The price at which Tom shuts down equals minimum average *variable* cost. Average variable cost equals total variable cost divided by the quantity produced. And, total variable cost equals total cost minus fixed cost. Tom's total fixed cost is $30, his total cost when zero tattoos are produced. When Tom produces 4 tattoos, his total variable cost is $90 – $30, which is $60 and so his average variable cost is $60 ÷ 4 = $15. This is the minimum average variable cost. As a result, Tom shuts down at any price less than $15 a tattoo.

When Tom shuts down, his loss equals his total fixed cost, which is $30; pages 377, 384.

■ CHECKPOINT 15.3

Fill in the blanks

In the long run, a perfectly competitive firm cannot make an economic profit, cannot incur an economic loss, and can make zero economic profit. In the long run, a perfectly competitive firm produces at minimum average total cost. Entry into an industry shifts the market supply curve rightward. Firms exit an industry when they are incurring an economic loss. A techno-

logical change results in perfectly competitive firms temporarily making an economic profit.

True or false

1. True; page 386
2. True; pages 387-388
3. True; pages 388-389
4. False; pages 389-390
5. True; page 392

Multiple choice

1. d; page 387
2. a; pages 387-388
3. b; pages 387-388
4. b; pages 388-389
5. e; pages 388-389
6. a; page 388
7. a; pages 387-389
8. b; pages 389-391

Complete the graph

■ **FIGURE 15.11**

Price and cost (dollars per unit)

1. Figure 15.11 shows a perfectly competitive firm in long-run equilibrium. The marginal revenue curve is horizontal at the price of $20. The firm produces 150 units because that is the quantity at which marginal revenue equals marginal cost. The firm makes zero economic profit because the price, $20 per unit, equals the average total cost, also $20 per unit; page 386.

■ **FIGURE 15.12**
Price and cost (dollars per unit)

2. a. At the price of $6, the marginal revenue curve is MR_1 in Figure 15.12. Firm 1 produces 20 units and makes zero economic profit because the $6 price equals average total cost. Firm 2 produces 35 units and makes an economic profit because the $6 price exceeds average total cost; pages 386, 389-390.

   b. Market supply increases and the price falls. Firm 1 now incurs an economic loss and Firm 2 makes a smaller economic profit; pages 390-391.

   c. In the long run, the new price will be $4 because that is the minimum of the new average total cost. Firm 1 will either have adopted the new technology and be making zero economic profit or will have exited the industry. Firm 2 will make zero economic profit; pages 390-391.

Short answer and numeric questions

1. Perfectly competitive firms cannot make an economic profit in the long run because the existence of an economic profit invites entry by new firms. As these new firms enter, the market supply increases, driving down the price and eventually eliminating the economic profit. If perfectly competitive firms incur an economic loss, they close because no firm will incur an economic loss in the long run. As some firms close, the price rises

and the economic loss of the surviving firms decreases and is eventually eliminated when enough firms have closed; pages 387-389.

2. Perfect competition is efficient. In a perfectly competitive market, equilibrium occurs at the intersection of the supply and demand curves. Key, however, the facts that the supply curve also is the marginal cost curve and the demand curve also is the marginal benefit curve. So the equilibrium quantity also is the quantity at which the marginal cost equals the marginal benefit, which is the efficient quantity; page 392.

3. Competition in the market for home delivered pizza keeps the price of home delivered pizza low. The producers of pizza would like to charge the highest price they can. However their price is limited by competition and it is this competition that protects you by keeping the price of home delivered pizza low.

Additional Exercises (also in MyEconLab Test A)

1. If the market price is $20 a tattoo, marginal revenue equals $20 a tattoo. The marginal cost of the fifth tattoo is the total cost of 5 tattoos minus the total cost of 4 tattoos, which is $110 − $90 = $20. So, Tom sells 5 tattoos an hour because the marginal cost of the fifth tattoo, $20, equals the marginal revenue. The average total cost of a tattoo equals the total cost divided by the quantity of tattoos, which is $110 ÷ 5 tattoos = $22 a tattoo. The price of a tattoo is $20 a tattoo, so Tom makes an economic "profit" of $20 minus $22, which is −$2 a tattoo. Tom sells 5 tattoos an hour, so his total economic "profit" equals −$2 × 5 tattoos, which is −$10. Tom incurs an economic loss of $10. Because firms are incurring an economic loss, tattoo firms exit the industry; pages 386-387.

2. In the long run, the price is equal to minimum average total cost, which is $22 a tattoo. In the long run, Tom sells five tattoos an hour because at this quantity price equals

minimum average total cost. In the long run, Tom makes zero economic profit; page 386.

3. The decrease in the fixed cost does not change Tom's marginal cost schedule, so in the short run there is no change in the price or quantity. In the long run, however, the number of firms producing tattoos increases because the existing firms make an economic profit as a result of the lower fixed costs. The new long-run price is $17.50 a tattoo, the minimum of the new, lower average total cost; page 390.

Chapter

Monopoly

16

CHAPTER CHECKLIST

In Chapter 16 we study how a monopoly chooses its price and quantity, discuss whether a monopoly is efficient or fair, and investigate how monopolies can be regulated.

1 Explain how monopoly arises and distinguish between single-price monopoly and price-discriminating monopoly.

A monopoly is a market with a single supplier of a good or service that has no close substitutes and in which natural, ownership, or legal barriers to entry prevent competition. A single-price monopoly is a monopoly that sells each unit of its output for the same price to all its customers. A price-discriminating monopoly is a monopoly that is able to sell different units of a good or service for different prices.

2 Explain how a single-price monopoly determines its output and price.

The demand curve for a monopoly is the downward sloping market demand curve. For a single-price monopoly, marginal revenue is less than price, so the marginal revenue curve lies below the demand curve. A monopoly maximizes profit by producing the quantity at which marginal revenue equals marginal cost and finding the highest price at which it can sell this output on the demand curve.

3 Compare the performance of a single-price monopoly with that of perfect competition.

Compared to perfect competition, a single-price monopoly produces a smaller output and charges a higher price. A monopoly is inefficient because it creates a deadweight loss. A monopoly redistributes consumer surplus so that the producer gains and the consumers lose. Rent seeking is the act of obtaining special treatment by the government to create an economic profit or divert consumer surplus or producer surplus away from others. Rent seeking aims to restrict competition and create a monopoly.

4 Explain how price discrimination increases profit.

To be able to price discriminate, a firm must be able to identify and separate different types of buyers and sell a product that cannot be resold. Price discrimination converts consumer surplus into economic profit so price discrimination increases the firm's profit. Perfect price discrimination leaves no consumer surplus but is efficient.

5 Explain why natural monopoly is regulated and the effects of regulation.

Regulation sets the prices a regulated firm can charge. The social interest theory of regulation is that regulation seeks an efficient use of resources; the capture theory is that regulation helps producers maximize economic profit. Natural monopolies are usually regulated. A marginal cost pricing rule sets price equal to marginal cost and achieves an efficient level of output but the regulated firm incurs an economic loss. An average cost pricing rule sets price equal to average total cost. The firm makes zero economic profit but there is a deadweight loss. Rate of return regulation sets the price so that the firm earns a target rate of return on its capital. Price cap regulation specifies the highest price the firm can set.

CHECKPOINT 16.1

■ **Explain how monopoly arises and distinguish between single-price monopoly and price-discriminating monopoly.**

Quick Review

• *Barrier to entry* Any constraint that protects a firm from competitors.

Additional Practice Problem 16.1

1. What is the source of the monopoly for each of the following situations? What sort of barrier to entry protects these producers?
   a. The U.S. Postal Service has a monopoly on first class mail delivery.
   b. DeBeer's, while not truly a monopoly, nonetheless controls about 80 percent of the world's diamond sales.
   c. Tampa Electric is the only electric utility company supplying power to Tampa, Florida.

Solutions to Additional Practice Problem 16.1

1a. The U.S. Postal Service derives its monopoly status by a government franchise to deliver first class mail. So the U.S. Postal Service is protected by a legal barrier to entry. Though it retains its franchise on first class mail delivery, it faces competition from the overnight services provided by FedEx, United Parcel Service, and others.

1b. DeBeers gained its monopoly power in diamond sales by buying up supplies of diamonds from sources throughout the world. So DeBeers is protected by an ownership barrier to entry.

1c. Tampa Electric has been granted a public franchise to be the only distributor of electricity in Tampa. Although Tampa Electric might be a natural monopoly, the public franchise, a legal barrier to entry, is perhaps the most immediate source of monopoly.

■ **Self Test 16.1**

Fill in the blanks

One of the requirements for monopoly is that there ____ (are; are no) close substitutes for the good. A ____ (legal; natural) monopoly exists when one firm can meet the entire market demand at a lower average total cost than two or more firms could. A monopoly that is able to sell different units of a good or service for different prices is a ____ (legal-price; natural-price; price-discriminating) monopoly.

True or false

1. A legal barrier creates a natural monopoly.
2. A firm experiences economies of scale along a downward-sloping long-run average total cost curve.
3. A monopoly always charges all customers the same price.

Multiple choice

1. A monopoly market has
   a. a few firms.
   b. a single firm.
   c. two dominating firms in the market.
   d. only two firms in it.
   e. some unspecified number of firms in it.

2. Two types of barriers to entry are called ____ barriers to entry and ____ barriers to entry.
   a. legal; illegal
   b. natural; legal
   c. natural; illegal
   d. natural; rent seeking
   e. ownership; rent seeking

3. A natural monopoly is one that arises from
   a. patent law.
   b. copyright law.
   c. a firm buying all of a natural resource.
   d. economies of scale.
   e. ownership of a natural resource.

4. A legal barrier is created when a firm
   a. has economies of scale, which allow it to produce at a lower cost than two or more firms.
   b. is granted a public franchise, government license, patent, or copyright.
   c. produces a unique product or service.
   d. produces a standardized product or service.
   e. has an ownership barrier to entry.

5. Pizza producers charge one price for a single pizza and almost give away a second one. This is an example of
   a. monopoly.
   b. a barrier to entry.
   c. behavior that is not profit-maximizing.
   d. price discrimination.
   e. rent seeking.

Short answer and numeric questions
1. What conditions define monopoly?
2. What are the two types of barriers to entry?
3. What are the two pricing strategies a monopoly can use? Why don't perfectly competitive firms have these same strategies?

Additional Exercises (also in MyEconLab Test A)
The following list has five different firms:
- A department store in a large downtown Houston shopping mall
- Tiffany, the upscale jeweler
- Wal-Mart
- The only shoe-shine stand licensed to operate in St. Louis airport
- The U.S. Postal Service

1. Which of the five firms are monopolies?
2. Which of the firms are natural monopolies and which are legal monopolies? Which can price discriminate, which cannot, and why?

CHECKPOINT 16.2

■ **Explain how a single-price monopoly determines its output and price.**

Quick Review
- *Marginal revenue* The change in total revenue resulting from a one-unit increase in the quantity sold.
- *Maximize profit* A single-price monopoly maximizes its profit by producing where $MR = MC$ and then using the demand curve to determine the price for this quantity of output.

Additional Practice Problems 16.2

Quantity (pizzas per hour)	Total cost (dollars per pizza)	ATC (dollars per pizza)	MC (dollars per pizza)
0	1.00		
1	6.00	___	___
2	13.00	___	___
3	22.00	___	___
4	33.00	___	

1. In a small town, Leonardo's Pizza is the sole restaurant. The table above gives Leonardo's total cost schedule. Complete the table.

Quantity demanded (pizzas per hour)	Price (dollars per pizza)	MR (dollars per pizza)
0	16.00	
1	14.00	___
2	12.00	___
3	10.00	___
4	8.00	

2. The table above gives the demand schedule for Leonardo's pizzas. Complete the table.
3. In a figure, plot Leonardo's demand curve, average total cost curve, marginal cost curve, and marginal revenue curve.
   a. What is Leonardo's equilibrium quantity and price?
   b. What is Leonardo's economic profit or loss? In the figure show the economic profit or loss.

Solutions to Additional Practice Problems 16.2
1. The completed table is above.

Quantity (pizzas per hour)	Total cost (dollars per pizza)	ATC (dollars per pizza)	MC (dollars per pizza)
0	1.00		5.00
1	6.00	6.00	7.00
2	13.00	6.50	9.00
3	22.00	7.33	11.00
4	33.00	8.25	

Quantity demanded (pizzas per hour)	Price (dollars per pizza)	Marginal revenue (dollars per pizza)
0	16.00	
		14.00
1	14.00	
		10.00
2	12.00	
		6.00
3	10.00	
		2.00
4	8.00	

2. The completed table is above.
3. The figure shows Leonardo's demand curve, average total cost curve, marginal cost curve, and marginal revenue curve.

3a. Both a monopoly and a perfectly competitive firm maximize their profit by producing the quantity at which marginal revenue equals marginal cost. So Leonardo's maximizes its profit by producing 2 pizzas per hour. The price, from the demand curve, is $12 per pizza.
3b. Leonardo's sells each pizza for $12.00. The average total cost for 2 pizzas is $6.50. So for each pizza Leonardo's makes an economic profit of $5.50 for a total economic profit of $5.50 per pizza × 2 pizzas, or $11.00. This economic profit is equal to the area of the darkened rectangle in the figure.

■ Self Test 16.2
Fill in the blanks

For each level of output, marginal revenue for a single-price monopoly is ____ (greater than; equal to; less than) price. When demand is inelastic, marginal revenue is ____ (positive; negative). A single-price monopoly maximizes profit by producing the quantity at which marginal revenue ____ (is greater than; equals; is less than) marginal cost and then finds the highest

price for which it can sell that output by using the ____ (demand; marginal revenue; average total cost) curve.

True or false

1. For a single-price monopoly, marginal revenue exceeds price.
2. Marginal revenue is always positive for a monopoly.
3. A single-price monopoly maximizes profit by producing the quantity at which marginal revenue equals marginal cost.

Multiple choice

1. For a single-price monopoly, price is
   a. greater than marginal revenue.
   b. one half of marginal revenue.
   c. equal to marginal revenue.
   d. unrelated to marginal revenue.
   e. always less than average total cost when the firm maximizes its profit.

2. A single-price monopoly can sell 1 unit for $9.00. To sell 2 units, the price must be $8.50 per unit. The marginal revenue from selling the second unit is
   a. $17.50.
   b. $17.00.
   c. $8.50.
   d. $8.00.
   e. $9.00.

3. When demand is elastic, marginal revenue is
   a. positive.
   b. negative.
   c. zero.
   d. increasing as output increases.
   e. undefined.

4. To maximize its profit, a single-price monopoly produces the quantity at which
   a. the difference between marginal revenue and marginal cost is as large as possible.
   b. marginal revenue equals marginal cost.
   c. average total cost is at its minimum.
   d. the marginal cost curve intersects the demand curve.
   e. the marginal revenue curve intersects the horizontal axis.

5. Once a monopoly has determined how much it produces, it will charge a price that
   a. is determined by the intersection of the marginal cost and average total cost curves.
   b. minimizes marginal cost.
   c. is determined by its demand curve.
   d. is independent of the amount produced.
   e. is equal to its average total cost.

Complete the graph

Quantity (hamburgers per hour)	Price (dollars)	Marginal revenue (dollars)
1	8.00	
2	7.00	____
3	6.00	____
4	5.00	____
5	4.00	

1. The table above gives the demand schedule for Bud's Burgers, a monopoly seller of hamburgers in a small town. Complete the table by calculating the marginal revenue.

   a. In Figure 16.1 draw the demand curve and marginal revenue curve.

   b. Suppose the marginal cost is $3 no matter how many hamburgers Bud's produces. Draw the marginal cost curve in the figure. To maximize his profit, how many burgers will Bud grill in an hour and what will be their price?

2. Figure 16.2 shows a monopoly's cost curves and its demand and marginal revenue curves. Label the curves. Identify the profit-maximizing quantity price. Is the monopoly making an economic profit or incurring an economic loss? Darken the area that shows the economic profit or economic loss.

■ **FIGURE 16.1**

Price and marginal revenue (dollars per hamburger)

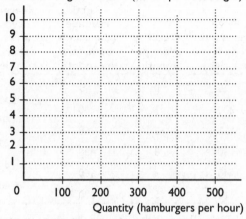

■ **FIGURE 16.2**

Price and cost (dollars per unit)

Short answer and numeric questions

1. What is the relationship between the elasticity of demand and marginal revenue?

2. Both perfectly competitive and monopoly firms maximize their profit by producing where $MR = MC$. Why do both use the same rule?

3. Why can a monopoly make an economic profit in the long run?

264 Part 6 · PRICES, PROFITS, AND INDUSTRY PERFORMANCE

Additional Exercises (also in MyEconLab Test A)

Price (thousands of dollars per ride)	Quantity (rides per month)	Total revenue (thousands of dollars per month)	Marginal revenue (thousands of dollars per ride)
220	0	0	
			200
200	1	200	
			160
180	2	360	
			120
160	3	480	
			80
140	4	560	
			40
120	5	600	

HotAir Balloon Rides is a single-price monopoly. The table shows the demand schedule for balloon rides (columns 1 and 2) and HotAir's total cost schedule (columns 2 and 3).

1. Calculate HotAir's total revenue and marginal revenue schedules.

2. Draw the demand curve and HotAir's marginal revenue curve.

3. Calculate HotAir's profit-maximizing output, price, and economic profit.

4. If the government imposes a fixed tax of $60,000 a month on HotAir, what are the new profit-maximizing output, price, and economic profit?

5. If instead of imposing a fixed tax on HotAir, the government taxes HotAir by $30,000 per ride, what are the new profit-maximizing output, price, and economic profit?

CHECKPOINT 16.3

■ **Compare the performance of a single-price monopoly with that of perfect competition.**

Quick Review

• *Monopoly and competition compared* Compared to perfect competition, a single-price monopoly produces less output and charges a higher price.

Additional Practice Problems 16.3

1. In River Bend, Ohio, the owners of the Acme cab company have convinced the city government to grant it a public franchise so it is the only cab company in town. Prior to this, the cab market had been perfectly competitive. The figure shows the market demand and marginal revenue curves for cab rides as well as the marginal cost curve.

a. Before the government granted Acme its monopoly, how many miles of taxi rides were driven and what was the price?

b. As a monopoly, how many miles of taxi rides will Acme drive? What is the price Acme sets?

c. What is the efficient number of miles?

d. On the graph, show the deadweight loss that results from Acme's monopoly.

2. Suppose that Acme is put up for sale. Looking at the entire future, say Acme's total economic profit is $2 million. If the bidding for Acme is a competitive process, what do you expect will be the price for which the company is sold? What result are you illustrating?

Solutions to Additional Practice Problems 16.3

1a. Before the monopoly was granted, the equilibrium number of miles and price were determined by the demand and supply curves. As the figure shows, 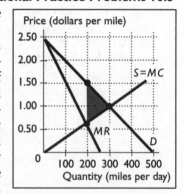 the number of miles was 300 miles per day and the price was $1.00 per mile.

1b. To maximize its profit, the figure shows that Acme drives 200 miles per day because that is the quantity at which marginal revenue equals marginal cost. The price is set from the demand curve and is $1.50 per mile.

1c. The efficient quantity is the quantity at which marginal benefit equals marginal cost. The demand curve is the marginal benefit curve, so the figure shows that the efficient quantity is 300 miles a day.

1d. Single-price monopolies create a deadweight loss because a monopoly produces where $MR = MC$ but efficiency requires production where $MB = MC$. The figure illustrates the deadweight loss as the darkened triangle.

2. Bidders are willing to pay up to $2 million for Acme because if they can buy it for any price less than $2 million, they receive an economic profit. The bidding is competitive, so the price of Acme will be bid up to $2 million and the winning bidder makes zero economic profit. This result demonstrates a rent-seeking equilibrium in which the rent-seeking costs exhaust the economic profit.

■ Self Test 16.3

Fill in the blanks

Compared to perfect competition, a single-price monopoly produces a _____ (larger; smaller) output and charges a _____ (higher; lower) price. A single-price monopoly _____ (creates; does not create) a deadweight loss. The act of obtaining special treatment by the government to create an economic profit is called _____ (government surplus; rent seeking). Rent seeking _____ (decreases; increases) the amount of deadweight loss.

True or false

1. A monopoly charges a higher price than a perfectly competitive industry.

2. A monopoly redistributes consumer surplus so that consumers gain and the producer loses.

3. The buyer of a monopoly always makes an economic profit.

Multiple choice

1. If a perfectly competitive industry is taken over by a single firm that operates as a single-price monopoly, the price will _____ and the quantity will _____.
   a. fall; decrease
   b. fall; increase
   c. rise; decrease
   d. rise; increase
   e. not change; decrease

■ FIGURE 16.3

Price and costs (dollars per gallon)

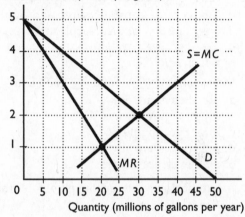

Quantity (millions of gallons per year)

2. Figure 16.3 shows the market for gasoline in a town. If the market is perfectly competitive, the price is _____ per gallon and if the market is taken over by a firm that operates as a single-price monopoly, the price is _____.
   a. $1; $2
   b. $1; $3
   c. $1; $1
   d. $2; $1
   e. $2; $3

3. Figure 16.3 shows the market for gasoline in a town. If the market is perfectly competitive, the quantity is _____ million gallons a year and if the market is taken over by a firm that operates as a single-price monopoly, the quantity is _____ million gallons a year.
   a. 50; 20
   b. 50; 30
   c. 30; 20
   d. 50; 10
   e. 20; 30

4. Comparing single-price monopoly to perfect competition, monopoly
   a. increases the amount of consumer surplus.
   b. has the same amount of consumer surplus.
   c. has no consumer surplus.
   d. decreases the amount of consumer surplus.
   e. decreases the amount of economic profit.

5. Is a single-price monopoly efficient?
   a. Yes, because it creates a deadweight loss.
   b. No, because it creates a deadweight loss.
   c. Yes, because consumers gain and producers lose some of their surpluses.
   d. Yes, because consumers lose and producers gain some of their surpluses.
   e. Yes, because it produces the quantity at which *MR=MC*.

6. Monopolies ____ fair and ____ efficient.
   a. are always; are not
   b. might be; are always
   c. might be; might be
   d. are always; are always
   e. are never; are always

7. In equilibrium, rent seeking eliminates the
   a. deadweight loss.
   b. economic profit.
   c. consumer surplus.
   d. demand for the product.
   e. opportunity to price discriminate.

Complete the graph

■ FIGURE 16.4
Price and costs (dollars per ostrich)

1. Figure 16.4 shows the market for ostrich farming, an industry that is initially perfectly competitive. Then one farmer buys all the other farms and operates as a single-price monopoly. In the figure, label the curves. What was the competitive price and quantity? What is the monopoly price and quantity? Darken the deadweight loss area.

Short answer and numeric questions

1. How does the quantity produced and the price set by a single-price monopoly compare to those in a perfectly competitive market?

2. What happens to consumer surplus with a single-price monopoly?

3. What is rent seeking? How does rent seeking affect society?

Additional Exercises (also in MyEconLab Test A)

■ FIGURE 16.5
Price and cost (dollars per ride)

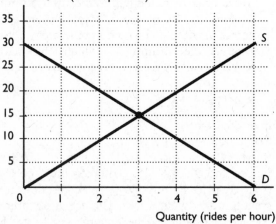

Quantity (rides per hour)

Sandy Cove is the only beach resort on a small island and the only beach activity it offers is jet ski rides. Figure 16.5 shows the marginal cost of a ride and the market demand for rides. The resort is single-price monopoly.

1. How many rides an hour are taken and what is the price of a ride?

2. Is the equilibrium number of rides the efficient quantity? Explain your answer.

3. What are the consumer surplus redistributed to the resort and the deadweight loss created because the resort has no competitors?

CHECKPOINT 16.4

■ **Explain how price discrimination increases profit.**

Quick Review

- *Price discrimination* Price discrimination is selling a good at a number of different prices.
- *Consumer surplus* The consumer surplus of a good is its marginal benefit, which equals the maximum price the consumer is willing to pay for the unit of the good, minus the price paid for it, summed over the quantity consumed.

Additional Practice Problems 16.4

1. Frequently the price of the first scoop of ice cream in a cone is less than the price of the second scoop. Why does the ice cream shop use this pricing strategy?
2. Why is the price to attend a movie less on a weekday afternoon than on a weekend evening?
3. How does price discrimination affect the amount of consumer surplus? The amount of the firm's economic profit?

Solutions to Additional Practice Problems 16.4

1. The ice cream store is price discriminating among units of the good by charging different prices for different scoops of ice cream. The store knows that consumers' marginal benefit from ice cream decreases as more is consumed, so the consumer is willing to pay less for the second scoop than for the first scoop. By charging less for the second scoop, the store will sell more scoops and increase its profit.
2. When the price to attend a movie is less on a weekday afternoon than on a weekend evening, the movie theater is practicing price discrimination among two groups of buyers. Each group has a different willingness to pay to see a movie. By setting two different prices, the movie theater maximizes profit by converting consumer surplus into economic profit.

3. Price discrimination decreases consumer surplus because it allows the business to set a price that is closer to the maximum the consumer is willing to pay. Price discrimination increases the firm's profit.

■ **Self Test 16.4**

Fill in the blanks

It is ____ (sometimes; never) possible for a monopoly to charge different customers different prices. The key idea behind price discrimination is to convert ____ (consumer surplus; producer surplus) into economic profit. Price discrimination results in consumers with a higher willingness paying a ____ (higher; lower) price than consumers with a lower willingness to pay. Perfect price discrimination results in ____ (the maximum; zero) consumer surplus and ____ (creates; does not create) a deadweight loss.

True or false

1. Price discrimination lowers a firm's profit.
2. Price discrimination converts producer surplus into consumer surplus.
3. With perfect price discrimination, the firm produces the efficient quantity of output and has a larger profit than it would if it did not price discriminate.

Multiple choice

1. Which of the following must a firm be able to do to successfully price discriminate?
   i. divide buyers into different groups according to their willingness to pay
   ii. prevent resale of the good or service
   iii. identify into which group (high willingness to pay or low willingness to pay) a buyer belongs
   a. ii only.
   b. i and ii.
   c. i and iii.
   d. iii only.
   e. i, ii, and iii.

2. Which of the following is (are) price discrimination?
   i. charging different prices based on differences in production cost
   ii. charging business flyers a higher airfare than tourists
   iii. charging more for the first pizza than the second
   a. i only.
   b. ii only.
   c. ii and iii.
   d. i and iii.
   e. i, ii, and iii.

3. When a monopoly price discriminates, it
   a. increases the amount of consumer surplus.
   b. decreases its economic profit.
   c. converts consumer surplus into economic profit.
   d. converts economic profit into consumer surplus.
   e. has no effect on the deadweight loss.

4. If a monopoly is able to perfectly price discriminate, then consumer surplus is
   a. equal to zero.
   b. maximized.
   c. unchanged from what it is with a single-price monopoly.
   d. unchanged from what it is in a perfectly competitive market.
   e. not zero but is less than with a single-price monopoly.

5. With perfect price discrimination, the quantity of output produced by a monopoly is ____ the quantity produced by a perfectly competitive market.
   a. greater than but not equal to
   b. less than
   c. equal to but not greater than
   d. not comparable to
   e. either greater than or equal to

Complete the graph

1. Figure 16.6 shows the cost and demand curves for a dry-cleaner that has a monopoly in a small town.
   a. In the figure, lightly darken the area of the

■ **FIGURE 16.6**

Price and cost (dollars per article of clothing)

Quantity (articles of clothing per day)

economic profit for a single-price monopoly. What is the amount of economic profit this firm makes?

b. Suppose the firm can price discriminate and set one price for the first 10 articles of clothing and another price for the second 10 articles of clothing. What prices would it set? Darken the additional economic profit the firm makes. What is the amount of the firm's economic profit now?

c. Suppose the firm is able to perfectly price discriminate. More heavily darken the additional economic profit the firm now makes. What is the amount of the firm's economic profit now?

Short answer and numeric questions

1. Explain the effect of price discrimination on consumer surplus and economic profit.

2. When does a price discriminating monopoly produce the efficient quantity of output?

Additional Exercises (also in MyEconLab Test A)

Consider the following situations in California:

- The weekend price of a hotel room is less than the mid-week price.
- Stand-by passengers can fly at lower fares than passengers who buy etickets.
- Colleges charge out-of-state students a higher tuition than those from California.

- A supermarket sells water for $2 a bottle or $18 for a box of 12 bottles.
- A bank charges a student a higher interest rate on a car loan than on a student loan.
- The price of water is higher for a car wash firm than it is for a farmer.
- A cell phone company offers free calls on the weekend.
- A museum offers discounts to students and senior citizens.

1. Which of the situations is *not* an example of price discrimination? Explain why not.

2. For the situations that *are* examples of price discrimination, explain how the discrimination is achieved.

CHECKPOINT 16.5

■ **Explain why natural monopoly is regulated and the effects of regulation.**

Quick Review

- *Marginal cost pricing rule* A price rule for a natural monopoly that sets price equal to marginal cost.
- *Average cost pricing rule* A price rule for a natural monopoly that sets price equal to average cost.

Additional Practice Problems 16.5

1. The figure shows the demand and cost curves for the local water distributing company. The company is a natural monopoly.

   a. If the company is unregulated, what price does it charge for water and how much is distributed? Does

   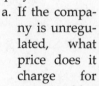

the firm have an economic profit, zero economic profit, or an economic loss?

b. If the company is regulated using an average cost pricing rule, what price does it charge for water and how much is distributed? Does the firm have an economic profit, zero economic profit, or an economic loss?

c. If the company is regulated using a marginal cost pricing rule, what price does it charge for water and how much is distributed? Does the firm have an economic profit, zero economic profit, or an economic loss?

2. The Airmail Act of 1934 awarded airline routes on the basis of competitive bidding. The airlines bid for routes (the bids were the fares the airline would charge) and the low bidder won. The Interstate Commerce Commission regulated the fares. Frequently, after having won a route, an airline was allowed to raise its fare to a profitable level.

The Civil Aeronautics Act was passed in 1938 and served to regulate airlines for the next four decades. There was complete control over entry and exit, as well as fare and route structure. Over this period of time, virtually no new airlines were allowed to enter the market. For two decades after World War II, utilization continued to decline until less than half of seating capacity was being utilized.

In 1978, deregulation occurred. Airlines were free to enter or exit and were also free to determine the fare they would charge. Since deregulation in 1978, passenger airline miles have more than doubled, prices have fallen, and mergers have occurred.

Which theory, the social interest or capture theory, best describes each of these three periods of the airline industry history?

Solutions to Additional Practice Problems 16.5

1a. An unregulated monopoly produces the quantity where marginal revenue equals marginal cost and the price is determined by the demand curve. In the figure on the next page, marginal revenue equals marginal cost when 2 thousand gallons of water per day are distributed. The price is $6 per thousand gallons. The firm makes an economic profit.

Price and cost
(dollars per thousand gallons)

1b. If an average cost pricing rule is used, price and quantity are determined by where the average total cost curve intersects the demand curve. From the figure, the price is $4 per thousand gallons and the quantity is 3 thousand gallons per day. The firm makes zero economic profit.

1c. If a marginal cost pricing rule is used, price and quantity are determined by where the marginal cost curve intersects the demand curve. From the figure, the price is $2 per thousand gallons and the quantity is 4 thousand gallons per day. The firm incurs an economic loss.

2. From 1934 to 1938, the competitive bidding suggests that social interest might have been more important than in the 1938 to 1978 period. But during the early four-year period, airlines were learning to expect a handout from government regulators.

During the four-decade era of the Civil Aeronautics Act, the industry is best described by the capture theory. Airlines were protected from competition by new entrants. They also faced little competition from existing airlines because fares were fixed. Competition took the form of frills, such as fancy dinners, champagne, and attractive accommodations and services.

Since 1978 airline behavior more typically resembles social interest theory and has as its legacy lower prices, higher capacity utilization, new low-fare entrants, bankruptcies, and mergers.

■ Self Test 16.5

Fill in the blanks

The theory that regulation seeks an efficient use of resources is the _____ (capture; social interest) theory, and the theory that regulation helps producers maximize economic profit is the _____ (capture; social interest) theory. With _____ (an average; a marginal) cost pricing rule, a natural monopoly incurs an economic loss. Regulated firms have an incentive to inflate their costs under _____ (rate of return; price cap) regulation.

True or false

1. Social interest theory assumes that the political process introduces regulation that eliminates deadweight loss.

2. A regulated natural monopoly produces the efficient quantity of output when it is regulated to use a marginal cost pricing rule.

3. Price cap regulation is designed to give firms the incentive to raise the price of their output, provided competition in the market increases.

Multiple choice

1. The theory that regulation seeks an efficient use of resources is the
   a. social interest theory.
   b. producer surplus theory.
   c. consumer surplus theory.
   d. capture theory.
   e. deadweight loss theory.

2. Which of the following best describes the capture theory of regulation?
   i. Regulation seeks an efficient use of resources
   ii. Regulation is aimed at keeping prices as low as possible
   iii. Regulation helps firms maximize economic profit
   a. i only.
   b. ii only.
   c. iii only.
   d. i and ii.
   e. i, ii, and iii.

3. When regulators require a natural monopoly to set a price that is equal to its marginal cost, the firm
   a. makes zero economic profit.
   b. makes an economic profit.
   c. incurs an economic loss.
   d. sets $P = MC = ATC$.
   e. makes either zero economic profit or an economic profit, depending on whether the firm's average total cost equals or is less than its marginal cost.

4. If a natural monopoly is told to set price equal to its average cost, then the firm
   a. is not able to set marginal revenue equal to marginal cost.
   b. automatically also sets price equal to marginal cost.
   c. will make a substantial economic profit.
   d. will incur an economic loss
   e. sets a price that is lower than its marginal cost.

■ **FIGURE 16.7**

Price and cost (dollars per month)

Quantity (thousands of households)

5. If the natural monopoly illustrated in Figure 16.7 was regulated using a marginal cost pricing rule, the price would be ____.
   a. $100
   b. between $100.01 and $200.00
   c. between $200.01 and $300.00
   d. between $300.01 and $400.00
   e. more than $400.01

6. If the natural monopoly illustrated in Figure 16.7 was regulated using an average total cost pricing rule, the price would be ____.
   a. $100
   b. between $100.01 and $200.00
   c. between $200.01 and $300.00
   d. between $300.01 and $400.00
   e. more than $400.01

7. If the natural monopoly illustrated in Figure 16.7 was unregulated, the price would be ____.
   a. $100
   b. between $100.01 and $200.00
   c. between $200.01 and $300.00
   d. between $300.01 and $400.00
   e. more than $400.01

Complete the graph

■ **FIGURE 16.8**

Price and cost (dollars per month)

Quantity (thousands of households)

1. Figure 16.8 shows both the average total cost curves of a cable TV company that is a regulated monopoly. Also given are the demand curve and marginal revenue curve.
   a. What price would the regulator set using the marginal cost pricing rule?
   b. What price would the regulator set using the average cost pricing rule?
   c. What price would the firm set if it was unregulated?

Short answer and numeric questions

1. Why doesn't the government regulate all industries?

2. What is the social interest theory of regulation? The capture theory?

3. What is the advantage of using a marginal cost pricing rule to regulate a natural monopoly? The disadvantage?

4. What is the goal of price cap regulation?

2. If the monopoly captures the regulator, how might the monopoly be regulated?

3. If the regulator sets a price cap such that the monopoly breaks even, what is the quantity produced and price at which it is sold? Would the regulated monopoly produce efficiently?

Additional Exercises (also in MyEconLab Test A)

■ **FIGURE 16.9**

Price (cents per can)

Quantity (thousands of cans per year)

An unregulated natural monopoly cans Mt. McKinley air, unique clean air that has no substitutes. The monopoly's total fixed cost is $30,000, and its marginal cost is 10 cents a can. Figure 16.9 illustrates the demand for Mt McKinley air.

1. How many cans of Mt. McKinley air does the monopoly sell and what is the price of a can of Mt. McKinley air?

SELF TEST ANSWERS

■ CHECKPOINT 16.1

Fill in the blanks

One of the requirements for monopoly is that there <u>are no</u> close substitutes for the good. A <u>natural</u> monopoly exists when one firm can meet the entire market demand at a lower average total cost than two or more firms could. A monopoly that is able to sell different units of a good or service for different prices is a <u>price-discriminating</u> monopoly.

True or false

1. False; pages 400-401
2. True; page 401
3. False; page 402

Multiple choice

1. b; page 400
2. b; page 400
3. d; page 400
4. b; page 401
5. d; page 402

Short answer and numeric questions

1. Monopoly occurs when there is a market with a single firm selling a good or service that has no close substitutes and in which the firm is protected by either a natural, ownership, or a legal barrier to entry; page 400.

2. Barriers to entry are anything that protects a firm from the entry of new competitors. Barriers to entry are either natural barriers, ownership barriers, or legal barriers; pages 400-401.

3. A monopoly can sell each unit of its output for the same price to all its customers or it can price discriminate by selling different units of its good or service at different prices. A perfectly competitive firm cannot affect the price so it must charge a single price determined by market demand and market supply; page 402.

Additional Exercises (also in MyEconLab Test A)

1. A large shopping mall in downtown Houston is not a monopoly because there are many other similar stores and malls nearby. Tiffany is not a monopoly because there are many other upscale jewelers. Wal-Mart is not a monopoly because there are many other similar retailers. The only shoe-shine stand licensed to operate in an airport is a monopoly. The U.S. Postal Service is a monopoly when it comes to first class mail; page 400.

2. The shoe-shine stand and U.S. Postal Service are legal monopolies. The shoe-shine stand and the U.S. Postal service can price discriminate because the service they produce cannot be resold; pages 400-402.

■ CHECKPOINT 16.2

Fill in the blanks

For each level of output, marginal revenue for a single-price monopoly is <u>less than</u> price. When demand is inelastic, marginal revenue is <u>negative</u>. A single-price monopoly maximizes profit by producing the quantity at which marginal revenue <u>equals</u> marginal cost and then finds the highest price for which it can sell that output by using the <u>demand</u> curve.

True or false

1. False; page 404
2. False; page 405
3. True; page 407

Multiple choice

1. a; page 404
2. d; page 404
3. a; page 405
4. b; page 407
5. c; page 407

Complete the graph

Quantity (hamburgers per hour)	Price (dollars)	Marginal revenue (dollars)
1	8.00	
		6.00
2	7.00	
		4.00
3	6.00	
		2.00
4	5.00	
		0.00
5	4.00	

■ FIGURE 16.10

Price and marginal revenue (dollars per hamburger)

1. The completed table is above.
   a. Figure 16.10 plots the demand and marginal revenue curves; page 407.
   b. Figure 16.10 shows the marginal cost curve. To maximize his profit, Bud produces the quantity at which marginal revenue equals marginal cost. So Bud prepares 300 hamburgers per hour. From the demand curve, the price of a hamburger is $6; pages 406-407.
2. The curves are labeled in Figure 16.11. The profit-maximizing quantity is 20 units and the price is $1,500. The economic profit equals the area of the dark rectangle; page 407.

Short answer and numeric questions

1. If demand is elastic, marginal revenue is positive; if demand is unit elastic, marginal revenue is zero; and if demand is inelastic, marginal revenue is negative; page 405.

■ FIGURE 16.11

Price and cost (dollars per unit)

2. Both perfectly competitive and monopoly firms maximize profit by producing where *MR* = *MC* because for *any* firm, a unit of output is produced if *MR* > *MC* and is not produced if *MR* < *MC*. As long as *MR* > *MC*, *any* firm increases its total profit by continuing to produce additional output until it reaches the point at which *MR* = *MC*; pages 406-407.

3. A monopoly can make an economic profit in the long run because it is protected by a barrier to entry. Other firms want to enter the market in order also to make some economic profit, but they cannot do so; page 407.

Additional Exercises (also in MyEconLab Test A)

Price (thousands of dollars per ride)	Quantity (rides per month)	Total revenue (thousands of dollars per month)	Marginal revenue (thousands of dollars per ride)
220	0	0	
			200
200	1	200	
			160
180	2	360	
			120
160	3	480	
			80
140	4	560	
			40
120	5	600	

1. The total revenue equals the price multiplied by the quantity and the marginal revenue equals the change in total revenue divided by the change in quantity. A table showing

HotAir's total revenue and marginal revenue is above; pages 404-405.

■ FIGURE 16.12

Price and marginal revenue (thousands of dollars per ride)

Quantity (rides per month)

2. Figure 16.12 illustrates HotAir's demand and marginal revenue curves; page 404.

3. HotAir's marginal cost equals marginal revenue at 2 1/2 rides a month, where both equal $120,000. From the demand curve, the price is $170,000 a ride. The total cost of 2 1/2 rides a month is $320,000. HotAir's total revenue equals the number of rides multiplied by the price per ride, which is (2 1/2 rides per month) × ($170,000) = $425,000. So the total economic profit is total revenue minus total cost, which is $425,000 − $320,000 = $105,000; pages 406-407.

4. As a result of the tax, HotAir's fixed cost changes, but its marginal cost does not. The profit-maximizing level of output is still 2 1/2 rides a month and the price still equals $170,000. The tax decreases HotAir's economic profit by $60,000 so the new economic profit is $45,000; pages 406-407.

5. A $30,000 per ride tax increases HotAir's marginal cost by $30,000 at every level of output. With the increase in the marginal costs, HotAir now sells 2 rides a month because this is the level at which the new marginal cost equals the marginal revenue (both equal $140,000). From the demand curve, HotAir sets a price of $180,000 a ride. Total

profit equals total revenue minus total cost. The total revenue is 2 rides × $180,000, which is $360,000. The total cost is $260,000 plus the tax of $60,000, which is $320,000. The new economic profit is $360,000 − $320,000 = $40,000; pages 406-407.

■ CHECKPOINT 16.3

Fill in the blanks

Compared to perfect competition, a single-price monopoly produces a <u>smaller</u> output and charges a <u>higher</u> price. A single-price monopoly <u>creates</u> a deadweight loss. The act of obtaining special treatment by the government to create an economic profit is called <u>rent seeking</u>. Rent seeking <u>increases</u> the amount of deadweight loss.

True or false

1. True; page 409
2. False; page 410
3. False; page 411

Multiple choice

1. c; page 409
2. e; page 409
3. c; page 409
4. d; page 410
5. b; page 410
6. c; page 411
7. b; page 412

Complete the graph

■ FIGURE 16.13

Price and cost (dollars per ostrich)

Quantity (thousands of ostriches per year)

1. Figure 16.13 shows that the perfectly compet-

itive price is $20 an ostrich and the quantity is 3,000 ostriches. The monopoly price is $30 an ostrich and the quantity is 2,000 ostriches a year. The deadweight loss is the dark triangular area; page 410.

Short answer and numeric questions

1. The price set by a monopoly exceeds the price in a competitive market and the quantity produced by a monopoly is less than the quantity produced in a competitive market; page 410.

2. Consumer surplus decreases with a single-price monopoly. Consumer surplus decreases because the monopoly produces less output and charges a higher price; page 410.

3. Rent seeking is the act of obtaining special treatment by the government to create economic profit or to divert consumer surplus or producer surplus away from others. Rent seeking harms society because in a competitive rent-seeking equilibrium, the amount of the deadweight loss increases; page 411.

Additional Exercises (also in MyEconLab Test A)

■ FIGURE 16.14

Price and cost (dollars per ride)

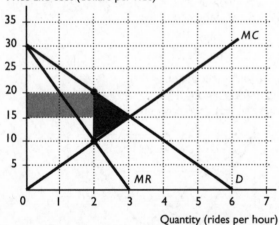

1. Figure 16.14 is helpful in answering this question. In Figure 16.14, the marginal revenue curve has been included. Marginal revenue equals marginal cost when 2 rides per hour are sold. The price per ride, from the demand is curve, is $20 per ride; page 409.

2. The number of rides is less than the efficient quantity. The efficient quantity is 3 rides per hour, where the marginal cost curve and marginal benefit curve (which is the same as the demand curve) intersect; page 410.

3. The consumer surplus when the market was perfectly competitive is the area of the triangle under the demand curve and above the equilibrium price, $15 per ride. The consumer surplus in this case equals 1/2 × 3 rides × $15, which is $22.50. The consumer surplus when the market is a monopoly is the area of the triangle under the demand curve and above the monopoly price, $20 per ride. The consumer surplus in this case equals 1/2 × 2 rides × $10, which is $10. Hence consumers lose a total $12.50 of consumer surplus. But not all of this amount is redistributed to the firm. Only $10—the area of the light grey rectangle in Figure 16.14—is redistributed to the firm. The remainder, $2.50, is lost as part of the deadweight loss.

The deadweight loss is equal to the area of the dark grey triangle in Figure 16.14. This area equals 1/2 × 1 ride × $10, which is $5; pages 410-411.

■ CHECKPOINT 16.4

Fill in the blanks

It is <u>sometimes</u> possible for a monopoly to charge different customers different prices. The key idea behind price discrimination is to convert <u>consumer surplus</u> into economic profit. Price discrimination results in consumers with a higher willingness paying a <u>higher</u> price than consumers with a lower willingness to pay. Perfect price discrimination results in <u>zero</u> consumer surplus and <u>does not create</u> a deadweight loss.

True or false

1. False; pages 414-416
2. False; page 414
3. True; page 417

Multiple choice

    1. e; page 414

    2. c; page 414

    3. c; pages 414-416

    4. a; page 417

    5. c; page 417

Complete the graph

■ FIGURE 16.15

Price and cost (dollars per article of clothing)

Quantity (articles of clothing per day)

    1. a. The economic profit is the light gray rectangle in Figure 16.15. The economic profit equals the area of the rectangle, which is $60 a day; page 415.

       b. The firm will set a price of $8 for each of the first 10 articles and $6 for each of the second 10 articles. The added profit is the darker gray rectangle for the first 10 articles. The total economic profit the firm now makes is $80 a day; page 416.

       c. The economic profit is increased by the addition of the three very dark gray areas. The economic profit is now $120 a day; page 417.

Short answer and numeric questions

    1. Price discrimination decreases consumer surplus and increases economic profit. Price discrimination allows the firm to charge a price closer to the maximum the consumer is willing to pay, which is the marginal benefit of the good. Consumer surplus is converted into economic profit; page 414.

    2. With perfect price discrimination, the monopoly increases output to the point at which price equals marginal cost. This output is identical to that of perfect competition. Deadweight loss with perfect price discrimination is zero. So perfect price discrimination produces the efficient quantity; page 417.

Additional Exercises (also in MyEconLab Test A)

    1. All are examples of price discrimination *except* the bank loan. Different interest rates reflect borrowers' different risks, which is a possible cost. Charging different interest rates is not price discriminating; page 414.

    2. For a firm to price discriminate it must be able to identify specific consumers' willingness to pay different prices and must be able to prevent the resale of the good or service. So if a firm can identify customers' willingness to pay different prices *and* if the firm can prevent resale of its good or service, then the firm can price discriminate.

For the hotel, weekend guests are likely vacation travelers with a lower willingness to pay than the mid-week guests, who are likely business travelers. The hotel can discriminate because it is not possible for the weekend guest to re-sell the room to a mid-week guest.

Stand-by passengers have a lower willingness to pay than passengers who buy the ticket in advance. The airline can discriminate because it is not possible for a stand-by traveler to re-sell the lower priced ticket to another traveler.

For the college, out-of-state students have a higher willingness to pay since they are willing to move far away from home to attend the college. The college can discriminate because it enforces residency requirements.

The supermarket is selling 12 bottles of water at an average price of $1.50 rather than the $2.00 price when it sells one bottle. The supermarket can discriminate because customers who purchase the 12 bottle box are highly unlikely to stand outside the supermarket reselling the water to customers who otherwise would buy only 1 bottle.

The water company is price discriminating by charging two different users different prices for the water. The water company can do so because it is not possible for a farmer to resell water to a car wash firm.

The cell phone company is price discriminating because it charges a lower fee for weekend calls, which are more likely pleasure calls with a lower willingness to pay, than it charges for weekday calls, which are more likely business calls, with a higher willingness to pay. The cell phone company can discriminate because it is not possible for a weekend call to be sold to a weekday caller.

The museum is price discriminating because it charges less to students and senior citizens, who likely have a lower willingness to pay, than to other visitors. The museum can discriminate because it is not possible for senior or student to resell the ticket to other visitors; page 414.

■ CHECKPOINT 16.5

Fill in the blanks

The theory that regulation seeks an efficient use of resources is the <u>social interest</u> theory, and the theory that regulation helps producers maximize economic profit is the <u>capture</u> theory. With <u>a marginal</u> cost pricing rule, a natural monopoly incurs an economic loss. Regulated firms have an incentive to inflate their costs under <u>rate of return</u> regulation.

True or false

1. True; page 421
2. True; page 422
3. False; page 425

Multiple choice

1. a; page 421
2. c; page 421
3. c; page 422
4. a; page 423
5. a; page 422
6. b; page 423
7. c; page 407

Complete the graph

1. a. Using marginal cost pricing, the regulator sets a price of $50 a month; page 421.
   b. Using average cost pricing, the regulator sets a price of $100 a month; page 423.
   c. The firm serves 20,000 households, where marginal revenue equals marginal cost, and sets the price at $150 a month; pages 406-407.

Short answer and numeric questions

1. The government does not regulate all industries because not all industries need to be regulated. Competitive industries do not need regulation because competition produces an efficient outcome. But a natural monopoly is not a competitive industry and so government regulation might help move the monopoly toward efficiency; pages 420-425.

2. The social interest theory of regulation is that the regulators pursue the public's interest by devising regulation that achieves an efficient use of resources. The capture theory of regulation is that the producers have "captured the regulators" and, as a result, the regulation helps producers maximize their economic profit; page 421.

3. The advantage of using a marginal cost pricing rule is that the firm produces the efficient quantity of output. The disadvantage is that the firm incurs an economic loss; page 422.

4. Price cap regulation gives regulated firms the incentive to cut their costs and produce efficiently, without exaggerating their costs or wasting resources; page 425.

Additional Exercises (also in MyEconLab Test A)

1. The firm produces 100,000 cans, which is the quantity at which marginal cost equals marginal revenue. The firm sets a price of $0.40 a can, which, as the demand curve shows, is the maximum price at which consumers are willing to buy the 200,000 cans produced; page 407.

2. If the monopoly can capture the regulator, the firm gets the regulator to allow it to maximize its economic profits. This outcome occurs when 100,000 cans are produced; page 420.

3. The monopoly produces 300,000 cans. When it is producing 300,000 cans, its price is $0.20 a can. And when 300,000 cans are produced, the company's average fixed cost is $0.10 a can and its average variable cost is equal to its marginal cost, $0.10 a can. So average total cost is $0.20 a can, which is equal to its price. The company is not producing efficiently. Only if the regulated monopoly produces 400,000 cans (where the demand curve crosses the marginal cost curve) does it produce an efficient outcome; pages 424-425.

Monopolistic Competition

Chapter 17

CHAPTER CHECKLIST

In Chapter 17 we study a market structure that lies between the extremes of perfect competition and monopoly: monopolistic competition.

1 Describe and identify monopolistic competition.

Monopolistic competition is a market structure in which a large number of firms compete; each firm produces a differentiated product; firms compete on product quality, price, and marketing; and firms are free to enter and exit. Product differentiation means making a product that is slightly different from the products of competing firms. Product differentiation allows the firm to compete on product quality, price, and marketing. There are no barriers to entry in monopolistic competition. The four-firm concentration ratio and the Herfindahl-Hirschman Index (HHI) measure the extent to which a market is dominated by a small number of firms. The four-firm concentration ratio is the percentage of the value of the sales accounted for by the four largest firms in the industry; the HHI is the square of the percentage market share of each firm summed over the 50 largest firms in the market. Small values of these indexes indicate competitive markets.

2 Explain how a firm in monopolistic competition determines its output and price in the short run and the long run.

A firm in monopolistic competition has a downward-sloping demand curve. The firm maximizes profit by producing the output at which marginal revenue equals marginal cost. Its price is determined from the demand curve and is the highest price for which the firm can sell the quantity it produces. In the short run, the firm might have an economic profit or an economic loss. Entry and exit result in zero economic profit in the long run. In the long run, a firm in monopolistic competition has excess capacity because it produces less than the efficient scale of output. In monopolistic competition price exceeds marginal cost, which indicates inefficiency, but the inefficiency arises from product variety, a gain for consumers.

3 Explain why advertising costs are high and why firms use brand names in monopolistic competition.

To try to make an economic profit, firms in monopolistic competition develop new products and incur huge costs to ensure that buyers appreciate the differences between their products and those of their competitors. Selling costs, such as advertising, increase a firm's *total* cost, but might lower *average* total cost if they increase the quantity sold by a large enough amount. Firms advertise to signal to the consumer the high quality of the product. Brand names also signal the consumer about the product's quality and give the firm the incentive to maintain the expected level of product quality. Advertising and brand names provide consumers with information, but the opportunity cost of the additional information must be weighed against the gain to the consumer, making the efficiency of monopolistic competition ambiguous.

CHECKPOINT 17.1

■ **Describe and identify monopolistic competition.**

Quick Review

- *Four-firm concentration ratio* The four-firm concentration ratio is the percentage of the value of sales accounted for by the four largest firms in the industry.

- *Herfindahl-Hirschman Index (HHI)* The HHI is the square of the percentage market share of each firm summed over the 50 largest firms (or summed over all the firms if there are fewer than 50) in a market.

Additional Practice Problem 17.1

Firm	Total revenue (millions of dollars)	Percent of total revenue (percent)
McDonald's	1,200	___
Burger King	600	___
Wendy's	600	___
Hardee's	300	___
Checker's	180	___
Other 20 smaller firms	720	___

1. The table gives some hypothetical data on sales in the fast-food hamburger market. Suppose that the total revenue of each of the 20 smallest firms is the same and each has total revenue of $36 million.
   a. Complete the table.
   b. Calculate the four-firm concentration ratio.
   c. Calculate the Herfindahl-Hirschman Index.
   d. Based on the hypothetical concentration ratios, in what market structure would you classify the fast-food hamburger market?

Solution to Additional Practice Problem 17.1

1a. The total revenue shares are in the table above. To calculate the total revenue shares, first determine the total revenue within the market, which is $3,600 million. A firm's total revenue equals its total revenue divided by $3,600 million and then multiplied by 100.

Firm	Total revenue (millions of dollars)	Percent of total revenue (percent)
McDonald's	1,200	33.3
Burger King	600	16.7
Wendy's	600	16.7
Hardee's	300	8.3
Checker's	180	5.0
Other 20 smaller firms	720	20.0

1b. The four-firm concentration ratio is the percentage of the total revenue accounted for by the four largest firms in the industry, which is 33.3 percent + 16.7 percent + 16.7 percent + 8.3 percent = 75.0 percent.

1c. To calculate the Herfindahl-Hirschman Index (HHI), we need to square and then sum the market shares of the firms. The market shares are equal to each firm's percentage of total revenue. Each of the 20 smaller firms has total revenue of $36 million, so each has a 1 percentage point market share. So the HHI = $(33.3)^2 + (16.7)^2 + (16.7)^2 + (8.3)^2 + (5.0)^2 + (1.0)^2 \times 20$ = 1,108.89 + 278.89 + 278.89 + 68.89 + 25.00 + 20.00, which is 1,780.56.

1d. Based on concentration ratios, the fast-food hamburger market is just on the borderline between monopolistic competition and oligopoly. To make a decision whether this industry is monopolistically competitive or an oligopoly, information about the presence or absence of barriers to entry is needed.

■ **Self Test 17.1**

Fill in the blanks

In monopolistic competition there are a ____ (large; small) number of firms producing ____ (identical; differentiated) products. Firms in monopolistic competition ____ (do; do not) compete on product quality. In monopolistic competition, barriers to entry ____ (do not exist; exist). The square of the percentage market share of each firm summed over the 50 largest firms (or summed over all firms if there are fewer than 50) is the ____ (50-firm concentration ratio; Herfindahl-Hirschman Index). Concentration ratios ____ (do; do not) measure barriers to entry.

True or false

1. Firms in monopolistic competition are free to enter or exit the market.

2. Each firm in monopolistic competition constantly tries to collude with its competitors.

3. The goods and services produced by firms in monopolistic competition all have virtually the same, if not identical, quality.

4. The larger the four-firm concentration ratio, the more competitive the industry.

5. Concentration ratios might overstate the degree of competition within an industry because concentration ratios take a national view of the market.

Multiple choice

1. In monopolistic competition there
   a. are a large number of firms.
   b. are several large firms.
   c. is one large firm.
   d. might be many, several, or one firm.
   e. are many firms but only a few buyers.

2. A firm in monopolistic competition has a _____ market share and _____ influence the price of its good or service.
   a. large; can
   b. large; cannot
   c. small; can
   d. small; cannot
   e. large; might be able to

3. Product differentiation means
   a. making a product that has perfect substitutes.
   b. making a product that is entirely unique.
   c. the inability to set your own price.
   d. making a product that is slightly different from products of competing firms.
   e. making your demand curve horizontal.

4. A firm in monopolistic competition has _____ demand curve.
   a. a downward-sloping
   b. an upward-sloping
   c. a vertical
   d. a horizontal
   e. a U-shaped

5. Firms in monopolistic competition compete on
   i. quality.
   ii. price.
   iii. marketing.
   a. i and ii.
   b. ii only.
   c. ii and iii.
   d. i and iii.
   e. i, ii, and iii.

6. The absence of barriers to entry in monopolistic competition means that in the long run firms
   a. make an economic profit.
   b. make zero economic profit.
   c. incur an economic loss.
   d. make either an economic profit or zero economic profit.
   e. make either zero economic profit or suffer an economic loss.

7. Each of the ten firms in an industry has 10 percent of the industry's total revenue. The four-firm concentration ratio is
   a. 80.
   b. 100.
   c. 1,000
   d. 40.
   e. 10.

8. Each of the four firms in an industry has a market share of 25 percent. The Herfindahl-Hirschman Index equals
   a. 3,600.
   b. 100.
   c. 625.
   d. 25.
   e. 2,500.

9. If the four-firm concentration ratio for the market for pizza is 28 percent, then this industry is best characterized as
   a. a monopoly.
   b. monopolistic competition.
   c. an oligopoly.
   d. perfect competition.
   e. oligoplistic competition.

10. The larger the four-firm concentration ratio, the ____ competition within an industry; the larger the Herfindahl-Hirschman Index, the ____ competition within an industry.
    a. more; more
    b. more; less
    c. less; more
    d. less; less
    e. The premise of the question is wrong because the four-firm concentration ratio applies only to markets with four firms in it and these markets are, by definition, not competitive.

Short answer and numeric questions

1. What conditions define monopolistic competition?

Firm	Total revenue (millions of dollars)	Percent of total revenue (percent)
Dell	1,000	____
HP	800	____
IBM	500	____
Toshiba	400	____
Other 46 smaller firms	2,300	____

2. The table gives some hypothetical data on sales in the desktop computer market. Suppose that the total revenue of each of the 46 smallest firms is the same and each has total revenue of $50 million.
    a. Complete the table.
    b. Calculate the four-firm concentration ratio.
    c. Calculate the Herfindahl-Hirschman Index.

3. Industry A has 1 firm with a market share of 57 percent and 43 other firms, each with a market share of 1 percent. Industry B has 4 firms, each with a market share of 15 percent, and 40 other firms, each with a market share of 1 percent.
    a. Calculate the four-firm concentration ratio for the two industries.
    b. Calculate the Herfindahl-Hirschman Index for the two industries.

Additional Exercises (also in MyEconLab Test A)

The table shows the total revenue of the six U.S. firms that make fine chocolates. Use this information to answer exercises 1, 2, and 3.

Firm	Total revenue (dollars)
Mayfair	30
Bond	40
Magic	10
All Nature	30
Truffles	60
Gold	30
Industry	**200**

1. Calculate the four-firm concentration ratio and the HHI.

2. What is the market structure of the chocolate industry? What would be the market structure of the chocolate industry if U.S. firms in the chocolate industry faced fierce competition from foreign suppliers?

3. What additional information would you need about the chocolate industry to be sure that it is an example of monopolistic competition?

4. Suppose that a new chocolate-making technology enables anyone with a kitchen to produce outstanding chocolates. How might the market structure of the chocolate industry change?

CHECKPOINT 17.2

■ **Explain how a firm in monopolistic competition determines its output and price in the short run and the long run.**

Quick Review
- *Profit maximization* A firm produces where marginal revenue equals marginal cost and determines the price from the demand curve.
- *Economic profit and economic loss*: Economic profit brings entry into the market and economic loss brings exit from the market.

Additional Practice Problems 17.2

1. The figure shows the demand and costs for Bernie's Burger barn, a firm in monopolistic competition.

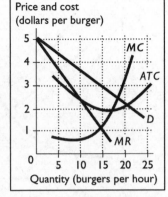

a. To maximize its profit, how many burgers does Bernie produce in an hour? What is the price Bernie sets for one of his burgers?

b. Is the firm making an economic profit or economic loss and, if so, how much?

c. Does this figure show the firm in the short run or the long run? Explain your answer.

2. The Piece A' Pie company is a pizza restaurant in competition with many other pizza restaurants. Piece A' Pie produces 50 pizzas an hour.

a. If Piece A' Pie's average total cost is $10 a pizza and its price is $12 a pizza, what is its economic profit?

b. If Piece A' Pie's average total cost is $12 a pizza and its price is $12 a pizza, what is its economic profit?

c. If Piece A' Pie's average total cost is $15 a pizza and its price is $12 a pizza, what is its economic profit?

d. Which of the three situations outlined in parts (a), (b), and (c) can represent a short-run equilibrium? A long-run equilibrium?

Solutions to Additional Practice Problems 17.2

1a. To maximize its profit, Bernie's will produce where $MR = MC$. So Bernie's produces 15 burgers per hour. Bernie's demand curve shows that Bernie will set a price of $3 for a burger.

1b. Bernie's is making an economic profit because its price is greater than its average total cost. Its economic profit equals the area of the darkened rectangle in the figure. Bernie's makes an economic profit of $1 (its price, $3, minus its average total cost, $2) on each

burger and so its total economic profit is $1 × 15 = $15.

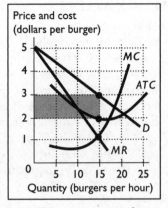

1c. Bernie's is in short-run equilibrium. It is not in long-run equilibrium because the firm is making an economic profit. Firms in monopolistic competition cannot make an economic profit in the long run; they can make an economic profit only in the short run.

2a. Piece A' Pie's economic profit on a pizza is equal to price minus average total cost. So Piece A' Pie makes an economic profit of $12 a pizza minus $10 a pizza, which is $2 a pizza. Piece A' Pie produces 50 pizzas an hour, so its total economic profit is $2 a pizza × 50 pizzas an hour, which is $100 an hour.

2b. Piece A' Pie's economic profit on a pizza is equal to price minus average total cost. So Piece A' Pie makes an economic profit of $12 a pizza minus $12 a pizza, which is zero dollars a pizza. Piece A' Pie makes zero economic profit so its owners earn a normal profit.

2c. Piece A' Pie's economic profit on a pizza is equal to price minus average total cost. So Piece A' Pie makes an economic profit of $12 a pizza minus $15 a pizza, which is −$3 a pizza. Piece A' Pie produces 50 pizzas an hour, so its total economic profit is −$3 a pizza × 50 pizzas an hour, which is −$150 an hour. So Piece A' Pie incurs an economic loss of $150 an hour.

2d. In the short run, depending on market conditions, a firm in monopolistic competition can make an economic profit, can make zero economic profit, or can incur an economic loss. Only the situation in part (b) can represent a long-run equilibrium. In the long run, the absence of barriers to entry means that firms in monopolistic competition make zero economic profit.

■ Self Test 17.2

Fill in the blanks

A firm in monopolistic competition produces the quantity where marginal revenue ____ (is greater than; equals; is less than) marginal cost. In the long run, a firm in monopolistic competition ____ (can; cannot) make an economic profit. A firm in monopolistic competition ____ (does not have; has) excess capacity in the long run. People value product variety and variety is ____ (free; costly) to produce.

True or false

1. A firm in monopolistic competition makes its output decision just like a monopoly and produces the quantity where marginal revenue equals marginal cost.
2. A firm in monopolistic competition can make an economic profit in the short run.
3. A firm in monopolistic competition can never incur an economic loss.
4. A firm in monopolistic competition has a positive markup.
5. In a broader view of efficiency, monopolistic competition brings gains for consumers.

Multiple choice

1. A firm in monopolistic competition maximizes profit by producing the quantity at which
   a. price and marginal revenue.
   b. price and marginal cost.
   c. demand and marginal cost.
   d. marginal revenue and marginal cost.
   e. price and average total cost.

2. Once a firm in monopolistic competition has determined how much to produce, the firm determines its price by referring to its
   a. demand curve.
   b. marginal cost curve.
   c. marginal revenue curve.
   d. average total cost curve.
   e. average variable cost curve.

■ **FIGURE 17.1**

Price and cost (dollars per lunch)

3. Figure 17.1 shows Louie's Lunches, a lunch counter in competition with many other restaurants. To maximize its profit, Louie's Lunches produces ____ lunches per day.
   a. 10
   b. 20
   c. 30
   d. between 31 and 40
   e. more than 40

4. Figure 17.1 shows Louie's Lunches, a lunch counter in competition with many other restaurants. To maximize its profit, Louie's Lunches sets a price of ____ per lunch.
   a. $2
   b. $4
   c. between $5.00 and $5.99
   d. $6
   e. more than $6.01

5. Figure 17.1 shows the costs and demand curves for Louie's Lunches. Louie's Lunches is in the ____ and is ____.
   a. short run; making an economic profit
   b. short run; making zero economic profit
   c. short run; incurring an economic loss
   d. long run; making an economic profit
   e. long run; making zero economic profit

6. A firm in monopolistic competition definitely incurs an economic loss if
   a. price equals marginal revenue.
   b. price is less than average total cost.
   c. marginal revenue equals marginal cost.
   d. marginal revenue is less than average total cost.
   e. price is greater than marginal cost.

7. In the long run, a firm in monopolistic competition
   a. makes zero economic profit.
   b. produces at a minimum average total cost.
   c. has deficient capacity.
   d. makes either zero economic profit or an economic profit.
   e. produces a quantity where its demand curve is upward sloping.

8. A firm's efficient scale of production is the output at which its
   a. marginal cost is at a minimum.
   b. average total cost is at a minimum.
   c. profit is maximized.
   d. marginal revenue is at a maximum.
   e. marginal revenue equals marginal cost.

9. In the long run, a firm in monopolistic competition ____ excess capacity and a firm in perfect competition ____ excess capacity.
   a. has; has
   b. has; does not have
   c. does not have; has
   d. does not have; does not have
   e. might have; might have

10. In the long run, a firm in monopolistic competition ____ a markup of price over marginal cost and a firm in perfect competition ____ a markup of price over marginal cost.
    a. has; has
    b. has; does not have
    c. does not have; has
    d. does not have; does not have
    e. might have; might have

11. Monopolistic competition is efficient when compared to
    a. perfect competition.
    b. complete product uniformity.
    c. the short run.
    d. the long run.
    e. None of the above answers is correct.

Complete the graph

■ **FIGURE 17.2**

1. Figure 17.2 shows the demand and marginal revenue curves for Seaside Pizza, a firm in monopolistic competition. Draw the average total cost curve and marginal cost curve so that Seaside's output is 40 pizzas a day and its economic profit is $160. Is this a short-run or long-run equilibrium?

■ **FIGURE 17.3**
Price and cost (dollars per pizza)

2. Figure 17.3 shows the demand and the marginal revenue curves for Surf Pizza, a firm in monopolistic competition. Draw the average total cost curve and marginal cost curve so that Surf's output is 20 pizzas a day and Surf's makes zero economic profit. Is this a short-run or long-run equilibrium?

Short answer and numeric questions

1. What rule do firms in monopolistic competition follow to determine their profit-maximizing quantity of output? How does this rule compare to the rule followed by a monopoly? To the rule followed by a firm in perfect competition?

2. Why do firms in monopolistic competition make zero economic profit in the long run?

3. Is monopolistic competition efficient?

Additional Exercises (also in MyEconLab Test A)

Lorie restrings tennis racquets. Her fixed costs are $1,000 a month, and it costs her $15 of labor to string one racquet. The table shows the demand schedule for Lorie's restringing services.

Price (dollars per racquet)	Quantity (racquets per month)
25	0
20	10
15	20
10	30
5	40
0	50

1. Calculate Lorie's profit-maximizing output, price, and economic profit.

2. Do you expect other firms to enter the tennis racquet restringing business and compete with Lorie?

3. What happens to the demand for Lorie's restringing services in the long run? What happens to Lorie's economic profit in the long run?

CHECKPOINT 17.3

■ **Explain why advertising costs are high and why firms use brand names in monopolistic competition.**

Quick Review

- *Selling costs* Selling costs such as advertising expenditures might lower average total cost if they increase the quantity sold by a large enough amount.

Additional Practice Problems 17.3

1. The figure to the right shows a firm in monopolistic competition.

   a. What quantity does the firm produce and what price does it set?

   b. How much is the firm's markup?

Price and cost (dollars per unit)

2. Selling costs are high in monopolistic competition. The table on the next page gives the costs of producing a pair of Nikes.

   a. The cost of producing the shoe in Asia is $20. The remaining costs are selling costs. What percentage of the retail price is selling costs?

b. When the shoes reach America, selling costs are the result of activity at Nike Headquarters and local retailing activity. What proportion of the $70 price is attributable to Nike and what proportion to local retailers?

Item	Cost (dollars)
Asia	
Materials	9.00
Labor	2.75
Capital	3.00
Profit	1.75
Shipping	0.50
Import duty	3.00
Nike	
Distribution	5.00
Advertising	4.00
R and D	0.25
Profit	6.25
Local	
Labor	9.50
Shop rent	9.00
Other costs	7.00
Profit	9.00

Solutions to Additional Practice Problems 17.3

1a. As the figure shows, the firm produces 30 units, because this is the quantity at which $MR = MC$, and sets its price from the demand curve at $6 per unit.

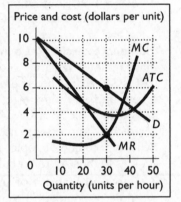

1b. The markup equals the difference between the price and the marginal cost. The price is $6 and the marginal cost is $2, so the markup is $4.

2a. Selling costs account for ($50 ÷ $70) × 100, which is 71.4 percent of the price.

2b. Nike accounts for ($15.50 ÷ $70) × 100, which is 22.1 percent of the price. Local retailers account for ($34.50 ÷ $70) × 100, which is 49.3 percent of the price.

■ Self Test 17.3

Fill in the blanks

Firms in monopolistic competition ____ (are; are not) continuously developing new prod-

ucts. In monopolistic competition, product improvement ____ (does; does not) equal its efficient level. Advertising costs ____ (are; are not) large in monopolistic competition. Advertising costs are a ____ (fixed; variable) cost and shift the average total cost curve ____ (downward; upward). Monopolistic competition ____ (definitely is; might be; definitely is not) efficient.

True or false

1. Firms in monopolistic competition develop new products without regard to cost.

2. Firms in monopolistic competition often undertake extensive advertising.

3. Because advertising increases the demand for a firm's product, increasing the amount of advertising shifts the firm's cost curves downward.

4. Brand names give the firm an incentive to achieve a high and consistent standard of quality.

5. Whether monopolistic competition is efficient depends on the value people place on product variety.

Multiple choice

1. Because economic profits are eliminated in the long run in monopolistic competition, to make an economic profit in some markets firms continuously
   a. shut down.
   b. exit the industry.
   c. develop and market new products.
   d. declare bankruptcy.
   e. decrease their costs by decreasing their selling costs.

2. A firm in monopolistic competition that introduces a new and differentiated product will temporarily have a ____ demand for its product and be able to charge ____.
   a. less elastic, a lower price than before
   b. less elastic, a higher price than before
   c. more elastic, a lower price than before
   d. more elastic, a higher price than before
   e. less elastic, the same price as before

3. Developing a new version of a product
   a. depends on the marketing department.
   b. always benefits the firm's customers.
   c. is based on the marginal cost and the marginal revenue of the development.
   d. is impossible in monopolistic competition.
   e. None of the above answers is correct.

4. Advertising costs and other selling costs are
   a. efficient.
   b. fixed costs.
   c. variable costs.
   d. marginal costs.
   e. considered as part of demand because they affect the demand for the good.

5. For a firm in monopolistic competition, selling costs
   a. increase costs and reduce profits.
   b. always increase demand.
   c. can change the quantity produced and lower the average total cost.
   d. can lower total cost.
   e. has no effect on the quantity sold.

6. If advertising increases the number of firms in an industry, each firm's demand
   a. increases.
   b. does not change.
   c. decreases.
   d. might increase or decrease depending on whether the new firms produce exactly the same product or a product that is slightly differentiated.
   e. None of the above answers is correct.

7. One reason a company advertises is to
   a. signal consumers that its product is high quality.
   b. lower its total cost.
   c. produce more efficiently.
   d. lower its variable costs.
   e. lower its fixed costs.

8. The efficiency of monopolistic competition
   a. is as clear-cut as the efficiency of perfect competition.
   b. depends on whether the gain from extra product variety offsets the selling costs and the extra cost that arises from excess capacity.
   c. comes from its excess capacity.
   d. is eliminated in the long run.
   e. is equal to that of monopoly.

Short answer and numeric questions
1. Why do firms in monopolistic competition engage in developing new products or new variations of existing products?

2. How might advertising lower average total cost?

3. How does advertising act as a signal?

4. Are advertising, brand names, and product differentiation efficient?

Additional Exercises (also in MyEconLab Test A)
Bianca bakes delicious cookies. Her total fixed cost is $40 a day, her average variable cost is $1 a bag, and she maximizes profit by selling 10 bags a day for $5 a bag. Now Bianca changes her recipe (at no cost) and bakes an even more delicious cookie. People prefer Bianca's new cookies to those of other bakers.

1. How will Bianca's price, quantity produced, and economic profit change?

2. Bianca estimates that if she spends $50 a day on advertising, she will be able to sell 25 bags a day at $5 a bag. If Bianca decides to advertise, will she increase her economic profit?

SELF TEST ANSWERS

■ CHECKPOINT 17.1

Fill in the blanks

In monopolistic competition there are a <u>large</u> number of firms producing <u>differentiated</u> products. Firms in monopolistic competition <u>do</u> compete on product quality. In monopolistic competition, barriers to entry <u>do not exist</u>. The square of the percentage market share of each firm summed over the 50 largest firms (or summed over all firms if there are fewer than 50) is the <u>Herfindahl-Hirschman Index</u>. Concentration ratios <u>do not</u> measure barriers to entry.

True or false

1. True; page 432
2. False; page 432
3. False; page 433
4. False; page 434
5. True; page 436

Multiple choice

1. a; page 432
2. c; page 432
3. d; page 432
4. a; page 433
5. e; page 433
6. b; page 433
7. d; page 434
8. e; page 435
9. b; page 435
10. d; pages 434-435

Short answer and numeric questions

1. Monopolistic competition occurs when a large number of firms compete; each firm produces a differentiated product, the firms compete on product quality; price, and marketing; and firms are free to enter and exit; page 432.

2 a. The total revenue shares are in the table above. The total revenue within the market is $5,000 million. A firm's total revenue share equals its total revenue divided by $5,000 million and then multiplied by 100.

Firm	Total revenue (millions of dollars)	Percent of total revenue (percent)
Dell	1,000	<u>20</u>
HP	800	<u>16</u>
IBM	500	<u>10</u>
Toshiba	400	<u>8</u>
Other 46 smaller firms	2,300	<u>46</u>

b. The four-firm concentration ratio is the percentage of the total revenue accounted for by the four largest firms in the industry, which is 20 percent + 16 percent + 10 percent + 8 percent = 54 percent; page 434.

c. To calculate the Herfindahl-Hirschman Index (HHI), square and then sum the market shares of the firms. The market shares are equal to each firm's percentage of total revenue. Each of the 20 smaller firms has total revenue of $50 million, so each has a 1 percentage point market share. The HHI = $(20)^2 + (16)^2 + (10)^2 + (8)^2 + (1)^2 \times 50 = 400 + 256 + 100 + 64 + 50$, which is 870; page 435.

3. a. The four-firm concentration ratios are the same for both industries, 60 percent; page 434.

b. The Herfindahl-Hirschman Index is 3,292 for Industry A and 940 for Industry B; page 435.

Additional Exercises (also in MyEconLab Test A)

1. The firms and the percentage of their total revenue shares are Truffles (30 percent), Bond (20 percent), Mayfair (15 percent), All Nature (15 percent), Gold (15 percent), and Magic (5 percent). The 4 largest are Truffles, Bond, and then any two of Mayfair, All Nature, and Gold. The four-firm concentration ratio is 30 + 20 + 15 + 15, which is 80. The HHI equals $30^2 + 20^2 + 15^2 + 15^2 + 15^2 + 5^2 = 2,000$; pages 434-435.

2. Based on the four-firm concentration ratio and the HHI alone, one would presume that the chocolate industry is an oligopoly. If chocolate firms face competition from for-

eign suppliers, the industry is more competitive than the four-firm concentration ratio and HHI suggest. In this case the industry might be monopolistic competition; page 436.

3. To be sure that the industry is monopolistic competition, we need to know the extent to which firms engage in product differentiation, whether firms are free to enter and exit, and the extent to which firms compete on product quality, price, and marketing; pages 432-433 .

4. The new technology lowers the barriers to entry. Probably there would be entry of new firms, so there would be greater product differentiation and fiercer competition on product quality, price, and marketing; page 432.

■ CHECKPOINT 17.2

Fill in the blanks

A firm in monopolistic competition produces the quantity where marginal revenue <u>equals</u> marginal cost. In the long run, a firm in monopolistic competition <u>cannot</u> make an economic profit. A firm in monopolistic competition <u>has</u> excess capacity in the long run. People value product variety and variety is <u>costly</u> to produce.

True or false
1. True; page 438
2. True; page 438
3. False; page 439
4. True; page 441
5. True; page 442

Multiple choice
1. d; page 438
2. a; page 438
3. b; page 438
4. d; page 438
5. c; page 439
6. b; page 439
7. a; page 440
8. b; page 441
9. b; page 441
10. b; page 441
11. b; page 442

Complete the graph
■ **FIGURE 17.4**
Price and cost (dollars per pizza)

1. Figure 17.4 shows the average total cost curve and marginal cost curve so that Seaside Pizza's output is 40 pizzas a day and economic profit is $160. The figure shows a short-run equilibrium because Seaside is making an economic profit; page 438.

■ **FIGURE 17.5**
Price and cost (dollars per pizza)

2. Figure 17.5 shows the average total cost curve and marginal cost curve so that Surf Pizza's output is 20 pizzas a day and it makes zero economic profit. The figure shows a long-run equilibrium because Surf is making zero economic profit; page 440.

Short answer and numeric questions

1. Firms in monopolistic competition produce the quantity at which marginal revenue equals marginal cost. This rule is the same rule that a monopoly and perfectly competitive firm follow; page 438.

2. There is no restriction on entry in monopolistic competition, so if firms in an industry are making an economic profit, other firms have an incentive to enter the industry. The entry of new firms decreases the demand for each firm's product. The demand curve and marginal revenue curve shift leftward. When firms in the industry are making zero economic profit, there is no new incentive for new firms to enter and the industry is in long-run equilibrium. Similarly, if firms in an industry are incurring an economic loss, they have an incentive to exit the industry and in the long run the remaining firms make zero economic profit; page 440.

3. In monopolistic competition, price exceeds marginal revenue and marginal revenue equals marginal cost, so price exceeds marginal cost—a sign of inefficiency. But this inefficiency arises from product differentiation. Consumers value variety and are they are willing to pay for it. So the loss that arises because marginal benefit exceeds marginal cost must be weighed against the gain that arises from greater product variety; page 442.

Additional Exercises (also in MyEconLab Test A)

1. Lorie maximizes profits by producing 10 racquets. Her marginal cost is $15 a racquet. Her marginal revenue between zero and 10 racquets is $20 and between 10 and 20 racquets is $10, so marginal revenue equals $15 at 10 racquets. Lorie's charges $20 a racquet, which is the price from the demand curve for the 10th racquet a month.

   Lorie's fixed cost is $1,000 and her variable cost is $150 ($15 a racquet multiplied by 10 racquets). Her total cost is $1,150 and her total revenue is $200. Lorie incurs an economic

loss of $200 − $1,150, which is $950; page 438.

2. Because of the economic loss, firms will not enter. Indeed, firms will *exit* the restringing business; pages 439-440.

3. In the long run, as other firms exit the market the demand for Lorie's restringing business will increase if she stays in the market. In the long run, Lorie's business will make zero economic profit. Lori will either leave the industry or if she remains open, the demand for her services increases as other firms leave and she earns a normal profit; page 440.

■ CHECKPOINT 17.3

Fill in the blanks

Firms in monopolistic competition <u>are</u> continuously developing new products. In monopolistic competition, product improvement <u>does not</u> equal its efficient level. Advertising costs <u>are</u> large in monopolistic competition. Advertising costs are a <u>fixed</u> cost and shift the average total cost curve <u>upward</u>. Monopolistic competition <u>might be</u> efficient.

True or false

1. False; page 444
2. True; page 445
3. False; page 446
4. True; page 447
5. True; page 449

Multiple choice

1. c; page 444
2. b; page 444
3. c; page 444
4. b; page 446
5. c; page 446
6. c; page 447
7. a; page 448
8. b; page 449

Short answer and numeric questions

1. Firms develop new products new versions of old products to increase the demand for

their product and make an economic profit; page 444.

2. Although advertising increases a firm's total costs, it also might increase sales. If the quantity sold increases by a large enough amount, it can lower *average* total cost of the quantity produced because the greater fixed cost is spread over an even greater amount of output; page 446.

3. Advertising sends a signal to the consumer that the product being advertised is high quality. Producers are willing to pay for expensive advertising only if they know that their product is of high enough quality that the consumer will buy it repeatedly; pages 448-449.

4. The bottom line on the question of whether advertising, brand names, and product differentiation are efficient is ambiguous. Advertising and product differentiation provide consumers with variety, which is a benefit. Brand names provide a signal to consumers, which also benefits consumers because they know the product's quality. But these benefits need to be weighed against the costs of advertising and product differentiation as well as the possibility that the actual differences between products might be very small; page 449.

Additional Exercises (also in MyEconLab Test A)

1. The increase in demand will increase the number of cookies sold and increase the price she charges. Her economic profit will increase; page 444.

2. If additional advertising enables sales to increase so that total revenue increases more than total cost, she can increase economic profit. In the case at hand, her total revenue will increase by $125 and her total cost will increase by $50 plus whatever is the increase in her variable costs of producing the cookies. Because her *AVC* when she produces 10 bags is only $1, it is likely that her variable costs will increase by less than $75, which means that advertising will be profitable; pages 445-447.

Oligopoly

Chapter 18

In Chapter 18 we study oligopoly, a market structure that lies between perfect competition and monopoly.

1 Describe and identify oligopoly and explain how it arises.

An oligopoly is a market structure in which a small number of firms compete because natural or legal barriers prevent the entry of new firms. A duopoly is a market with only two firms. Because there are a small number of firms in the market, the firms are interdependent: each firm's actions affect the other firms. Firms in oligopoly have a temptation to form a cartel and collude to limit output, raise price, and increase economic profit. The key feature to identifying an oligopoly is uncovering whether the firms are so few that they recognize the interdependence among them.

2 Explain the dilemma faced by firms in oligopoly.

Firms in oligopoly can make the same economic profit as a monopoly *if* they act together in a cartel to restrict output to the monopoly level. In the cartel, each firm can make a bigger economic profit for itself by increasing its production, but this action decreases the economic profit of the other firms. The dilemma faced by firms in an oligopoly cartel is that if each firm in the cartel increases output to maximize its profit, then every firm ends up making a smaller economic profit.

3 Use game theory to explain how price and quantity are determined in oligopoly.

Game theory is the tool economists use to analyze strategic behavior. Games have rules, strategies, and payoffs. Strategies are all the possible actions of each player in a game. The prisoners' dilemma is a game between two prisoners that shows why it is hard to cooperate, even when it would be beneficial to both players to do so. The Nash equilibrium of a game occurs when each player takes the best possible action given the action of the other player. The Nash equilibrium of the prisoners' dilemma game is each confesses, which is not the best outcome for the prisoners. The duopolists' dilemma is like the prisoners' dilemma: the firms reach a Nash equilibrium in which they produce more and have lower profit than if they restricted production. In a repeated game, a punishment strategy can produce a monopoly output, a monopoly price, and an economic profit.

4 Describe the antitrust laws that regulate oligopoly.

Antitrust law regulates and prohibits certain kinds of market behavior. The Sherman Act of 1890 was the first federal antitrust law in the United States. Section 1 outlaws "every contract, combination in the form of a trust or otherwise, or conspiracy in restraint of trade." Section 2 declares that "every person who shall monopolize, or attempt to monopolize, ... shall be deemed guilty of a felony." The Clayton Act, Robinson-Patman Act, and Celler-Kefauver Act prohibit practices if they "substantially lessen competition or create monopoly." Price fixing is *always* illegal. But resale price maintenance and tying arrangements are more controversial because they *might* lead to efficiency.

CHECKPOINT 18.1

■ **Describe and identify oligopoly and explain how it arises.**

Quick Review

- *Oligopoly* An oligopoly is characterized by having a small number of firms competing with natural or legal barriers preventing the entry of new firms.

Additional Practice Problems 18.1

1. What is the key difference between oligopoly and monopolistic competition?

2. What does it mean for firms to be interdependent? Why are firms in oligopoly interdependent?

Solutions to Additional Practice Problems 18.1

1. The key difference between oligopoly and monopolistic competition is that oligopoly is characterized by having only a small number of interdependent firms. Monopolistic competition has a large number of competing firms. Because there are only a few firms in oligopoly and because they are interdependent, the firms in oligopoly face the temptation to collude, which is an incentive absent from monopolistic competition.

2. Firms are interdependent when one firm's actions have an impact on another firm's profit. Firms in oligopoly are interdependent because there are only a few firms. In this case, one firm's actions have a major effect on the profits of its (few) competitors.

■ Self Test 18.1

Fill in the blanks

In oligopoly a ____ (large; small) number of firms compete. A ____ (cartel; duopoly) is a group of firms acting together to limit output, raise price, and increase economic profit. A market with an HHI that ____ (lies between 1,000 and 1,800; is greater than 1,800) is usually an oligopoly.

True or false

1. Oligopoly is a market in which a small number of firms compete.

2. The aim of a cartel is to lower price, increase output, and increase economic profit.

3. Only legal barriers to entry can create oligopoly.

4. Economies of scale can limit the number of firms that are in a market.

5. A market in which the HHI exceeds 1,800 is usually an oligopoly.

Multiple choice

1. Oligopoly is a market structure in which
   a. many firms each produce a slightly differentiated product.
   b. one firm produces a unique product.
   c. a small number of firms compete.
   d. many firms produce an identical product.
   e. the number of firms is so small that they do not compete with each other.

2. The fact that firms in oligopoly are interdependent means that
   a. there are barriers to entry.
   b. one firm's profits are affected by other firms' actions.
   c. they can produce either identical or differentiated goods.
   d. there are too many of them for any one firm to influence price.
   e. they definitely compete with each other so that the price is driven down to the monopoly level.

3. Collusion results when a group of firms
   i. act separately to limit output, lower price, and decrease economic profit.
   ii. act together to limit output, raise price, and increase economic profit.
   iii. in the United States legally fix prices.
   a. i only.
   b. ii only.
   c. iii only.
   d. i and iii.
   e. ii and iii.

x

4. A cartel is a group of firms
   a. acting separately to limit output, lower price, and decrease economic profit.
   b. acting together to limit output, raise price, and increase economic profit.
   c. legally fixing prices.
   d. acting together to erect barriers to entry.
   e. that compete primarily with each other rather than the other firms in the market.

5. A market with only two firms is called a
   a. duopoly.
   b. two-firm monopolistic competition.
   c. two-firm monopoly.
   d. cartel.
   e. two-firm quasi-monopoly.

6. The efficient scale of one firm is 20 units and the average total cost at the efficient scale is $30. The quantity demanded in the market as a whole at $30 is 40 units. This market is
   a. a natural duopoly.
   b. a legal duopoly.
   c. a natural monopoly.
   d. a legal monopoly.
   e. monopolistically competitive.

7. Even though four firms can profitably sell hotdogs downtown, the government licenses only two firms. This market is a
   a. natural duopoly.
   b. legal duopoly.
   c. natural monopoly.
   d. legal monopoly.
   e. market-limited oligopoly.

8. To determine if a market is an oligopoly, we need to determine if
   a. the market's HHI is less than 900.
   b. there are many firms in the market.
   c. the firms are so few that they recognize their mutual interdependencies.
   d. the firms make identical or differentiated products.
   e. cartels are legal in their market.

Short answer and numeric questions
1. What conditions define oligopoly?
2. Firms in oligopoly are interdependent. Firms

in monopolistic competition are not. What accounts for the difference?
3. What is a cartel?
4. How does the HHI for monopolistic competition compare to the HHI for oligopoly?

Additional Exercises (also in MyEconLab Test A)
1. Identify an oligopoly market in which you bought something recently.
2. Why are the firms that make boxes of chocolates on the borderline between oligopoly and monopolistic competition?

CHECKPOINT 18.2

■ Explain the dilemma faced by firms in oligopoly.

Quick Review
- *Duopoly* A market with only two firms.
- *Range of outcomes* The price and quantity in a duopoly can range from the competitive outcome to the monopoly outcome.

Practice Problem 18.2
1. Isolated Island has two natural gas wells, one owned by Tom and the other owned by Jerry. Each well has a valve that controls the rate of flow of gas, and the marginal cost of producing gas is zero. The table gives the demand schedule for gas on this island. Suppose Tom and Jerry agree to operate as a monopoly. A

Price (dollars per unit)	Quantity demanded (units per day)
12	0
11	1
10	2
9	3
8	4
7	5
6	6
5	7
4	8
3	9
2	10
1	11
0	12

monopoly produces 6 units and charges $6 a unit. Tom and Jerry agree that each will produce 3 units and charge $6. There are no fixed costs.
   a. If neither Tom nor Jerry cheat on the agreement what is Tom's profit? Jerry's

profit? The combined profit?

b. Suppose Tom decides to cheat on the agreement by producing 4 units. Jerry sticks to the agreement. If 7 units are produced, what is the price? What is Tom's profit? Jerry's profit? The combined profit?

c. Why would Tom ever consider cheating on the agreement he made with Jerry?

Solutions to Additional Practice Problem 18.2

1a. Profit is equal to total revenue because total cost is zero. Tom's profit is $18, Jerry's profit is $18, and the combined profit is $36.

1b. If 7 units are produced, the price is $5 a unit. Tom's profit on his 4 units is $20 and Jerry's profit on his 3 units is $15. The combined profit is $35.

1c. Tom considers cheating because cheating increases his profit. Tom realizes that if he alone cheats, his profit will be more, $20 versus $18. Jerry's profit falls more than Tom's rises but Tom is concerned only about his own profit.

■ Self Test 18.2

Fill in the blanks

When a duopoly charges the perfectly competitive price, each firm receives _____ (no; positive) economic profit. When a duopoly charges the monopoly price, economic profit is _____ (maximized; minimized).

True or false

1. In a duopoly, the highest price that the firms might set is the perfectly competitive price.

2. The only possible outcome for a duopoly is the monopoly outcome.

3. Once a duopoly has achieved the monopoly outcome, neither firm can increase its total profit.

4. A duopoly is currently making, in total, the same economic profit as a monopoly. If one firm increases its output, the economic profit of the other firm increases.

5. A duopoly's total profit is the largest when it produces more than the monopoly level of output.

Multiple choice

■ FIGURE 18.1

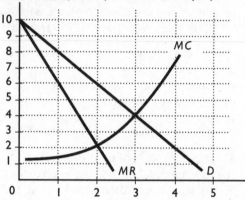

Price and cost (dollars per bottle of shampoo)

Quantity (millions of bottles of shampoo per day)

1. Suppose only two companies make shampoo. Figure 18.1 shows the market demand curve and associated marginal revenue curve. It also shows the combined marginal cost curve of the two companies. If these companies formed a cartel that operated as a monopoly, production is _____ million bottles of shampoo and the price is _____ per bottle of shampoo.
   a. 5; $4
   b. 2; $6
   c. 3; $6
   d. 2; $2
   e. 3; $4

2. Suppose the two companies that make shampoo illustrated in Figure 18.1 operate as perfect competitors. In this case, production is _____ million bottles of shampoo and the price is _____ per bottle of shampoo.
   a. 5; $4
   b. 2; $6
   c. 3; $6
   d. 2; $2
   e. 3; $4

3. For a duopoly, the highest price is charged when the duopoly achieves
   a. the competitive outcome.
   b. the monopoly outcome.
   c. an outcome between the competitive outcome and the monopoly outcome.
   d. its noncooperative equilibrium.
   e. Both answers (a) and (d) are correct because both refer to the same price.

4. For a duopoly, the smallest *total* quantity is produced when the duopoly achieves
   a. the competitive outcome.
   b. the monopoly outcome.
   c. an outcome between the competitive outcome and the monopoly outcome.
   d. its noncooperative equilibrium.
   e. Both answers (a) and (d) are correct because both refer to the same quantity.

5. For a duopoly, the maximum *total* profit is reached when the duopoly produces
   a. the same amount of output as the competitive outcome.
   b. the same amount of output as the monopoly outcome.
   c. an amount of output that lies between the competitive outcome and the monopoly outcome.
   d. more output than the competitive outcome.
   e. less output than the monopoly outcome.

6. If a duopoly has reached the monopoly outcome, a firm can increase its profit if it and it alone ____ its price and ____ its production.
   a. raises; increases
   b. raises; decreases
   c. lowers; increases
   d. lowers; decreases
   e. raises; does not change

7. If a duopoly has reached the monopoly outcome and only one firm increases its production, that firm's profit ____ and the other firm's profit ____.
   a. increases; increases
   b. increases; decreases
   c. decreases; increases
   d. decreases; decreases
   e. increases; does not change

8. Suppose a duopoly had reached the monopoly outcome and then the first firm increased its production. If the second firm next increases its production, the second firm's profit ____ and the first firm's profit ____.
   a. increases; increases
   b. increases; decreases
   c. decreases; increases
   d. decreases; decreases
   e. increases; does not change

9. If both firms in a duopoly increase their production by one unit beyond the monopoly output, each firm's profit ____ and the *total* profit of the duopoly ____.
   a. increases; increases
   b. does not change; does not change
   c. decreases; decreases
   d. does not change; increases
   e. decreases; does not change

10. The very best outcome possible for the firms in a duopoly is to produce the
    a. monopoly level of output.
    b. perfectly competitive level of output.
    c. amount of output that maximizes total revenue.
    d. amount of output that minimizes total cost.
    e. equilibrium level of output if the game is not repeated.

Complete the graph

Quantity (thousands of newspapers per day)	Price (cents)	Marginal revenue (cents)
0	60	60
2	50	40
4	40	20
6	30	0
8	20	−20

1. Anytown, USA has two newspapers that have a duopoly in the local market. The table contains information on the market demand and marginal revenue for newspapers. Marginal cost of a newspaper is 20 cents.

   a. Graph the demand curve, marginal revenue curve, and marginal cost curve in Figure 18.2.

■ FIGURE 18.2

Price and marginal revenue (cents per newspaper)

Quantity (thousands of newspapers per day)

   b. What price and quantity represent the competitive outcome?

   c. What price and quantity represent the monopoly outcome?

   d. What range of price and quantity represent the potential duopoly outcomes?

Short answer and numeric questions

1. In oligopoly, one firm's profit-maximizing actions might decrease its competitors' profits. Why is this fact a problem for firms in oligopoly?

2. Why do firms in an oligopoly have an incentive to form a cartel that boosts the price and decreases the output?

3. Why does a firm have the incentive to cheat on a collusive agreement to limit production and raise the price?

Additional Exercises (also in MyEconLab Test A)

Isolated Island has three natural gas wells, one owned by Tom, one owned by Jerry, and one owned by Joey. The table gives the demand schedule for gas on this island. The marginal cost of producing gas is zero. Use this information to answer Exercises 1 and 2.

Price (dollars per unit)	Quantity demanded (units per day)
12	0
11	1
10	2
9	3
8	4
7	5
6	6
5	7
4	8
3	9
2	10
1	11
0	12

1. What is the price of gas and the quantity produced if Tom, Jerry, and Joey form a cartel and maximize their joint profit?

2. If Tom, Jerry, and Joey are forced to sell at the perfectly competitive price, what will be the price of gas and the quantity produced?

Duracell and Energizer are the only major producers of batteries. Each company has developed a long-lasting battery and aggressively advertises it. The two firms are locked in a duopolists' dilemma.

3. Describe the dilemma facing Duracell and Energizer.

4. Suppose that Duracell and Energizer secretly were to form a cartel. What do you predict would happen to the price of a battery? How would the two firms change their advertising and research and development budgets?

CHECKPOINT 18.3

■ **Use game theory to explain how price and quantity are determined in oligopoly.**

Quick Review

- *Game theory* The tool that economists use to analyze strategic behavior—behavior that recognizes mutual interdependence and takes account of the expected behavior of others.
- *Nash equilibrium* An equilibrium in which each player takes the best possible action given the action of the other player.

Additional Practice Problem 18.3

1. Coke and Pepsi are engaged in an advertising game. They each know that if they both limit their advertising, they will make the maximum attainable joint economic profit of $400 million, divided so that each has an economic profit of $200 million. They also know that if either of them advertises while the other does not, the one advertising makes an economic profit of $300 million and the one that not advertising incurs an economic loss of $100 million dollars. And they also know that if they both advertise, they both make zero economic profit.

   a. Construct a payoff matrix for the game that Coke and Pepsi must play.

   b. Find the Nash equilibrium. How is this game similar to the prisoners' dilemma?

   c. What is the equilibrium if this game is played repeatedly?

   d. Suppose that Coke and Pepsi are both playing a tit-for-tat strategy and that last time both did not advertise. Today, however, Coke really needs some extra income. So Coke advertises. What takes place today and in the future?

Solution to Additional Practice Problem 18.3

1a. A payoff matrix is a table that shows payoffs for every possible action by each player, Coke and Pepsi, given every possible action by the other player. The payoff matrix is given

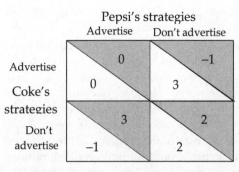

above. The number in each square is the economic profit in millions of dollars.

1b. To find the Nash equilibrium of a game, place yourself in the position of the first player. Ask yourself "what if" your opponent takes one action: What will you do? Then ask "what if" the opponent takes the other action: now what will you do? This analysis allows you to determine the first player's action. Then place yourself in the position of the second player and repeat the "what if" analysis to determine the second player's action. So, to find Coke's strategy, ask what Coke will do for each of Pepsi's choices. If Pepsi advertises (the first column of the payoff matrix), Coke advertises because that gives Coke a larger profit ($0 versus a loss of $1 million). If Pepsi does not advertise (the second column of the payoff matrix), Coke advertises gallons because that gives Coke a larger profit ($3 million versus $2 million). Regardless of Pepsi's action, Coke advertises. Similar reasoning shows that Pepsi also advertises. So the Nash equilibrium is for each to advertise and make zero economic profit. The game is similar to a prisoners' dilemma game because there is a conflict between each player's incentives to do what is best for the player versus what is best for both of them taken together. In the prisoners' dilemma game, both prisoners confess, leading to the worst joint outcome. In this game, both players advertise, again leading to the worst joint outcome.

1c. In a repeated game, Coke and Pepsi both do not advertise and make the maximum joint economic profit. This outcome occurs if they use a tit-for-tat strategy.

1d. Today, Coke makes an economic profit of $3 million and Pepsi incurs an economic loss of $1 million. But in the second year, Pepsi will advertise. Coke might go back to not advertising to induce Pepsi to not advertise in the third year. So in the second year, Pepsi makes an economic profit of $3 million and Coke incurs an economic loss of $1 million. Over the two years, Coke makes a total economic profit of $2 million (and Pepsi also makes a total economic profit of $2 million.) But if Coke had not "cheated" on the agreement and advertised in the first year, then over the two years Coke's total economic profit would have been $4 million, not just $2 million. So, by cheating on the agreement Coke makes more profit immediately but over the longer haul makes less profit.

■ Self Test 18.3

Fill in the blanks

Game theory is the main tool that economists use to analyze ____ (irrational; strategic) behavior. Games feature ____, ____, and ____. The Nash equilibrium is ____ (always; not always) the best possible equilibrium for the players. Game theory shows that duopolists ____ (can; cannot) always reach the best possible equilibrium. In a ____ (repeated; single-play) game, a tit-for-tit strategy can be used. The ____ (larger; smaller) the number of firms, the harder it is for an oligopoly to maintain the monopoly output.

True or false

1. Game theory is used to analyze strategic behavior.

2. A prisoners' dilemma has no equilibrium.

3. A Nash equilibrium is the best outcome for all players in a prisoners' dilemma game.

4. The monopoly outcome is more likely in a repeated game than in a one-play game.

5. If firms in oligopoly play a repeated game and end up restricting their output, then oligopoly is efficient.

Multiple choice

1. One of the main tools economists use to analyze strategic behavior is
   a. the Herfindahl-Hirschman Index.
   b. game theory.
   c. cartel theory.
   d. the collusion index.
   e. dual theory, which is used to study duopolies.

2. A Nash equilibrium occurs
   a. when each player acts without considering the actions of the other player.
   b. when each player takes the best possible action given the action of the other player.
   c. only when players use the tit-for-tat strategy.
   d. only if the game is played in Nashville, TN.
   e. when each player takes the action that makes the combined payoff for all players as large as possible.

3. Game theory reveals that
   a. the equilibrium might not be the best solution for the parties involved.
   b. firms in oligopoly are not interdependent.
   c. each player looks after what is best for the industry.
   d. if all firms in an oligopoly take the action that maximizes their profit, then the equilibrium will have the largest possible combined profit of all the firms.
   e. firms in an oligopoly choose their actions without regard for what the other firms might do.

4. The prisoners' dilemma game
   a. shows that prisoners are better off if they cooperate.
   b. shows it is easy to cooperate.
   c. has an equilibrium in which both prisoners are made as well off as possible.
   d. would have the same outcome even if the prisoners can communicate and cooperate.
   e. has an equilibrium in which one prisoner is made as well off as possible and the other prisoner is made as worse off as possible.

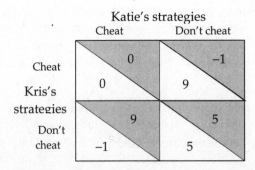

Katie's strategies

5. Katie and Kris are duopolists who formed a collusive agreement to boost prices and decrease production. Their payoff matrix is above and the entries are millions of dollars of economic profit. They now have the choice of cheating on the agreement or not cheating. If Kris cheats, then
   a. Kris definitely makes an economic profit of $9 million.
   b. Kris definitely makes $0.
   c. Kris definitely incurs an economic loss of $1 million.
   d. Kris definitely makes an economic profit of $5 million.
   e. Kris might make an economic profit of $9 million or might make $0 depending on what Katie does.

6. Based on the payoff matrix above, the Nash equilibrium is for
   a. Kris to cheat and Katie to cheat.
   b. Kris to not cheat and Katie to not cheat.
   c. Kris to cheat and Katie to not cheat.
   d. Kris to not cheat and Katie to cheat.
   e. Kris and Katie to invite a third person to determine what each of them should do.

7. Based on the payoff matrix above, in the Nash equilibrium the total economic profit that Katie and Kris make together is ____ million.
   a. $8
   b. $9
   c. $10
   d. $0
   e. −$1

8. A collusive agreement to form a cartel is difficult to maintain because
   a. each firm can increase its own profits by cutting its price and selling more.
   b. forming a cartel is legal but frowned upon throughout the world.
   c. supply will decrease because of the high cartel price.
   d. demanders will rebel once they realize a cartel has been formed.
   e. each firm can increase its profit if it decreases its production even more than the decrease set by the cartel.

9. Firms in oligopoly can achieve an economic profit
   a. always in the long run.
   b. if they cooperate.
   c. only if the demand for their products is inelastic.
   d. only if the demand for their products is elastic.
   e. if they reach the non-cooperative equilibrium.

10. When duopoly games are repeated and a "tit-for-tat" strategy is used,
    a. the competitive outcome is more likely to be reached than when the game is played once.
    b. the monopoly outcome is more likely to be reached than when the game is played once.
    c. both firms begin to incur economic losses.
    d. one firm goes out of business.
    e. because the game is repeated it is impossible to predict whether the competitive or the monopoly outcome is more likely.

11. Oligopoly is
    a. always efficient.
    b. efficient only if the firms cooperate.
    c. efficient only if the firms play non-repeated games.
    d. generally not efficient.
    e. efficient only if the firms innovate.

Complete the graph

Cameron's strategies

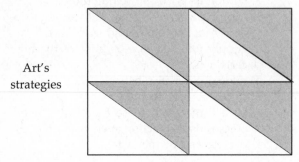

Art's
strategies

1. Art and Cameron own the only two movie theaters in a town. They have recently (illegally) agreed to boost their ticket prices. If they both comply with the agreement, both make $1 million of economic profit. If one cheats by lowering his price, the cheater makes $1.5 million of economic profit and the other incurs an economic loss if $0.5 million. If they both cheat by lowering their prices, each makes zero economic profit.
   a. Complete the payoff matrix above.
   b. What is the Nash equilibrium?

Intel's strategies

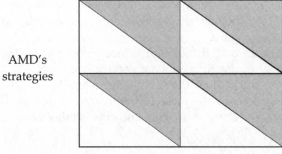

AMD's
strategies

2. Intel and AMD are involved in a game to determine the amount they will spend on research and development. If they each spend $2 billion, each has an economic profit of zero. If they each spend $1 billion, each has an economic profit of $500 million. And if one spends $2 billion and the other spends $1 billion, the one spending $2 billion has an eco-

nomic profit of $1,500 million and the other has an economic loss of $100 million.
   a. Complete the payoff matrix above.
   b. What is the Nash equilibrium of this game?

Short answer and numeric questions

1. What are "strategies" in game theory?
2. In a prisoners' dilemma, why don't the players cooperate?
3. In the duopolists' dilemma, why don't the players cooperate?
4. How does the number of players in a game affect its outcome?

Additional Exercises (also in MyEconLab Test A)

Bud and Wise are racing to develop a new brand of coconut milk that they both believe will be the next big soft drink. Bud and Wise know that if they both develop the new product, they will both make zero economic profit; if only one of them develops the new product, that firm will make an economic profit of $2 million a week and the other will incur an economic loss of $1 million a week; and if neither of them develops the new product, both will make zero economic profit.

1. Construct a payoff matrix for this game.
2. Find the Nash equilibrium.
3. Is there any chance of cooperation in this research and development game?

CHECKPOINT 18.4

■ **Describe the antitrust laws that regulate oligopoly.**

Quick Review
- *Sherman Act* The first U.S. antitrust law, Section 1 of the Sherman Act prohibits conspiring with others to restrict competition and Section 2 outlaws attempts to monopolize.
- *Clayton Act* The second antitrust law, the Clayton Act prohibits certain business

practices if they substantially lessen competition or create monopoly.

Additional Practice Problem 18.4

1. Cooperative agreements among firms such as the New York Yankees and the Chicago White Sox that limit the number of games played and that restrict the number of teams for which an athlete can play show cartel-like behavior. Except for professional sports teams, cartels are generally illegal in the United States. For instance, Microsoft and Hewlett Packard do not draft college graduates and so they cannot agree that a particular college graduate will work for Microsoft and not Hewlett Packard. Why do you think the Supreme Court made a decision in the case of professional sporting teams to permit cartel-like behavior?

Solution to Additional Practice Problem 18.4

1. Under competitive conditions, rich teams such as the New York Yankees, with plenty of fans and lucrative media contracts, would be able to purchase all the best players. Putting all the best players on a single team would prevent another team from winning. The teams unable to win would be unable to entice fans to their stadiums. The entire sports industry would die if only one team were profitable and dominant. This situation is unlike the case with Microsoft and Hewlett Packard because if one of these firms becomes dominant, its absolute dominance would not spell the end of the industry. The sports leagues, in an exception to general American policy, are allowed to have league rules that seek to apportion talent equally to preserve the competitive nature of the sport.

■ Self Test 18.4

Fill in the blanks

The first antitrust law in the United States was the ____ (Clayton; Sherman) Act and, in part, it outlaws ____ (attempts to monopolize; monopolies; oligopolies). The Clayton Act ____ (does not prohibit; prohibits) acquiring a competitor's shares if this act substantially lessens competition or creates monopoly. Resale price mainte-nance ____ (always leads; does not always lead) to inefficiency. Economists generally believe that predatory pricing is ____ (common; uncommon). The ____ (higher; lower) a market's Herfindahl-Hirschman Index, the more likely the Federal Trade Commission will challenge a merger.

True or false

1. The Sherman Act outlaws contracts and conspiracies in restraint of trade.

2. The Clayton Act outlaws all price discrimination.

3. Price fixing is *always* illegal.

4. Resale price maintenance always leads to efficiency.

5. The Federal Trade Commission uses the four-firm concentration ratio as the guideline to determine which mergers it will examine and possibly block.

Multiple choice

1. The first antitrust act was____ passed in ____.
   a. the Clayton Act; 1890
   b. the Sherman Act; 1890
   c. the Clinton Act; 1999
   d. the Rockefeller Act; 1890
   e. the Clayton Act; 1914

2. The Clayton Act
   a. replaced the Sherman Act.
   b. along with its amendments, outlawed several business practices if they substantially lessened competition or created monopoly.
   c. along with its amendments, prohibited all business practices that substantially lessen competition or create monopoly.
   d. was the first anti-trust law in the United States.
   e. was repealed in 1985.

3. Which of the following is (are) prohibited if it substantially lessens competition or creates a monopoly?
   i.   price discrimination
   ii. tying arrangements
   iii. exclusive dealing
   a. i only.
   b. ii only.
   c. ii and iii.
   d. iii only.
   e. i, ii, and iii.

4. If Polka Cola agrees to sell its cola to a retailer only if the retailer also buys a lemon-lime drink, Polka Up, then Polka Cola is engaged in
   a. a tying arrangement.
   b. a requirement contract.
   c. an exclusive deal.
   d. territorial confinement.
   e. price discrimination.

5. Which of the following is *always* illegal?
   a. possessing a very large market share
   b. selling at a price below other producers because of efficiency
   c. price fixing
   d. attempting to merge with a competitor
   e. price discrimination

6. Resale price maintenance
   a. can lead to efficiency by preventing low-price shops from being free riders.
   b. can lead to inefficiency by preventing low-price shops from being free riders.
   c. is always legal.
   d. is a clear example of predatory pricing.
   e. is an example of a tying arrangement.

7. Predatory pricing occurs when a firm sets a ____ price to drive competitors out of business with the intention of then setting a ____ price.
   a. monopoly; high
   b. monopoly; low
   c. low; monopoly
   d. low; low
   e. high; monopoly

8. In the case against Microsoft, it was claimed that combining Internet Explorer and Windows was
   a. predatory pricing.
   b. an illegal tying agreement.
   c. creating one product that is convenient for the consumers.
   d. illegal territorial confinement.
   e. an inefficient resale maintenance agreement.

9. In a concentrated industry with a Herfindahl-Hirschman Index that exceeds 1,800, the Federal Trade Commission will challenge any merger that increases the Herfindahl-Hirschman index by a minimum of
   a. 50 points.
   b. 100 points.
   c. 1,000 points.
   d. 1,800 points.
   e. 10,000 points.

Short answer and numeric questions

1. General Motors is a huge company, with total revenue exceeding $150 billion a year. Why doesn't the government challenge General Motors and take it to court for antitrust violations?

2. Airlines routinely price discriminate, charging pleasure travelers a significantly lower price than business travelers. The Clayton Act, however, mentioned price discrimination as one of the business practices it covers and prohibits. Why can airlines routinely price discriminate?

3. What is the law about price fixing?

Company	Market share (percent)
Acme	27
ABC	18
Banks	10
Cooper	8
37 individual firms	I each

4. The table above has a list of companies that make up the market for steel, along with each companies' share of the market.

a. What is the Herfindahl-Hirschman Index for this market? How would you describe the competitiveness of this market?

b. If Acme acquires Banks, what is the new Herfindahl-Hirschman Index? Would the Department of Justice challenge this acquisition? Why or why not? How would you describe the competitiveness of this market if the merger occurs?

Additional Exercises (also in MyEconLab Test A)

1. In 1911, Standard Oil Company was found guilty under the Sherman Act and was ordered to divest itself. Some of the oil companies that were created as a result of the 1911 order have now merged to form large companies. Why do you think Standard Oil Company was found guilty under the Sherman Act while recent oil company mergers have been approved?

SELF TEST ANSWERS

■ CHECKPOINT 18.1

Fill in the blanks

In oligopoly a <u>small</u> number of firms compete. A <u>cartel</u> is a group of firms acting together to limit output, raise price, and increase economic profit. A market with an HHI that <u>is greater than 1,800</u> is usually an oligopoly.

True or false

1. True; page 432
2. False; page 432
3. False; page 432
4. True; page 433
5. True; page 434

Multiple choice

1. c; page 432
2. b; page 432
3. b; page 432
4. b; page 432
5. a; page 432
6. a; page 433
7. b; page 434
8. c; page 434

Short answer and numeric questions

1. Oligopoly occurs when a small number of firms compete and natural or legal barriers prevent the entry of new firms; page 432.
2. The difference is because there are only a small number of firms in oligopoly. Because there are only a small number of firms, one firm's actions affect the profits of all its (few) competitors; page 432.
3. A cartel is a group of firms acting together to limit output, raise price, and increase economic profit; page 432.
4. The HHI for monopolistic competition is less than that for oligopoly. For monopolistic competition, the HHI usually lies between 1,000 and 1,800. For oligopoly, the HHI usually lies above 1,800; page 434.

Additional Exercises (also in MyEconLab Test A)

1. Some common oligopoly markets are CPUs for computers, long-distance telephone service, cellular telephone service, automobiles, and cigarettes.
2. The HHI is relatively high for the chocolate industry, but there are a large number of chocolate producers. So based on the HHI, the industry seems oligopoly but based on the large number of firms (and the point that often the relevant market is local rather than national) the industry might be monopolistic competition; page 435.

■ CHECKPOINT 18.2

Fill in the blanks

When a duopoly charges the perfectly competitive price, each firm receives <u>no</u> economic profit. When a duopoly charges the monopoly price, economic profit is <u>maximized</u>.

True or false

1. False; page 437
2. False; page 437
3. False; page 437
4. False; page 437
5. False; pages 436-437

Multiple choice

1. b; page 436
2. e; page 436
3. b; page 437
4. b; page 437
5. b; page 437
6. c; page 437
7. b; page 437
8. b; page 438
9. c; page 438
10. a; page 438

Complete the graph

■ FIGURE 18.3

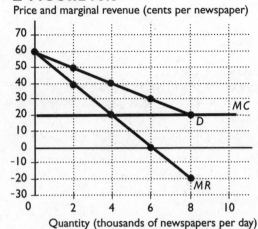

Price and marginal revenue (cents per newspaper)

Quantity (thousands of newspapers per day)

1. a. The curves are graphed in Figure 18.3.

    b. The competitive equilibrium is 8,000 newspapers a day and a price of 20¢ a newspaper; page 436.

    c. The monopoly equilibrium is 4,000 newspapers a day and a price of 40¢ a newspaper; pages 436-437.

    d. The exact price and quantity can't be predicted, but it will be somewhere between the competitive and monopoly outcomes. The price will be between 40¢ and 20¢ a newspaper and the output will be between 4,000 and 8,000 newspapers a day; pages 436-438.

Short answer and numeric questions

1. The point that one firm's actions can decrease another firm's profits is what makes competition difficult in an oligopoly. While the firms might be better off cooperating, each firm trying to increase its profit takes actions that lead the profits of its competitors to decrease, so that all the firms wind up worse off; pages 436-438.

2. If the firms can form and maintain a cartel that boosts the price and decreases the output, all the firms' profits can increase; page 437.

3. Every firm has the incentive to cheat on an output-limiting agreement because if it and it alone cheats by boosting its output and cutting its price, its economic profit will increase; page 437.

Additional Exercises (also in MyEconLab Test A)

1. The price equals $6. The profit-maximizing price does not depend on the number of firms in the cartel, though the more firms in the cartel, the lower is each firm's production quota; page 436.

2. The price equals zero and the quantity produced is 12 units a day; pages 436-437.

3. The dilemma is that if *both* firms reduced their advertising, *both* firms' profit would increase. But if only *one* firm cut its advertising, its profit would plunge while its competitor would make a fortune. Because neither firm can trust the other to follow through on an agreement to cut advertising, both advertise heavily even though there is a better outcome possible for both firms; page 438.

4. If Duracell and Energizer adhere to the cartel agreement to restrict output, the price of a battery will rise. To the extent that one or both firms cheat on the agreement, the price of a battery will be less than when both firms comply. If the firms comply with the cartel agreement, advertising expenditure as well as research and development expenditure will be cut. To the extent that one or both firms cheat on the agreement, advertising expenditure and research and development expenditure will be greater than when both firms comply; pages 437-438.

■ CHECKPOINT 18.3

Fill in the blanks

Game theory is the main tool that economists use to analyze <u>strategic</u> behavior. Games feature <u>rules</u>, <u>strategies</u>, and <u>payoffs</u>. The Nash equilibrium is <u>not always</u> the best possible equilibrium for the players. Game theory shows that duopolists <u>cannot</u> always reach the best possible equilibrium. In a <u>repeated</u> game, a tit-for-tat strategy can be used. The <u>larger</u> the number of firms, the harder it is for an oligopoly to maintain the monopoly output.

True or false
1. True; page 441
2. False; pages 442-443
3. False; page 443
4. True; page 446
5. False; page 446

Multiple choice
1. b; page 441
2. b; page 442
3. a; page 443
4. a; page 443
5. e; page 442
6. a; page 444
7. d; page 444
8. a; page 444
9. b; page 444
10. b; page 446
11. d; page 446

Complete the graph

Cameron's strategies

1. a. The completed payoff matrix is above. The payoffs are in millions of dollars; page 442.
   b. The Nash equilibrium is for both Cameron and Art to cheat on the collusive agreement and each make zero economic profit; page 444.

2. a. The completed payoff matrix is above. The payoffs are in millions of dollars; page 442.
   b. The Nash equilibrium is for both Intel and AMD to spend $2 billion on research and development and each make zero economic profit; page 444.

Short answer and numeric questions
1. Strategies are all the possible actions of each player. In the prisoners' dilemma game, strategies are "to confess" or "to deny;" in the Airbus/Boeing duopoly game, strategies are "to produce 4 airplanes a week" or "to produce 3 airplanes a week;" page 442.

2. In the prisoners' dilemma game, the players do not cooperate because they do not see cooperation as being in their best interest. Regardless of what the second player does, the first player is better off confessing. Regardless of what the first player does, the second player is better off confessing. Because it is in each player's separate best interest to confess rather than cooperate by denying, both players confess; pages 441-443.

3. In the duopolists' dilemma game, the players do not cooperate for precisely the same reason they do not cooperate in the prisoners' dilemma game: The players do not see cooperation as being in their best interest. As a result, because each player's profit-maximizing actions harm the other player, the equilibrium can be the worst outcome for both; page 444.

4. The more players in a game, the harder it is to maintain the monopoly outcome; page 444.

Additional Exercises (also in MyEconLab Test A)

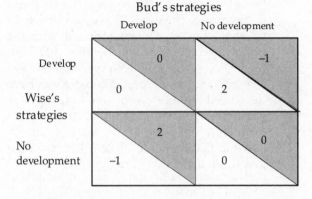

Bud's strategies

1. The payoff matrix is above with the entries in millions of dollars. If Bud and Wise both develop the drink, each makes zero economic profit. If neither develops, both make zero economic profit, while if one develops and the other does not, the developer makes $2 million economic profit and the non-developer incurs an economic loss of $1 million; page 442.

2. The game has a Nash equilibrium in which both develop the drink. For instance, if Wise develops, Bud wants to develop the drink because otherwise he loses $1 million. And if Wise does not develop the drink, Bud wants to develop the drink so that he can make an economic profit of $2 million. No matter what Wise does, Bud will develop the drink. Similar reasoning shows that Wise, too, will develop the drink; pages 442-443 .

3. There is a chance of cooperation in this research and development game if the game is played repeatedly and cheating on the agreement is punished using a tit for tat strategy; page 446.

■ CHECKPOINT 18.4

Fill in the blanks

The first antitrust law in the United States was the <u>Sherman</u> Act and, in part, it outlaws <u>attempts to monopolize</u>. The Clayton Act <u>prohibits</u> acquiring a competitor's shares if this act substantially lessens competition or creates monopoly. Resale price maintenance <u>does not always lead</u> to inefficiency. Economists generally believe that predatory pricing is <u>uncommon</u>. The <u>higher</u> a market's Herfindahl-Hirschman Index, the more likely the Federal Trade Commission will challenge a merger.

True or false

1. True; page 450
2. False; page 450
3. True; page 449
4. False; pages 449-450
5. False; page 453

Multiple choice

1. b; page 449
2. b; page 450
3. e; page 450
4. a; page 450
5. c; page 449
6. a; pages 449-450
7. c; page 451
8. b; page 452
9. a; page 453

Short answer and numeric questions

1. General Motors is, indeed, a huge company. But it competes with other huge companies in a gigantic market, the new car market. Ford has total revenue over $140 billion a year; Toyota's total revenue is comparable. In fact, in 2008 General Motors was bailed out by the government and, even so, in 2009 General Motors was forced to declare bankruptcy. General Motors suffered this fate because its other huge competitors were better at meeting consumer demand at lower cost than could GM. Antitrust laws deal with markets where there is little competition, not with markets where the many competitors are large; pages 449, 453.

2. The Clayton Act prohibited several businesses practices *only if* they "substantially lessen competition or create monopoly." Price discrimination by the airlines does not substantially lessen competition or create a monopoly. Price discrimination by the airlines is legal; page 450.

3. The law about price fixing is clear: It is *always* illegal. If price fixing can be proven, the firms are automatically guilty because there can be no acceptable excuse; page 449.

4. a. HHI = $27^2 + 18^2 + 10^2 + 8^2 + 37 = 1,254$. Because this falls between 1,000 and 1,800, the market is moderately concentrated; page 453.

   b. HHI = $37^2 + 18^2 + 8^2 + 37 = 1,794$. The Federal Trade Commission would challenge this acquisition because it increases the index by more than 100 points. After this merger, the market remains moderately concentrated; page 453.

Additional Exercises (also in MyEconLab Test A)

1. The Standard Oil Company was broken up years ago because the courts believed that it was restraining trade to an unreasonable level. In recent years, some of these individual firms have merged. These actions are a result of the market changing. This outcome would be analogous to the government allowing fragmented portions of the old AT&T to merge. The communications market has changed and new types of competitors have developed. In the petroleum industry, the government has decided that the merged firms now represent a *more* efficient operation and that they face sufficient competition to restrain their behavior; page 453.

Markets for Factors of Production

Chapter 19

In this chapter we study demand, supply, and equilibrium in factor markets.

1 Explain how the value of marginal product determines the demand for a factor of production.

The four factors of production are labor, capital, land (natural resources), and entrepreneurship. Natural resources are either renewable or nonrenewable. The wage rate is the price of labor services, the (capital) rental rate is the price of capital services, and the (land) rental rent is the price of the services of land. The demand for a factor of production is derived from the demand for the goods and services it is used to produce. The value of marginal product is the value to a firm of hiring one more unit of a factor of production and equals the price of a unit of output multiplied by the factor's marginal product. To maximize its profit, a firm hires labor up to the point at which the value of marginal product of labor equals the wage rate. A firm's demand for labor curve is its value of marginal product curve. The demand for labor changes and the demand for labor curve shifts when the price of the firm's output changes, the prices of other factors of production change, or technology changes.

2 Explain how wage rates and employment are determined and how labor unions influence labor markets.

An individual's labor supply curve can be backward bending at higher wage rates so that an increase in the wage rate decreases the quantity of labor supplied. The key factors that change the supply of labor are the adult population, preferences, and time spent in school and training. In a competitive labor market, the equilibrium between the demand for labor and the supply of labor determines the wage rate and employment. A labor union is an organized group of workers that aims to increase the wages of its members. Labor unions try to increase the demand for their members' labor (by increasing the value of marginal product of union members and by supporting minimum wage laws, immigration restrictions, and import restrictions). Unions also try to restrict the supply of non-union labor.

3 Explain how capital and land rental rates and natural resource prices are determined.

The demand for capital is based on the value of marginal product of capital. Equilibrium in the capital market determines the capital rental rate and quantity of capital. The quantity of land is fixed, so the supply of each particular block of land is perfectly inelastic. Equilibrium in the land market determines the land rental rate. The proven reserves of a nonrenewable resource increase over time because advances in technology enable ever less accessible sources to be discovered. The supply of a nonrenewable resource in any given time period is perfectly elastic at the price that gives the owners the same expected profit as selling it in the next time period. The Hotelling Principle is the proposition that the price of a nonrenewable natural resource is expected to rise at a rate equal to the interest rate.

CHECKPOINT 19.1

■ **Explain how the value of marginal product determines the demand for a factor of production.**

Quick Review

- *Factors of production* The four factors of production are labor, capital, land, and entrepreneurship.
- *Value of marginal product* The value to a firm of hiring one more unit of a factor of production, which equals the price of a unit of output multiplied by the marginal product of the factor of production.

Additional Practice Problems 19.1

1. Tell whether each of the following are land, labor, capital, or entrepreneurship.
   a. oil
   b. an oil worker
   c. an oil platform in the Gulf of Mexico
   d. the Chief Executive Officer of Exxon
   e. a professor
   f. a beach in Florida

2. Casey's lawn service, The Other Side of the Fence, hires workers to mow lawns. The market for lawn mowing is perfectly competitive, and the price of mowing a lawn is $20.00.

Workers	Lawns per day
1	3
2	7
3	14
4	18
5	20
6	21

The labor market is competitive, and the wage rate is $40 a day. The table shows the workers' total product, *TP:*

   a. Calculate the marginal product of hiring the third worker.
   b. Calculate the value of marginal product of the third worker.
   c. Complete the table to the right showing the value of marginal product.

Workers	Value of the MP
1	____
2	____
3	____
4	____
5	____
6	____

   d. How many workers will Casey hire to maximize his profit?
   e. How many lawns a day will Casey mow to maximize its profit?
   f. What is Casey's total revenue if he hires 4 workers? What is Casey's total revenue if he hires 5 workers? What is the change in total revenue if Casey hires 5 workers?
   g. How does the increase in Casey's total revenue from hiring the 5th worker compare to the value of marginal product of the 5th worker?

Solutions to Additional Practice Problems 19.1

1a. Oil is a gift of nature and therefore is land.

1b. An oil well worker is labor.

1c. The oil platform is capital.

1d. The Chief Executive Officer is in charge of running Exxon and so is entrepreneurship.

1e. The professor is labor.

1f. The beach is a gift of nature and is land.

2a. The marginal product of hiring the third worker equals the total product of hiring three workers, which is 14 lawns, minus the total product of hiring two workers, which is 7 lawns. So the marginal product of hiring the third worker is 7 lawns.

2b. To calculate the value of marginal product, multiply the marginal product of the third worker by the price of mowing a lawn. The value of marginal product of the third worker is 7 lawns a day × $20.00, which is $140 a day.

2c. The completed table is to the right.

Workers	Value of the MP
1	$60
2	$80
3	$140
4	$80
5	$40
6	$20

2d. To answer this practice problem, recall that to maximize profit, a firm hires labor up to the point at which the value of marginal product equals the wage rate. So, to maximize his profit, Casey hires up to the point at which the value of marginal product equals the wage rate. The wage rate is $40 a day and the answer to part (c) shows that the value of marginal product of the fifth worker is also $40 a day. So Casey hires 5 workers.

2e. To maximize its profit, Casey hires 5 workers and the 5 workers mow 20 lawns.

2f. When Casey hires 4 workers, Casey's company mows 18 lawns. Total revenue is 18 lawns a day × $20, which is $360 a day. When Casey hires 5 workers, Casey's company mows 20 lawns a day. Total revenue is 20 lawns a day × $20, which is $400 a day. Casey's total revenue increases by $40 when Casey hires the fifth worker.

2g. The change in Casey's total revenue equals the value of marginal product of the fifth worker.

■ Self Test 19.1

Fill in the blanks

The factors of production are ____, ____, ____, and ____. The value of marginal product equals the marginal product of the factor of production times the ____ (factor's price; price of a unit of output). The value of marginal product of labor ____ (decreases; increases) as more workers are hired. The quantity of labor demanded by a firm is the quantity at which the value of marginal product of labor equals the ____ (wage rate; price of a unit of output). When the price of the firm's output increases, the demand for labor ____ (decreases; increases) and the demand for labor curve shifts ____ (rightward; leftward).

True or false

1. As a factor of production, coal is considered to be land.

2. The demand for labor is derived from the demand for the goods and services that the labor is hired to produce.

3. A firm's demand for labor curve is also its value of marginal product curve.

4. A rise in the wage rate decreases the quantity of labor demanded.

Multiple choice

1. The four factors of production that produce goods and services are
   a. labor, capital, profits, and entrepreneurship.
   b. money, labor, rent, and profit.
   c. labor, capital, land, and entrepreneurship.
   d. wages, interest, rent, and profit.
   e. wages, prices, quantities, and employment.

2. The wage rate paid to labor is
   a. a factor output.
   b. a factor price.
   c. a factor input.
   d. an input of the workforce.
   e. part of the firm's normal profit.

3. The demand for labor is derived from the
   a. supply of labor.
   b. wage rate.
   c. supply of the good the labor is used to produce.
   d. demand for the goods and services the labor helps produce.
   e. supply of all the other factors of production that can be substituted for labor.

4. The value of marginal product of labor is equal to the marginal product of labor ____ the price of a unit of output.
   a. divided by
   b. multiplied by
   c. minus
   d. plus
   e. squared and then multiplied by

5. The rule for maximizing profit is to hire labor up to the point at which the value of marginal product of labor
   a. equals the wage rate.
   b. is greater than the wage rate.
   c. is less than the wage rate.
   d. is a mirror image of the wage rate.
   e. equals the price of the product produced.

6. Which of the following is true?
   a. The value to a firm of hiring another worker is the worker's value of marginal product.
   b. A firm will hire more workers if the wage rate is greater than the value of marginal product.
   c. The value of marginal product is the cost of hiring a worker.
   d. The value of marginal product increases as more workers are hired.
   e. The value of marginal product equals the price of the good produced divided by the marginal product.

7. An increase in the price of a firm's output leads to a
   a. movement up along the demand for labor curve.
   b. movement down along the demand for labor curve.
   c. rightward shift of the demand for labor curve.
   d. leftward shift of the demand for labor curve
   e. rightward shift of the supply of labor curve.

Complete the graph

Quantity of labor (workers)	Marginal product (lawns per week)	Value of marginal product 1 (dollars)	Value of marginal product 2 (dollars)
1	13	___	___
2	12	___	___
3	11	___	___
4	10	___	___
5	9	___	___

1. Gene's Lawn Service hires workers to mow lawns. The market for lawns is perfectly competitive and Gene charges $25 a lawn. The table above shows the workers' marginal product schedule.
   a. Calculate the value of marginal product for each quantity of workers and record your answers in the "Value of marginal product 1" column. In Figure 19.1, plot Gene's demand for labor curve. Label it LD_1.

■ **FIGURE 19.1**

Wage rate (dollars per week)

b. Suppose the price of mowing a lawn rises to $30 per lawn. Calculate the new value of marginal products and record them in the "Value of marginal product 2" column. In Figure 19.1, plot Gene's new demand for labor curve and label it LD_2. How did the increase in the price of mowing a lawn change Gene's demand for labor curve?

■ **FIGURE 19.2**

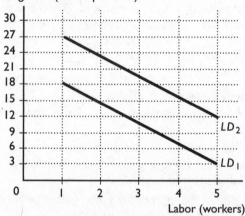

Wage rate (dollars per hour)

2. Figure 19.2 shows the labor demand curves for two groups of labor.
   a. Which group of labor, group 1 or group 2, has a larger value of its marginal product?
   b. What does the difference in the value of marginal product between the two groups equal?

Short answer and numeric questions

1. For what are factors of production used?

2. Petroleum is categorized as what type of factor of production?

3. Why does the value of marginal product decrease as more workers are employed?

4. What is the relationship between the demand for labor curve and the value of marginal product curve?

5. What factors change the demand for labor and shift the demand for labor curve?

Additional Exercises (also in MyEconLab Test A)

Greg's Grooming hires workers to groom dogs. The market for dog grooming is perfectly competitive, and the price is $20 a dog. The labor market is competitive, and the wage rate is $40 a day. The table shows the workers' total product schedule.

Workers	Groomings per day
1	4
2	7
3	11
4	16
5	20
6	23
7	25

1. Calculate the marginal product of hiring the third worker and the value of marginal product of the third worker.

2. How many workers will Greg's hire to maximize its profit and how many dogs a day will Greg's groom?

3. If the wage rate rises to $60 a day, how many workers will Greg's hire?

4. Greg installs a machine that doubles the workers' productivity. If the price of a grooming falls to $10, how many workers will Greg's hire at $40 a day?

5. More and more people shop on the Internet. What are three types of labor for which the demand will continue to increase and three types for which the demand will continue to decrease? Explain your answer.

CHECKPOINT 19.2

■ **Explain how wage rates and employment are determined and how labor unions influence labor markets.**

Quick Review

- *Changes in the demand for labor* The demand for labor depends on the price of the firm's output, the prices of other factors of production, and technology.

- *Changes in the supply of labor* The key factors that change the supply of labor are the adult population, preferences, and time spent in school and training.

Additional Practice Problems 19.2

1. Why does an individual labor supply curve bend backward?

2. Tell how each of the events given below affects the labor market. Draw a labor supply and labor demand diagram to determine the effect on the equilibrium wage rate and employment.

   a. More workers reach retirement age and retire.

   b. New technology increases workers' productivity.

   c. Suppose that the price of clothing falls. What is the impact of this change in the labor market for textile workers.

Solutions to Additional Practice Problems 19.2

1. To see how the wage rate influences the quantity of labor supplied, think about Emma's labor supply decision. Emma enjoys leisure time but, if her boss offers her $12 an hour, Emma chooses to work 30 hours a week. This wage rate is high enough to make Emma regard this use of her time as the best available to her. If Emma were offered a higher wage rate, she would want to work even longer hours, but only up to a point. If Emma is offered $25 an hour, she would be willing to work a 40-hour week. But if the wage rate is increased above $25 an hour, Emma would cut back on her work hours and take more leisure. Emma's labor supply curve eventually bends backward.

2a. When more workers reach retirement age and then retire, the supply of labor decreases. The labor supply curve shifts leftward, as shown in the figure by the shift from LS_0 to LS_1. As a result, the equilibrium wage rate rises and the equilibrium quantity of employment decreases.

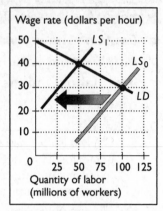

2b. By making workers more productive, the new technology, increases the demand for labor. The labor demand curve shifts rightward, in the figure from LD_0 to LD_1. The equilibrium wage rate rises and the equilibrium amount of employment increases.

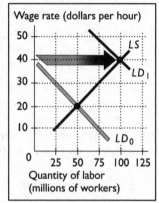

2c. A fall in the price of clothing decreases the value of marginal pro-duct of textile workers. As a result, the demand for labor decreases and the labor demand curve shifts leftward, from LD_0 to LD_1 in the figure. The equilibrium wage rate falls and the equilibrium amount of employment decreases.

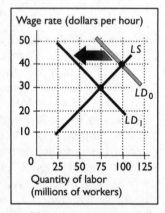

■ Self Test 19.2

Fill in the blanks

An individual's ____ (demand; supply) of labor curve bends backward. An increase in the adult population ____ (decreases; increases) the supply of labor. If the wage rate exceeds the equilibrium wage rate, the quantity of labor supplied is ____ (greater than; less than) the quantity of labor demanded. Unions try to ____ (increase; decrease) the demand for their members' labor and ____ (increase; decrease) the supply of non-union labor.

True or false

1. An individual's supply of labor curve shows that the quantity of labor supplied always increases when the wage rate rises.

2. An increase in college enrollment decreases the supply of low-skilled labor.

3. If the wage rate is less than the equilibrium wage rate, the wage rate will rise to eliminate the surplus of labor.

4. Compared to a competitive labor market, unions boost their members' wages.

5. Unions are likely to support import restrictions.

Multiple choice

1. An individual's labor supply curve eventually bends backward because at a high enough wage rate,
   a. people are willing to work more hours.
   b. employers are willing to hire more workers.
   c. people desire more leisure time.
   d. very few workers are hired.
   e. more people enter the labor market to search for jobs.

2. How does an increase in the adult population affect the labor market?
   a. The demand for labor will become more inelastic.
   b. The supply of labor will decrease.
   c. The supply of labor will increase.
   d. The demand for labor will decrease.
   e. The demand for labor will increase.

3. The supply of labor curve shifts leftward if
    a. the population increases.
    b. the demand for labor curve shifts leftward.
    c. the supply of labor increases.
    d. the wage rate falls.
    e. the supply of labor decreases.

4. If the wage rate is above the equilibrium wage rate, the quantity of labor demanded is ____ the quantity of labor supplied.
    a. greater than
    b. less than
    c. equal to
    d. the negative of
    e. not comparable to

5. The more people who remain in school for full-time education and training, the ____ is the ____ low-skilled labor.
    a. smaller; demand for
    b. smaller; supply of
    c. larger; supply of
    d. larger; demand for
    e. less elastic; demand for

6. If the supply of labor decreases, then the equilibrium wage rate ____ and equilibrium employment ____.
    a. does not change; decreases
    b. rises; increases
    c. rises; decreases
    d. falls; increases
    e. falls; decreases

7. Of the following, a union is *least* likely to support
    a. an increase in the minimum wage rate.
    b. laws that restrict immigration into the country.
    c. on-the-job training that makes their members more productive.
    d. laws that increase the quantity of the nation's imports.
    e. programs that boost the demand for the goods and services their members produce.

Complete the graph

■ **FIGURE 19.3**

1. Figure 19.3 shows Hank's supply of labor curve. At what wage rate does an increase in the wage rate decrease the quantity of labor Hank supplies?

■ **FIGURE 19.4**

2. Figure 19.4 shows the labor market for Internet security programmers. Suppose that more companies start conducting more of their business on the Internet and so need more Internet security. In Figure 19.4, illustrate the effect in the market for these programmers. What happens to the equilibrium wage rate and number of programmers?

Short answer and numeric questions

1. How does an increase in the adult population change the supply of labor?

2. If more people decide to obtain an advanced education, after they graduate what is the effect on the supply of high-skilled labor? What is the effect on the equilibrium wage rate for high-skilled workers?

3. Why do labor unions support increases in the minimum wage rate even though their members are generally paid more than the minimum wage?

Additional Exercises (also in MyEconLab Test A)

1. Ski instructors are skilled workers. Consider the market for ski instructors in the greater Salt Lake City region and explain how that market would change if ski holidays became more popular.

2. What do you think the effect of Internet commerce has been on the markets for truck drivers, couriers, and sales clerks?

3. Why does the United Farm Workers union want the government to limit the immigration of farm workers from Mexico?

CHECKPOINT 19.3

■ **Explain how capital and land rental rates and natural resource prices are determined.**

Quick Review

- *Renewable natural resources* Natural resources that can be used repeatedly.
- *Nonrenewable natural resources* Natural resources that can be used only once and that cannot be replaced once they have been used.

Additional Practice Problem 19.3

1. Petroleum is a nonrenewable natural resource and is constantly being used. Additionally, there are new technologies being developed that allow petroleum to be discovered in new locations and also new technologies being developed that make more efficient use of petroleum. What effects do these changes have on the known reserves of petroleum, the demand for petroleum, and the price of petroleum?

Solution to Additional Practice Problem 19.3

1. Using a natural resource such as petroleum decreases its known reserves, which, by itself, raises the price. But new technologies that lead to the discovery of previously unknown reserves increase the known reserves, which, by itself, lowers the price. And the new technologies that enable a more efficient use of a nonrenewable natural resource decrease the demand for the resource, which, by itself, lowers the price. So whether the known reserves increase or decrease and whether the price rises or falls depends on which of the effects is larger.

■ Self Test 19.3

Fill in the blanks

The higher the rental rate of capital, the ____ (greater; smaller) the quantity of capital demanded. The supply of each particular block of land is perfectly ____ (elastic; inelastic). Over time, advances in technology ____ (increase; decrease) the proven reserves of a nonrenewable natural resource. The Hotelling Principle is the result that as time passes, the price of a nonrenewable natural resource ____ (rises at a random rate; rises at the same rate as the interest rate; does not change).

True or false

1. If the supply of capital increases, the rental rate of capital rises.

2. The demand for land is perfectly elastic, and the supply of land is perfectly inelastic.

3. Because new natural gas deposits are always being discovered, natural gas is a renewable natural resource.

4. The price of a natural resource can only rise over time.

Multiple choice

1. The supply of each particular block of land is
   a. perfectly elastic.
   b. unit elastic.
   c. elastic but not perfectly elastic.
   d. perfectly inelastic.
   e. inelastic but not perfectly inelastic.

2. The equilibrium quantity of capital is
   a. determined by only the supply of capital because the supply is perfectly inelastic.
   b. determined by only the supply of capital because the supply is perfectly elastic.
   c. expected to increase at the same rate as the interest rate.
   d. determined by the supply of capital and the demand for capital.
   e. the only factor of production whose quantity is not determined in a market.

3. A natural resource is nonrenewable if it
   a. never has to rest.
   b. can be used repeatedly.
   c. cannot be replaced once it has been used.
   d. is available at a price of zero.
   e. has a perfectly elastic supply.

4. Oil is an example of
   a. a nonrenewable natural resource.
   b. a renewable natural resource.
   c. physical capital.
   d. a resource for which the true value cannot be measured.
   e. a resource with a perfectly inelastic demand.

5. The demand for a nonrenewable resource is
   a. determined by the value of its marginal product.
   b. fixed and cannot change.
   c. perfectly inelastic.
   d. perfectly elastic.
   e. not defined because the resource can be used only once.

6. A producer's supply of a nonrenewable natural resource is
   a. always decreasing because the resource is always being used.
   b. perfectly inelastic.
   c. perfectly elastic.
   d. not relevant because nonrenewable resources are used only once.
   e. is determined by the value of the resource's marginal product.

Complete the graph

Rent (dollars per acre per month)	Land demanded (thousands of acres)
400	10
350	20
300	30
250	40
200	50

1. The table above shows the demand schedule for land. The supply of land is fixed at 20,000 square acres.
   a. In Figure 19.5, label the axes and graph the demand and the supply curve of land.

■ **FIGURE 19.5**

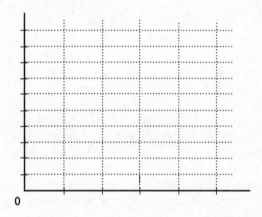

   b. What is the equilibrium rent and quantity?
   c. Suppose the demand decreases so that the quantity of land demanded decreases by 10 thousand acres at each rent. What is the new equilibrium rent and quantity? Comment on the change in the rent and the change in the quantity.

Short answer and numeric questions

Capital rental rate (dollars)	Demand for capital (billions of dollars)	Supply of capital (billions of dollars)
400	150	90
500	130	100
600	110	110
700	90	120
800	70	130

1. The table above gives the demand and sup-

ply schedules for capital.

a. What is the equilibrium rental rate and quantity of capital?

b. Suppose that population growth increases the quantity of capital demanded by $20 billion at each rental rate and also increases the quantity of capital supplied by $20 billion at each rental rate. Now what is the equilibrium rental rate and quantity of capital?

2. There are billions of barrels of petroleum still in the ground. Why, then, is petroleum considered a nonrenewable natural resource?

3. Explain the role played by the interest rate play in how the price of a nonrenewable natural resource changes over time.

4. The Eye on Your Life discussed salaries of different professions. When you are thinking about a major and a possible career, probably salary implications ought to play some role. And you can use the demand and supply model to help make informal predictions about the future prospects of different career paths. For instance, the U.S. population is aging and older people tend to use more hospital care. How will this fact affect the future job prospects and salary of a person going into nursing?

Additional Exercises (also in MyEconLab Test A)

1. New technology has allowed oil to be pumped from much deeper offshore oil fields than before. For example, 28 deep ocean rigs operate in the deep waters of the Gulf of Mexico. What effect do you think deep ocean sources have had on the world oil price? Who will benefit from drilling for oil in the Gulf of Mexico? Explain your answer.

2. Water is a natural resource that is plentiful in Canada but not plentiful in Arizona and southern California. If Canadians start to export bulk water to Arizona and southern California, what do you predict will be the effect on the price of bulk water? Will Canada eventually run out of water?

3. In the 1970s, few people drank bottled spring water and the major producers of bottled spring water were in Europe. Today, lots of people drink bottled spring water. How has this increase in the demand for spring water been satisfied? Will this increase in demand lead to some springs running dry?

4. As cities grow, good farmland is being replaced by urban sprawl. Why do farmers sell their land to urban developers?

SELF TEST ANSWERS

■ CHECKPOINT 19.1

Fill in the blanks

The factors of production are <u>labor</u>, <u>capital</u>, <u>land</u>, and <u>entrepreneurship</u>. The value of marginal product equals the marginal product of the factor of production times the <u>price of a unit of output</u>. The value of marginal product of labor <u>decreases</u> as more workers are hired. The quantity of labor demanded by a firm is the quantity at which the value of marginal product of labor equals the <u>wage rate</u>. When the price of the firm's output increases, the demand for labor <u>increases</u> and the demand for labor curve shifts <u>rightward</u>.

True or false

1. True; page 484
2. True; page 485
3. True; pages 486-487
4. True; pages 486-487

Multiple choice

1. c; page 484
2. b; page 484
3. d; page 485
4. b; page 485
5. a; pages 486-487
6. a; page 486
7. c; page 488

Complete the graph

Quantity of labor (workers)	Marginal product (lawns per week)	Value of marginal product 1 (dollars)	Value of marginal product 2 (dollars)
1	13	325	390
2	12	300	360
3	11	275	330
4	10	250	300
5	9	225	270

1. a. The completed table is above. Figure 19.6 plots the demand for labor curve LD_1; pages 485-487.

   b. The completed table is above. Figure 19.6 plots the demand for labor curve LD_2. The increase in the price of mowing a lawn in-

■ FIGURE 19.6

Wage rate (dollars per week)

Labor (workers)

creases Gene's demand for labor and his demand for labor curve shifts rightward; page 488.

2. a. Group 2's value of marginal product is higher because its demand curve lies to the right of group 1's demand curve; page 486.

   b. Because the demand curve is the same as the value of marginal product curve, the vertical distance between the two demand curves equals the difference in the value of marginal product. So group 2's value of marginal product is $7.50 more per hour than group 1's value of marginal product; pages 486-487

Short answer and numeric questions

1. Factors of production are used to produce goods and services; page 484.
2. Petroleum is a gift of nature, so as a factor of production it is included as land; page 484.
3. The value of marginal product equals the price of a unit of the output multiplied by the marginal product of the factor of production. As more of the factor of production is employed, marginal product decreases, and as a result, the value of marginal product also decreases; pages 485-486.
4. The demand for labor curve and the value of marginal product curve are the same; pages 486-487.

5. Three factors change the demand for labor and shift the demand for labor curve: changes in the price of the firm's output, changes in the prices of other factors of production, and changes in technology; page 488.

Additional Exercises (also in MyEconLab Test A)

1. The marginal product of the third worker is 4 groomings a day. The value of marginal product of the third worker is (4 groomings a day) × ($20 a grooming), which is $80 a day; page 485.

2. Greg will hire 7 workers because the value of marginal product of the seventh worker is $40 a day, (2 groomings a day × $20 a grooming) which equals the wage rate. When Greg hires 7 workers, 25 dogs are groomed a day; pages 487-488.

3. If the wage rate rises to $60, Greg hires 6 workers. The value of marginal product of the sixth worker is $60, which equals the new wage rate; page 488.

4. With the increase in productivity and the fall in the price of a dog grooming, Greg hires 7 workers. The value of marginal product of the seventh worker equals the marginal product, which is now 4 groomings a day, multiplied by the price of a grooming, which is now $10. So the value of marginal product of the seventh worker is (4 groomings a day) × ($10 a grooming) = $40, which is equal to the wage rate; pages 485-486 .

5. As more people use the Internet, computer sales increase. These computers will break and need repair. The demand for PC producers and repair people increases. As more firms enter the Internet market, they hire Web-page designers. The demand for Web-page designers also increases. The demand for other types of workers decreases. As more people use the Internet for news, the demand for newspapers decreases so newspapers lay off people. If more sales are transacted via the Internet, fewer sales clerks are needed. Fewer customer service representatives are needed as people use the Internet to get product information; page 488.

■ CHECKPOINT 19.2

Fill in the blanks

An individual's <u>supply</u> of labor curve bends backward. An increase in the adult population <u>increases</u> the supply of labor. If the wage rate exceeds the equilibrium wage rate, the quantity of labor supplied is <u>greater than</u> the quantity of labor demanded. Unions try to <u>increase</u> the demand for their members' labor and <u>decrease</u> the supply of non-union labor.

True or false

1. False; page 490
2. True; page 492
3. False; pages 492-493
4. True; page 494
5. True; page 495

Multiple choice

1. c; page 490
2. c; page 492
3. e; page 492
4. b; pages 492-493
5. b; page 492
6. c; page 493
7. d; page 495

Complete the graph

■ **FIGURE 19.7**

Wage rate (dollars per hour)

1. Figure 19.7 shows that for wage rates exceeding $60 an hour, Hank decreases the quantity of labor he supplies as the wage rate rises; page 490.

■ FIGURE 19.8

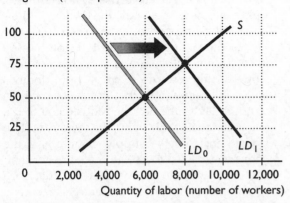

Wage rate (dollars per hour)

2. In Figure 19.8 the demand for Internet security programmers increases. The demand for labor curve shifts rightward from LD_0 to LD_1. The equilibrium wage rate rises and the quantity of these programmers employed increases; pages 492-493.

Short answer and numeric questions

1. An increase in the adult population increases the supply of labor; page 492.

2. As more people obtain advanced degrees the supply of high-skilled labor increases. The equilibrium wage rate for high-skilled labor falls; pages 492-493.

3. Unions support hikes in the minimum wage because lower-skilled workers, who are paid the minimum wage, are substitutes for higher-skilled union labor. If the wage rate that must be paid lower skilled workers increases, some firms will hire instead higher-skilled union labor, thereby increasing the demand for union labor; page 495.

Additional Exercises (also in MyEconLab Test A)

1. If ski holidays become more popular, the demand for ski instructors increases. The number of ski instructors employed increases and the wage rate rises; page 492.

2. The demand for truck drivers and couriers increases. As a result, the number of truck drivers and couriers employed increases and the wage rate rises. The demand for sales clerks in stores decreases as more transactions take place via the Internet. As a result, the number of sales clerks employed decreases and the wage rate falls; page 492.

3. Farm workers from Mexico are substitutes for the labor of the members of the United Farm Workers union. If fewer immigrants are allowed in from Mexico, the demand for the labor of the members of the United Farm Workers union increases so that employment and wages paid to the union members both rise; page 495.

■ CHECKPOINT 19.3

Fill in the blanks

The higher the rental rate of capital, the smaller the quantity of capital demanded. The supply of each particular block of land is perfectly inelastic. Over time, advances in technology increase the proven reserves of a nonrenewable natural resource. The Hotelling Principle is the result that as time passes, the price of a nonrenewable natural resource rises at the same rate as the interest rate.

True or false

1. False; page 497
2. False; page 498
3. False; page 499
4. False; page 500

Multiple choice

1. d; page 498
2. d; page 497
3. c; page 499
4. a; page 499
5. a; page 499
6. c; page 500

Complete the graph

1. a. Figure 19.9 (on the next page) shows the completed figure; page 498.

   b. The equilibrium rent is $350 an acre per month and the equilibrium quantity is 20,000 acres; page 498.

■ **FIGURE 19.9**

c. The decrease in demand lowers the equilibrium rent to $300 per acre and the equilibrium quantity remains 20,000 acres. The change in demand changed *only* the rent; the quantity is unchanged. Because the supply is perfectly inelastic, changes in demand change only the rent and do not affect the quantity; page 498.

Short answer and numeric questions

1. a. The equilibrium rental rate is $600 because this is the rental rate at which the quantity of capital demanded equals the quantity of capital supplied. The equilibrium quantity of capital is $110 billion; page 497.

   b. In this question, both the demand and supply of capital have increased by the same amount. So the equilibrium rental rate remains the same, $600, and the equilibrium quantity of capital increases to $130 billion; page 497.

2. Petroleum is a nonrenewable natural resource because once any particular barrel is used, that barrel cannot be used again; page 499.

3. The Hotelling Principle is the result that the price of a nonrenewable resource is expected to rise at a rate that equals the interest rate. The explanation for this result lies in the behavior of the owners of the resource: They can either sell the resource and invest the proceeds in an interest bearing asset or else

hold the resource and sell it next period. If the price is expected to rise at a rate that is less than the interest rate, the owners will increase their supply today in order to use the proceeds to buy an interest bearing asset. The supply will continue to increase, which lowers the resource's price, until today's price falls enough so that its rate of increase from today to the next period is equal to the interest rate. At this point, the owners will no longer increase the supply. Similarly, if the price is expected to rise at a rate greater than the interest rate, the owners will decrease their supply in order to hold the resource and enjoy the high return. The supply will continue to decrease, which raises the resource's price, until today's price rises enough so that its rate of increase from today to the next period is equal to the interest rate. At this point, the owners will no longer decrease the supply. So the equilibrium, which occurs when the owners are neither increasing nor decreasing the supply (that is, the supply curve is not shifting) occurs only when the price of the resource is expected to rise at a rate that equals the interest rate; page 501.

4. A large fraction of nurses are hired by hospitals. As the nation ages and more individuals require hospital care, the demand for nurses is likely to increase. The increase in the demand for nurses will raise the salary paid nurses and increase the quantity employed. So by using the supply and demand model, it is possible to make an informed prediction that the career possibilities of nurses are fairly bright; page 499.

Additional Exercises (also in MyEconLab Test A)

1. The deep ocean oil fields increased the supply of oil and have kept oil prices from rising higher than they have. The people benefiting from the new technology are the owners of the oil rigs and the firms selling this oil. Consumers also benefit because the price of oil is lower. If oil is drilled from the Gulf of Mexico, the owners and producers of this oil will

benefit as will consumers of oil; pages 500-501.

2. With the increased supply, the price of water will fall in Arizona and California. Water is a renewable resource in Canada so it will not run out; pages 484, 499.

3. The increased demand for bottled water has encouraged land owners to sell the spring water produced on their land. Springs are renewable resources and will not run dry; pages 484, 499.

4. Farmers sell their land to urban developers because they believe their return from selling the land is greater than they will receive from farming. The price offered for the land is high because the demand for land to use for development is high; page 498.

Chapter 20

Economic Inequality

CHAPTER CHECKLIST

1 Describe the economic inequality in the United States.

Market income is a household's wages, interest, rent, and profit earned in factor markets before paying taxes. Money income is market income plus cash payments from the government. Income and wealth are distributed unequally. The extent of inequality is measured using a Lorenz curve. A Lorenz curve graphs the cumulative percentage of income (or wealth) against the cumulative percentage of households. The farther the Lorenz curve is from the 45° line of equality, the more unequally income (or wealth) is distributed. In the United States, inequality has increased over the past few decades and economic mobility, moving up or down 1 quintile in the distribution of income, has decreased. Education, household size, and martial status are important factors affecting a household's income. Poverty is a state in which a household's income is too low to buy the quantities of food, shelter, and clothing that are deemed necessary. Poverty rates for blacks and Hispanics exceed those for white households. The longer poverty lasts, the larger the problem for the household. For more than 20 percent of poor households poverty lasts for more than a year.

2 Explain how economic inequality arises.

Human capital is people's accumulated skill and knowledge. Differences in skills lead to differences in earnings. High-skilled labor has a greater value of marginal product than low-skilled labor, so at a given wage rate, the quantity of high-skilled labor demanded exceeds that of low-skilled labor. Skills are costly to acquire, so at a given wage rate, the quantity of high-skilled labor supplied is less than that of low-skilled labor. The equilibrium wage rate of high-skilled labor is higher than that of low-skilled labor. Discrimination according to race or sex is another possible source of inequality. High income people typically own large amounts of physical and financial capital while some have great entrepreneurial ability. Personal and family characteristics also affect an individual's income.

3 Explain how governments redistribute income and describe the effects of redistribution on economic inequality.

The government redistributes income using income taxes, income maintenance programs, and subsidized services. Income maintenance programs include Social Security, unemployment compensation, and welfare programs. The distribution of disposable income (income after taxes and benefits) is more equal than the market distribution. Utilitarianism suggests that more equality is fairer. But government redistribution weakens work incentives both for the recipient and the wage earner, which create the big tradeoff between equity and efficiency. A major challenge is to insure that welfare programs do not weaken the incentives to acquire human capital; the current approach attempts to avoid weakening these incentives. The negative income tax is a redistribution scheme that provides every household with a guaranteed minimum annual income and taxes all earned income above the minimum at a fixed rate.

CHECKPOINT 20.1

■ **Describe the economic inequality in the United States.**

Quick Review

• *Lorenz curve* A curve that graphs the cumulative percentage of income (or wealth) against the cumulative percentage of households. The farther the Lorenz curve is from the line of equality, the greater is the inequality.

Additional Practice Problems 20.1

1978	
Households	**Income (percentage)**
Lowest 20 percent	4.3
Second 20 percent	10.3
Third 20 percent	16.9
Fourth 20 percent	24.7
Highest 20 percent	43.8

1. The table above shows the distribution of money income in the United States in 1978:

   a. Draw the Lorenz curve for the United States in 1978.

   b. Was the distribution of income in the United States more or less equal than in recent years?

2. The figure shows the Lorenz curves for three nations, *A, B,* and *C.* In which nation is income distributed the most unequally? The most equally? In which nation is average income the highest?

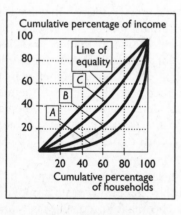

Solutions to Additional Practice Problems 20.1

1a. When drawing a Lorenz curve, the key is that it plots the *cumulative* percentage of income against the *cumulative* percentage of households. To create a Lorenz curve calculate cumulative percentages, which is done

1978	
Households (cumulative percent)	**Income (cumulative percent)**
20 percent of households	4.3
40 percent of households	14.6
60 percent of households	31.5
80 percent of households	56.2
100 percent of households	100.0

by adding the income owned by *all* the people who fall in the income group in and below the percentage being considered. So, to draw the Lorenz curve, we first need to calculate the cumulative percentage of households and the cumulative percentage of income. The table above has these percentages. The Lorenz curve in the figure plots the cumulative percentage of income and cumulative percentage of households in the above table.

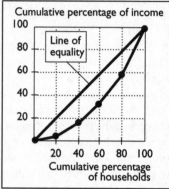

1b. The distribution of income in the United States in recent years has become less equal that what it was in 1978.

2. Income is distributed the most unequally in nation *A* because its Lorenz curve is farthest from the line of equality. Income is distributed the most equally in nation *C* because its Lorenz curve is the closest to the line of equality. Based on the Lorenz curves it is impossible to determine in which nation average income is the highest. Lorenz curves give information about the distribution of income, *not* about its amount.

■ Self Test 20.1

Fill in the blanks

In the United States, the poorest 20 percent of households receive less than _____ (4; 12) percent of money income and the richest 20 percent receive about ____ (25; 50) percent of money income. A Lorenz curve for income plots the ____ (percentage; cumulative percentage) of income against the cumulative percentage of households. Since 1970, the distribution of income and wealth has become ____ (less; more) unequal in the United States. Education has a ____ (small; large) role in influencing a household's income. The poverty level of income in the United States for a family of four is approximately ____ ($22,000; $30,000; $35,000). A little more than ____ (20; 50; 75) percent of households that live in poverty do so for more than a year.

True or false

1. The Lorenz curve always lies above the line of equality.
2. Since 1970, the percentage of the money income received by the richest 20 percent of households decreased.
3. Inequality of annual income overstates the degree of lifetime inequality.
4. When it comes to determining household income, education is a more important characteristic than is race.
5. In the United States, poverty is distributed equally across the races, with approximately 15 percent of households of each race living in poverty.

Multiple choice

1. Which of the following is correct about the United States?
   a. Income is equally distributed.
   b. Wealth is equally distributed.
   c. Income is equally distributed but wealth is unequally distributed because of inheritances.
   d. Both wealth and income are unequally distributed.
   e. Both wealth and income are equally distributed.

■ FIGURE 20.1

Cumulative percentage of income

Cumulative percentage of households

2. In Figure 20.1, the richest 20 percent of households receive ____ percent of total income.
   a. 20
   b. 100
   c. 80
   d. 40
   e. 60

3. If the income distribution is more unequal than the wealth distribution, then the
   a. Lorenz curve for income will be farther away from the line of equality than the Lorenz curve for wealth.
   b. government has imposed a higher tax rate on income.
   c. Lorenz curve for wealth will be farther away from the line of equality than the Lorenz curve for income.
   d. Lorenz curve for wealth will lie above the Lorenz curve for income.
   e. It is not possible to draw the Lorenz curve for wealth on the same figure with the Lorenz curve for income.

4. In the United States in 2004, the wealthiest 1 percent of households owned approximately ____ percent of all wealth.
   a. 1
   b. 13
   c. 27
   d. 34
   e. 88

5. In the United States since 1970, the share of money income received by the richest 20 percent of households has ____ and the share received by the lowest 20 percent of households has ____.
   a. increased; not changed
   b. not changed; increased
   c. not changed; decreased
   d. decreased; increased
   e. increased; decreased

6. The inequality of annual income
   a. overstates the degree of lifetime inequality.
   b. understates the degree of lifetime inequality.
   c. cannot change from one year to the next.
   d. is about the same as the amount of lifetime inequality.
   e. cannot be compared to the amount of lifetime inequality.

7. Of all the characteristics that lead to income inequality, the factor with the largest impact is
   a. race.
   b. sex.
   c. age.
   d. education.
   e. location.

8. Which of the following statements about poverty is (are) correct?
   i. Blacks and Hispanics have higher poverty rates than whites.
   ii. Over the last 40 years, poverty rates for all groups have generally increased.
   iii. Most household spells of poverty last much longer than 1 year.
   a. i only.
   b. ii only.
   c. iii only.
   d. ii and iii.
   e. i, ii, and iii.

Complete the graph

Household percentage	Percentage of income	Cumulative percentage of income
Lowest 20 percent	5.0	_____
Second 20 percent	9.0	_____
Third 20 percent	20.0	_____
Fourth 20 percent	26.0	_____
Highest 20 percent	40.0	_____

■ **FIGURE 20.2**

1. The table above has data for the nation of Beta. Complete the table by calculating the cumulative percentages for the last column. In Figure 20.2, plot the Lorenz curve for Beta.

Short answer and numeric questions

1. Can a Lorenz curve ever lie above the line of equality? Why or why not?

2. What does the distance between a Lorenz curve for income and the line of equality tell about the distribution of income?

3. How has the distribution of income and the amount of economic mobility changed in the United States over the past few decades?

4. What is poverty? How many Americans live in poverty? How have poverty rates changed over the last few decades?

Additional Exercises (also in MyEconLab Test A)

Table 20.1(a) on page 508 of the textbook shows the distribution of income in the United States. On the next page of this Study Guide, the top table shows the distribution of income in Canada and the bottom table shows the distribution of income in the United Kingdom.

Distribution of income in Canada	
Households	Income (percentage)
Lowest 20 percent	7.4
Second 20 percent	13.2
Third 20 percent	18.1
Fourth 20 percent	24.9
Highest 20 percent	36.4

Distribution of income in the United Kingdom	
Households	Income (percentage)
Lowest 20 percent	3
Second 20 percent	5
Third 20 percent	14
Fourth 20 percent	25
Highest 20 percent	53

1. Create a table that shows the cumulative percentages of households and income in the United Kingdom.

2. Draw the Lorenz curves for the United Kingdom and the United States. Compare the distribution of income in the United Kingdom with that in the United States. Which distribution is more unequal?

3. Draw the Lorenz curves for the United Kingdom and Canada. Compare the distribution of income in the United Kingdom with that in Canada. Which distribution is more unequal?

CHECKPOINT 20.2

■ **Explain how economic inequality arises.**

Quick Review

- *Demand for high-skilled labor and low-skilled labor* The vertical distance between the demand curve for low-skilled labor and the demand curve for high-skilled labor is equal to the value of marginal product of skill.
- *Supply of high-skilled labor and low-skilled labor* The vertical distance between the supply curve of low-skilled labor and the supply curve of high-skilled labor is equal to the compensation that high-

skilled workers require for the cost of acquiring the skill.

Additional Practice Problems 20.2

1. What is the opportunity cost of acquiring a skill?

2. The figure shows the demand and supply curves for high-skilled and low-skilled labor at the beginning of the 1990s. Since then, new technology has increased the value of marginal product of skill. In the figure, show the effect of this change. Is the income difference between high-skilled labor and low-skilled labor greater now or in 1990?

Solutions to Additional Practice Problems 20.2

1. The opportunity cost of acquiring a skill includes actual expenditures on tuition and books, as well as costs in the form of lost or reduced earnings while the skill is being acquired. When a person goes to school full time, that cost is the total earnings forgone. When a person receives on-the-job training, he or she is paid a lower wage than one who is doing a comparable job but not undergoing training. In this case, the cost of acquiring the skill is equal to the wage paid to a person not being trained minus the wage paid to a person being trained.

2. High-skilled labor has a higher value of marginal product than low-skilled labor. The technology changes increased the value of marginal product even more. The demand for high-skilled labor increased and

the demand curve shifted rightward. As the figure shows, the wage rate paid high skilled-workers increased. So the income difference between high-skilled labor and low-skilled labor is greater now than in 1990.

■ Self Test 20.2

Fill in the blanks

The demand curve for high-skilled workers lies ____ (above; below) the demand curve for low-skilled workers and the supply curve of high-skilled workers lies ____ (above; below) the supply curve for low-skilled workers. The wage rate paid high-skilled workers is ____ (greater; less) than the wage rate paid low-skilled workers. On the average, men earn ____ (more; less) than women. Entrepreneurial ability ____ (can; cannot) account for why some people become very wealthy.

True or false

1. At a given wage rate, the quantity of high-skilled labor demanded exceeds the quantity of low-skilled labor demanded.
2. The horizontal distance between the demand curve for high-skilled labor and the demand curve for low-skilled labor measures the value of marginal product of skill.
3. The greater the cost of acquiring a skill, the greater is the vertical distance between the supply curve of high-skilled labor and the supply curve of low-skilled labor.
4. The wage rate paid high-skilled workers exceeds that paid low-skilled workers.
5. Discriminating against some group of workers has no cost to a prejudiced employer.

Multiple choice

1. Differences in skills
   i. can arise from differences in education and/or from differences in on-the-job training.
   ii. can lead to large differences in earnings.
   iii. result in different demand curves for high-skilled and low-skilled labor.
   a. i only.
   b. ii only.
   c. ii and iii.
   d. i and iii.
   e. i, ii, and iii.

2. The cost of acquiring a skill accounts for why the
   a. demand for high-skilled workers is different than the demand for low-skilled workers.
   b. supply of high-skilled workers is different than the supply of low-skilled workers.
   c. demand for high-skilled workers is different from the supply of high-skilled workers.
   d. demand for high-skilled workers is different from the supply of low-skilled workers.
   e. supply curves of high-skilled and low-skilled workers cross.

3. If decreased student aid increases the cost of acquiring skills, the equilibrium wage rate paid high-skilled workers ____ and the employment of high-skilled workers ____.
   a. rises; decreases
   b. rises; does not change
   c. falls; decreases
   d. rises; increases
   e. falls; does not change

4. If the value of marginal product of skill increases, the wage rate paid high-skilled workers ____ and the employment of high-skilled workers ____.
   a. might rise, fall, or not change; decreases
   b. falls; decreases
   c. rises; decreases
   d. rises; increases
   e. does not change; increases

■ **FIGURE 20.3**

Wage rate (dollars per hour)

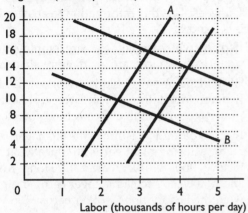

Labor (thousands of hours per day)

5. Figure 20.3 shows supply and demand curves for high-skilled and low-skilled labor. The curve labeled *A* is the supply curve for ____ workers and the curve labeled *B* is the demand curve for ____ workers.
   a. both high-skilled and low-skilled; both high-skilled and low-skilled
   b. high-skilled; high-skilled
   c. high-skilled; low-skilled
   d. low-skilled; high-skilled
   e. low-skilled; low-skilled

6. Figure 20.3 shows supply and demand curves for high-skilled and low-skilled labor. The wage rate paid high-skilled workers is ____ per hour and the wage rate paid low-skilled workers is ____ per hour.
   a. $14; $10
   b. $16; $14
   c. $14; $10
   d. $16; 10
   e. $16; $8

7. If discrimination against women decreases their value of marginal product, then women will have ____ wage rate than men and there will be ____ high-paying jobs for women.
   a. a lower; more
   b. a higher; fewer
   c. a lower; fewer
   d. a higher; more
   e. the same; fewer

8. Inequality in the distribution of income and wealth is increased by
   a. the point that the children of the poorest find it difficult to get into college.
   b. saving to redistribute an uneven income over the life cycle.
   c. marrying outside one's own socioeconomic class.
   d. donating money to charities.
   e. the U.S. income tax.

Complete the graph

■ **FIGURE 20.4**

Wage rate (dollars per hour)

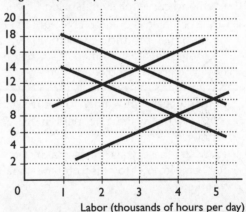

Labor (thousands of hours per day)

1. Figure 20.4 shows demand and supply curves for high-skilled and low-skilled workers.
   a. Label the demand curve for the high-skilled workers D_H and the demand curve for low-skilled workers D_L. Label the supply curves similarly, using S_H and S_L.
   b. What is the value of marginal product of skill?

c. What is the compensation required for the cost of acquiring the skill?

d. What is the equilibrium wage rate for high-skilled workers and low-skilled workers?

■ **FIGURE 20.5**

Wage rate (dollars per hour)

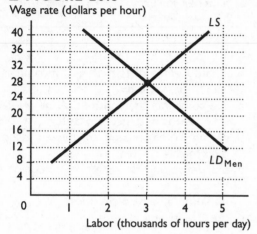

2. Suppose that the supply of labor for men and women is identical and Figure 20.5 shows this supply curve, labeled *LS*. It also shows the demand curve for men, labeled *LD*Men.

a. If that men and women have equal values of marginal products but employers are prejudiced against women. As a result, at any wage rate employers demand 2,000 fewer hours of female labor. Draw the demand curve for women in Figure 20.5.

b. What is the wage rate paid men? Paid women?

c. How do these wage rates make it costly for employers to discriminate against women?

Short answer and numeric questions

1. a. How does the demand for high-skilled workers compare to the demand for low-skilled workers? How does the supply of high-skilled workers compare to the supply of low-skilled workers?

b. How does the wage rate of high-skilled workers compare to the wage rate of low-skilled workers?

c. How does the quantity of high-skilled workers employed compare to the quantity of low-skilled workers employed?

2. Why is discrimination costly for a prejudiced employer?

Additional Exercises (also in MyEconLab Test A)

In the United States in 2000, 2 million people worked full-time in protective services and were paid an average of $600 a week. At the same time, 7 million people worked as full-time machine operators and were paid an average of $450 a week. Use this information to answer Exercises 1 and 2.

1. Explain why people who are employed in protective services are paid more than machine operators.

2. Explain why fewer people are employed in protective services than as machine operators.

3. In Canada and Australia, the manager of a manufacturing plant earns 20 times what the factory floor worker earns. In Hong Kong and Malaysia, such a manager earns 40 times what the factory floor worker earns. Can you explain this difference?

CHECKPOINT 20.3

■ **Explain how governments redistribute income and describe the effects of redistribution on economic inequality.**

Quick Review

- *Market income* Market income equals income earned from factors of production with no government redistribution.

- *Disposable income* Disposable income is market income plus cash benefits from the government minus taxes.

- *Median voter theory* The theory that governments pursue policies that make the median voter as well off as possible,

Additional Practice Problem 20.3

Households	Income (millions of dollars per year)	Income (percentage of total income)
Lowest 20 percent	5	2.5
Second 20 percent	15	7.5
Third 20 percent	35	17.5
Fourth 20 percent	55	27.5
Highest 20 percent	90	45.0

1. The table above shows the distribution of market income in an economy.

   a. Suppose the government imposes a proportional income tax of 10 percent upon everyone. It then distributes the funds it collects by paying benefits to the bottom two percentile income groups. The lowest 20 percent group receives one half of the funds collected and the second lowest receives the other half. Calculate the income shares of each 20 percent of households after the tax and the benefits are paid.

   b. Draw the Lorenz curves for this economy before and after taxes and benefits. Have the government's taxes and benefits made the distribution more or less equal?

Solution to Additional Practice Problem 20.3

Household percentage	Tax paid (millions of dollars)	Income after tax and benefits (millions of dollars)	Income (percentage of total income)
Lowest 20 percent	0.5	14.5	7.25
Second 20 percent	1.5	23.5	11.75
Third 20 percent	3.5	31.5	15.75
Fourth 20 percent	5.5	49.5	24.75
Highest 20 percent	9.0	81.0	40.50

1a. To solve this practice problem, subtract the amount paid as income tax and add the income received as benefits to obtain the new amount of income of each group. Then construct the Lorenz curve for the new income shares. In the above table, the second column shows the tax paid by each group. Total taxes collected are $20 million. The lowest and second lowest 20 percentile groups each receive half of this amount, so each receives $10 million in benefits. The third column

adds benefits to the market income and subtracts the tax. The last column has the income shares. To find a group's income share divide income after tax and benefits by total income, which is $200 million, and multiply by 100.

Household percentage	Cumulative percentage (before)	Cumulative percentage (after)
Lowest 20 percent	2.50	7.25
Second 20 percent	10.00	19.00
Third 20 percent	27.50	34.75
Fourth 20 percent	55.00	59.50
Highest 20 percent	100.00	100.00

1b. The table above has the cumulative percentage of income before tax and benefits and after tax and benefits. The cumulative percentages are plotted in the

Lorenz curve in the figure. The Lorenz curve after the taxes and benefits is closer to the line of equality so the government's taxes and benefits have made the distribution of income more equal.

■ Self Test 20.3

Fill in the blanks

Governments redistribute income using ____ taxes, ____ maintenance programs, and ____ services. Education is an example of a ____. A household's ____ (market; money) income is the income it earns in factor markets before taxes and excluding government redistribution. A household's ____ (market; money) income is its market income plus money benefits paid by the government. The distribution of income after taxes and benefits is ____ (more; less) equal than the distribution of market income. Redistribution of income creates the big tradeoff between ____ (equity; tax revenue) and ____ (efficiency; redistribution). The ____ (median voter theory; utilitarianism voter theory) says that programs, such as redistribution programs, and also taxes are such that they make the median voter as ____ (poor; well) off as possible. A tax and redistribution plan that provides every household with a guaranteed minimum annual income and taxes all market income at a fixed rate is called a ____ (negative; fair; constant) income tax.

True or false

1. In general, U.S. federal and state taxes are progressive.

2. Subsidized services from the government go to only households with below-average incomes.

3. The distribution of income after taxes and benefits is more equal than the market distribution of income.

4. The redistribution of income creates the big tradeoff between earning an income and losing welfare benefits.

5. Under a negative income tax, some households would receive more money from the government than they would pay in taxes.

Multiple choice

1. Which of the following is a way income is redistributed in the United States?
   i.   subsidizing services
   ii. income taxes
   iii. income maintenance programs
   a. i only.
   b. ii only.
   c. ii and iii.
   d. ii and iii.
   e. i, ii, and iii.

2. A ____ tax is one that taxes income at an average rate that increases with the level of income.
   a. regressive
   b. progressive
   c. flat
   d. consumption
   e. proportional

3. Of the following types of income tax systems, the one that provides the greatest amount of redistribution from the rich to the poor is a
   a. progressive income tax.
   b. proportional income tax.
   c. regressive income tax.
   d. flat-rate income tax.
   e. money-income tax.

4. The three major types of income maintenance programs are
   a. Social Security programs, unemployment compensation, and welfare programs.
   b. food stamps, unemployment compensation, and agricultural price supports.
   c. student loans, rent control, and welfare programs.
   d. corporate welfare, minimum wages, and affirmative action laws.
   e. minimum wages, food stamps, and student loans.

5. A household's income earned from the markets for factors of production and with no government redistribution is its
   a. money income.
   b. welfare.
   c. market income.
   d. exploitative income.
   e. factored income.

6. The median voter theorem says government
   a. must redistribute income.
   b. does not face the big tradeoff.
   c. ought to use progressive taxes.
   d. cannot affect the distribution of income.
   e. policies aim to make the median voter as well off as possible.

7. When government redistributes income, one dollar collected from a rich person translates into ____ received by a poor person.
   a. one dollar
   b. less than one dollar
   c. more than one dollar
   d. zero dollars
   e. either exactly one dollar or, with some programs, more than one dollar

8. With a negative income tax that has a $10,000 guaranteed minimum income and a 25 percent tax rate, a household that has earned income of $16,000 has a total income of
   a. $16,000.
   b. $22,000.
   c. $26,000.
   d. $24,000.
   e. $10,000.

Short answer and numeric questions

1. Would progressive or regressive income taxes redistribute more money from the rich to the poor? Why?

2. What are the nation's three main types of income maintenance programs?

3. Currently the government more heavily taxes high-income households and transfers money to low-income households. What are the likely reactions of the recipients of the money? Of the taxpayers? How do these reactions reflect the big tradeoff?

4. Suppose a negative income tax plan is passed so that a household is guaranteed an income of $20,000 and market income is taxed at a rate of 25 percent.
   a. What is the total income of a household that has a market income of $20,000?
   b. What is the total income of a household that has a market income of $60,000?

Additional Exercises (also in MyEconLab Test A)

Households	Income (millions of dollars per year)
Lowest 20 percent	5
Second 20 percent	10
Third 20 percent	18
Fourth 20 percent	28
Highest 20 percent	39

Households	Income tax (percent)	Benefits (millions of dollars)
Lowest 20 percent	0	10
Second 20 percent	10	8
Third 20 percent	18	3
Fourth 20 percent	28	0
Highest 20 percent	39	0

1. An economy is given in the tables to the above. The top table shows the distribution of market income in an economy. The government initially redistributes income by collecting income taxes and paying benefits shown in the second table. The government lowers the tax rate on the third 20 percent to 15 percent, on the fourth 20 percent to 25 percent, and on the highest 20 percent to 30 percent but benefits are unchanged.
   a. Calculate the income shares of each 20 percent of households after tax and redistribution.
   b. Draw this economy's Lorenz curve before and after taxes and benefits.

2. Suppose the government increases the benefits paid to the lowest 20 percent to $12 million, to the second 20 percent to $10 million, and to the third 20 percent to $5 million but keeps the tax rates unchanged. Calculate the income shares of each 20 percent of households after tax and redistribution.

SELF TEST ANSWERS

■ CHECKPOINT 20.1

Fill in the blanks

In the United States, the poorest 20 percent of households receive less than <u>4</u> percent of money income and the richest 20 percent receive about <u>50</u> percent of money income. A Lorenz curve for income plots the <u>cumulative percentage</u> of income against the cumulative percentage of households. Since 1970, the distribution of income and wealth has become <u>less;</u> unequal in the United States. Education has a <u>large</u> role in influencing a household's income. The poverty level of income in the United States for a family of four is approximately <u>$22,000</u>. A little more than <u>20</u> percent of households that live in poverty do so for more than a year.

True or false

1. False; page 509
2. False; page 510
3. True; page 511
4. True; page 512
5. False; page 513

Multiple choice

1. d; page 509
2. e; page 509
3. a; page 509
4. d; page 508
5. e; page 510
6. a; page 511
7. d; page 512
8. a; page 513

Complete the graph

1. The table and Lorenz curve (in Figure 20.6) are in the next column. In the table, the cumulative percentage of income for any income group equals its percentage of income plus the percentages of income of all groups lower than it. The Lorenz curve plots these cumulative percentages of income against the cumulative percentage of households; pages 508-509.

Household percentage	Percentage of income	Cumulative percentage of income
Lowest 20 percent	5.0	<u>5.0</u>
Second 20 percent	9.0	<u>14.0</u>
Third 20 percent	20.0	<u>34.0</u>
Fourth 20 percent	26.0	<u>60.0</u>
Highest 20 percent	40.0	<u>100.0</u>

■ FIGURE 20.6

Cumulative percentage of income

Cumulative percentage of households

Short answer and numeric questions

1. A Lorenz curve can never lie above the line of equality. The Lorenz curve plots the cumulative percentage of income against the cumulative percentage of households. Because the households are arranged by order of income, the cumulative percentage of income must always be less than the cumulative percentage of households; pages 508-509.

2. The farther the Lorenz curve from the line of equality, the less equal the distribution of income; page 509.

3. The distribution of income has become less equal in the United States over the last few decades. The distribution of income changed because higher income groups have gained more income than the lower income groups. Economic mobility has decreased over the same years. Fewer families are now moving up or down 1 or more quintile in the distribution of income and more families are remaining in the same quintile; page 510.

4. Poverty is a state in which a household's income is too low to buy the quantities of food, shelter, and clothing that are deemed necessary. In 2010 46 million Americans lived in poverty. Over the last several decades, poverty rates for whites and blacks have generally decreased, while poverty rates for Hispanics at first rose and then decreased, strikingly, during the 1990s; pages 513-514.

Additional Exercises (also in MyEconLab Test A)

Households	Income (cumulative percentage)
Lowest 20 percent	3
Second 20 percent	8
Third 20 percent	22
Fourth 20 percent	47
Highest 20 percent	100

1. The cumulative distribution of income for the United Kingdom is in the table above.

■ FIGURE 20.7

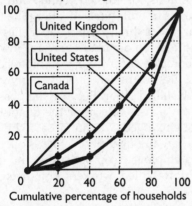

Cumulative percentage of income

2. The Lorenz curves are in Figure 20.7. Income is distributed *slightly* more equally in the United States than in the United Kingdom. The only real differences are in the second and fourth quintiles but the Lorenz curves are otherwise virtually identical; page 509.

3. The Lorenz curves are in Figure 20.7. The distribution of income is more unequal in the United Kingdom than in Canada. The U.K. Lorenz curve is farther from the line of equality than is the Canadian Lorenz curve so the distribution of income in the U.K. is

less equally distributed than in Canada; page 509.

■ CHECKPOINT 20.2

Fill in the blanks

The demand curve for high-skilled workers lies <u>above</u> the demand curve for low-skilled workers and the supply curve of high-skilled workers lies <u>above</u> the supply curve for low-skilled workers. The wage rate paid high-skilled workers is <u>greater</u> than the wage rate paid low-skilled workers. On the average, men earn <u>more</u> than women. Entrepreneurial ability <u>can</u> account for why some people become very wealthy.

True or false

1. True; pages 516-517
2. False; page 517
3. True; pages 516-517
4. True; pages 516-517
5. False; page 519

Multiple choice

1. e; pages 516-517
2. b; pages 516-517
3. a; pages 517-518
4. d; pages 517-518
5. c; page 517
6. e; page 517
7. c; page 519
8. a; page 520

Complete the graph

1. a. Figure 20.8 on the next page labels the curves; page 517.
   b. The value of marginal product of skill is $4 an hour because that is the vertical distance between the demand curve for high-skilled workers and the demand curve for low-skilled workers; page 517.
   c. The compensation required for the cost of acquiring the skill is $8 an hour because that is the vertical distance between the supply curve for high-skilled workers and the supply curve for low-skilled workers; page 517.

■ **FIGURE 20.8**

Wage rate (dollars per hour)

Labor (thousands of hours per day)

d. The equilibrium wage rate for high-skilled workers is $14 an hour and the equilibrium wage rate for low-skilled workers is $8 an hour; page 517.

■ **FIGURE 20.9**

Wage rate (dollars per hour)

Labor (thousands of hours per day)

2. a. Figure 20.9 has the demand curve for women. It lies to the left of the demand curve by men by 2,000 hours of labor at every wage rate; page 519.

b. Men are paid a wage of $28 an hour and women are paid a wage of $20 an hour; page 519.

c. If a firm discriminates against women, it costs the firm $28 an hour to hire a man when it could get the same output if it hired a woman for $20. A discriminating

firm's costs are higher as a result of its discrimination; page 519.

Short answer and numeric questions

1. a. Because the value of marginal product of high-skilled workers exceeds that of low-skilled workers, the demand for high-skilled workers exceeds the demand for low-skilled workers. Because skills are costly to attain, the supply of high-skilled workers is less than the supply of low-skilled workers; pages 516-517.

b. The demand for high-skilled workers exceeds the demand for low-skilled workers and the supply of high-skilled workers is less than the supply of low-skilled workers. So the wage rate received by high-skilled workers exceeds the wage rate received by low-skilled workers; page 517.

c. The quantity of high-skilled workers employed compared to the quantity of low-skilled workers employed depends on the positions of the demand and supply curves of both types of labor. The demand curve for high-skilled labor lies to the right of the demand curve for low-skilled labor. The supply curve of high-skilled labor lies to the left of the supply curve of low-skilled labor. Because the positions of these curves determine the quantity of labor employed, we cannot say with certainty how the quantity of high-skilled workers employed compares that the quantity of low-skilled workers employed; page 518.

2. Discrimination is costly for employers. Discrimination means that they hire the high-wage, favored group of workers rather than the low-wage, not favored group of workers. The firm's costs are higher than necessary and hence its profit is less than it could be. The reduced profit is the opportunity cost a prejudiced employer must pay; page 519.

Additional Exercises (also in MyEconLab Test A)

1. The value of marginal product for protective services and therefore the demand for labor for protective services exceeds that of ma-

chine operators. Likely the supply of labor for protective services is less than that for machine operators. As a result of the higher demand and lower supply, people working in protective services are paid more than people working as machine operators; page 517.

2. If the demand for labor for protective services is only slightly greater than the demand for machine operators and the supply of labor for protective services is much less than the supply of labor for machine operators, then the equilibrium quantity of machine operators exceeds the equilibrium quantity of people working in protective services; page 517.

3. The difference in pay is a result of the fact that managerial skills are in much smaller supply in Hong Kong and Malaysia. There are many low-skilled factory floor workers in Hong Kong and Malaysia. There are few high-skilled managers. As a result, the equilibrium wage rate paid to the few high-skilled managers in Hong Kong and Malaysia is many times greater than the wage rate paid to the many low-skilled factory floor workers; page 517.

■ CHECKPOINT 20.3

Fill in the blanks

Governments redistribute income using <u>income</u> taxes, <u>income</u> maintenance programs, and <u>subsidized</u> services. Education is an example of a <u>subsidized service</u>. A household's <u>market</u> income is the income it earns in factor markets before taxes and excluding government redistribution. A household's <u>money</u> income is its market income plus money benefits paid by the government. The distribution of income after taxes and benefits is <u>more</u> equal than the distribution of market income. Redistribution of income creates the big tradeoff between <u>equity</u> and <u>efficiency</u>. The <u>median voter theory</u> says that programs, such as redistribution programs, and also taxes are such that they make the median voter as <u>well</u> off as possible. A tax and re-

distribution plan that provides every household with a guaranteed minimum annual income and taxes all market income at a fixed rate is called a <u>negative</u> income tax.

True or false

1. True; page 522
2. False; page 523
3. True; page 524
4. True; page 525
5. True; page 527

Multiple choice

1. e; page 522
2. b; page 522
3. a; page 522
4. a; page 522
5. c; page 523
6. e; page 526
7. b; page 525
8. b; page 527

Short answer and numeric questions

1. A progressive income tax will redistribute more income away from the rich to the poor. A progressive income tax has a higher average tax rate as income rises. As a result, the rich pay a greater amount of taxes than do the poor because the rich have more income and because the average tax rate on that income is higher; page 522.

2. The three types of income maintenance programs are Social Security programs, unemployment compensation, and welfare programs; page 522.

3. The recipients of the money payments likely will work less. If they were to work more, they might earn enough to move into a higher tax bracket and lose the money the government is giving to them. The taxpayers also will tend to work less. On both counts, people work less and so the nation's total income decreases. These effects illustrate the force of the big tradeoff: By making incomes more equal, the government program has blunted people's incentives to work, lessened

economic efficiency, and decreased the over-all size of the nation's income; page 525.

4. a. The household receives its $20,000 guar-anteed income. Then, on its market in-come of $20,000, it pays ($20,000 × 25 per-cent) = $5,000 in taxes, leaving $15,000 in income after taxes. Its total income is $20,000 + $15,000 = $35,000. This house-hold receives a "negative income tax" payment of $15,000; page 527.

   b. The household receives its $20,000 guaran-teed income. Then, on its market income of $60,000, it pays ($60,000 × 25 percent) = $15,000 in taxes, leaving $45,000 in income after taxes. Its total income is $20,000 + $45,000 = $65,000. This household receives a "negative income tax" payment of $5,000; page 527.

Additional Exercises (also in MyEconLab Test A)

Households	Market income (millions of dollars)	Tax paid (millions of dollars)	Benefits received (millions of dollars)
Lowest 20 percent	5.0	0.0	10
Second 20 percent	10.0	1.0	8
Third 20 percent	18.0	2.7	3
Fourth 20 percent	28.0	7.0	0
Highest 20 percent	39.0	11.7	0

Households	Income after tax and benefits (millions of dollars)	Income (percentage)
Lowest 20 percent	15.0	15.2
Second 20 percent	17.0	17.2
Third 20 percent	18.3	18.6
Fourth 20 percent	21.0	21.3
Highest 20 percent	27.3	27.7

1. a. The top table shows the market income, taxes paid, and benefits received by the 5 percentile groups. The second table then shows the income after the tax is subtract-ed and the benefits added. It also shows the percentage of this adjusted income that each group receives.

   b. Figure 20.10 shows the Lorenz curves be-fore and after taxes and benefits. To draw

■ FIGURE 20.10

Cumulative percentage of income

these Lorenz curves, calculate the cumula-tive percentage chares. For instance, after taxes and benefits, the lowest 20 percent have 15.2 percent of total income and the lowest 40 percent have 32.4 percent (15.2 + 17.2). The remaining the cumulative per-centages are calculated similarly.

Households	Market income (millions of dollars)	Tax paid (millions of dollars)	Benefits received (millions of dollars)
Lowest 20 percent	5.0	0.0	12
Second 20 percent	10.0	1.0	10
Third 20 percent	18.0	3.2	5
Fourth 20 percent	28.0	7.8	0
Highest 20 percent	39.0	15.2	0

Households	Income after tax and benefits (millions of dollars)	Income (percentage)
Lowest 20 percent	17.0	17.0
Second 20 percent	19.0	19.0
Third 20 percent	19.8	19.8
Fourth 20 percent	20.2	20.2
Highest 20 percent	23.8	23.8

2. The top table shows the market income, tax-es paid, and benefits received by the 5 per-centile groups. The second table then shows the income after the tax is subtracted and the benefits added. It also shows the percentage of this adjusted income that each group re-ceives.